Requirements Analysis and System Design

Developing Information Systems with UML

Pearson Education

We work with leading authors to develop the
strongest educational materials in computer science,
bringing cutting-edge thinking and best learning
practice to a global market.

Under a range of well-known imprints, including
Addison Wesley, we craft high quality print and
electronic publications which help readers to
understand and apply their content,
whether studying or at work.

To find out more about the complete range of our
publishing please visit us on the World Wide Web at:
www.pearsoneduc.com

Requirements Analysis and System Design

Developing Information Systems with UML

LESZEK A. MACIASZEK

Macquarie University, Sydney, Australia

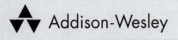
Addison-Wesley

An imprint of Pearson Education

Harlow, England · London · New York · Reading, Massachusetts · San Francisco · Toronto · Don Mills, Ontario · Sydney
Tokyo · Singapore · Hong Kong · Seoul · Taipei · Cape Town · Madrid · Mexico City · Amsterdam · Munich · Paris · Milan

Pearson Education Limited
Edinburgh Gate
Harlow
Essex CM20 2JE
England

and Associated Companies throughout the world

Visit us on the World Wide Web at:
http://www.pearsoneduc.com

First published 2001

ISBN 0 201 70944 9

British Library Cataloguing-in-Publication Data
A catalogue record for this book is available from the British Library

Library of Congress Cataloging-in-Publication Data applied for
A catalog record for this book can be obtained from the Library of Congress

10 9 8 7 6 5 4 3
06 05 04 03 02

Typeset by 35 in 10/13pt Garamond MT
Printed and bound in Great Britain by Biddles Ltd, *www.biddles.co.uk*

To my Mother

In memory of my Father

To my Family

Brief contents

Contents

2   Underpinnings of Requirements Analysis   29

6 Underpinnings of System Design 196

7 User Interface Design   244

9   Program and Transaction Design   319

Trademark Notice

The following are trademarks or registered trademarks of their respective companies:

Acrobat is a trademark of Adobe Systems Incorporated; ActiveX, Outlook, PowerPoint and Windows are trademarks of Microsoft Corporation; DB2 and IBM are trademarks of International Business Machines Corporation; Java is a trademark of Sun Microsystems, Inc.; Informix is a trademark of Informix Corporation; Macintosh is a trademark of Apple Computer, Inc.; Netscape is a trademark of Netscape Communications Corporation; Oracle is a trademark of Oracle Corporation; PowerDesigner and Sybase are trademarks of Sybase, Inc.; Rational Rose is a trademark of Rational Software Corporation; UniSQL is a trademark of Cincom Systems, Inc.; Unix and Motif are trademarks of The Open Group.

Preface

Outline of the book

The development of an information system (IS) – from its inception to the first release to stakeholders – comprises three iterative and incremental phases: analysis, design, and implementation. This book describes the methods and techniques used in the first two phases. The implementation issues are only addressed to the extent to which they need to be considered in the design phase. Testing and change management are addressed in the final chapter.

The text concentrates on object-oriented software development. The Unified Modeling Language (UML) is used to capture modeling artifacts. Emphasis is placed on the development by elaboration where the same modeling language (UML) is used throughout the development lifecycle. Analysts, designers, and programmers 'speak' the same language, although perhaps use the dialects (profiles) of the language fitting their individual needs.

The early applications of object technology targeted graphical user interfaces (GUIs) and focused on the speed of developing new systems and the speed of program execution. In this book, I emphasize the application of object technology in IS development. The challenge is the large volume of data, complex data structures, shared access to information by many concurrent users, transaction processing, changing requirements, etc. The main advantage of object technology in IS environments is in facilitating software maintenance and scalability.

Developing information systems is synonymous with doing analysis and design 'in-the-large'. No IS project can succeed without following strict development processes and without understanding the underlying software architectures. The development is large-scale, object-oriented, iterative and incremental. The software architecture is based on a client/server solution, where the client is a workstation with GUI and the server stores a database. Client and server run in separate processes and communicate via object messaging. A server database can be relational, object-relational, or purely object-oriented.

The book proposes a detailed approach to analysis and design of information systems with UML. The book identifies ways to:

1. harness the complexity of large system models;
2. improve software architectures;
3. facilitate software readability, maintainability and scalability;
4. promote layered structuring of objects;
5. handle component integration;
6. improve modeling of collaboration between GUI and persistent database objects, etc.

Distinguishing features

This book has a number of features which, when combined, create a unique offering. The 'teach-by-example' approach is the cornerstone of the text. The main discussion is based on examples and a guided tutorial drawn from five application domains *University Enrolment, Video Store, Contact Management, Telemarketing,* and *OnLine Shopping.* The examples are independent. They build up into case studies that can be extended or diversified through questions formulated at the end of most chapters (Exercise Questions). Some exercises refer to a sixth application domain – *Advertising Expenditure Measurement.*

To facilitate self-education, the guided tutorial (OnLine Shopping) and the case studies are formulated using the question-and-answer principle. A separate section at the beginning of the book, 'Book Activity Diagrams' offers diagrams that link the question-and-answer steps used in the tutorial and in the case studies. The book activity diagrams can serve as an alternative table of contents for examples scattered in the text.

The book discusses principles, methods and techniques of good analysis and good design. Special attention is paid to the design phase. Design is not treated as a straightforward transformation from analysis. The book acknowledges the difficulties and intricacies of large-scale object-oriented client/server system development. In many ways, the book takes a fresh look at the 'design-in-the-large,' at iterative and incremental development of large systems, and at capabilities and limitations of tools and methods in large software production.

A unique character of the book comes from a balanced blend of practical explanation and theoretical insight. A major premise is to avoid unnecessary over-complication, but without the loss of rigor. The book 'speaks' from experience. Topics that are not relevant to industry or that are only of research interest have been excluded.

The book is on the 'cutting-edge' of information technology. It uses the latest standard in system modeling – UML. It addresses the latest developments in database technology, including object-relational databases. In this context, the Internet-driven shift from 'thick-clients' (i.e. large desktop computers) back to server-based computing is acknowledged. The analysis and design principles discussed in the text apply equally well to conventional client/server solutions and to modern component-based distributed applications.

Software development is not amenable to 'black–white,' 'true–false,' 'zero–one' solutions. Good software solutions come from good business analysts and system designers/programmers, not from blindly applied algorithms. A policy of the book is *to warn* the reader about *potential* difficulties that the advocated approach cannot entirely resolve. In consequence it is hoped that readers will apply their acquired knowledge with care and will not assume unrealistic expectations of the ease with which the approach can be applied (and thereby, possibly, fail more dramatically).

In summary, the distinguishing features of the book are:

1. The book relates the theories to reality – in the form of practical problems and limitations, which will have to be addressed when applying the approach 'in the field.'

2. The book gives special attention to the design phase. Design is *not* treated as a straightforward transformation from analysis and it acknowledges the difficulties and intricacies of large-scale client/server system development.

3. A wealth of nontrivial examples and exercises with all solutions are included in the book or the supplementary materials. The Instructor's Manual is not an afterthought – it has been written concurrently with the text and is meticulous.

Intended readership

In tune with the growing demand for university courses to be more relevant to industry practice, this textbook is aimed at students and practitioners alike. This has been a difficult task but, it is hoped, it has been successfully achieved. To ensure a *lasting educational benefit*, the implementation aspects of software development are discussed in non-vendor-specific terms (although commercial CASE tools have been used in illustrations and solutions).

The book is aimed at computer science and information systems curricula. As it contains both 'high-level' system modeling topics and 'low-level' user interface and database design issues, the book should be attractive to courses in *systems analysis, systems design, software engineering, databases, object technology*, and to *software project* courses that require students to develop a system following the development lifecycle: from requirements determination to GUI and database implementation. The book is designed for a one-semester course, but it can potentially be used over two one-semester courses – one on requirements analysis and the other on system design.

For the practitioners' audience, the presented theories are related to realities. Most problem statements, examples and exercises are drawn from the consulting practice of the author. We have adopted a policy of warning the reader of potential difficulties or limitations with advocated approaches. The following categories of practitioners are likely to benefit most from the book: *business and system analysts, designers, programmers, system architects, project leaders and managers, reviewers, testers, technical writers*, and *industry trainers*.

Organization of the book

The book provides comprehensive coverage of object-oriented analysis and design of information systems. The material is presented in an order consistent with modern development processes. The book consists of ten chapters. The coverage is balanced between analysis and design. The first five chapters address the analysis issues and the last five design and related considerations.

Readers with varying amounts of background knowledge should be able to accommodate the text. Two chapters in the book are dedicated to an explanation of the underpinnings of analysis and design. The remaining chapters assume that the reader understands these underpinnings. The reader has a choice of studying the 'underpinnings' chapters in detail or of using them for review only.

The book has several features to improve its clarity and to break the monotony of the text, in particular:

- Sections are small.

- Example and problem statements are placed in frames to distinguish them from the rest of the text. A graphical icon (see below) in the page margin also marks the beginning of each example.

- Page margins are used to:
  - number and caption figures and tables,
  - show graphical icons to identify examples in the text and end-of-chapter questions, as per the icon key below:

ICON KEY

- Examples
- Review questions
- Exercise questions

Supplementary materials

A comprehensive package of supplementary material is provided on the companion websites. Most of the web documents are freely available to the readers, but some material is password-protected for the benefit of instructors who have adopted the textbook in their teaching. The home page for the book is simultaneously maintained at:

http://www.booksites.net/maciaszek
http://www.comp.mq.edu.au/books/maciaszek

The web package includes:

1. **Instructor's Manual** with:
   - *Lecture Slides* in Microsoft PowerPoint and Acrobat Read (.pdf) formats.
   - *Answers and Solutions* manual containing annotated answers and solutions to all review and exercise questions from the end of each chapter. The organization of the manual corresponds to the textbook structure. The questions from the textbook are repeated in the manual. Answers and solutions follow the questions.

2. **Student's Resources** with printable lecture slides in Acrobat Read format.

3. **Self-education Resources** with Rational Rose (.mdl) and PowerDesigner (.pdm) model files containing solutions to the guided tutorial, the case studies and all other modeling examples in the textbook.

4. **Errata** page dedicated to corrections of errors and omissions in the book.

5. **For More Information** page to point the reader to the latest ideas and trends in the textbook's subject area. Also, to identify courses that adopted the book and which are prepared to share their web facilities with other readers.

Your comments, corrections, suggestions for improvements, contributions, etc. are very much appreciated. Please, direct any correspondence to:

Leszek A. Maciaszek
Department of Computing
Macquarie University
Sydney
NSW 2109
Australia
leszek@ics.mq.edu.au
http://www.comp.mq.edu.au/~leszek/
phone: +61 2 9850-9519
facsimile: +61 2 9850-9551
courier: North Ryde, Herring Road, Bld. E6A, Room 319

Acknowledgements

The writing of this book would be impossible without my interactions with friends, colleagues, students, industry gurus, and all the other people who, consciously or not, have shaped my knowledge in the subject area. I am truly indebted to all of them. An attempt to list all their names would be injudicious and impractical – please accept a blanket 'thank you.' However, even in the little space available for acknowledgements, a few 'mates' must be mentioned:

- Keith Mansfield, Mary Lince and the staff of Pearson Education – for recognizing the potential of this book and bringing it to the international market.

- Stephen Bills and his staff at ACNielsen AdEx, Sydney, Australia, in particular: Steven Grotte, Kevin Mathie, Cameron Murray, James Rees, Jovan Spoa, and Eric Zurcher – for providing me with a production IS development testbed for this book.

- My friends and colleagues in the Department of Computing at Macquarie University in Sydney Australia – for their support in the making of this book.

- The formal (unknown to me) and informal reviewers – for invaluable feedback that has greatly benefited the book.

- The staff at Rational, Oracle and Sybase – for providing me with the CASE and database software indispensable to the development of tutorials, case studies and examples.

The publishers are grateful to the following for permission to reproduce copyright material:

Figure 2.34 reproduced with the permission of Gateway, Inc. © Gateway, Inc.; Figures 7.1, 7.2, 7.4, 7.6, 7.7, 7.8, 7.9, 7.11, 7.12, 7.13, 7.14, 7.15, 7.16, 7.17, 7.19, 7.20, 10.6, 10.7, 10.8, 10.9, 10.10, 10.11 and 10.12 reproduced with the permission of ACNielsen; Figure 7.10 reproduced with the permission of Macquarie University.

A Companion Website accompanies *Requirements Analysis and System Design* by Leszek A. Maciaszek.

Visit the ***Requirements Analysis and System Design*** Companion Website at www.booksites.net/maciaszek

Here you will find valuable teaching and learning material including:

For Lecturers:
- Lecture slides in PowerPoint or Acrobat format.
- Solutions manual containing annotated answers and solutions to all review and exercise questions from the end of each chapter.

For Students and Lecturers:
- Rational Rose and PowerDesigner model files containing solutions to the guided tutorials, case studies and all other modeling examples in the textbook.
- Updates page with links to latest trends and others working in the subject area.

Book Activity Diagrams

Requirements analysis and system design is an applied knowledge. As such, it cannot just be learned by reading textbooks. The only effective way of learning it is by doing it, making mistakes, analyzing the mistakes, and trying to avoid them on a future assignment. This textbook has been written with this observation in mind.

The book is full of examples, including a guided tutorial and four case studies. However, the examples have been formulated to permit the reader's self-education, experimentation, making mistakes or arriving at alternative solutions. The reader is always invited to have a go at it before looking at a provided solution. After all 'Good judgment comes from experience. Experience comes from bad judgment' (Jim Horning).

The book activity diagrams provide the maps that link each example. A formal modeling technique (UML Activity Diagrams) has been used in construction of these diagrams but no knowledge of the technique is required to use the diagrams. Each *rounded rectangle* (a UML state) refers to a *section* in the book with an example. *Arrows* that (directly or indirectly) point to a rectangle come from the *prerequisite examples*. The labels on these arrows define all *activities* that would have to be accomplished before attempting the example.

The ways in which the book activity diagrams can be used are diverse and limited only by the imagination of the reader. They can be used:

- to combine examples in a tutorial or case study into a coherent unit to be addressed in a consecutive and uninterrupted learning effort;
- to quickly locate the previous examples and solutions necessary to undertake the next task;
- to select some modeling activities and ignore others for targeted and customized learning;
- to develop student assignments, etc.

The book activity diagrams are integrated with the exercises at the end of each chapter. The exercises extend the ideas developed in the in-text examples. The best way to locate examples referred to in an exercise and to get an idea of the knowledge required to solve that exercise's problems, is to look at the relevant activity diagram.

OnLine Shopping (Guided Tutorial)

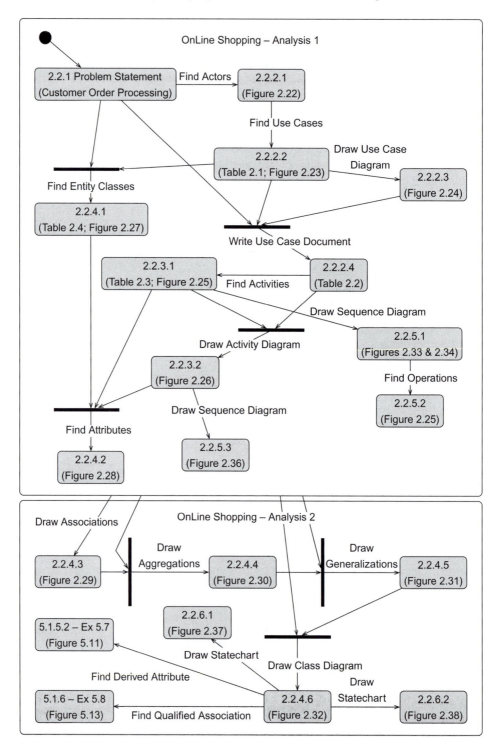

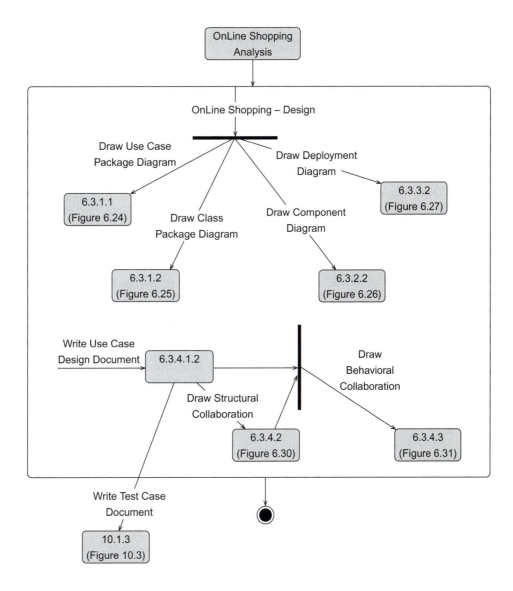

University Enrolment (Case Study)

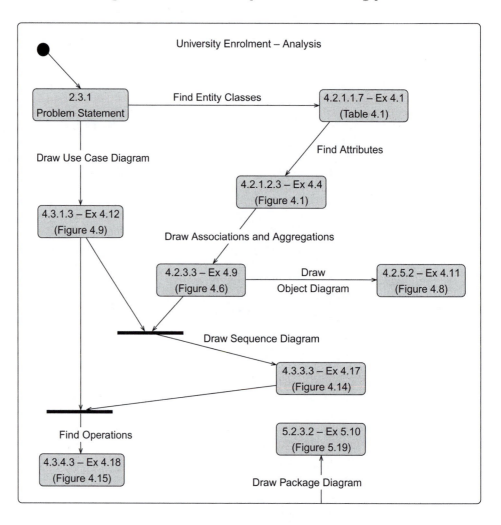

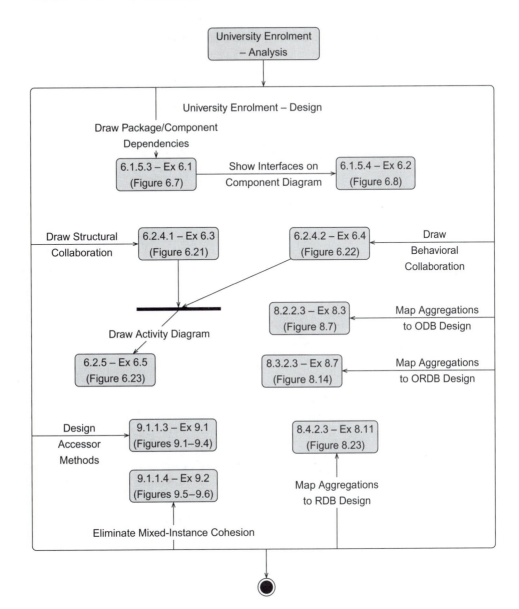

Video Store (Case Study)

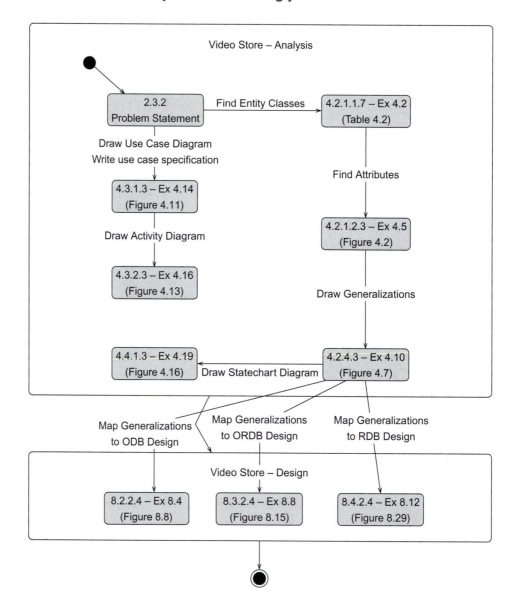

Contact Management (Case Study)

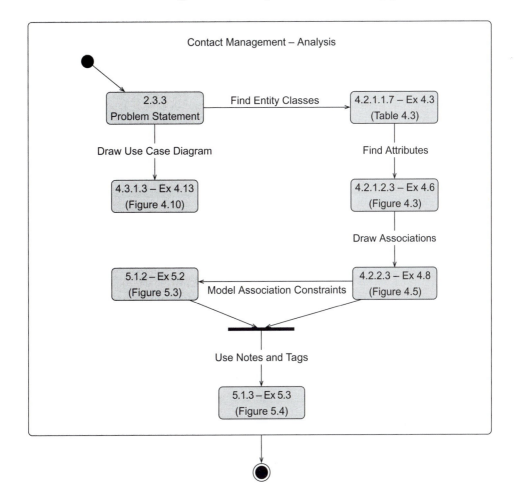

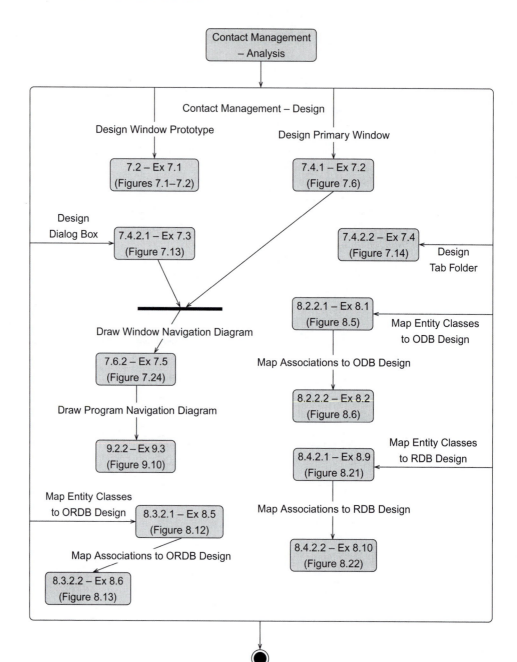

Telemarketing (Case Study)

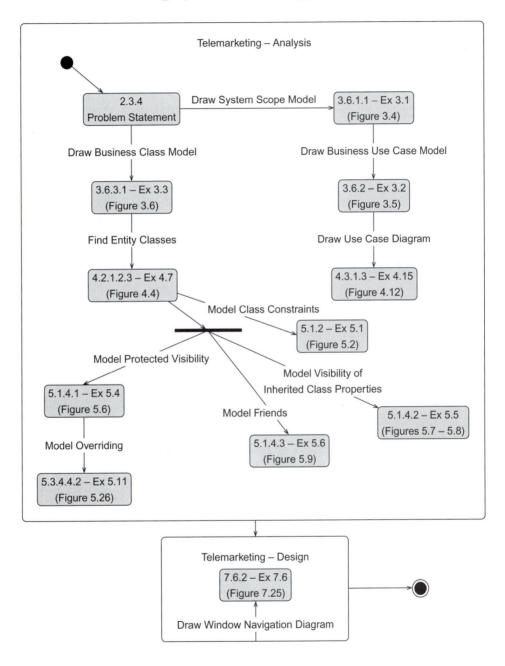

Software Process

The intention of this chapter is to describe – at an overview level – a number of strategic issues in the software development process. Since the topic is treated at an overview level and some issues are contentious, the reader does not have to agree with the author to benefit from the rest of the book (and possibly re-evaluate his/her opinion when reaching the end of the text).

The educational value of this chapter is in introducing the reader to processes and approaches that underlie modern software development. The reader may already be familiar with many of the ideas and topics discussed in this chapter from experience, everyday use of computers or from reading related literature. Such a reader may choose to skim this chapter and proceed to Chapter 2.

1.1 The nature of software development

The literature on Information Systems (IS) management is full of examples of failed projects, exceeded deadlines and budgets, faulty solutions, unmaintainable systems, etc. The 1998 version of the frequently quoted CHAOS research report by the Standish Group maintains that almost three out of four software projects fail in one or more of the above areas. The paramount questions are: What causes software projects to fail? What are the symptoms of project problems and what is the treatment?

To address these questions, we first need to understand the nature of software development. In a now classic paper, Brooks (1987) identified the essence and accidents of software engineering. The *essence* of software engineering is embodied in the difficulties inherent in the software itself. These difficulties can only be acknowledged – they are not amenable to breakthroughs or 'silver bullets.' According to Brooks, the essence of software engineering is a consequence of the inherent software complexity, conformity, changeability, and invisibility.

The four 'essential difficulties' of software define a software development invariant. The invariant states simply that software is a product of a creative act of development – a craft or an art in the sense of that activity performed by an artisan rather than a fine artist. In a typical state of affairs, software is not a result of a repetitive act of manufacturing.

Once the invariant of software development is understood, one should address the *accidents* of software engineering – the difficulties due to software production practices, amenable to human intervention. We group various 'accidental difficulties' into three categories:

1. Stakeholders.

2. Process.

3. Modeling language and tools.

1.1.1 The software development invariant

Software is *developed* rather than *manufactured* (Pressman, 1997). Of course, one cannot deny that advances in software engineering introduce more certainty to development practices, but (unlike in traditional engineering) the success of a software project cannot be guaranteed.

Algorithms, code libraries, reusable classes, software components, etc. are incomplete solutions for what we need to describe when developing information systems. The challenge is in putting together little pieces of the problem into a coherent *enterprise system* that meets the needs of complex business processes.

Software practices encourage the development of systems from customizable software packages – *commercial-of-the-shelf* (COTS) solutions or *Enterprise Resource Planning* (ERP) systems. A software package can deliver a routine accounting, manufacturing or human resources system. The emphasis is changed from 'developing from scratch' to 'customizing' the software, but the production process is equally groundbreaking.

Conceptual constructs (models) for a final solution, so that they satisfy the specific needs of an organization, have to be created for any system developed from scratch. Once created, software package functionality is customized to correspond to the conceptual constructs. Programming tasks may be different, but requirements analysis and system design activities are similar to those in development from scratch. After all, a conceptual construct (model) is the same under many possible representations (implementations).

Even more importantly, it is unlikely that an organization can find a software package to automate its *core business* activities. A core business activity of a telephone company is telephony, not human resources or accounting. What makes an organization tick (and compete) must be developed from scratch (or redeveloped from an existing *legacy system*). As noticed by Szyperski (1998, p. 5): 'Standard packages create a level playing field and the competition has to come from other areas.'

Of course, in every case, the development process should take advantage of *component technology* (Szyperski, 1998; Allen and Frost, 1998). A component is an executable unit of software with well-defined functionality (services) and communication protocols (interfaces) to other components. Components can be configured to satisfy application requirements. Currently most influential component technologies are:

- *Common Object Request Broker Architecture* (CORBA) from Object Management Group (OMG).

- *Distributed Component Object Model* (DCOM) from Microsoft.

- *Enterprise JavaBeans* (EJB) from Sun.

Packages, components and similar techniques do not change the essence of software production. In particular, the principles and tasks of requirements analysis and system design remain invariant. A final software product can be assembled from standard and custom-made components but the 'assembly' process is still an art. Frankly, as Pressman (1997) observes, we do not even have software 'spare parts' to replace broken components in systems 'on the road.'

1.1.2 Stakeholders

Stakeholders are people who have a stake in a software project. Any person affected by the system or who has influence on system development is a stakeholder. There are two main groups of stakeholders:

- Customers (users and system owners); and

- Developers (analysts, designers, programmers, etc.).

We prefer to use the term *customer* rather than *user*. This distinction is certainly valid from the system development perspective. Firstly, the customer is the person who pays for the development and is responsible for making decisions. Secondly, even if the customer is not always right, the customer's requirements cannot be arbitrarily changed or rejected by developers – any conflicting, unfeasible or illegal requirements must be renegotiated with customers.

This said, we have to acknowledge that the term *user* (to mean *customer*) is much more popular and we will not shy away from this later on. We will refrain, however, from using the awkward term *end-user* that has historically referred to a *user representative* selected to interact with developers (in lieu of a *real user*).

Information systems are *social systems*. They are developed by people (developers) for people (customers). Success of a software project is determined by social factors – technology is secondary. There are many examples of technically inferior systems that work and benefit customers. The inverse is not true. A system with no benefit (perceived or real) to the customer will be abandoned no matter how technically brilliant.

In a typical situation, the main causes of software failure can be traced to the stakeholder factor. On the *customer* end, projects fail because (e.g. Pfleeger, 1998):

- customer needs are misunderstood or not fully captured;

- customer requirements change too frequently;

- customers are not prepared to commit sufficient resources to the project;

- customers do not want to cooperate with developers;

- customers have unrealistic expectations;

- the system is no longer of benefit to customers.

Projects also fail because the *developers* may not be up to the task. With the escalation in software complexity, there is a growing recognition that skills and knowledge of developers are critical. Good developers can deliver a solution. Great developers can deliver much better solutions much quicker and cheaper. As the famous one-liner from Fred Brooks says: 'Great designs come from great designers.' (Brooks, 1987, p. 13).

Excellence and commitment of developers is the factor which contributes most to software quality and productivity. To ensure that a software product is successfully delivered to a customer, and, more importantly, to reap productivity benefits from it, a software organization must follow some obvious steps with regard to developers (Brooks, 1987; Yourdon, 1994):

- hire the best developers;
- provide ongoing training and education to existing developers;
- encourage exchange of information and interaction among developers so that they stimulate each other;
- motivate developers by removing obstacles and channeling the efforts into productive work;
- offer an exciting working environment (this tends to be much more important to people than an occasional salary increase);
- align personal goals with organizational strategies and objectives;
- emphasize teamwork.

1.1.3 Process

A software development *process* determines activities and organizational procedures to enhance collaboration in the development team so that a quality product is delivered to the customers. A process model:

- states an order for carrying out activities;
- specifies what development artifacts are to be delivered and when;
- assigns activities and artifacts to developers;
- offers criteria for monitoring a project's progress, for measuring the outcomes, and for planning future projects.

Development processes cannot be standardized or codified to be automatically embraced by an organization. Each organization has to develop its own process model or customize it from a generic process template, such as the template provided by the Rational Software Corporation and known as the *Rational Unified Process* (Kruchten, 1999).

The process adopted by an organization must be aligned with its development culture, social dynamics, developers' knowledge and skills, managerial practices, customers' expectations, project sizes, and even kinds of application domains. Because all these factors are subject to change, an organization may need to diversify its process model and create variants of it for each software project. For example, depending on the developers' familiarity with the modeling methods and tools, special training courses may need to be included in the process.

Project size has probably the greatest influence on the process. In a small project (of ten or so developers), a formal process may not be needed at all. Such a small team is likely to communicate and respond to changes informally. In larger projects, an informal communication network will not suffice and a well-defined process for controlled development is necessary.

1.1.3.1 *Iterative and incremental process*

Modern software development processes are invariably *iterative* and *incremental*. System models are refined and transformed through analysis, design and implementation phases – details are added in successive *iterations*, changes and improvements are introduced as needed, and *incremental releases* of software modules maintain user satisfaction and provide important feedback to modules still under development.

As the *Rational Unified Process* states: 'An iterative process is one that involves managing a stream of executable releases. An incremental process is one that involves the continuous integration of the system's architecture to produce these releases, with each new release embodying incremental improvements over the other.' (Booch *et al.*, 1999, p. 33.)

The success of an iterative and incremental process is predicated on early identification of the *system's architectural modules*. The modules should be of similar size, be highly cohesive and have minimal overlaps (coupling). The order in which the modules are to be implemented is also important. Some modules may not be able to be *released* if they depend for information or computation on other modules yet to be developed. Unless iterative and incremental development is planned and controlled, it can degenerate to 'ad-hoc hacking' with no control over the project's real progress.

1.1.3.2 *Capability maturity model*

A major challenge for every organization engaged in software production is to improve its development process. Naturally enough, to introduce process improvements, the organization has to know what the problems are with its current process. *Capability Maturity Model* (CMM) is a popular method for process assessment and improvement (CMM, 1995).

CMM has been specified by the Software Engineering Institute (SEI) at Carnegie Mellon University in Pittsburgh, USA. Originally used by the US Department of Defense to assess IT capabilities of organizations bidding for defense contracts, it is now widely used by the IT industry in America and elsewhere.

CMM is essentially a *questionnaire* that an IT organization fills in. The questionnaire is followed by a verification and attestation process, which assigns the organization to one of the five CMM levels. The higher the level, the better the process maturity in the organization.

FIGURE 1.1

Process maturity
levels in CMM.

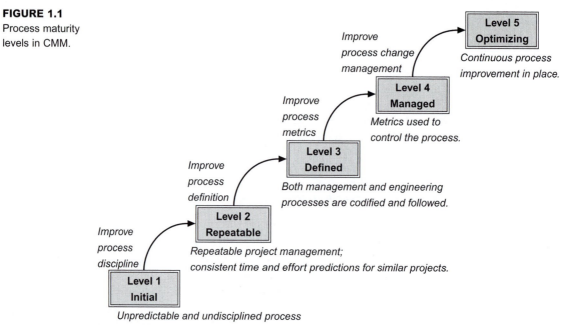

Figure 1.1 defines the levels, gives a short description of the main features of each level, and indicates the main areas of process improvement necessary for the organization to achieve a higher level.

Arthur (1992) calls the levels of maturity 'the stairway to software excellence.' The five steps on the stairway are: chaos, project management, methods and tools, measurement, and continuous quality improvement.

Experience has shown that it takes several years to progress one level up on the maturity scale. Most organizations are at Level 1, some at Level 2; very few are known to be at Level 5. The following few questions show the difficulty of the task. An organization that wants to be at CMM Level 2 must provide positive answers to all these questions (and more) (Pfleeger, 1998):

■ Does the Software Quality Assurance function have a management-reporting channel separate from the software development project management?

■ Is there a software configuration control function for each project that involves software development?

■ Is a formal process used in the management review of each software development prior to making contractual commitments?

■ Is a formal procedure used to produce software development schedules?

■ Are formal procedures applied to estimating software development cost?

■ Are statistics on software code and test errors gathered?

■ Does senior management have a mechanism for the regular review of the status of software development projects?

■ Is a mechanism used for controlling changes to the software requirements?

1.1.3.3 ISO 9000

There are other process improvement models besides CMM. Of particular interest is the ISO 9000 series of quality standards, developed by the International Organization for Standardization. The ISO standards apply to the *quality* management and the *process* to produce a quality product. The standards are generic – they apply to any industry and all types of businesses, including software development.

The main premise of the ISO 9000 standards is that if the process is right then the process outcome (product or service) will also be right. 'The objective of quality management is to produce quality products by building quality into the products rather than testing quality into the products.' (Schmauch, 1994, p. 1.)

As per our earlier discussion about the process, the ISO standards do not enforce or specify processes. The standards provide models of *what* must be accomplished, not *how* activities must be performed. An organization requesting an ISO certification (also called registration) must say what it does, do what it says, and demonstrate what it has done (Schmauch, 1994).

A litmus test for an ISO certified organization is that it should be able to make a quality product or provide a quality service even if its entire workforce were replaced. To this aim the organization has to *document and record* all its activities. Written procedures must be defined for each activity, including what to do when things go wrong or customers complain.

As with CMM, the ISO certification can only be granted after an *on-site audit* by an ISO registrar. These audits are then repeated at regular intervals. Organizations are forced into the scheme through competitive forces stipulated by customers demanding that the suppliers of products and services be certified.

1.1.4 Modeling language and tools

Stakeholders and processes are two elements in the triangle for success. The third element consists of a modeling language and tools. Modeling artifacts have to be communicated (language) and documented (tools).

Developers need a *language* to build visual and other models and discuss them with customers and fellow developers. The language should allow the construction of models at varying levels of abstraction to present proposed solutions at different levels of detail.

The language should have a strong *visual* component as per the popular saying that 'a picture is worth a thousand words.' It should also have strong *declarative semantics*, i.e. it should allow capturing 'procedural' meaning in 'declarative' sentences. We should be able to communicate by saying 'what' needs to be done rather than 'how' to go about doing it.

Developers also need a *tool* for Computer-Assisted Software Engineering (CASE). A CASE tool enables storage and retrieval of models in a central repository and graphical and textual manipulation of models on a computer screen. Ideally, a repository should provide for a shareable multi-user (i.e. multi-developer) access to models. Typical functions of a *CASE repository* are to:

- coordinate access to models;
- facilitate collaboration between developers;
- store multiple versions of models;
- identify differences between versions;
- allow to share the same concepts in different models;
- check consistency and integrity of models;
- generate project reports and documents;
- generate data structures and programming code (forward engineering);
- generate models from existing implementation (reverse engineering), etc.

Note that a CASE-generated program is frequently just a code skeleton – computational algorithms need to be coded by programmers in the usual way.

1.1.4.1 *Unified modeling language*

'The Unified Modeling Language (UML) is a general-purpose visual modeling language that is used to specify, visualize, construct, and document the artifacts of a software system.' (Rumbaugh *et al.*, 1999, p. 3.) UML was developed by the Rational Software Corporation to unify the best features of earlier methods and notations. In 1997, Object Management Group (OMG) approved it as a standard modeling language. Since then, UML has been further developed and has been widely adopted by the IT industry.

UML is independent of any software development process, although Rational has later proposed a matching process called *Rational Unified Process* (Kruchten, 1998). Clearly enough a process that adopts UML must support an *object-oriented approach* to software production. UML is not appropriate for old-style structured approaches that result in systems implemented with procedural programming languages, such as COBOL.

UML is also independent of implementation technologies (as long as they are object-oriented). This makes UML somewhat deficient, in our opinion, in supporting the detailed design phase of the development lifecycle. By the same token, however, this makes UML resilient to frequent changes in implementation platforms.

UML language constructs allow modeling the static structure and dynamic behavior of a system. A system is modeled as a set of collaborating *objects* (software modules) that react to external events to perform tasks of benefit to customers (users). Individual models emphasize some aspects of the system and ignore aspects that are emphasized in other models. Together, all models provide a complete description for the system.

The UML models can be categorized into three groups:

- *State models* (that describe the static data structures);

- *Behavior models* (that describe object collaborations); and

- *State change models* (that describe the allowed states for the system over time).

UML also contains a few *architectural constructs* that allow modularizing the system for iterative and incremental development.

1.1.4.2 CASE and process improvement

Process improvement is much more than the introduction of new methods and techniques. In fact, the introduction of new methods and techniques to organization at a low level of process maturity can bring more harm than good.

An example in point is the CASE technology. An *integrated* CASE tool can allow multiple developers to collaborate and share design information in order to produce new design artifacts. Such a CASE tool imposes certain processes that the development team has to obey to take advantage of this technology. But, if the development team has not been capable so far to improve its processes, it is extremely unlikely that it will assimilate the process dictated by the CASE tool. As a result, the potential productivity and quality gains offered by the new technology will not materialize.

The above discussion must not mislead you into thinking that CASE technology is a 'risky business'. It may not give you the expected benefits if you attempt to use it to drive the entire development team and the team is not prepared to follow necessary processes. However, the same CASE methods and techniques would always bring personal productivity and quality improvements to individual developers who use the technology on their own local workstations. Modeling software artifacts with pencil and paper only makes good sense in a classroom, never on real projects.

1.2 System planning

Information system projects have to be planned for. They have to be identified, classified, ranked and selected for initial development, for improvement, or perhaps for elimination. The question is: Which IS technologies and applications will return the most value to the business? Ideally, the decision as to which way to go should be based on *business strategy* and on careful and methodical planning (Bennett *et al.*, 1999; Hoffer *et al.*, 1999; Maciaszek, 1990).

Business strategy can be determined through various processes known as *strategic planning*, *business modeling*, *business process reengineering*, *strategic alignment*, *information resource management*, or similar. It is not our aim to explain differences in the various approaches. Suffice to say that all these approaches undertake to study fundamental business processes in an organization in order to determine a long-term vision for the business and then to prioritize business issues that can be resolved by the use of information technology.

This said, there are many organizations, in particular many small organizations, with no clear business strategy. Such organizations are likely to decide on information systems development by simply identifying the current most pressing business problems that need to be addressed. If external environment or internal business conditions change, the existing information systems have to be modified again. While this approach has obvious disadvantages, it allows small organizations to refocus quickly on their current situation – either to take advantage of new opportunities or to rebuff new threats.

Large organizations cannot afford constant changes of business directions. In reality, they frequently dictate directions for other organizations in the same line of business. To some degree, they can mold the environment to their *current* needs. However, large organizations have to look carefully into the *future*. They have to use a planning-based approach for identifying development projects. These are typically large projects that take a long time to complete. They are too cumbersome to be easily changed or replaced. They need to accommodate or even target future opportunities and threats.

System planning can be carried out in a number of different ways. A traditional approach is nicknamed *SWOT – Strengths, Weaknesses, Opportunities, Threats*. Another popular strategy is based on *VCM – Value Chain Model*. More modern variations for developing a business strategy are known as *BPR – Business Process Reengineering*. The information needs of an organization can also be assessed by using blueprints for *Information System Architecture* (ISA). Such blueprints can be obtained by analogy from descriptive frameworks that proved successful in disciplines other than IT – for example, in the construction industry.

All system planning approaches have an important common denominator – they are concerned with *effectiveness* (doing the right thing) rather than *efficiency* (doing things right). Efficiently solving a wrong problem does not do much good!

1.2.1 SWOT approach

The SWOT (Strengths, Weaknesses, Opportunities, Threats) approach allows the identification, classification, ranking and selection of IS development projects in a manner that is aligned with an organization's strengths, weaknesses, opportunities and threats. This is a top-down approach that starts with the determination of an organization's mission.

The *mission statement* captures the unique character of an organization and specifies its vision of where it wants to be in the future. In a good mission statement emphasis is placed on customer needs rather than on products or services that an organization delivers.

The mission statement and a business strategy developed from it takes into consideration the *internal company strengths and weaknesses* in the areas of management, production, human resources, finance, marketing, research and development, etc. These strengths and weaknesses must be carefully negotiated, agreed upon and prioritized. A successful organization can, at all times, identify a current set of strengths and weaknesses that guide the development of its business strategy.

The identification of internal company strengths and weaknesses is a necessary, but not sufficient, condition for successful business planning. An organization does not function in a vacuum – it depends on external economic, social, political, and technological factors. An organization has to know of *external opportunities* to be taken advantage of and *external threats* to be avoided. These are factors that an organization cannot control but knowledge of them is essential in determining the organization's objectives and goals.

Organizations pursue one or very few *objectives* at any given time. Objectives are normally long-term (three to five years) or even 'timeless.' Typical examples of objectives are to improve customer satisfaction, to introduce new services, to address competitive threats, to increase control over suppliers, etc. Each strategic objective must be associated with specific *goals*, usually expressed as annual targets. For example, the objective 'to improve customer satisfaction' can be supported by the goal of fulfilling customer orders more quickly – within two weeks, say.

Objectives and goals require management *strategies* and specific *policies* for the implementation of these strategies. Such managerial instruments would adjust organizational structures, allocate resources and determine development projects, including information systems.

1.2.2 VCM approach

The VCM (Value Chain Model) assesses competitive advantage by analyzing the full chain of activities in an organization – from raw materials to final products sold and shipped to customers. The chain metaphor reinforces the point that a single weak link will cause the whole chain to break.

The model serves the purpose of understanding which value chain configurations will yield the greatest competitive advantage. The IS development projects can then target those segments, operations, distribution channels, marketing approaches, etc. that give the most competitive advantage.

In the original VCM approach (Porter, 1985), organizational functions are categorized into *primary activities* and *support activities*. The primary activities create or add value to a final product. They are divided into five successive stages: (1) inbound logistics, (2) operations, (3) outbound logistics, (4) sales and marketing, (5) services.

The support activities do not add value, at least directly. They are still essential but they do not enrich the product. The support activities include: (1) administration and infrastructure, (2) human resource management, (3) research and development, and – perhaps not surprisingly – (4) IS development.

While VCM is a useful tool for IS planning, the omnipresent computerization can facilitate business changes that can in turn create competitive advantages. In other words, *IT can transform organizations' value chains*. A self-reinforcing loop between IT and VCM can be established.

Porter and Millar (1985) identify five steps that an organization can take to exploit IT opportunities:

1. Assess the information intensity of products and processes.

2. Assess the role of IT in industry structure.

3. Identify and rank ways in which IT could create a competitive advantage.

4. Consider how IT could create new businesses.

5. Develop a plan to take advantage of IT.

1.2.3 BPR approach

The BPR (Business Process Reengineering) approach to system planning is based on the premise that today's organizations must reinvent themselves and abandon the functional decomposition, hierarchical structures and operational principles that they are now using.

The concept was introduced in 1990 by Hammer (1990) and Davenport and Short (1990) and it immediately generated interest as well as controversy. An extended description of BPR can be found in the books by the originators (Hammer and Champy, 1993; Davenport, 1993).

Most organizations today are structured in *vertical units* focused on functions, products or regions. These structures and work styles can be traced back to the eighteenth century and to Adam Smith's principle of the division of labor and the consequent fragmentation of work. No one employee or department is responsible for a *business process* which is defined as '. . . a collection of activities that takes one or more kinds of input and creates an output that is of value to the customer' (Hammer and Champy, 1993).

BPR challenges Smith's industrial principles of the division of labor, hierarchical control and economies of scale. In today's world, organizations must be able to adapt quickly to market changes, new technologies, competitive factors, customer demands, etc.

Rigid organizational structures in which business processes have to cut across many departments are obsolete. Organizations must focus on business processes rather than individual tasks, jobs, people, or departmental functions. These processes cut *horizontally* across the business and end at points of contact with customers. 'The most visible difference between a process enterprise and a traditional organization is the existence of process owners' (Hammer and Stanton, 1999).

The main objective of BPR is to radically redesign business processes in an organization (hence, BPR is sometimes known as a *process redesign*). Business processes have to be identified, streamlined and improved. The processes are documented in *workflow diagrams* and subjected to a *workflow analysis*. Workflows capture the flow of events, documents and information in a business process and can be used to calculate time, resources and costs needed for these activities.

The major hurdle in implementing BPR in organizations lies in the need to embed a horizontal process in a traditional vertical management structure. A serious BPR initiative requires changing the organization around the development teams as the primary organizational units. These teams are responsible for one or more end-to-end business processes.

Sometimes a radical change is unacceptable. The traditional structures cannot be changed overnight. A radical push can meet with defiance and potential benefits of BPR can be compromised. Under such circumstances, an organization can still benefit from modeling business processes and attempting just to improve them, rather than reengineer. The term Business Process Improvement (BPI) is used to characterize such an initiative (Allen and Frost, 1998).

Once business processes are defined, the process owners would require Information Technology (IT) support to further improve the efficiency of these processes. The resulting IS development projects would concentrate on implementing the identified workflows. The combination of *effectiveness* of BPR and *efficiency* of IT can give dramatic improvements in all contemporary measures of an organization's performance, such as quality, service, speed, cost, price, competitive advantage, flexibility, etc.

1.2.4 ISA approach

Unlike the already described approaches, ISA (Information Systems Architecture) is a bottom-up approach that offers a *neutral architectural framework* for IS solutions that can suit a variety of business strategies. As such, the ISA approach does not include a system planning methodology. It simply offers a framework that leverages most business strategies.

The ISA approach has been introduced in a seminal paper by Zachman (1987) and later extended by Sowa and Zachman (1992). An insignificantly modified version of the original paper has been published again in Zachman (1999).

The ISA framework is represented as a table of thirty cells organized into five rows (labeled 1 through 5) and six columns (labeled A through F). The rows represent the different *perspectives* used in the construction of a complex engineering product, such as an information system. These perspectives are those of five major 'players in the game,' the five IS participants:

1. Planner (determines the scope of the system);
2. Owner (defines an enterprise conceptual model);
3. Designer (specifies a system physical model);
4. Builder (provides detailed technological solutions);
5. Subcontractor (delivers system components).

The six columns represent the six different *descriptions* or *architectural models* that each of the participants 'plays with.' Like perspectives, descriptions are quite different from each other but at the same time they are intrinsically related to one another. The descriptions provide answers to six questions that each participant is concerned with:

A.   *What* is the thing made of? (i.e. data, in the case of IS);

B.   *How* does the thing function? (i.e. business processes);

C.   *Where* is the thing located? (i.e. location of processing components);

D.   *Who* works with the thing? (i.e. the users);

E.   *When* does the thing occur? (i.e. the scheduling of events and states);

F.   *Why* is the thing taking place? (i.e. the motivation of the enterprise).

The combination of perspectives and descriptions in thirty cells provides a powerful taxonomy that establishes a complete architecture for an IS development. The vertical perspectives may differ in detail, but more importantly, they differ in essence and they employ different modeling representations. Different models emphasize different viewpoints of the participants. Likewise, the horizontal descriptions are prepared for different reasons. They each answer one of the six questions.

The most attractive feature of the ISA approach comes from providing a framework that is likely to be flexible enough to accommodate future changes in business conditions and resources. This is because an ISA solution is not derived from any particular business strategy. It is just a framework for a complete description of an IS system. The framework draws from experiences of more established disciplines – some with a thousand or so years of history (such as classical architecture).

1.2.5 Systems for three management levels

Associated with system planning is the recognition that an organization has three management levels:

1.   Strategic;

2.   Tactical; and

3.   Operational.

The three levels are characterized by a unique focus of decision making, by a distinct set of required IS applications, and by a specific support required from IT. It is the task of system planning to define a blend of IS applications and IT solutions that are most effective for an organization at a particular point in time. Table 1.1 defines the issues involved in matching decision-making levels to IS applications and IT solutions (cp. Jordan and Machesky, 1990; Robson, 1994).

IS applications and IT solutions that offer the greatest returns to an organization are those at the *strategic level*. However, these are also solutions that are most difficult to implement – they use 'bleeding-edge' technology and demand very skillful and specialized design. After all, these are the systems that can give an organization a competitive advantage in the marketplace.

At the other end of the spectrum, systems in support of the *operational management level* are quite routine, use conventional database technology, and are frequently customized from

TABLE 1.1 IS and IT support for different levels of decision making.

Level of decision making	Focus of decision making	Typical IS applications	Typical IT solutions
Strategic	Strategies in support of organizational long-term objectives	Market and sales analysis, Product planning, Performance evaluation	Data mining, Knowledge management
Tactical	Policies in support of short-term goals and resource allocation	Budget analysis, Salary forecasting, Inventory scheduling, Customer service	Data warehouse, Analytical processing, Spreadsheets
Operational	Day-to-day staff activities and production support	Payroll, Invoicing, Purchasing, Accounting	Database, Transactional processing, Application generators

pre-packaged solutions. These systems are unlikely to provide a competitive edge, but without them the organization is not able to function properly.

Every modern organization has a full suite of operational-level systems, but only the best-managed organizations have an integrated set of strategic-level IS applications. The main technology for storing and retrieving data for high-level strategic and tactical decision making is known as *data warehouse* (Kimball, 1996).

1.3 Software lifecycle phases

Software development follows a life cycle. The term is so popular that it is frequently written as one word – *lifecycle*. The lifecycle is an orderly set of activities conducted and managed for each development project. The processes and methods are the machinery for a lifecycle implementation. The lifecycle identifies the *phases* along which the software product moves – from initial inception to phasing it out.

The software development lifecycle can be presented at different levels of phase granularity. At a *coarse level of granularity*, the lifecycle can include only three phases:

1. Analysis.

2. Design.

3. Implementation.

The *analysis phase* concentrates on system requirements. Requirements are determined and specified. Function and data models for the system are developed and integrated. Non-functional requirements and other system constraints are also captured.

The *design phase* divides into two major sub-phases: architectural and detailed design. In particular, the client/server program design that integrates user interface and database objects is explained. Various design issues that influence a system's understandability, maintainability and scalability are raised and documented.

The *implementation phase* contains the coding of client application programs and server databases. Incremental and iterative implementation processes are emphasized. *Round-trip engineering* between design models and the implementation of client applications and server databases is essential to a successful product delivery.

In a nutshell, analysis is about what to do, design is how to do it using the available technology, and implementation is doing it (in the sense that a tangible software product is delivered).

At a *refined level of granularity*, the lifecycle can be divided into the following seven phases:

1. Requirements Determination.

2. Requirements Specification.

3. Architectural Design.

4. Detailed Design.

5. Implementation.

6. Integration.

7. Maintenance (and eventual phasing-out).

Some authors include also *Planning* and *Testing* as two additional phases. In our opinion, these two important activities are *not* separate lifecycle phases because they span the whole lifecycle. A software project management plan is drawn up early in the process, significantly enriched after the specification phase, and evolving through the rest of the lifecycle. Similarly, testing is most intensive after implementation but it also applies to software artifacts produced in every other phase.

1.3.1 Requirements determination phase

Kotonya and Sommerville (1998) define a *requirement* as 'a statement of a system service or constraint.' A *service statement* describes how the system should behave with regard to an individual user or with regard to the whole user community. In the latter case, a service statement really defines a *business rule* that must be obeyed at all times (e.g. 'fortnightly salaries are paid on Wednesdays'). A service statement may also be some computation that the system must carry out (e.g. 'calculate salesperson commission based on the sales in the last fortnight using a particular formula').

A *constraint statement* expresses a restriction on the system's behavior or on the system's development. An example for the former may be the security constraint: 'only direct managers can see the salary information of their staff.' An example for the latter may be: 'we must use Sybase development tools.'

Notice that sometimes the distinction between a constraint statement on the system's behavior and a business rule service statement is blurred. This is not a problem as long as all requirements are identified and duplications eliminated.

The task of the requirements determination phase is to determine, analyze and negotiate requirements with the customers. The phase involves various techniques of gathering information from the customers. It is a concept exploration through structured and unstructured interviews of users, questionnaires, study of documents and forms, video recording, etc. An ultimate technique of the requirements phase is *rapid prototyping* of the solution so that difficult requirements can be clarified and misunderstandings are avoided.

Requirements analysis includes negotiations between developers and customers. This step is necessary to eliminate contradicting and overlapping requirements, and also to conform to the project budget and deadline.

The product of the requirements phase is a *requirements document*. This is mostly a narrative text document with some informal diagrams and tables. No formal models are included except perhaps a few easy and popular notations which can be easily grasped by the customers and which can facilitate the developer–customer communication.

1.3.2 Requirements specification phase

The requirements specification phase begins when the developers start modeling the requirements using a particular method (such as UML). A CASE tool is used to enter, analyze and document the models. As a result, the Requirements Document is enriched with graphical models and CASE-generated reports. In essence, a *specifications document* (the *specs* in the jargon) replaces the requirements document.

The two most important specification techniques in object-oriented analysis are class diagrams and use case diagrams. These are techniques for data and function specifications. A typical specification document will also describe other requirements, such as performance, 'look and feel,' usability, maintainability, security, and also political and legal requirements.

Specification models can and will overlap. They allow the proposed solution to be viewed from many different angles so that specific aspects of the solution are emphasized and analyzed. Consistency and completeness of requirements are also carefully checked.

Ideally, the specification models should be independent from the hardware/software platform on which the system is to be deployed. *Hardware/software considerations* impose heavy restrictions on the vocabulary (and therefore expressiveness) of the modeling language. Moreover, the vocabulary may be difficult for customers to understand, thus inhibiting developer–customer communication.

This said, some of the constraint statements would, in fact, be imposing hardware/software considerations on developers. Moreover, the customers themselves may be expressing their requirements in relation to a particular hardware/software technology, or even demanding a particular technology. The lesson is: avoid hardware/software considerations, if you can.

1.3.3 Architectural design phase

The specification document is like a *contract* between developers and customers for delivery of the software product. It lists all the requirements that the software product must satisfy. Specifications are now handed over to system architects and designers to develop lower-level models of a system's architecture and its internal workings. Design is done in terms of the software/hardware platform on which the system is going to be implemented.

The description of the system in terms of its modules is called *architectural design*. The architectural design includes decisions about the solution strategies for the client and server aspects of the system.

The description of the internal workings of each module (use case) is called *detailed design*. It develops detailed algorithms and data structures for each module. These algorithms and data structures are tailored to all (both reinforcing and obstructive) constraints of the underlying implementation platform.

The architectural design is concerned with the selection of a solution strategy and with the modularization of the system. The *solution strategy* needs to resolve client (user interface) and server (database) issues as well as any *middleware* needed to 'glue' client and server. The decision on basic building blocks (modules) is relatively independent from a solution strategy but the detailed design of the modules must conform to a selected client/server solution.

Client/server models are frequently extended to provide a *three-tier architecture* where application logic constitutes a separate layer. The middle-tier is a logical tier and as such may or may not be supported by separate hardware. Application logic is a process that can run on either the client or the server, i.e. it can be compiled into the client or server process and implemented as Dynamic Link Library (DLL), Application Programming Interface (API), Remote Procedure Calls (RPC), etc. (Next, 1996).

1.3.4 Detailed design phase

Architectural design describes the product in terms of its modules. *Detailed design* describes each module. In a typical IS development, the modules are allocated either to a client component or to a server component. Application designers are responsible for the former; database designers would develop the latter.

The *user interface* (client) design must conform to the GUI design guidelines provided by the creator of a particular GUI interface (Windows, Motif, Macintosh). Such guidelines are normally provided online as part of the electronic GUI documentation (e.g. Windows, 2000).

A major principle for an object-oriented GUI design is that the *user is in control*, not the program. The program reacts to randomly generated user events and provides the necessary software services. Other GUI design principles are the consequence of this fact. (Of course, 'the user is in control' principle should not be taken literally – the program would still validate the user's privileges and might disallow certain user's actions.)

The *database design* defines objects of the database server – most likely a relational (or possibly object-relational) server. Some of these objects are data containers (tables, views, etc.). Other objects are procedural (stored procedures, triggers, etc.).

1.3.5 Implementation phase

Implementation of an information system involves *installation* of purchased software and *coding* of custom-written software. It also involves other important activities, such as loading of test and production databases, testing, user training, hardware issues, etc.

A typical organization of an implementation team distinguishes two groups of programmers: one responsible for client programming and the other in charge of server database programming. Client programs implement windows, application logic and call server database programs (stored procedures) as needed. The responsibility for database consistency and for transactional correctness lies with server programs.

In a true spirit of iterative and incremental development, the design of *user interfaces* is sometimes prone to implementation changes. Application programmers may opt for a different appearance of implemented windows to conform to the vendor's GUI principles, to facilitate programming or to improve the user's productivity.

Similarly, server *database* implementation may force changes to design documents. Unforeseen database problems, difficulties with programming of stored procedures and triggers, concurrency issues, integration with client processes, performance tuning, etc. are just a few reasons why the design may need to be modified.

1.3.6 Integration phase

Incremental development implies *incremental integration* of software modules. The task is not trivial. For large systems, module integration can take more time and effort than any one of the earlier lifecycle phases, including implementation. As Aristotle observed: 'The whole is more than the sum of the parts.'

Module integration must be carefully planned from the very beginning of the software lifecycle. Software units, to be individually implemented, must be identified in early stages of system analysis. They need to be re-addressed in detail during architectural design. The sequence of implementation must allow for the smoothest possible incremental integration.

The main difficulty with the incremental integration is in intertwined reflexive dependencies between the modules. In a well-designed system such *coupling* of modules is minimized. Nevertheless, every so often, two modules depend on each other so that neither can function in isolation.

What can we do if we need to deliver one module before the other is ready? The answer lies in writing special code to temporarily 'fill the gaps' so that all modules can be integrated. Programming routines to simulate the activity of the missing module are called *stubs*.

Unlike conventional software systems, based on the notion of the main program, in modern object-oriented event-driven systems there is no central intelligence (main program). In modern systems, there is no clearly defined integration structure. Conventional top-down or bottom-up integration strategies do not apply to modern systems.

Object-oriented systems must be *designed for integration*. Each module should be as independent as possible. Dependencies between modules should be identified and minimized in the analysis and design phases. Ideally, each module should constitute a single thread of processing that executes as a response to a particular customer need. The use of stubs as replacement operations should be avoided when possible. If not properly designed, the integration phase will result in chaos and will put at risk the entire development project.

1.3.7 Maintenance phase

Maintenance follows a successful handover to a customer of each incremental software module and eventually of the entire software product. Maintenance is not only an inherent part of the software lifecycle – it accounts for most of it as far as IT personnel time and effort is concerned. Schach (1996) estimates that 67% of lifecycle time is spent on software maintenance.

Maintenance consists of three distinct stages (Maciaszek, 1990):

1. Housekeeping.
2. Adaptive maintenance.
3. Perfective maintenance.

Housekeeping relates to routine maintenance tasks necessary to keep the system accessible to users and operational. *Adaptive maintenance* involves monitoring and auditing of the system's operation, adjusting its functionality to satisfy the changing environment, and adapting it to meet performance and throughput demands. *Perfective maintenance* refers to redesigning and modifying the system to accommodate new or substantially changed requirements.

Eventually, the continuing maintenance of a software system becomes unsustainable and the system has to be phased out. *Phasing out* would normally happen due to reasons that have little to do with the *usefulness* of the software. The software is probably still useful, but it has become unmaintainable. Schach (1996) lists four reasons why the software may have to be phased out:

1. proposed changes go beyond the immediate capability of perfective maintenance;
2. the system is out of maintainers' control and the effects of changes cannot be predicted;
3. there is lack of documentation to base future software extensions on;
4. the implementation hardware/software platform has to be replaced and no migration path is available.

1.3.8 Project planning in the software lifecycle

A familiar maxim says that if you can't plan it, you can't do it. Planning spans the software project lifecycle. It begins once the *system planning* activities determine the business strategy for the organization and the software projects are identified. *Project planning* is the activity of estimating the project's deliverables, costs, time, risks, milestones, and resource requirements. It also includes the selection of development methods, processes, tools, standards, team organization, etc.

Project planning is a moving target. It is not something you do once and never change. Within the framework of a few *fixed constraints*, project plans evolve with the lifecycle.

Typical constraints are *time* and *money* – each project has a clear deadline and a tight budget. One of the first tasks in project planning is to assess whether the project is feasible under the time, budget and other constraints. If it is feasible then the constraints are documented and can only be changed in the course of a formal approval process.

Project feasibility is assessed with several factors in mind (Hoffer *et al.*, 1999; Whitten and Bentley, 1998):

- *Operational feasibility* re-addresses the issues originally undertaken in *system planning* when the project was identified; it is the study of how the proposed system will affect organizational structures, procedures and people.
- *Economic feasibility* assesses costs and benefits of the project (known also as the cost–benefit analysis).
- *Technical feasibility* assesses practicality of the proposed technical solution and availability of technical skills, expertise, and resources.
- *Schedule feasibility* assesses the reasonability of the project timetable.

Not all constraints are known or could be evaluated at the time of project initiation. Additional constraints will be discovered during the requirements phase and will undergo feasibility studies. These will include legal, contractual, political, and security constraints.

Subject to feasibility assessment, a *project plan* will be constructed and will constitute the guidance for project and process management. The issues addressed in the project plan include (Whitten and Bentley, 1998):

- Project scope;
- Project tasks;
- Directing and controlling the project;
- Quality management;
- Metrics and measurement;
- Project scheduling;
- Allocation of resources (people, material, tools);
- People management.

1.3.9   Metrics in the software lifecycle

Measuring development time and effort and taking other *metrics* of project artifacts is, in fact, an important part of *project and process management*. Although an important part, it is frequently neglected in organizations at low levels of process maturity. The price is high. Without measuring the past, the organization is not able to plan accurately for the future.

Metrics are usually discussed in the context of *software quality* and *complexity* – they apply to the quality and complexity of the *software product* (Henderson-Sellers, 1996; Pressman, 1997). Metrics are used to measure such factors of quality as correctness, reliability, efficiency, integrity, usability, maintainability, flexibility, and testability. For example, software reliability can be evaluated by measuring the frequency and severity of failures, and in the meantime, between failures, the accuracy of output results, the ability to recover from failure, etc.

An equally important application of metrics is measuring the development models (*development products*) at different phases of the lifecycle. Metrics are then used to assess the effectiveness of the *process* and to improve the quality of work at various lifecycle phases.

Typical metrics that apply to the *software process* and can be taken at various lifecycle phases are (Schach, 1996):

- Requirements volatility (percentage of requirements which changed by the time the requirements phase had finished). This may reflect on the difficulty of obtaining requirements from the customers.

- Requirements volatility after the requirements phase. This may point to a poor quality requirements document.

- Prediction of 'hot spots' and 'bottlenecks' in the system (frequency at which the users attempt to execute different functions in the prototype of the software product).

- The size of the specification document generated by the CASE tool, and other more detailed metrics from the CASE repository, such as the number of classes in a class model. If taken on a few past projects with known cost and time to completion, these metrics provide an ideal planning 'database' to predict time and effort on future projects.

- Record of fault statistics, when they were introduced to the product and when they were discovered and rectified. This may reflect on the thoroughness of quality assurance, review processes, and testing activities.

- Average number of tests before a test unit is considered acceptable for integration and release to customers. This may reflect on the programmers' debugging procedures.

1.3.10   Testing in the software lifecycle

Like project planning or metrics taking, *testing* is an activity that spans the software lifecycle. It is not just a separate phase after the implementation. It is much too late to start testing what we have done so far after the software product is implemented. The escalating cost of fixing faults introduced in earlier lifecycle phases is likely to be exorbitant (Schach, 1996).

Testing activities should be carefully planned. To start with *test cases* have to be identified. Test cases (or test plans) define the test steps to be undertaken in an attempt to 'break' the software model or product.

Test cases should be defined for each functional module (*use case*) described in the requirements document. Relating test cases to use cases establishes a *traceability* path between tests and user requirements. To be testable, a software artifact must be traceable.

Naturally enough, every developer tests products of their work. However, original developers are somewhat blind-folded by the work they have done to produce the software artifact in the first place.

To be most effective, a third party should conduct testing methodically. The task can be assigned to the Software Quality Assurance (SQA) group in the organization. The group should include some of the best developers in the organization. Their job is to test, not to develop. The SQA group (not original developers) is then charged with the responsibility for product quality.

The more testing we do in early development phases, the better the payoff. Requirements, specifications and any documents (including program source code) can be tested in *formal reviews* (so-called *walkthroughs* and *inspections*).

Formal reviews are carefully prepared meetings that target a particular part of the documentation or system. An appointed reviewer studies a document beforehand and raises various questions. The meeting decides if a question is in fact a fault, but there is no attempt to offer an immediate solution to the problem. The original developer will later address the fault. Provided that the meetings are friendly and finger pointing is avoided, the 'team synergy' will lead to early detection and correction of many faults.

Once software prototypes and first versions of the software product are made available, *execution-based testing* can be undertaken. There are two kinds of execution-based testing:

- Testing to specs (black-box testing).
- Testing to code (white-box or glass-box testing).

Testing to specs treats the program itself as a black box about which nothing is known except that it takes some input and produces some output. The program is given some input and the resulting output is analyzed for presence of errors. Testing to specs is particularly useful to discover incorrect or missing requirements.

Testing to code 'looks through' the program logic to derive the input needed to *exercise* various execution paths in the program. Testing to code complements testing to specs – the two tests tend to discover different categories of error.

Incremental development implies not only incremental integration of software modules, but also *incremental* or *regression testing*. Regression testing is the re-execution of the previous test cases on the same *baseline data set* after a previously released software module has been incrementally extended. The assumption is that the old functionality should remain the same and should not have been broken by an extension.

Regression testing can be well supported by *capture-playback tools* that allow capturing the user's interactions with the program and playing them back without further user intervention.

The main difficulty with regression testing is the enforcement of the baseline data set. Incremental development does not just extend the procedural program logic, but it also extends (and modifies) underlying data structures. An extended software product may force changes to the baseline data set, thus ruling out sensible comparison of results.

1.4 Software development approaches

The 'software revolution' has introduced some significant changes to the way software products work. In particular, software has become much more *interactive*. The tasks and behavior of a program can be dynamically adapted to the user's requests.

The *procedural* logic of a COBOL-like program of the past was inflexible and not very responsive to unexpected events. Once started, the program executed to completion in a more-or-less deterministic fashion. Occasionally, the program could request some information from the user and follow a different execution branch. In general, however, the interaction with the user was limited and the number of different execution paths pre-fixed. The program was in control, not the user.

With the advent of modern graphical user interfaces (GUIs) things have dramatically changed. The GUI programs are *event-driven* and execute in a random and unpredictable fashion dictated by user-generated events from a keyboard, mouse, or other input devices.

In a GUI environment, the user is (largely) in control of program execution, not vice versa. Behind every event, there is a software *object* that knows how to service that event in the current state of the program's execution. Once the service is accomplished, the control returns to the user.

Different styles of program demand different approaches to software development. Conventional software has been well served by the so-called *structured approach*. Modern GUI systems require object programming and the *object approach* is the best way to design such systems.

1.4.1 Structured approach

The *structured approach* to systems development was popularized (and de facto standardized) in the 1980s. The approach is based on two techniques: DFD (data flow diagrams) for process modeling and ERD (entity relationship diagrams) for data modeling.

The structured approach is *function-centric* and treats DFDs as a driving development force. More recently, and as the direct result of the popularity of the relational database model, the importance of DFDs in structured development has faded and the approach has become more *data-centric* with emphasis placed on ERDs.

The combination of DFDs and ERDs delivers relatively complete analysis models that capture all the system's functions and data at a desirable level of abstraction independently of software/hardware considerations. The analysis model is transformed later into a design model, expressed typically in relational database terms. The implementation phase can then follow.

The structured approach to analysis and design is characterized by a number of features, some of which are not well aligned with modern software engineering:

■ The approach tends to be *sequential and transformational* rather than iterative and incremental (i.e. the approach does not facilitate a seamless development process through iterative refinement and incremental software delivery).

■ The approach tends to deliver inflexible solutions that satisfy the set of identified business functions but which can be hard to scale up and extend in the future.

■ The approach assumes development from scratch and it does not support reuse of pre-existing components.

The transformational nature of the approach introduces a considerable risk of misinterpreting original user requirements down the development track. This risk is exacerbated by the progressive need to trade off the relatively declarative semantics of analysis models for procedural solutions in design models and implementation code (this is because the analysis models are semantically richer than the underlying design and implementation models).

1.4.2 Object-oriented approach

The *object-oriented approach* to systems development was popularized in the 1990s. The Object Management Group approved a standard for it (UML – Unified Modeling Language).

Compared to the structured approach, the object-oriented approach is more *data-centric* – it evolves around class models. In the analysis phase, classes do not need to have operations defined – only attributes. The growing significance of *use cases* in UML shifts the emphasis slightly from data to functions.

There is a perception that developers use object approaches because of technical advantages of the object paradigm, such as abstraction, encapsulation, reuse, inheritance, message passing, polymorphism, etc. These technical properties can lead to greater reusability of code and data, shorter development times, increased programmer's productivity, improved software quality, greater understandability, etc.

While attractive, these advantages of object technology do not always materialize in practice. Nevertheless, we do use objects today and will be using them tomorrow. The reasons have to do with the new style of *event-driven* programming supported by modern graphical user interfaces (GUIs).

Other reasons for the popularity of the object approach have to do with addressing the needs of newly *emerging applications* and with the preferred ways to fight *application backlogs*. Two of the most important new categories of applications that demand object technology are *workgroup computing* and *multimedia systems*. The idea of stopping the application backlog from growing, via the concept known as 'object wrapping,' has proved to be both attractive and workable.

The object approach to systems development follows the *iterative and incremental* process. A single model (and a single design document) is 'elaborated' through analysis, design and implementation phases – details are added in successive iterations, changes and refinements are introduced as needed, and incremental releases of selected modules maintain user satisfaction and provide additional feedback to other modules.

Development by elaboration is possible because all development models (analysis, design, and implementation) are semantically rich and based on the same 'language' – the underlying vocabulary is essentially the same (classes, attributes, methods, inheritance, polymorphism, etc.). Note, however, that if the implementation is based on a relational database, there is still a need for a complex and risky transformation (because the underlying semantics of the relational model is quite poor by comparison).

The object approach alleviates the most important shortcomings of the structured approach but it does introduce a few new problems.

- The analysis phase is conducted on an even higher level of abstraction and – if the implementation server solution assumes a relational database – the *semantic gap* between the concept and its implementation can be significant. Although the analysis and design can be conducted in an iterative and incremental fashion, eventually the development reaches the implementation stage, which requires transformation to a relational database. If the implementation platform is an object or object-relational database, then the transformation from design is much easier.

- *Project management* is difficult. Managers measure development progress by clearly defined work breakdown structures, deliverables and milestones. In object development through 'elaboration' there are no clear boundaries between phases, and project documentation continuously evolves. An attractive solution to this difficulty lies in dividing the project into small modules and managing the progress by frequent executable releases of these modules (some of these releases can be internal, some others – delivered).

- Another major problem with object approaches relates to the increased *complexity* of the solution, which in turn affects software maintainability and scalability.

The difficulties with the object approach do not change the fact that 'the future isn't what it used to be,' in Arthur Clarke's words. There is no going back to the procedural style of programming reminiscent of batch COBOL applications. All stakeholders in IS development projects are aware of the Internet, e-commerce, computer games, and other interactive applications.

New software applications are much more complex to build and the structured approach is inadequate for the task. The object-oriented approach is currently the only known method to harness the development of new event-driven highly interactive software.

Summary

In this chapter we have looked at strategic issues of the software development process. For some readers the content of this chapter may have amounted to little more than 'motherhood' statements. For readers with some experience in software development, the chapter could have delivered additional cerebral ammunition. For all readers, the intent of the chapter was to serve (not necessarily gently) as an introduction to the much more comprehensive discussions to come.

The *nature* of software development is that of a *craft* or even *art*. An outcome of a software project cannot be completely ascertained at its start. The main *accidental difficulty* in software development relates to *stakeholders* – a software product must give a tangible benefit to stakeholders; it will fail, otherwise. The triangle for success includes, in addition to the stakeholders' factor, a sound *process* and the support of a *modeling language and tools*.

Software development is concerned with delivering an *efficient* software product. *System planning* precedes software development and determines which products can be most *effective* to the organization. There are various ways in which the system planning can be conducted. Four popular approaches were discussed: SWOT, VCM, BPR, and ISA. Systems that support the *strategic* level of decision making offer the greatest effectiveness. These are also systems that create the greatest challenges to software developers.

Software development follows a *lifecycle*. In this book we concentrate on two phases of the lifecycle: *analysis* and *design*. Other phases include implementation, integration and maintenance. The software development comprises a range of other important activities such as project planning, collection of metrics, testing and change management. We do not consider any of those to be a separate phase because they occur repeatedly throughout the lifecycle.

In the past, software products were *procedural* – a programmed procedure executed its task more-or-less sequentially and predictably and it then terminated. The *structured development approach* has been successfully used for production of such systems.

Modern software products are *object-oriented* – a program consists of programming objects that execute randomly, unpredictably and the program does not terminate unless closed by the user. The objects 'hang around' waiting for user-generated events to start a computation, they may request services of other objects to complete the task, and then get idle again, but alert – just in case a user generates another event. Modern GUI-based client/server IS applications are object-oriented and the *object-oriented development approach* is best equipped for production of such applications. The rest of the book concentrates on the object-oriented approach.

Review questions

R1 Based on your experiences with software products, how would you interpret Fred Brooks's observation that the *essence of software engineering* is determined by inherent software complexity, conformity, changeability, and invisibility? How would you explain these four factors? How is software engineering different from traditional engineering, such as civil or mechanical engineering?

R2 We have argued that *software production is an art or craft*. We can supplement this observation with the quotation that 'Art is a collaboration between God and the artist, and the less the artist does, the better' (André Gide). What lesson, if any, is this quotation providing to software developers? Do you agree with it?

R3 Explain the difference between software *packages* and *components*. What do you think are the future prospects for these two technologies?

R4 Recall the definition of a *stakeholder*. Is a software vendor or a technical support person a stakeholder? Explain.

R5 Which *CMM level of maturity* is needed for the organization to be able to respond successfully to a crisis situation? Explain.

R6 When explaining the SWOT approach to system planning we remarked: 'in a good mission statement emphasis is placed on customer needs rather than on products or services that an organization delivers.' Please explain and exemplify how targeting products or services in the *mission statement* can defeat the *effectiveness* objective of system planning.

R7 BPR makes a clear distinction between a *business process* and a *business function*. What is this distinction? Give an example of a business process that cuts horizontally across an organization.

R8 Compare the concepts of *value chain* and *business process*.

R9 Why is an understanding of *ISA* important to system development?

R10 What are the three *management levels*? Consider a banking application that monitors the usage patterns of a credit card by its holder in order to block the card automatically when the bank suspects a misuse (theft, fraud, etc.). Which management level is addressed by such an application? Give reasons.

R11 Explain the difference between the *requirements* and the *specification* phase.

R12 Explain the relationship of the two design phases (*architectural design* and *detailed design*) to the first two phases of the lifecycle – the requirements phase and the specification phase.

R13 What do you understand by the undertaking that an object-oriented system should be *designed for integration*?

R14 System planning and software metrics are inherently correlated. Explain this supposition.

R15 Explain the relationship between traceability and testing.

R16 What are the main modeling techniques in the structured development approach?

R17 What are the main reasons for the shift from the structured to object-oriented development approach?

Chapter 2

Underpinnings of Requirements Analysis

The emphasis in this book is on object-oriented software production. This does not come cheaply as the object-oriented development demands a good understanding of object technology. Without an in-depth appreciation of object technology, a developer will not be able to use the UML correctly as the single and omnipresent modeling language.

The main difficulty in learning object technology relates to the absence of an obvious starting point and the lack of a clear path of investigation. There is not a top-down or bottom-up learning approach that we know of. By necessity, the approach has to be a sort of 'middle-out'. No matter how much we advance the learning process, we seem always to be in the middle of that learning (as new issues keep emerging). The first major test for the successful learning process is passed when the reader understands the in-depth meaning of the fact that in an object-oriented system 'everything is an object.'

This chapter aims at gauging the right level of information to provide to the reader before diving into the subject. This chapter covers the prerequisites for requirements analysis in two parallel ways. Firstly, we explain the fundamentals of object technology. Secondly, we 'teach-by-example' and provide a guided tutorial in analysis modeling using a familiar application domain – OnLine Shopping via the Internet.

2.1 Fundamentals of object technology

A good way to explain object-orientation in information systems is by providing an analogy with real-life concrete objects. The world around us consists of *objects* in a particular *state* determined by current values of the object's attributes.

For example, a coffee mug on my desk is in a `filled` *state* because it is shaped to hold liquids and there is still coffee in it. When there is no more coffee in it, the state of the mug can be defined as `empty`. If it falls on the floor and breaks, it will be in a `broken` state.

My coffee mug is rather passive – it does not have *behavior* of its own. However, the same cannot be said of my dog or a eucalyptus tree outside my window. My dog barks, the tree grows, etc. So, some real-life objects have behavior.

All real-life objects have also *identity* – a fixed property by which we identify one object from another. If I had two coffee mugs on my desk from the same mug set, I could say that the two mugs are *equal* but *not identical*. They are equal because they have the same values for all their properties (so, they are the same size and shape, are black, and are empty). However, in object-oriented parlance, they are not identical because there are two of them and I have a choice of which one to use.

Real-life objects that possess the three properties (state, behavior, identity) build up *natural behavioral systems*. Natural systems are by far the most *complex systems* that we know. No computer system has come close to the inherent complexity of an animal or a plant.

Despite their complexity, natural systems tend to work – they exhibit interesting behavior, can adjust to external and internal changes, can evolve over time, etc. The lesson is obvious. Perhaps we should construct *artificial systems* by emulating the structure and behavior of natural systems (cp. Maciaszek *et al.*, 1996b).

Artificial systems are models of reality. A coffee mug on my computer screen is as much a model of the real 'thing' as is a dog or a eucalyptus tree on my screen. A coffee mug can, therefore, be modeled with behavioral properties. It can, for example, fall on the floor if knocked over. The 'fall' action can be modeled as a behavioral *operation* of the mug. Another consequential operation of the mug may be to 'break' when hitting the floor. Most, if not all, objects in a computer system 'come alive' – they have behavior.

2.1.1   Instance object

An object is an *instance* of a 'thing.' It may be one of the many instances of the same 'thing.' My mug is an instance in the set of possible mugs.

A generic description of a 'thing' is called a *class*. Hence, an object is an instance of a class. But, as we will see in Section 2.1.6, a class itself may also need to be instantiated – it may be an object. For this reason, we need to distinguish between an *instance object* and a *class object*.

For brevity, an instance object is frequently called an *object* or an *instance*. It is confusing to call it an 'object instance.' An object-oriented system consists of collaborating objects. Everything in an object-oriented system is an object, be it an object of an instance (*instance object*) or an object of a class (*class object*).

As an aside, and as a consequence of the above discussion, we do not advocate using the term 'object class.' Yes, a class is a template for objects with the same attributes and operations, but a class itself can be instantiated as an object (and we would not like to call such a creation an 'object class object').

2.1.1.1   *Object notation*

The UML notation for an object is a rectangle with two compartments. The upper compartment contains the name of an object and the name of a class to which the object belongs. The syntax is:

`objectname: classname.`

The lower compartment contains the list of attribute names and values. The types of attributes can also be shown using the syntax:

`attributename: type = value.`

Figure 2.1 demonstrates a `Course` object named `c1`. The object has two attributes. The types of the attributes are not shown – they have been specified in the definition of the class.

FIGURE 2.1
Instance object.

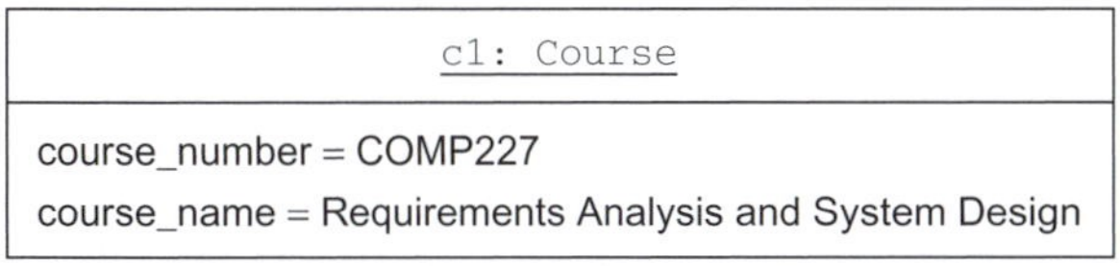

c1: Course
course_number = COMP227 course_name = Requirements Analysis and System Design

It is important to note that the object notation does not provide a 'compartment' for listing the *operations* that an instance object can execute. This is because the operations are identical for all instance objects and it would be redundant to store them repeatedly in each instance object. Operations may be stored in a *class object* or they may be associated with instance objects by other means (implemented in the underlying object-oriented system software).

2.1.1.2 *How do objects collaborate?*

The number of objects of a particular class can be very large. It is impractical and infeasible to visualize many objects on a diagram. Objects are only drawn to exemplify a system at a point in time or to exemplify how they *collaborate* over time to do certain tasks. For example, to order products a *collaboration* may need to be established between a `Stock` object and a `Purchase` object.

System tasks are performed by sets of objects that invoke *operations* (behavior) on each other. We say that they exchange *messages*. The messages trigger operations on objects that can result in the change of objects' states and can invoke other operations.

Figure 2.2 shows the flow of messages between four objects. The brackets after the message names indicate that a message can take parameters (like in a traditional programming call to a function). The object `Order` requests the object `Shipment` to ship the order. To do so, `Shipment` instructs the object `Stock` to subtract an appropriate quantity of products. The object `Stock` is then analyzing the new inventory levels and if the stock is low, it requests the object `Purchase` to reorder more products.

Although we explained the above object collaboration as a sequence of activities and we even numbered the messages, in general the flow of messages does not impose a strict temporal order on the activation of objects. For example, `analyzeStockLevels` or `reorderProducts` can execute in any sequence, possibly independently of `shipOrder` and `subtractProduct`. For these reasons, we shall abandon the numbering of messages when discussing the object collaboration at the design level (Section 6.2).

FIGURE 2.2
Object
collaboration.

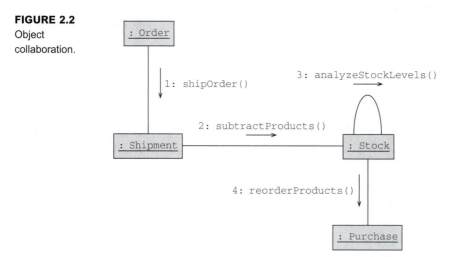

2.1.1.3 *How do objects identify each other?*

The question is how an object knows the *identity* of another object to which it wants to send a message. How does an Order object know its Shipment object so that the message shipOrder reaches its destination?

The answer is that each object is given an *object identifier* (OID) when it is created. The OID is an object *handle* – a unique number that remains with the object for its entire life. If an object X wants to send a message to an object Y then X has to somehow know the OID of Y.

There are two practical solutions to establishing OID *links* between objects. The solutions involve:

■   persistent OID links; and

■   transient OID links.

The distinction between these two kinds of link has to do with the longevity of objects. Some objects live only as long as the program executes – they are created by the program and destroyed during the program execution or when the program finishes its execution. These are *transient objects*. Other objects outlive the execution of the program – they are stored in the persistent disk storage when the program finishes and they are available for the next execution of the program. These are *persistent objects*.

2.1.1.3.1 Persistent link

A *persistent link* is an object reference (or a set of object references) in one object in persistent storage that links that object to another object in persistent storage (or to the set of other objects). Hence, to persistently link a Course object to its Teacher object, the object Course must contain a link attribute the value of which is the OID of the object Teacher. The link is persistent because the OID is physically stored in the object Course, as shown in Figure 2.3.

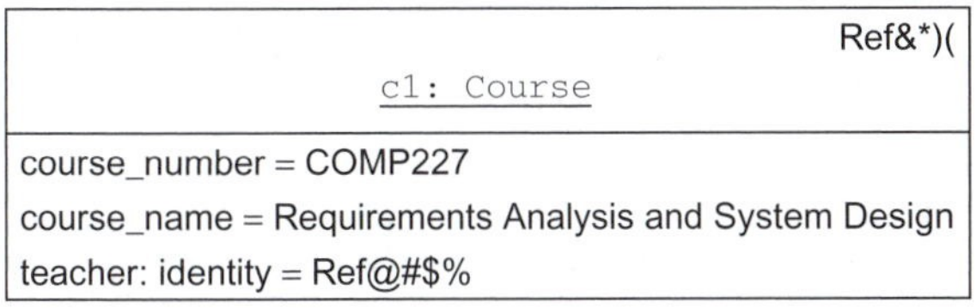
Ref&*)(
c1: Course
course_number = COMP227
course_name = Requirements Analysis and System Design
teacher: identity = Ref@#$%

FIGURE 2.3 Implementation of a persistent link.

The OID of object `c1` is marked here as `Ref&*)(`. The object contains a link attribute named `teacher`. The type of this attribute is `identity`. Its value is a magic number `Ref@#$%` – the disk address where the object `Teacher` is *persistently* stored.

Once the objects `Course` and `Teacher` are transferred to the program's memory, the value of the `teacher` attribute will be *swizzled* to a memory pointer, thus establishing a memory-level collaboration between the objects. (Swizzling is not the UML term – it is used in object databases (see Section 8.2) where the transfers of objects between the persistent storage and the transient memory are frequent.)

Figure 2.3 illustrates how persistent links are typically implemented. However, in the UML modeling, the links between objects are drawn as in Figure 2.4. The links are represented as *instances of an association* between the objects `Course` and `Teacher`.

Normally, collaboration links allow for *navigation* in both directions. Each `Course` object is linked to its `Teacher` object, and a `Teacher` object can navigate to `Course` objects. It is possible, though not frequent, to allow only for navigation in one direction.

Once an object is persistently linked to another object, it can send a message along the link to request a *service* from the other object. That is, an object can invoke an *operation* on another object by sending a *message* to it. In a typical scenario, to point to an object, the sender will use a program's variable containing a link value (OID value) of that object.

For example, a *message* sent by an object `Teacher` to find the name of an object `Course` could look like:

```
crs_ref.getCourseName(out crs_name)
```

In the example, the specific object of class `Course` that will execute `getCourseName` is pointed to by the current value of the link variable `crs_ref`. The output (`out`) argument

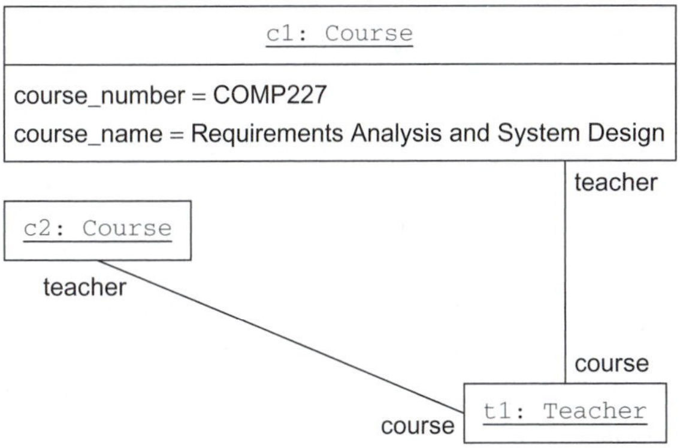
c1: Course
course_number = COMP227
course_name = Requirements Analysis and System Design
teacher
c2: Course
teacher
course
course
t1: Teacher

FIGURE 2.4 Persistent links in UML object model.

crs_name is a variable to be initialized with the value returned by the operation getCourseName implemented in the class Course.

2.1.1.3.2 Transient link

What if we have not defined a persistent link between Course and Teacher, and we still need to send a message from object t1 to object c1 to invoke the operation getCourseName? The application program must have other means to find out the identity of object c1 and create a *transient link* from object t1 to object c1 (Riel, 1996).

Fortunately, a programmer has many techniques that can lead to initialization of the variable crs_ref with an OID of memory-resident object c1. To start with, it is possible that earlier in the program a link between objects c1 and t1 has been established and crs_ref still holds the correct OID. For example, the program has executed a search operation on the teacher's t1 availability and the timetable for courses and has determined that the teacher t1 should teach the course c1.

An alternative possibility is that a program has access to a persistently stored table that maps course numbers to teacher names. It can then search on Course objects to find all courses taught by the teacher t1 and request the user to determine the course that the message getCourseName is to be sent to.

It is also possible that the very task of a program is to create courses and teachers before storing them in a database. There is no persistent link between teachers and courses, but the user enters the information so that each course clearly identifies a teacher in charge. The program can then store the transient links in the program's variables (such as crs_ref) and these variables can be later used (during the same program execution) to send messages between Teacher and Course objects.

In short, there are programmatic and user-driven techniques to establish transient links between objects that have not been persistently linked by associations between relevant classes. *Transient links* are program variables that contain OID values of objects that are currently in the program's memory. The mapping (*swizzling*) between the transient and persistent OIDs should be the responsibility of the underlying programming environment, such as an object database system.

2.1.2 Class

A *class* is the descriptor for a set of objects with the same attributes and operations. It serves as a *template* for object creation. Each object created from the template contains the attribute *values* that conform to attribute *types* defined in the class. Each object can invoke operations defined in its class.

Graphically, a class is represented as a rectangle with three compartments separated by horizontal lines, as shown in Figure 2.5. The top compartment holds the class name. The middle compartment declares all attributes for the class. The bottom compartment contains definitions of operations.

FIGURE 2.5
Class
compartments.

FIGURE 2.6
Attributes.

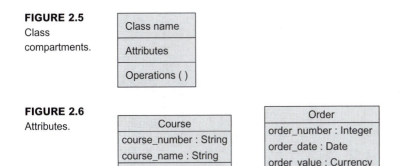

2.1.2.1 *Attribute*

An attribute is the *type-value* pair. Classes define *attribute types*. Objects contain *attribute values*. Figure 2.6 illustrates two classes with attribute names and attribute types defined.

An attribute type can be a built-in *primitive type* or it can be another *class*. A primitive type is the type directly understood and supported by an underlying object-oriented software environment. All attribute types in Figure 2.6 designate primitive types.

2.1.2.1.1 Attribute type that designates a class

An attribute type can also designate a class. In a particular object of the class, such an attribute contains an object identifier (OID) value pointing to an object of another class. In UML analysis models, attributes with class-based types (rather than primitive types) are not listed in the middle class compartment. Instead, the *associations* between classes represent them. Figure 2.7 shows such an association between two classes.

The two names on the association line (`the_shipment` and `the_order`) represent so-called rolenames. A *rolename* identifies the meaning for the association end and it is used to *navigate* to an object of the other class in the association.

In the implemented system, the rolename (on the opposite end of the association) becomes a class attribute whose type is the class pointed to by the rolename. Figure 2.8 shows two classes from Figure 2.7 as they are going to be eventually implemented.

2.1.2.1.2 Attribute visibility

As noted in Section 2.1.1.2, objects collaborate by sending messages to each other. A message invokes a class operation. The operation services the calling object's request by accessing attribute values in its own object. For this scenario to be possible, the operations must be *visible* to the outside objects (messages must see the operations). Such operations are said to have *public visibility*.

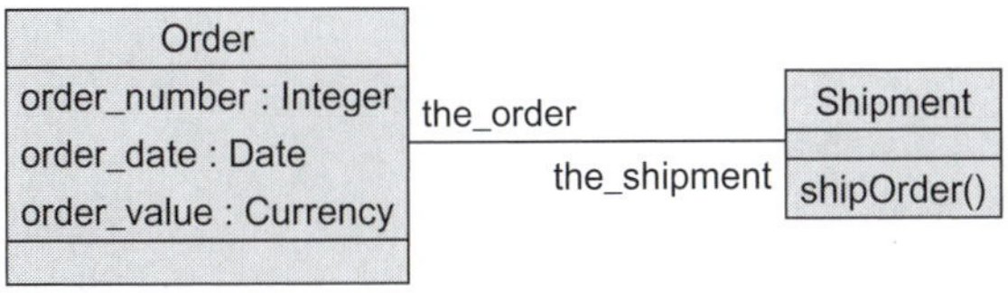

FIGURE 2.7
Rolenames that
designate
classes (analysis
model).

Order		Shipment
order_number : Integer	the_order	
order_date : Date		Shipment
order_value : Currency	the_shipment	shipOrder()

Order
order_number : Integer
order_date : Date
order_value : Currency
the_ shipment : Shipment
Shipment
the_order : Order
shipOrder()

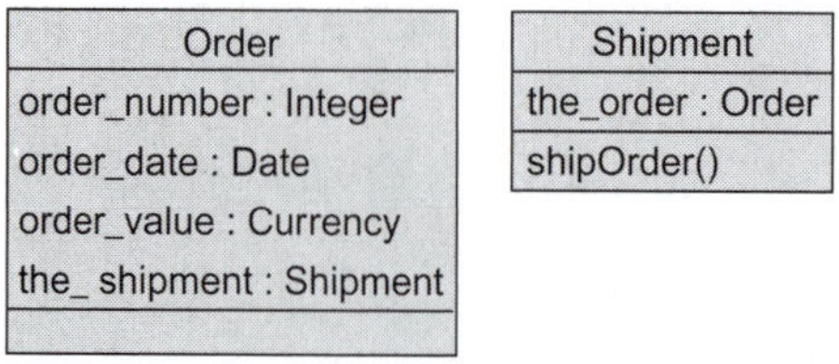

FIGURE 2.8 Attributes that designate classes (implementation model).

Purchase
–purchase_number : String
–purchase_date : Date
–purchase_value : Currency
+reorderProducts()
Purchase
purchase_number : String
purchase_date : Date
purchase_value : Currency
reorderProducts()

FIGURE 2.9 Private attributes and public operations.

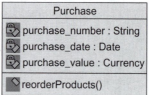

In a pure object-oriented system (as exemplified by the Smalltalk programming environment), most operations are *public* but most attributes are *private*. Attribute values are hidden from other classes. Objects of one class can only request the services (operations) published in the public interface of another class. They are not allowed to directly manipulate other objects' attributes.

We say that operations *encapsulate* attributes. Note, however, that the encapsulation applies to classes. One object cannot hide (encapsulate) anything from another object of the same class.

The visibility is normally designated by a plus or minus symbol:

+ for public visibility;
– for private visibility.

These symbols are replaced in some CASE tools by graphical icons. Figure 2.9 demonstrates two graphical representations to signify attribute visibility.

2.1.2.2 Operation

An object contains data (attributes) and algorithms (operations) to act on these data. An operation is declared in a class. A procedure that implements the operation is called a *method.*

An operation (or the method, to be precise) is invoked by a message sent to it. The name of the message and the name of the operation are the same. The operation can contain a list of parameters that can be set to specific values in the message call. The operation can return a value to the calling object.

The operation name together with a list of formal argument types is called the *signature* of an operation. The signature must be unique within a class. This means that a class may have many operations with the same name, provided that the lists of parameter types vary.

2.1.2.2.1 Operations support object collaboration

An object-oriented program executes by reacting to random events from the user. The events come from the keyboard, mouse clicks, menu items, action buttons, and any other input

FIGURE 2.10
Operations to
support object
collaboration.

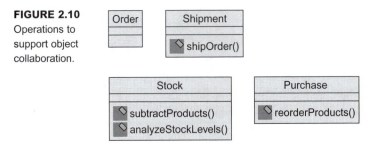

devices. A user-generated *event* converts to a *message* sent to an *object*. To accomplish a task many objects may need to collaborate. Objects collaborate by invoking *operations* in other objects (see Section 2.1.1.2).

Figure 2.10 shows operations in classes necessary to support the object collaboration demonstrated in Figure 2.2. Each message in Figure 2.2 requires an operation in the class designated by the message's destination. The class Order does not have any operations in this simple example. An object of the class Order initiates the object collaboration. The Order object requests that a Shipment object ship it. As a result of the shipment, the stock may need to be replenished with new products.

2.1.2.2.2   Operation visibility and scope

The principles of *operation visibility* are not different to attribute visibility (see Section 2.1.2.1.2). The visibility of an operation defines whether the operation is visible to objects of classes other than a class that defines the operation. If it is visible then its visibility is *public*. It is *private*, otherwise. The icons in front of operation names in Figure 2.10 denote public visibility.

Most operations in an object-oriented system would have public visibility. For an object to provide a service to the outside world, the 'service' operation must be visible. However, most objects will also have a number of internal housekeeping operations. These will be given private visibility. They are only accessible to objects of a class in which they have been defined.

The operation visibility needs to be distinguished from an *operation scope*. The operation may be invoked on an *instance object* (Section 2.1.1) or it may be invoked on a *class object* (Section 2.1.6). In the former case, the operation is said to have the *instance scope*. In the latter case – the *class scope*. For example, the operation to find an employee's age has the instance scope, but the operation to calculate the average age of all employees has the class scope.

2.1.3   Association

An *association* is one kind of relationship between classes. Other kinds of relationships include: generalization, aggregation, dependency and a few more.

The association relationship provides a linkage between objects of given classes. Objects needing to communicate with each other can use the linkage. Typically, messages between objects are sent along association relationships.

FIGURE 2.11
Association.

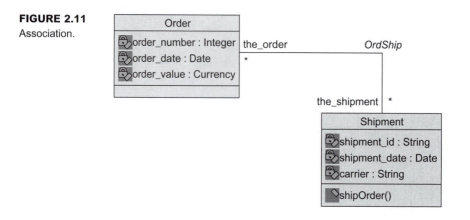

Figure 2.11 shows the relationship named `OrdShip` between classes `Order` and `Shipment`. The relationship allows for an `Order` object to be shipped (to be linked to) more than one `Shipment` object (indicated by the asterisk *). Also a `Shipment` object can carry (be linked to) more than one `Order` object.

2.1.3.1 Association degree

Association degree defines the number of classes connected by an association. The most frequent association is of *degree two*. This is called a *binary association*. The association in Figure 2.11 is binary.

Association can also be defined on a single class. This is called a *unary* (or *singular*) *association* (Maciaszek, 1990). The unary association establishes links between objects of a single class.

Figure 2.12 is a typical example of a unary association. It captures a hierarchical structure of employment. An `Employee` object is `managed_by` one other `Employee` object or by nobody (i.e. an employee who is, say, the Chief Executive Officer (CEO) is not managed by anybody). An `Employee` object is the `manager_of` many employees, unless the employee is at the bottom of the employment ladder and is not managing anybody.

Associations of degree 3 (*ternary associations*) are also possible, although not recommended (Maciaszek, 1990).

FIGURE 2.12
Unary
association.

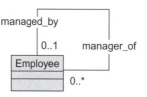

2.1.3.2 Association multiplicity

Association multiplicity defines how many objects may fill the position identified by a *rolename*. The multiplicity states how many objects of a target class (pointed to by the rolename) can be associated with a single object of the source class.

FIGURE 2.13
Association
multiplicity.

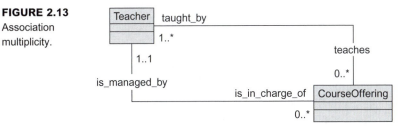

The multiplicity is shown as a range of integers n1..n2. The integer n1 defines the minimum number of connected objects, and n2 – the maximum number (the maximum number can be an asterisk * if we do not know the precise maximum integer value). If we do not want to specify the minimum number, but we know that it could be many connected objects then we do not specify the minimum number at all (as in Figure 2.11).

The most frequent multiplicities are:

```
0..1
0..*
1..1
1..*
*
```

Figure 2.13 demonstrates two associations on the classes Teacher and CourseOffering. One association captures the assignment of teachers to current course offerings. The other determines which teacher is in charge of an offering. A teacher can teach many offerings or none (e.g. if a teacher is on leave). One or more teachers teach a course offering. One of these teachers is in charge of the offering. In general, a teacher can be in charge of many course offerings or none. One and only one teacher manages a course offering.

The association multiplicity in UML is an overloaded term. The 'zero' and 'one' minimum multiplicity can be seen as a different semantic notion called the *membership* or *participation* (Maciaszek, 1990). The 'zero' minimum multiplicity signifies an *optional membership* of an object in the association. The 'one' multiplicity signifies a *mandatory membership*. For example, a CourseOffering object must be managed by a Teacher object.

The membership property has some interesting semantics of its own. For example, a particular mandatory membership may additionally imply that the membership is *fixed*, i.e. once an object is linked to a target object in the association it cannot be reconnected to another target object in the same association.

2.1.3.3 *Association link and extent*

The association *link* is an instance of the association. It is a *tuple* of references to objects. The tuple can be a *set* of references or a *list* (ordered set) of references. In general the tuple can contain one reference only. The link represents also the *rolename*, as discussed earlier. The *extent* is a set of links.

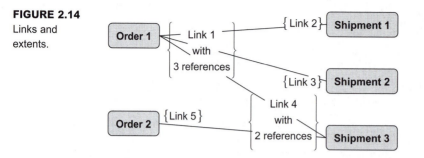

Figure 2.14 is a particular instantiation of the association OrdShip in Figure 2.11. There are five links in Figure 2.14. Hence the extent of the association is five.

The understanding of association links and extents is important to the overall comprehension of the association concept, but the links and extents are not meant to be modeled, obtained at run time or otherwise apparent.

2.1.3.4 Association class

Sometimes an association has attributes (and/or operations) of its own. Such an association must be modeled as a class (because attributes can only be defined in a class). Each object of an *association class* has attribute values and links to the objects of associated classes. Because an association class is a class, it can be associated with other classes in the model in the normal way.

Figure 2.15 shows the association class Assessment. An object of the class Assessment stores a list of marks, a total mark and a grade obtained by a Student in a ClassOffering.

The type of the attribute mark is List(Number). This is a so-called *parameterized type*. Number is the parameter of the class List, where List defines an ordered set of values. The attribute mark contains the list of all marks that a student obtained in a class offering. That is, if a student 'Fred' takes the course offering 'COMP227' there will eventually be a list (an ordered set) of marks for him on that course offering. That list of marks will be stored in an Assessment object that represents the association between 'Fred' and 'COMP227'.

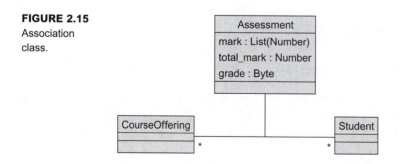

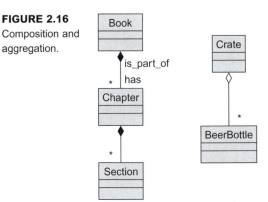

FIGURE 2.16
Composition and aggregation.

2.1.4 Aggregation and composition

Aggregation is a *whole-part relationship* between a class representing an assembly of components (*superset class*) and the classes representing the components (*subset classes*). A superset class contains a subset class (or classes).

The containment property can be strong (*aggregation by value*) or weak (*aggregation by reference*). In UML, the aggregation by value is called *composition*, and the aggregation by reference is simply called *aggregation*.

From the system modeling perspective, the aggregation is a special kind of association with additional semantics. In particular, the aggregation is transitive and asymmetric. *Transitivity* means that if class A contains class B and class B contains class C, then A contains C. *Asymmetry* means that if A contains B, then B cannot contain A.

Composition has an additional property of *existence dependency*. An object of a subset class cannot exist without being linked to an object of the superset class. This implies that if a superset object is deleted (destroyed), then its subset objects must also be deleted.

The *composition* is signified by the *filled diamond* 'adornment' on the end of the association line connected to the superset class. The *aggregation*, that is not a composition, is marked with the *hollow diamond*. Note, however, that the hollow diamond can also be used if the modeler does not want to make the decision if the aggregation is a composition, or not.

Figure 2.16 shows a composition on the left, and a normal aggregation on the right. Any `Book` object is a composition of `Chapter` objects, and any `Chapter` is a composition of `Section` objects. A `Chapter` object does not have an independent life; it exists only within the `Book` object. The same cannot be said about `BeerBottle` objects. The `BeerBottle` objects can exist outside of their container – a `Crate` object.

2.1.5 Generalization

Generalization is a *kind-of relationship* between a more generic class (*superclass* or *parent*) and a more specialized kind of that class (*subclass* or *child*). The subclass is a kind of superclass. An object of the subclass can be used where the superclass is allowed.

FIGURE 2.17
Generalization.

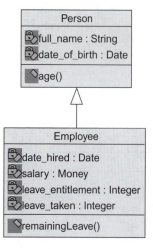

Generalization makes it unnecessary to restate already defined properties. The attributes and operations already defined for a superclass may be *reused* in a subclass. A subclass is said to *inherit* the attributes and methods of its parent class. Generalization facilitates incremental specification, exploitation of common properties between classes and better localization of changes.

A generalization is drawn as a hollow triangle on the relationship end connected to the parent class. In Figure 2.17, `Person` is the superclass and `Employee` is the subclass. The class `Employee` inherits all attributes and operations of the class `Person`. The inherited properties are not visibly shown in the subclass box – the generalization relationship forces the inheritance in the background.

Note that inheritance applies to classes, not to objects. It applies to types, not to values. The class `Employee` inherits the definitions of attributes `full_name` and `date_of_birth`. An object of the class `Employee` can be later instantiated with values for these attributes (because the attributes exist in `Employee` objects alongside four other attributes: `date_hired`, `salary`, `leave_entitlement` and `leave_taken`).

2.1.5.1 *Polymorphism*

A method inherited by a subclass is frequently used as is in that subclass. The operation `age()` works identically for the objects of classes `Person` and `Employee`. However, there are times when an operation needs to be *overridden* (modified) in a subclass to correspond to semantic variations of the subclass.

For example, `Employee.remainingLeave()` is computed by subtracting `leave_taken` from `leave_entitlement` (Figure 2.17). However, the employee who is a manager gains a yearly `leave_supplement`. If we now add the class Manager to the generalization hierarchy (as shown in Figure 2.18), the operation `Manager.remainingLeave()` would override the operation `Employee.remainingLeave()`. This is indicated in Figure 2.18 by duplicating the operation name in the subclass.

FIGURE 2.18
Polymorphism.

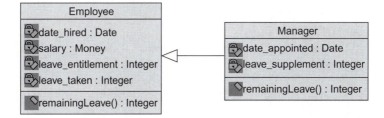

FIGURE 2.18
Polymorphism.

The operation `remainingLeave()` has been *overridden*. There are two implementations (two *methods*) of the operation. We can now send the message `remainingLeave()` to an `Employee` object or to a `Manager` object and we will get a different method executed. We may not even know or care which object is targeted: `Employee` or `Manager` – the proper method will execute. The operation `remainingLeave()` is *polymorphic*.

2.1.5.2 Inheritance

Polymorphism is of only limited use in the absence of inheritance. *Inheritance* permits incremental description of a subclass by reusing and then extending the superclass descriptions. The operation `Manager.remainingLeave()` is probably implemented by invoking the functionality of `Employee.remainingLeave()` and then by adding `leave_supplement` to the value returned from `Employee.remainingLeave()`.

Multiple classes in an inheritance hierarchy may declare the same operation. Such an operation has many implementations (*methods*) but the same *signature* – the name, and the number and types of its parameters (if any). The polymorphic behavior relies on inheritance.

2.1.5.2.1 Multiple inheritance

A subclass can inherit from more than one superclass. *Multiple inheritance* can lead to inheritance conflicts that have to be explicitly resolved by the programmer.

In Figure 2.19, the class `Tutor` inherits from the classes `Teacher` and `PostgraduateStudent`. `Teacher` in turn inherits from `Person` and so does `PostgraduateStudent` (via `Student`). As a result, `Tutor` would inherit twice the attributes and operations of `Person` unless the programmer instructs the programming environment to inherit only once by using either the left or right inheritance path (or unless the programming environment enforces some default behavior, acceptable to the programmer, that eradicates the duplicated inheritance).

2.1.5.2.2 Multiple classification

In most current object-oriented programming environments, an object can belong to only one class. This is a troublesome restriction because in reality objects can belong to multiple classes.

Multiple classification is different from multiple inheritance. In multiple classification an object is simultaneously the instance of two or more classes. In multiple inheritance a class may have many superclasses, but a single class must be defined for each object.

FIGURE 2.19
Multiple
inheritance.

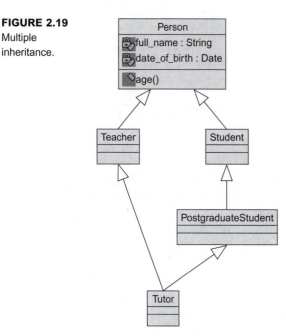

In the multiple inheritance example in Figure 2.19, each `Person` object (such as `Mary` or `Peter`) belongs to a single class (the most *specific* class that applies to it). If `Mary` is a `PostgraduateStudent`, but not a `Tutor`, then `Mary`'s class is `PostgraduateStudent`.

The problem arises if `Person` is specialized in a few orthogonal hierarchies. For example, a `Person` can be an `Employee` or `Student`, `Male` or `Female`, `Child` or `Adult`, etc. Without multiple classification, we would need to define classes for each legal combination between the orthogonal hierarchies to have, for example, a class for a `Person` object who is a child female student (i.e. the class that could be called `ChildFemaleStudent`) (Fowler and Scott, 2000).

2.1.5.2.3 Dynamic classification

In most current object-oriented programming environments, an object cannot change its class after it has been instantiated (created). This is another troublesome restriction because in reality objects do change classes dynamically.

`Dynamic classification` is a direct consequence of multiple classification. An object does not only belong to multiple classes but it can gain or lose classes over its lifetime.

Under the dynamic classification scheme, a `Person` object can be just an employee one day and a manager (and employee) another day. Without dynamic classification, the business changes such as promotion of employees are hard (or even impossible) to model *declaratively* in the class diagram. They would have to be modeled procedurally in state diagrams or similar modeling techniques.

Regrettably, UML does not support modeling of dynamic or multiple classification. This aligns it with the similar lack of support in programming environments. Consequently, our explanations and examples are not enhanced with graphical models.

FIGURE 2.20
Abstract class
with abstract
operation.

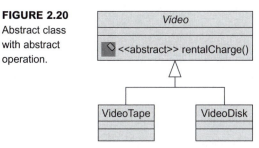

2.1.5.3 Abstract class

Abstract class is an important modeling concept that follows on from the notion of inheritance. An abstract class is a parent class that will not have direct instance objects. Only subclasses of the abstract parent class can be instantiated.

In a typical scenario, a class is abstract because at least one of its operations is abstract. An *abstract operation* has its *signature* (the name and the list of formal arguments) defined in the abstract parent class, but the implementation of the operation (the method) is deferred to *concrete* child classes.

The reason why an abstract class cannot instantiate objects is because it has at least one abstract operation. If we allowed an abstract class to create an object then a message to that object's abstract operation would cause a run-time error (because there would not be an implementation for the abstract operation in the class of that object).

A class can only be abstract if it is a superclass that is completely partitioned into subclasses. The partitioning is complete if the subclasses contain all possible objects that can be instantiated in the inheritance hierarchy. There are no 'stray' objects (Page-Jones, 2000). The class Person in Figure 2.19 is not abstract because we may want to instantiate objects of Person that are not teachers or students. It is also possible that we may want to add more subclasses of Person in the future (such as AdminEmployee).

Figure 2.20 shows the abstract class Video (in UML, the name of the abstract class is shown in italics). The class contains the abstract operation rentalCharge(). Understandably, rental charges are calculated differently for video tapes and for video disks. There will be two different implementations of rentalCharge() – in classes VideoTape and VideoDisk.

Abstract classes may not have objects, but they are very useful in modeling. They create a high-level modeling 'vocabulary' without which the modeling language would be deficient.

2.1.6 Class object

In passing, we made the distinction between *instance objects* and *class objects*. A *class object* is an object with class-scope attributes and/or class-scope operations. The class-scope implies here a global attribute or operation that applies to the class itself, not to any instance object.

Since in a pure object-oriented system the storage is provided in objects, we need a class object to store global attributes and operations. The most common *class-scope attributes* are

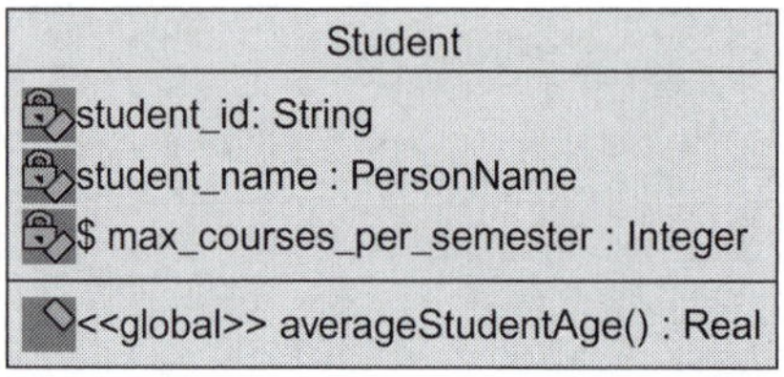

FIGURE 2.21

Class with class-scope attributes and operations.

Student
⬠⬦ student_id: String
⬠⬦ student_name : PersonName
⬠⬦ $ max_courses_per_semester : Integer
⬦ <<global>> averageStudentAge() : Real

attributes that hold default values or aggregate values (such as sums, counts, averages). The most common *class-scope operations* are operations to create and destroy instance objects and operations that calculate aggregate values.

Figure 2.21 shows the class `Student` with a class-scope attribute (`max_courses_per_semester`) and a class-scope operation (`averageStudentAge()`). Every student has the same allowed maximum number of courses per semester and therefore that number should be stored in the class object. The operation to calculate average age of students has the global scope because it needs to access individual ages of students (in `Student` instance objects) to be able to determine the average age of all students.

UML recommends that the class-scope attributes and operations be underlined in a class rectangle. In Figure 2.21, a '$' character in front of the attribute name signifies a class-scope (or *static*) attribute. The UML *stereotype* notation with the name `global` inside the brackets (<< >>) has been used to identify a class-scope (or *static*) operation.

2.2 Guided tutorial in analysis modeling

This section presents a quick tutorial in UML visual modeling using a simple example. The purpose is to demonstrate various UML diagrams and to show how they fit together. Each UML diagram emphasizes a particular *view* on the system. To understand the system in its entirety, multiple UML diagrams, representing different views, have to be developed and integrated.

At the most generic level, we can distinguish three kinds of UML models – each with its own set of diagrams and related constructs:

1. *The state model*, which represents the *static view* of the system – it models *data requirements*. The state model represents data structures and their relationships. The main visualization technique for state modeling is the class diagram.

2. *The behavior model*, which represents the *operational view* of the system – it models *function requirements*. The behavior model represents business transactions, operations and algorithms on data. There are several visualization techniques for behavior modeling – use case diagram, sequence diagram, collaboration diagram, and activity diagram.

3. *The state change model*, which represents the *dynamic view* of the system – it models object evolution over time. The state change model represents possible changes to object states (where the *state* is defined by the current values of an object's attributes and associations

with other objects). The main visualization technique for state change modeling is the statechart diagram.

2.2.1 OnLine Shopping

The Internet has revolutionized the ways in which we do business. To remain competitive, organizations have to be present on the Internet and have to extend their business applications to include electronic commerce (e-commerce). The changes are extensive on applications' *front ends*, but the underlying *back end* databases still have to perform quite conventional business transaction processing.

Our quick tutorial refers to an *online shopping application*. We are mostly concerned with the back end of the application – accepting a customer's online order, the processing and filling of the order, invoicing, and the shipment of goods to a customer.

The tutorial is contrived to serve the purpose of demonstrating the UML visual modeling methods. The presented sequence of modeling activities is also contrived to show dependencies between UML diagrams.

The sequence of activities must not be interpreted as the recommended *process*. In reality, the process is *iterative and incremental* (Section 1.1.3.1). The over-reliance in the tutorial on the use case modeling is not a true reflection of software development practices. The class modeling would normally be conducted in parallel with the use case modeling.

Tutorial statement: OnLine Shopping
Customer order processing

A *computer manufacturer* offers the possibility of purchasing computers via the Internet. The customer can select a computer on the manufacturer's web page. The computers are classified into servers, desktops and portables. The customer can select a standard configuration or can build a desired configuration online. The configurable components (such as memory) are presented as picklists of available options. For each new configuration, the system can calculate price.

To place an order, the customer must fill out the shipment and payment information. Acceptable payment methods are credit cards and checks. Once the order has been entered, the system sends a confirmation e-mail message to the customer with details of the order. While waiting for the arrival of the computer, the customer can check the order status online at any time.

The back end order processing consists of the steps needed to verify the customer's credentials and payment method, to request the ordered configuration from the warehouse, to print an invoice, and to request the warehouse to ship the computer to the customer.

2.2.2 Use case modeling

System behavior is what a system does when responding to external events. In UML, the outwardly visible and testable system behavior is captured in use cases. A *use case* performs a business function that is *outwardly visible* to an actor and that can be separately *testable* later in the development process.

An *actor* represents whoever or whatever (person, machine, etc.) that interacts with a use case. The actor interacts with the use case in expectation of receiving a useful result.

A use case diagram is a visual representation of actors and use cases together with any additional definitions and specifications. A use case diagram is not just a diagram but also a fully documented model of the system's intended behavior. The same understanding applies to other UML diagrams. Unless stated otherwise, the notion of *UML diagram* is synonymous with *UML model.*

2.2.2.1 Actors

Actors and use cases are determined from the analysis of function requirements. Function requirements are materialized in use cases. Use cases satisfy function requirements by providing a result of value to an actor. It is immaterial whether the business analyst chooses to first identify actors and then use cases or the other way around. In this tutorial, we have chosen first to identify the actors.

A typical graphical image for an actor is a 'stick person' (see below). In general, an actor can be shown as a *class* rectangular symbol. Like a normal class, an actor can have attributes and operations (events that it sends or receives).

Analysis tutorial: Step 1 (OnLine Shopping)

Refer to the Tutorial statement above (p. 47) and consider the following extended requirements to find *actors* in the OnLine Shopping application:

1. The customer uses the manufacturer's online shopping web page to view the standard configuration of the chosen server, desktop or portable computer. The price is also shown.

2. The customer chooses to view the details of the configuration, perhaps with the intention of buying it as is or to build a more suitable configuration. The price for each configuration can be computed at the customer's request.

3. The customer may choose to order the computer online or may request that the salesperson contact him/her to explain order details, negotiate the price, etc. before the order is actually placed.

4. To place the order, the customer must fill out an online form with shipment and invoice address, and with payment details (credit card or check).

5. After the customer's order has been entered into the system, the salesperson sends an electronic request to the warehouse with details of the ordered configuration.

6. The details of the transaction, including an order number and customer account number, are e-mailed to the customer, so that the customer can check the status of the order online.

7. The warehouse obtains the invoice from the salesperson and ships the computer to the customer.

Figure 2.22 shows the three actors that are manifestly present in the specifications. The actors are Customer, Salesperson, and Warehouse.

FIGURE 2.22
Actors (OnLine Shopping).

Customer   Salesperson   Warehouse

2.2.2.2 *Use cases*

A *use case* represents a complete unit of functionality of value to an actor. An actor who does not communicate with a use case is meaningless, but the converse is not necessarily true (i.e. a use case that does not communicate with an actor is allowed). There may be some use cases that generalize or specialize main use cases and do not directly interact with actors. They are used internally in the use case model and assist the main use cases in providing results to actors.

Use cases can be derived from the identification of tasks of the actor. The question to ask is: 'What are the actor's responsibilities towards the system and expectations from the system?' Use cases can also be determined from direct analysis of function requirements. In many instances, a *function requirement* maps directly to a *use case*.

Analysis tutorial: Step 2 (OnLine Shopping)

Refer to Step 1 (p. 48) of the tutorial and find *use cases* in the online shopping application.

To address this tutorial problem, we can construct a table that assigns the function requirements to the actors and the use cases. Note that some potential business functions may not be in the scope of the application – they are not to be transformed to use cases.

Table 2.1 assigns the function requirements listed in Step 1 of the tutorial to the actors and the use cases. The warehouse's tasks of configuring the computer and shipping it to the customer are *out-of-scope* functions.

Figure 2.23 demonstrates the UML graphical notation for use cases. A use case is drawn as an ellipse with the name inside the ellipse or below it. Other representations are also

TABLE 2.1 Assignment of requirements to actors and use cases (OnLine Shopping).

Req#	Requirement	Actor	Use case
1	The customer uses the manufacturer's online shopping web page to view the standard configuration of the chosen server, desktop or portable computer. The price is also shown.	Customer	Display Standard Computer Configuration
2	The customer chooses to view the details of the configuration, perhaps with the intention of buying it as is or to build a more suitable configuration. The price for each configuration can be computed on the customer's request.	Customer	Build Computer Configuration
3	The customer may choose to order the computer online or may request that the salesperson contact him/her to explain order details, negotiate the price, etc. before the order is actually placed.	Customer, Salesperson	Order Configured Computer, Request Salesperson Contact
4	To place the order, the customer must fill out an online form with shipment and invoice address, and with payment details (credit card or check).	Customer	Order Configured Computer, Verify and Accept Customer Payment
5	After customer's order has been entered into the system, the salesperson sends an electronic request to the warehouse with details of the ordered configuration.	Salesperson, Warehouse	Inform Warehouse About Order
6	The details of the transaction, including order number and customer account number, are e-mailed to the customer, so that the customer can check the status of the order online.	Salesperson, Customer	Order Configured Computer, Update Order Status
7	The warehouse obtains the invoice from the salesperson and ships the computer to the customer.	Salesperson, Warehouse	Print Invoice

FIGURE 2.23
Use cases
(OnLine
Shopping).

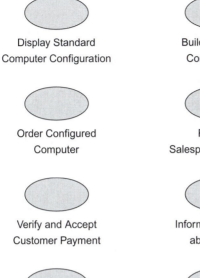

Display Standard
Computer Configuration

Build Computer
Configuration

Order Configured
Computer

Request
Salesperson Contact

Verify and Accept
Customer Payment

Inform Warehouse
about Order

Update
Order Status

Print Invoice

possible, including a class rectangle, so that any attributes and operations of the use case can be listed.

2.2.2.3 Use case diagram

The use case diagram assigns use cases to actors. It also allows the user to establish relationships between use cases, if any. These relationships are discussed in Chapter 4 (see Section 4.3.1.2).

The use case diagram is the principal visualization technique for a behavioral model of the system. The diagram elements (use cases and actors) need to be further described to provide a complete *use case model* (see Section 2.2.2.4).

Analysis tutorial: Step 3 (OnLine Shopping)

Refer to the previous steps of the tutorial and draw a *use case diagram* for the online shopping application.

A solution to this tutorial step can be directly obtained from the information contained in the previous steps. The only additional consideration may be the relationships between use cases. The diagram is presented in Figure 2.24. The meaning of the <<extend>> relationship is that the use case Order Configured Computer can be extended by Customer with the use case Request Salesperson Contact.

FIGURE 2.24
Use case
diagram (OnLine
Shopping).

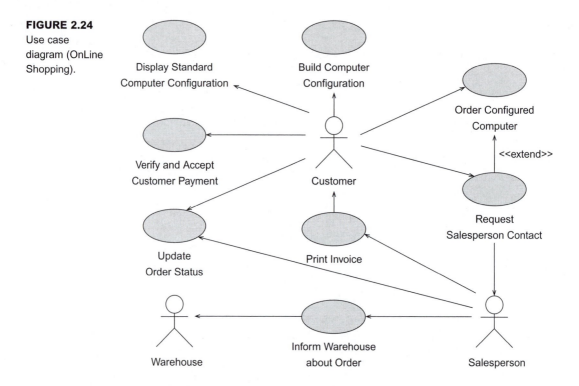

2.2.2.4 *Documenting use cases*

Each use case has to be described in a *flow of events* document. This textual document defines what the system has to do when the actor activates a use case. The structure of a *use case document* can vary, but a typical description would contain (cp. Quatrani, 2000):

- *Brief description*
- *Actors* involved
- *Preconditions* necessary for the use case to start
- *Detailed description* of flow of events that includes:
    - *Main flow* of events, that can be broken down to show:
        - *Subflows* of events (subflows can be further divided into smaller subflows to improve document readability)
    - *Alternative flows* to define exceptional situations
- *Postconditions* that define the state of the system after the use case ends

The use case document evolves with the development progress. In the early stage of requirements determination, only a brief description is written. Other parts of the document are written gradually and iteratively. A complete document emerges at the end of the requirements specification phase. At that stage, the prototypes of GUI screens can be added to the document. Later on, the use case document will be used to produce the user documentation for the implemented system.

Analysis tutorial: Step 4 (OnLine Shopping)

Refer to the previous tutorial steps and write a *use case document* for the use case `Order Configured Computer`. Use your general knowledge of typical order processing tasks to derive details not stated in the requirements.

The solution to this tutorial step is presented in a tabular form (Table 2.2). This is not the usual way of documenting use cases. Use case documents can contain many pages (ten or so on average) and a normal document structure, complete with a table of contents, would be the norm.

TABLE 2.2   Narrative specification for use case 'Order configured computer' (OnLine Shopping).

Use case	Order configured computer
Brief description	This use case allows a `Customer` to enter a purchase order. This includes providing a shipment and invoice address as well as payment details.
Actors	`Customer`
Preconditions	`Customer` points an Internet browser to the computer manufacturer's order entry web page. The page displays the details of a configured computer together with its price.
Main flow	The use case begins when the `Customer` decides to order the configured computer by choosing the `Continue` (or similarly named) function when the order details are displayed on the screen. The system requests that the `Customer` enter the purchase details, including: name of the salesperson (if known), shipment details (customer's name and address), invoice details (if different from shipment details), a payment method (credit card or check), and any comments. The `Customer` chooses the `Purchase` (or similarly named) function to send the order to the manufacturer. The system assigns a unique order number and a customer account number to the purchase order and it stores the order information in the database. The system e-mails the order number and the customer number to the `Customer`, together with all order details, as the confirmation of the order's acceptance.
Alternative flows	The `Customer` activates the `Purchase` function before providing all mandatory information. The system displays an error message and it requests that the missing information be supplied. The `Customer` chooses the `Reset` (or similarly named) function to revert to an empty purchase form. The system allows the `Customer` to enter the information again.
Postconditions	If the use case was successful, the purchase order is recorded in the system's database. Otherwise, the system's state is unchanged.

2.2.3 Activity modeling

The *activity model* can graphically represent the flow of events of a use case. Introduced only in the later versions of UML, the activity models fill a gap between a high-level representation of system behavior in *use case models* and much lower-level representation of behavior in *interaction models* (sequence and collaboration diagrams).

The activity diagram shows the steps of a computation. Each step is a *state* of doing something. For that reason, the execution steps are called *activity states*. The diagram depicts which steps are executed in sequence and which can be executed concurrently. The flow of control from one activity state to the next is called a *transition*.

If a use case document has been completed then activity states can be discovered from the description of the *main and alternative flows*. There is, however, an important difference between the use case description and the activity model. Use case descriptions are written from an *outside actor's perspective*. Activity models take an *inside system's viewpoint*.

Activity models can have other uses in system development apart from modeling use cases (cp. Fowler and Scott, 2000). They can be used to understand a business process at a high level of abstraction before any use cases are produced. Alternatively, they can be used at a much lower level of abstraction to design complex sequential algorithms or to design concurrency in multi-threaded applications.

2.2.3.1 Activities

If the activity modeling is used to visualize the sequencing of activities in a use case then activity states can be established from the use case document. As noted, the activities should be named from the system's perspective, not the actor's viewpoint.

An activity state is represented in UML by a rounded rectangle. To be precise, the same graphical symbol is used to visualize an *activity state* and *action state*. The distinction between activity and action is that of the time scale. *Activity* takes time to complete; *action* is so quick that – on our time scale – it is considered to take no time at all. (Consequently, in the statechart models (Section 2.2.6), activities can be only defined within *object states*, but actions can also appear on transitions between object states.)

Analysis tutorial: Step 5 (OnLine Shopping)

Refer to Step 4 (p. 53) of the tutorial. Analyze the main and alternate flows in the use case document. Find activities for the use case `Order Configured Computer` in the online shopping application.

Table 2.3 lists the statements in the main and alternative flows of the use case document and identifies activity states. Note the system's (not actor's) viewpoint in naming activities.

The activities identified in Table 2.3 are drawn in Figure 2.25.

TABLE 2.3 Finding activities in main and alternative flows.

No.	Use case statement	Activity state
1	The use case begins when the `Customer` decides to order the configured computer by choosing the `Continue` (or similarly named) function when the order details are displayed on the screen.	`Display Current Configuration; Get Order Request`
2	The system requests that the `Customer` enter the purchase details, including: name of the salesperson (if known), shipment details (customer's name and address), invoice details (if different from shipment details), a payment method (credit card or check), and any comments.	`Display Purchase Form`
3	The `Customer` chooses the `Purchase` (or similarly named) function to send the order to the manufacturer.	`Get Purchase Details`
4	The system assigns a unique order number and a customer account number to the purchase order and it stores the order information in the database.	`Store Order`
5	The system e-mails to the `Customer` the order number and the customer number, together with all order details, as the confirmation of the order's acceptance.	`Email Order Details`
6	The `Customer` activates the `Purchase` function before providing all mandatory information. The system displays an error message and it requests that the missing information be supplied.	`Get Purchase Details; Display Purchase Form`
7	The `Customer` chooses the `Reset` (or similarly named) function to revert to an empty purchase form. The system allows the `Customer` to enter the information again.	`Display Purchase Form`

2.2.3.2 *Activity diagram*

The *activity diagram* shows transitions between activities. Unless the activity diagram represents a continuous loop, the diagram will have an initial activity state and one or more final activity states. A solid filled circle represents the *initial state*. The *final state* is shown using a 'bull's eye' symbol.

Transitions can *branch* and *merge*. This creates *alternative* computation *threads*. A diamond box shows the branch condition.

Transitions can also *fork* and *rejoin*. This creates *concurrent* (parallel) computation *threads*. The fork/join of transitions is represented by a bar line. Note that an activity diagram without

FIGURE 2.25
Activities for use case 'Order configured computer' (OnLine Shopping).

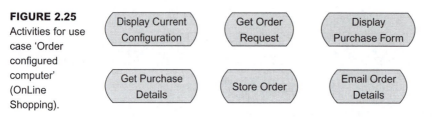

concurrent processes resembles a conventional *flowchart*. (Concurrent behavior is not taken advantage of in the tutorial. It is demonstrated in Section 4.3.2.)

Analysis tutorial: Step 6 (OnLine Shopping)

Refer to Steps 4 (p. 53) and 5 (p. 54) of the tutorial and draw an *activity diagram* for the use case `Order Configured Computer` in online shopping application.

To draw the diagram, the activities identified in Step 5 of the tutorial have to be connected by transition lines, as demonstrated in Figure 2.26. `Display Current Configuration` is the initial activity state. The *recursive transition* on this state recognizes the fact that the display is continuously refreshed until the next transition fires (to `Get Order Request`). This may be interpreted as the recognition of this state to be an *activity*, not an *action*.

FIGURE 2.26
Activity diagram for use case 'Order configured computer' (OnLine Shopping).

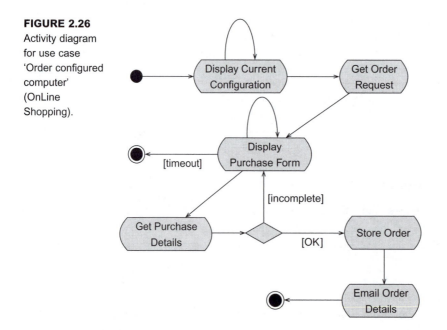

When in the state `Display Purchase Form`, the `timeout` condition finishes the execution of the activity model. Alternatively, the state `Get Purchase Details` is activated. If the purchase details are incomplete, the system again enters the state `Display Purchase Form`. Otherwise, the system gets into the state `Store Order`, followed by the state `Email Order Details` (that leads to a final state).

Note that only these branch conditions that appear (always) on exits from an activity state are shown. The branch conditions that are internal to an activity state are not explicit on the diagram. They can be inferred from the presence of multiple exit transitions, possibly with a guarded condition name in square brackets on the transition (such as `[timeout]` on exit from `Display Purchase Form`).

2.2.4 Class modeling

The *system state* is what a system consists of. The state is the function of the system's information content at a point in time – it is the function of the system's current set of instance objects (see Section 2.1.1).

The definition for an internal state of the system is given in *class models*. The class modeling elements include classes themselves, attributes and operations of classes, associations, aggregation and composition, and generalization (see Sections 2.1.2, 2.1.3, 2.1.4, and 2.1.5). A *class diagram* provides a combined visual representation for these modeling elements.

We remind you again that although in the tutorial we discuss class modeling after use case modeling, in practice these two activities are typically conducted in parallel (see Section 3.2). The two models feed each other with supplementary information. Use cases facilitate class discovery and vice versa – class models can lead to the discovery of overlooked use cases.

2.2.4.1 *Classes*

In the discussion so far, we have used classes to define *business objects*. Our class examples have all been long-lived (persistent) business entities, such as `Order`, `Shipment`, `Customer`, `Student`, etc. These are the classes that define the *database model* for an application domain. For that reason, such classes are frequently called *entity classes* (model classes). They represent persistent database objects.

The *entity classes* define the essence of any information system. Requirements analysis is interested predominantly in entity classes. However, for the system to function other classes are needed as well. The system needs classes that define GUI objects (such as screen forms) – called the *boundary classes* (view classes). The system also needs classes that control the program's logic – the *control classes* (see Section 5.2.3).

Depending on a particular modeling approach, the boundary and control classes may or may not be addressed in any detail in requirements analysis. Modeling of these classes may be delayed until the system design phase.

> ### 📁 Analysis tutorial: Step 7 (OnLine Shopping)
>
> Refer to the requirements defined in the tutorial statement (Section 2.2.1) and in Step 1 of the tutorial (Section 2.2.2.1). Find candidate *entity classes* in the online shopping application.

Following the approach taken in finding actors and use cases (see Table 2.1), we can construct a table that assists in finding classes from the analysis of function requirements. Table 2.4 assigns the function requirements listed in Step 1 of the tutorial to the entity classes.

TABLE 2.4 Assignment of requirements to entity classes (OnLine Shopping).

Req#	Requirement	Entity class
1	The customer uses the manufacturer's online shopping web page to view the standard configuration of the chosen server, desktop or portable computer. The price is also shown.	Customer, Computer (StandardConfiguration, Product)
2	The customer chooses to view the details of the configuration, perhaps with the intention to buy it as is or to build a more suitable configuration. The price for each configuration can be computed at the customer's request.	Customer, ConfiguredComputer (ConfiguredProduct), ConfigurationItem
3	The customer may choose to order the computer online or may request that the salesperson contact him/her to explain order details, negotiate the price, etc. before the order is actually placed.	Customer, ConfiguredComputer, Order, Salesperson
4	To place the order, the customer must fill out an online form with shipment and invoice address, and with payment details (credit card or check).	Customer, Order, Shipment, Invoice, Payment
5	After the customer's order has been entered into the system, the salesperson sends an electronic request to the warehouse with details of the ordered configuration.	Customer, Order, Salesperson, ConfiguredComputer, ConfigurationItem
6	The details of the transaction, including the order number and the customer account number, are e-mailed to the customer, so that the customer can check the status of the order online.	Order, Customer, OrderStatus
7	The warehouse obtains the invoice from the salesperson and ships the computer to the customer.	Invoice, Shipment

FIGURE 2.27
Classes (OnLine
Shopping).

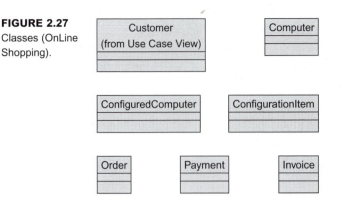

Finding classes is an iterative task and the initial list of candidate classes is likely to change. Answering a few questions may help to determine whether a concept in the requirements is a candidate class. The questions are:

1. Is the concept a container for data?
2. Does it have separate attributes that will take on different values?
3. Would it have many instance objects?
4. Is it in the scope of the application domain?

The list of classes in Table 2.4 still poses many questions. For example:

1. What's the difference between ConfiguredComputer and Order? After all, we are not going to store ConfiguredComputer unless Order for it has been placed, or are we?
2. Is the meaning of Shipment in Req# 4 and Req# 7 the same? Probably not. Do we need the Shipment class if we know that the shipment is the warehouse responsibility and it is therefore out of the scope? (Section 2.2.2.2.)
3. Could not ConfigurationItem be just a set of attributes in ConfiguredComputer?
4. Is OrderStatus a class or an attribute of Order?
5. Is Salesperson a class or an attribute of Order and Invoice?

Answering these and similar questions is not easy and requires an in-depth knowledge of application requirements. For the purpose of this tutorial, we have chosen the list of classes as shown in Figure 2.27. Note that the class Customer has already appeared as an *actor* in the use case diagram – hence the annotation 'from use case view'.

2.2.4.2 *Attributes*

The structure of a class is defined by its *attributes* (Section 2.1.2.1). The analyst must have some appreciation of the attribute structure when initially declaring a class. In practice, main attributes are usually allocated to a class immediately after the class has been added to the model.

Analysis tutorial: Step 8 (OnLine Shopping)

Refer to Steps 5, 6 and 7 of the tutorial. Think about attributes for the classes in Figure 2.27. Consider only *attributes with primitive types* (Section 2.1.2.1).

Figure 2.28 shows the classes with primitive attributes. Only most interesting attributes have been shown. Attributes of `ConfigurationItem` warrant brief explanation. The attribute `item_type` will have values such as processor, memory, screen, hard drive, etc. The attribute `item_descr` will further describe the item type. For example, the processor in the configuration may be an Intel 600 MHz with 256 k cache.

Admittedly and understandably, there is a significant amount of arbitrary decisions in defining attributes in Figure 2.28. Other interpretations are possible and indeed likely if a reader attempts an independent solution to this tutorial step.

2.2.4.3 Associations

Associations between classes establish pathways for easy object collaboration (Section 2.1.3). In the implemented system, the associations will be represented with attribute types that

FIGURE 2.28
Primitive attributes (OnLine Shopping).

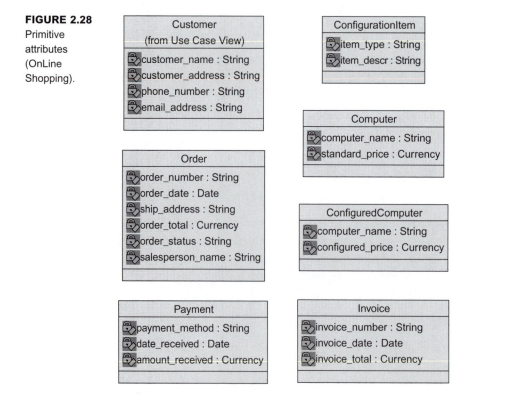

FIGURE 2.29
Associations
(OnLine
Shopping).

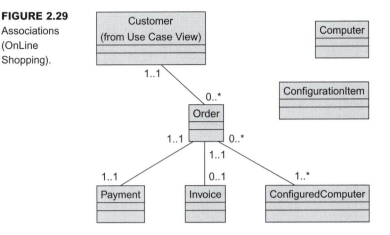

designate associated classes (Section 2.1.2.1.1). In the analysis model, the association lines represent associations.

Analysis tutorial: Step 9 (OnLine Shopping)

Refer to the previous steps of the tutorial. Consider the classes in Figure 2.28. Think what access paths between these classes are required by the use cases. Add *associations* to the class model.

Figure 2.29 shows the most apparent associations between the classes. We made a few assumptions when determining association *multiplicities* (Section 2.1.3.2). Order is from a single Customer, but Customer may place many Orders. Order is not accepted unless the Payment has been specified (hence, one-to-one association). Order does not have to have an associated Invoice, but Invoice is always related to a single Order. An Order is for one or many ConfiguredComputers. A ConfiguredComputer may be ordered many times or not at all.

2.2.4.4 Aggregations

Aggregation and composition are stronger forms of associations with ownership semantics (Section 2.1.4). In a typical commercial programming environment, aggregations and compositions are likely to be implemented like associations – with attribute types that designate associated classes (Section 2.1.2.1.1).

Analysis tutorial: Step 10 (OnLine Shopping)

Refer to the previous steps of the tutorial. Consider the models in Figure 2.28 and 2.29. Add *aggregations* to the class model.

FIGURE 2.30
Aggregations
(OnLine
Shopping).

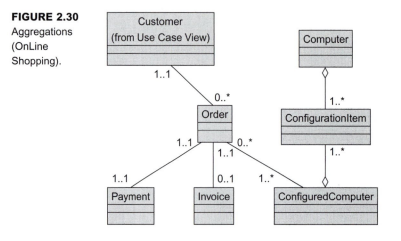

Figure 2.30 adds two aggregation relationships to the model. `Computer` has one or more `ConfigurationItems`. Likewise, `ConfiguredComputer` consists of one or many `ConfigurationItems`.

2.2.4.5   *Generalizations*

Generalization is a powerful software reuse technique, but it can also greatly simplify and clarify the model (Section 2.1.5). The simplification in the model is semantic not graphical. Generalization will normally create extra generic classes (frequently *abstract*). The simplification is achieved by the added precision with which the existing classes can be associated with the most applicable (i.e. at the most suitable abstraction level) classes in the generalization hierarchy.

Analysis tutorial: Step 11 (OnLine Shopping)

Refer to the previous steps of the tutorial. Consider the models in Figure 2.28 and 2.30. Think how you can extract any common attributes in the existing classes into a higher-level class. Add *generalizations* to the class model.

Figure 2.31 shows a modified model with the class `Computer` changed to a generic *abstract* class for two *concrete* subclasses `StandardComputer` and `ConfiguredComputer`. `Order` and `ConfigurationItem` are now linked to `Computer` and `Computer` can be either `StandardComputer` or `ConfiguredComputer`.

2.2.4.6   *Class diagram*

The class diagram is the heart and soul of an object-oriented system. In this tutorial, we have only demonstrated the *static modeling* ability of the class model.

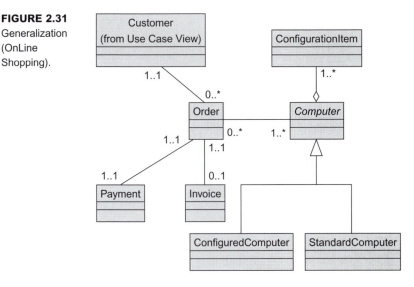

FIGURE 2.31
Generalization
(OnLine
Shopping).

We have not added as yet any operations to the classes. The operations belong more to the design than analysis realm. When operations are eventually included in classes, the class model implicitly defines the system *behavior*.

Analysis Tutorial: Step 12 (OnLine Shopping)

Refer to the previous steps of the tutorial. Combine the models in Figures 2.28 and 2.31 to show a complete class diagram. Modify attribute content of classes as necessitated by the introduction of the generalization hierarchy.

Figure 2.32 is the class diagram for the 'OnLine Shopping' application. It is not a complete solution, e.g. more attributes would be required in a pragmatic solution.

2.2.5 Interaction modeling

Interaction modeling captures interactions between objects needed to execute a use case. Interaction models are used in more advanced stages of requirements analysis, when a basic class model is known, so that the references to objects are backed by the class model.

The above observation underpins the main distinction between the activity modeling (see Section 2.2.3) and the interaction modeling. Both capture the behavior of a single use case (usually). However, the *activity modeling* is done at a higher level of abstraction – it shows the sequencing of events without assigning the events to objects. The *interaction modeling* shows the sequencing of events (messages) between collaborating objects.

There are two kinds of interaction diagram – the sequence diagram and the collaboration diagram. They can be used interchangeably and, indeed, many CASE tools support an

FIGURE 2.32
Class diagram
(OnLine
Shopping).

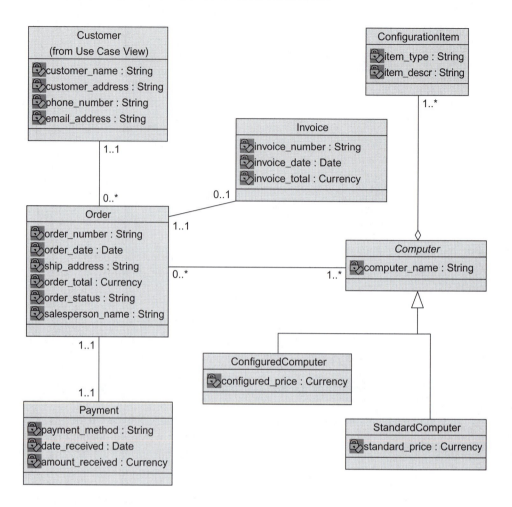

automatic conversion from one model to the other. The difference is in emphasis. The sequence models concentrate on time sequences and the collaboration models emphasize object relationships (cp. Rumbaugh *et al.*, 1999).

In this book, we elected to use sequence diagrams in requirements analysis and collaboration diagrams in system design. This is consistent with the prevailing IS development practice.

2.2.5.1 *Interactions*

An *interaction* is a set of *messages* in some behavior that are exchanged between *objects* across *links* (persistent or transient links (Section 2.1.1.3)). The sequence diagram is a two-dimensional graph. Objects are shown along the horizontal dimension. Sequencing of messages is shown top to bottom on the vertical dimension. Each vertical line is called the object's *lifeline* (see Figure 2.33).

An arrow represents each *message* from a calling object (*sender*) to an operation (method) in the called object (*target*). As a minimum, the message is named. *Actual arguments* of the message and other control information can also be included. The actual arguments correspond to the *formal arguments* in the method of the target object.

The actual argument can be an *input argument* (from the sender to the target) or an *output argument* (from the target back to the sender). The input argument may be identified by the keyword in (if there is no keyword then the input argument is assumed). The output argument is identified with the keyword out. The inout arguments are also possible but they are rare in object-oriented solutions. The message getCourseName (see Section 2.1.1.3.1), sent to an object identified by variable crs_ref, has one output argument and no input arguments:

```
crs_ref.getCourseName(out crs_name)
```

Showing the *return* of control from the target to the sender object is not necessary. The message arrow to the target object implies automatic return of control to the sender. The target knows the OID of the sender.

A message can be sent to a *collection* of objects (a collection could be a set, list, array of objects, etc.). This is frequently the case when a calling object is linked to multiple receiver objects (because the multiplicity of the association is one-to-many or many-to-many). An *iteration marker* – an asterisk in front of the message label – indicates iterating over a collection.

Analysis tutorial: Step 13 (OnLine Shopping)

Refer to the activity diagram in Figure 2.26. Consider the first step in the diagram, Display Current Configuration. **Construct a sequence diagram for this step.**

A sequence diagram for 'display current configuration' is shown in Figure 2.33. The outside actor (Customer) chooses to display the configuration of a computer. The message openNew is sent to an object ConfWin of the class ConfigurationWindow. The message results in *creating* (*instantiating*) a new aConfWin object. (ConfigurationWindow is a *boundaryclass* (Section 2.2.4.1).)

The object aConfWin needs to 'display itself' with the configuration data. To this aim, it sends a message to the object aComp:Computer. In reality, aComp is an object of the class StandardComputer or ConfiguredComputer. Computer is an abstract class (Figure 2.31 in Section 2.2.4.5).

The object aComp uses the output argument item_rec to 'compose itself' from ConfigurationItem objects. It then sends the configuration items in bulk to aConfWin as an argument i_recset of displayComputer message. The object aConfWin can now display itself. The screen display will be similar to Figure 2.34.

Note that the picklist fields in Figure 2.34 show the standard configuration items at the beginning. However, the picklists are populated with other non-standard items that a

FIGURE 2.33
Sequence diagram for activity 'display current configuration' (OnLine Shopping).

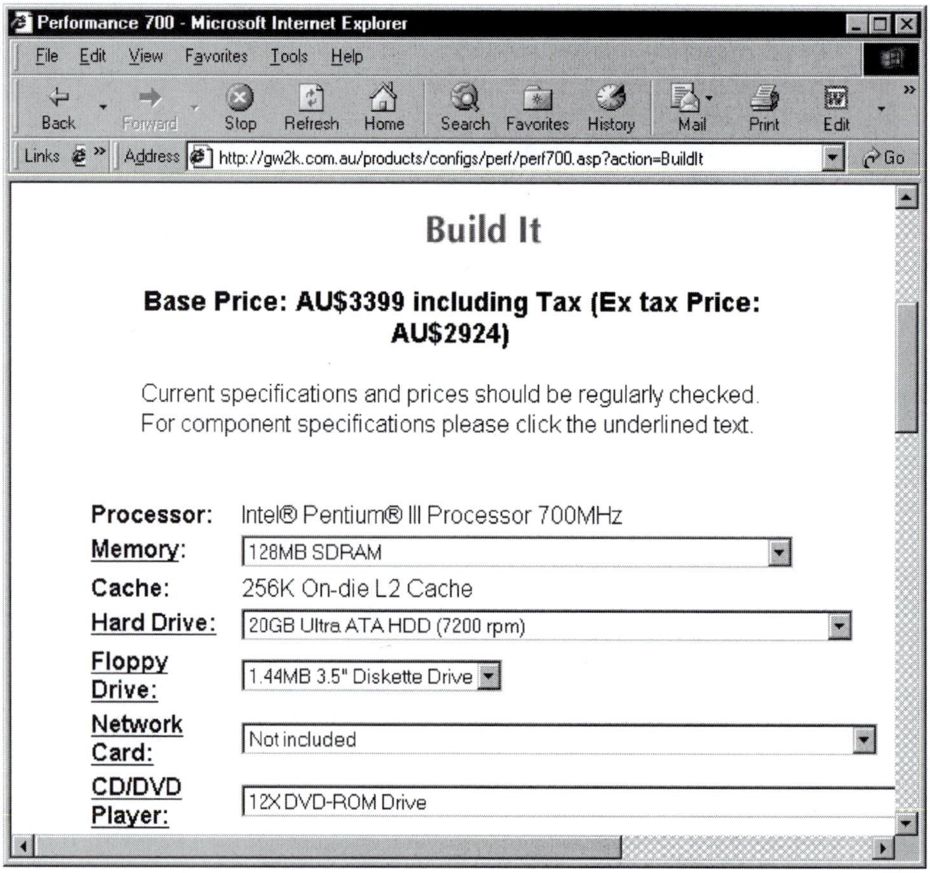

FIGURE 2.34
Example configuration window (OnLine Shopping) (courtesy of Gateway, Sydney, Australia).

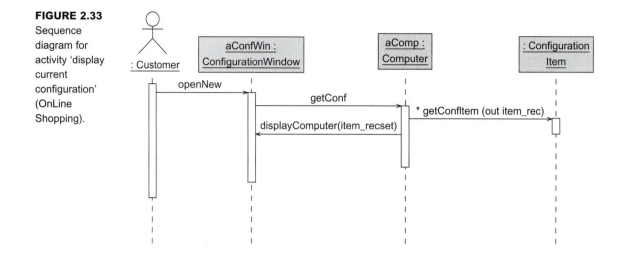

customer can select to create a new permissible configuration. The sequence diagram in Figure 2.33 does not model how and when the picklists are filled with data.

2.2.5.2 *Operations*

Although the introduction of *operations* to classes is frequently delayed to the design phase, we will illustrate in this tutorial that examining the interactions can lead to the discovery of operations. The dependency between interactions and operations is straightforward. Each *message* invokes an operation in the called object. The operation has the same name as the message.

Of course, this one-to-one mapping between *messages* in interaction models and *methods* in implemented classes can only be sustained if the interaction model constitutes a detailed technical design – something neither possible nor desirable in the analysis phase.

As an aside we observe that similar one-to-one mapping exists between *messages* and *associations*, when a message is sent between *persistent* (*model*) objects. These messages should be supported by persistent links (Section 2.1.1.3.1). Therefore, the presence of a message in a sequence diagram stipulates the need for an association in the class diagram.

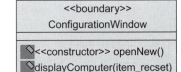

Analysis tutorial: Step 14 (OnLine Shopping)

Refer to the class diagram in Figure 2.32 and to the sequence diagram in Figure 2.33. For each interaction message in the sequence diagram add an operation to a relevant class in the class diagram. Do not redraw the whole class diagram – only show the classes extended with operations.

The solution to this simple tutorial step is shown in Figure 2.35. Three affected classes are shown. ConfigurationWindow is a boundary class. Two other classes are entity classes representing persistent database objects. The operation openNew is stereotyped as a *constructor operation*. This means that openNew will be implemented as a constructor method that instantiates new objects of the class.

FIGURE 2.35
Using interactions to add operations to classes (OnLine Shopping).

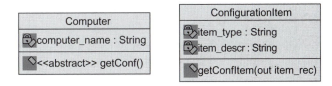

The class `Computer` is an *abstract class*. `getConf` is an abstract operation to be inherited by subclasses (`ConfiguredComputer` and `StandardComputer`). These subclasses provide their own implementations of `getConf`.

2.2.5.3 *Sequence diagram*

As mentioned, a separate sequence diagram is frequently constructed for each use case. Since each use case is likely to be also expressed in an activity diagram, a sequence diagram can be built for each activity diagram. Providing multiple correlated viewpoints on the same system is the cornerstone of a good modeling.

Analysis tutorial: Step 15 (OnLine Shopping)

Refer to the activity diagram in Figure 2.26 and construct a sequence diagram for it. To simplify the diagram do not show the exchange of messages between `Computer` and `ConfigurationItem` objects.

Also, do not visualize subclass objects – assume that a `Computer` object is either a `StandardComputer` or `ConfiguredComputer`.

Show only activation messages. Returns are implicit. There is no need to specify operation arguments or other control information.

Figure 2.36 is a solution to the above questions. The sequence diagram has been split into two parts for readability (`Order` and `OrderWindow` lifelines are repeated in the two parts).

The sequence diagram is largely self-explanatory. The first two messages are explained in Step 13 of the tutorial. The message `acceptConf` results in the `prepareForOrder` message sent to an `:Order` object. This creates a transient `:Order` object that is displayed in `:OrderWindow`.

On the customer's acceptance of the order details (`submitOrder`), `:OrderWindow` instigates (`storeOrder`) the creation of a persistent `:Order` object. The `:Order` object then links itself to the ordered `:Computer` and to relevant `:Customer` and `:Payment` objects. Once these objects are persistently linked in the database, the `:Order` object sends the `emailOrder` message to the outside actor `Customer`.

Note the double use of `:Customer` as an outside *actor object* and an inside *class object*. This is a frequent dichotomy in modeling. Customer is both external and internal to the system. It is external because it interacts with the system from the outside. However, the information about the customer must be kept in the system to recognize that the external customer is a legitimate internal entity that the system knows about.

2.2.6 **Statechart modeling**

An *interaction model* provides a detailed specification for a use case. A *statechart model* gives a detailed description of a class – dynamic changes of class states, to be more precise. These dynamic changes describe typically the behavior of an object across several use cases.

FIGURE 2.36
Sequence
diagram for
activity diagram
'Order
Configured
Computer'
(OnLine
Shopping).

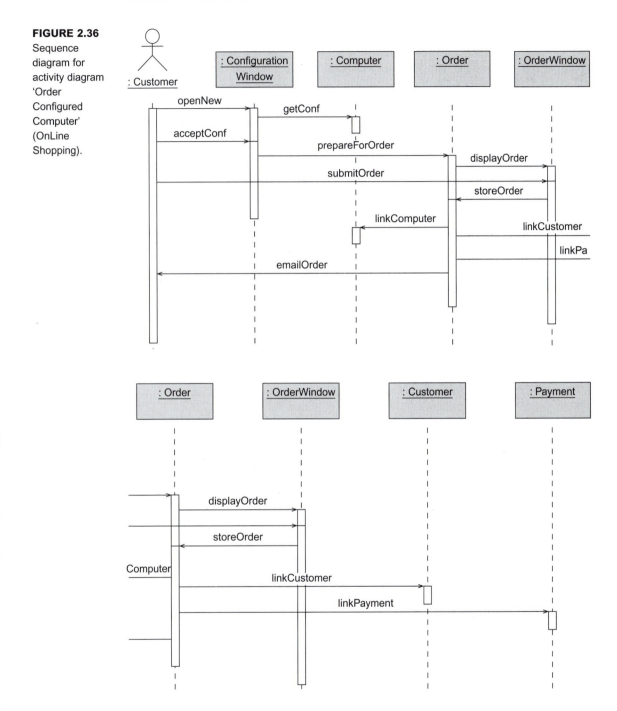

A *state* of an object is designated by the current values of the object's attributes (both primitive attributes and attributes that designate other classes). A *statechart model* captures possible states in which a class can be – it effectively captures the life history of the class. An object is one and the same during its lifetime – its identity never changes (Section 2.1.1.3). However, the state of an object changes.

A statechart diagram is a bipartite graph of *states* (rounded rectangles) and *transitions* (arrows) caused by *events*. The underlying concepts of states and events are the same concepts that we know from activity diagrams. The difference is that 'the states of the activity graph represent the states of executing the computation, not the states of an ordinary object' (Rumbaugh *et al.*, 1999, p. 81).

2.2.6.1 States and transitions

Objects change values of their attributes but not all such changes cause *state transitions*. Consider a `BankAccount` object and an associated business rule that the bank fees on an account are waived when the account's `balance` exceeds $100,000. We can say that `BankAccount` then enters a `privileged` state. It is in a `normal` state otherwise. The account's `balance` changes after each withdrawal/deposit transaction, but the *state* changes only when the balance goes above or below $100,000.

The above example captures the essence of state modeling. We construct state models for classes that have interesting state changes, not any state changes. What is 'interesting,' or not, is a business modeling decision. A statechart diagram is a model of business rules. The *business rules* are invariable over some periods of time. They are relatively independent of particular use cases. In fact, use cases must also conform to business rules.

Analysis tutorial: Step 16 (OnLine Shopping)

Consider the class `Invoice` in the online shopping application. We know from the use case model that a customer specifies the payment method (credit card or check) for the computer when the purchase form is filled out and submitted to the vendor. This results in the generation of an order and subsequently in the preparation of an invoice. However, the use case diagram has not clarified when the payment is actually received with relation to the invoice. We can assume, for example, that the payment can be made before or after the invoice is issued and that partial payments are allowed.

From the class model we know that the invoice for the order is prepared by a salesperson, but it is eventually handed over to the warehouse. The warehouse sends the invoice to the customer together with the computer shipment. It is important that the payment status of the invoice is maintained in the system so that invoices are properly annotated.

Draw a statechart diagram that captures possible invoice states as far as payments are concerned.

FIGURE 2.37
States and
events for the
class Invoice
(OnLine
Shopping).

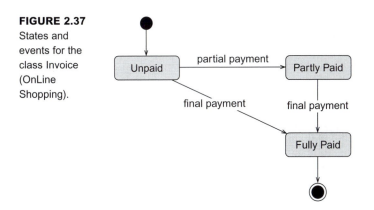

Figure 2.37 is a statechart model for the class `Invoice`. The initial state of `Invoice` is `Unpaid`. There are two possible transitions out of the `Unpaid` state. On the `partial payment` event, the `Invoice` object goes into the `Partly Paid` state. Only one `partial payment` is allowed. The `final payment` event, when in an `Unpaid` or `Partly Paid` state, fires a transition to `Fully Paid` state. This is the final state.

2.2.6.2 *Statechart diagram*

A statechart diagram is normally attached to a class, but in general, it can be attached to other modeling concepts, e.g. a use case. When attached to a class, the diagram determines how objects of that class react to events. More precisely, it determines – for each object state – what *action* the object will perform when it receives an event. The same object may perform a different action for the same event depending on the object's state. The action's execution will typically cause a state change.

The complete description of a *transition* consists of three parts:

```
event (parameters) [guard] / action .
```

Each part is optional. It is possible to omit all of them, if the transition line by itself is self-explanatory.

The event is a quick occurrence that affects an object. It can have parameters, e.g. `mouse button clicked (right_button)`. The event can be guarded by a condition, e.g. `mouse button clicked (right_button) [inside the window]`. Only when the condition evaluates to 'true' does the event fire and affect the object.

The distinction between an event and a guard is not always obvious. The distinction is that the *event* 'happens' and it may be even saved before the object is ready to handle it. At that point, the *guard* condition is evaluated to determine if a transition should fire.

The *action* is a short atomic computation that executes when the transition fires. An action can also be associated with a state. In general, an action is an object's response to a detected event. The states can additionally contain longer computations – called *activities*.

States can be composed of other states – *nested states*. The *composite state* is abstract – it is simply a generic label for all nested states. A transition taken out of a composite state's boundary means that it can fire from any of the nested states. This improves the clarity and brevity of the diagram. Of course, a transition out of a composite state's boundary can also be fired from a nested state.

Analysis tutorial: Step 17 (OnLine Shopping)

Refer to the previous steps of the tutorial. Consider the class `Order` in the online shopping application. Think about states in which `Order` can be – starting from its submission to the system and culminating in its fulfillment.

Consider that an ordered computer can be in stock or it may need to be individually configured to satisfy your requirements. You may also specify some day in the future that you want to receive the computer, even if the computer is in stock.

You are allowed to cancel your order any time prior to the computer's shipment. You don't need to model any penalty that may be involved in late canceling.

Draw a statechart diagram for the class `Order`.

A statechart diagram for `Order` is shown in Figure 2.38. The initial state is `New Order`. This is one of the `Pending` states – the other being `Back Order` and `Future Order`. There are two possible transitions out of any of the three states nested in the `Pending` state.

FIGURE 2.38
State diagram for the class Order (OnLine Shopping).

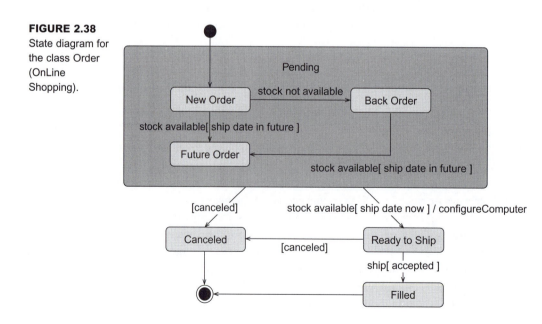

The transition into the `Canceled` state is guarded by the condition `[canceled]`. It would be possible – without violating the statechart modeling rules – to replace the guard by the event `cancel`. The transition to the state `Ready to Ship` is labeled with a complete description containing the event, guard and action.

2.3 Problem statements for case studies

To exemplify various modeling activities throughout the book, let us introduce four case studies. The case studies are presented using a similar approach as that used in the OnLine Shopping tutorial – the questions are defined and then the solutions are given. This allows the reader to attempt a solution and then compare it with the solution offered. The case studies are:

1. University Enrolment.

2. Video Store.

3. Contact Management.

4. Telemarketing.

2.3.1 University Enrolment

The University Enrolment is a classic textbook example (cp. Quatrani, 2000; Stevens and Pooley, 2000). It is a surprisingly complex application domain with a rich set of business rules that change relatively frequently, yet historical information has to be carefully maintained with relation to business rules in force at different times.

No two universities are the same. Each has its own interesting peculiarities that can be used in case studies to emphasize particular aspects of system analysis and design. The emphasis in our case study is on the intricacies of state modeling with regard to handling the time dimension (temporal information) and capturing business rules in data structures.

Problem statement 1: University Enrolment

A medium-size university offers a number of undergraduate and postgraduate degrees to full-time and part-time students. The educational structure of the university consists of divisions. Divisions contain several departments. While a single division administers each degree, the degree may include courses from other divisions. In fact, the university prides itself on the freedom of choice given to students in selecting courses towards their degrees.

The flexibility of course selection puts strains on the university enrolment system. Individually tailored programs of study must not contradict the rules governing the degree, such as the structure of prerequisite courses required so that the student can qualify for the degree's compulsory courses. A student's choice of courses may be restricted by timetable clashes, maximum class sizes, etc.

The flexibility of education offered by the university has been the main reason behind the steady growth in student numbers. However, to maintain its traditional strength, the current enrolment system – still partly manual – has to be replaced by a new software solution. The preliminary search for an off-the-shelf software package has not been successful. The university enrolment system is sufficiently unique to warrant the in-house development.

The system is required to assist in pre-enrolment activities and to handle the enrolment procedures. The pre-enrolment activities must include the mail-outs of last semester's examination grades to students together with any enrolment instructions. During enrolment sessions, the system must accept the students' proposed programs of study and validate them for prerequisites, timetable clashes, class sizes, special approvals, etc. Resolutions to some of the problems may require consultation with academic advisers or academics in charge of course offerings.

2.3.2 Video Store

Our second case study is a routine business application typical of small businesses. It is the application to support the operation of a small video store. The video store keeps in stock a wide-ranging tape and disk library of current and popular movies. The main operation of the store is rental services.

A typical computer system to support a small video store would be customized from off-the-shelf software or customized from some other proprietary solution. The system would be set on one of the popular database management systems available for a small-business computer.

Although with the database software underneath, the system may be initially deployed on a single machine. The GUI development is likely to be done with a simple fourth generation language (4GL) with screen painting, code generation capability, and a simple connection to the database.

A distinguishing aspect of the video store as a case study is the extensive chain of activities – from ordering of videos through stock management to the accounting associated with video rentals. In a way, it is a small-scale *value chain* operation (see Section 1.2.2).

Problem statement 2: Video Store

A new video store intends to offer rentals of video tapes and disks to the wider public. The store management is determined to launch its operations with the support of a computer system. The management has already sourced a number of small-business software packages that might be suitable for customization and further development. To assist with the package selection, the store hired a business analyst whose job is to determine and specify the requirements.

The video store will initially keep a stock of about a thousand video tapes and five hundred video disks. The inventory has already been ordered from one supplier, but more suppliers will be approached in future orders. All video tapes and disks will be bar coded so that a scanning machine integrated with the system can support the rentals and returns. The customer membership cards will also be bar coded.

Existing customers will be able to place reservations on videos to be collected at a specific date. The system must have a flexible search engine to answer customer enquiries, including enquiries about movies that the video store does not stock (but may order them on request).

2.3.3 Contact Management

Contact Management is a 'hot' application domain. Frequently known under the acronym CMS (Contact or Customer Management System), contact management is an important component of Enterprise Resource Planning (ERP) systems. The ERP systems automate so-called *back office* business transaction processing applications. Three typical components of an ERP system are: accounting, manufacturing, and human resources. CMS belongs to the human resources component.

The ERP systems are very large customizable solutions. Some people refer to them as mega-packages. Naturally enough, a CMS component of an ERP solution can be very complex. In our case study, we address only a small portion of the CMS problem area.

Contact management applications are characterized by interesting GUI solutions through which the employees of Customer Relations, or a similarly named department, can schedule their activities with regard to customers. In essence, the contact management system's GUI acts as a diary to record customer-related tasks and events and keep track of their progress.

The diary has to be database-driven to allow dynamic scheduling and monitoring of tasks and events across many employees. Like most human resource systems, contact management applications require a sophisticated authorization scheme to control access to sensitive information.

Problem statement 3: Contact Management

A market research company has an established customer base of organizations that buy market analysis reports. Some larger customers have also purchased specialized reporting software from the company. These customers are then provided with raw and pre-aggregated information for their own report generation.

The company is constantly on the search for new customers, even if the new customers may only be interested in one-off, narrowly targeted market reports. Since the prospective customers are not quite customers yet, the company prefers to call them contacts – hence, *contact* management system (contacts are prospective, actual and past customers).

A new contact management system is to be developed internally and be available to all employees in the company, but with varying levels of access. The employees of the Customer Services Department will take the ownership of the system. The system will permit flexible scheduling and re-scheduling of contact-related activities so that the employees can successfully collaborate to win new customers and foster existing relationships.

2.3.4 Telemarketing

Many organizations market their products and services by telemarketing, i.e. by directly contacting customers over the telephone. A telemarketing system needs to support an elaborated process of scheduling the phone calls to telemarketers, facilitating the conversation, and recording conversation outcomes.

Special aspects of a telemarketing system are heavy reliance on the database capability to actively schedule and dynamically re-schedule the phone calls while supporting concurrent conversations. Another interesting aspect is the capability to dial the scheduled phone numbers automatically.

Problem statement 4: Telemarketing

A charitable society sells lottery tickets to raise funds. The fundraising is done in *campaigns* to support currently important charitable causes. The society keeps a list of past contributors (*supporters*). For each new campaign, a subset of these supporters is pre-selected for telemarketing and/or direct mail contact.

The society uses some innovative schemes to gain new supporters. The schemes include special *bonus campaigns* to reward supporters for bulk buying, for attracting new contributors, etc. The society does not randomly target potential supporters by using telephone directories or similar means.

> To support its work, the society decided to contract out the development of a new telemarketing application. The new system is required to support up to fifty telemarketers working simultaneously. The system must be able to schedule the phone calls according to pre-specified priorities and other known constraints.
>
> The system is required to dial up the scheduled phone calls. Unsuccessful connections must be re-scheduled and tried again later. Telephone callbacks to supporters must also be arranged. The conversation outcomes, including ticket orders and any changes to supporter records, ought to be maintained.

Summary

In this chapter we have managed to cover quite a lot of ground. We explained the fundamental terminology and concepts of object technology. We have provided a large volume of illustrations to explain object modeling, including a complete tutorial. For a novice to the topic the task must have been daunting. The rewards will come in the next chapters.

An object system consists of collaborating *instance objects*. Each object has a state, behavior, and identity. The latter may well be the most essential for proper understanding of object systems – it is also the most difficult to appreciate for people with some luggage of experience in conventional computer applications. Navigate along *links* is the modus operandi of object technology – something that a reader educated on the relational database technology will have real difficulty to digest.

A *class* is the template for object creation. It defines the *attributes* that an object can contain and the *operations* that an object can invoke. Attributes can have primitive types or can designate other classes. The attributes that designate other classes declare the *associations*. The association is one kind of relationship between classes. Other kinds are *aggregation* and *generalization*.

The generalization relationship provides the basis for *polymorphism* and *inheritance*. Commercial programming environments can support *multiple inheritance*, but it is unlikely that they will support *multiple* or *dynamic classification*. Related to inheritance is the notion of *abstract class*. A class may have attributes or operations that apply to the class itself, not to any one of its instance objects. Such attributes and operations require the notion of a *class object*.

The concepts of object technology have been reinforced in the *guided tutorial* centered on application development for OnLine Shopping. The tutorial introduced the entire suite of UML modeling techniques – use case modeling, activity modeling, class modeling, interaction modeling, and statechart modeling. The techniques have been presented at a relatively high level of abstraction and many modeling details have been omitted. This will be rectified in the following chapters.

Finally, we defined the problem statements for four *case studies* to be used later (alongside the guided tutorial) to exemplify and explain more sophisticated analysis and design modeling. The case studies relate to the University Enrolment, Video Store, Contact Management and Telemarketing application domains.

Review questions

R1   Why do we need to distinguish between an instance object and a class object?

R2   What is an object identifier?

R3   What is the distinction between a transient object and a persistent object?

R4   What are a transient link and a persistent link? How are they used during the program execution?

R5   What does it mean that an attribute type designates a class? Give an example.

R6   Why are most attributes private and most operations public in a good object model?

R7   What is the difference between the operation visibility and scope?

R8   In what modeling situations must an association class be used? Give an example.

R9   What is the difference between the composition and aggregation?

R10   Explain the observation that in a typical object programming environment the inheritance applies to classes, not to objects.

R11   What is the connection between overriding and polymorphism?

R12   What is the signature?

R13   How is the multiple classification different from multiple inheritance?

R14   What are the modeling benefits of an abstract class?

R15   Explain the main characteristics and principal differences between a state model, behavior model, and state change model.

R16   Can an actor have attributes and operations? Explain.

R17   Explain the role and place of activity diagrams in system modeling.

R18   What is the difference between a branch and a fork in activity diagrams? Give an example.

R19   What are entity classes?

R20   What is an actual argument and what is a formal argument?

R21   What is the difference between an action and an activity in statechart diagrams? Exemplify.

Exercise questions

E1   Refer to Figure 2.13 (Section 2.1.3.2). Suppose that a course offering includes lectures and tutorials and that it is possible that one teacher is in charge of the lecturing portion of the course offering and another teacher is in charge of the tutorials.

Modify the diagram in Figure 2.13 to capture the above fact.

E2   Refer to Figure 2.15 (Section 2.1.3.4).

Provide an alternative model that does not use an association class and that does not use a ternary association (as we have not recommended the use of ternary associations). Describe semantic differences, if any, between the model in Figure 2.15 and your new model.

E3   Refer to Figure 2.19 (Section 2.1.5.2.1).

Extend the example by adding attributes to the classes `Teacher`, `Student`, `PostgraduateStudent`, and `Tutor`.

E4   *OnLine Shopping* – refer to Step 2 (Section 2.2.2.2).

Point 6 in Table 2.1 says that the customer is to be e-mailed so that s/he can check the order status online. There is no use case that shows this happening. Should there be? Explain.

E5   *OnLine Shopping* – refer (for a pattern) to Step 2 (Section 2.2.2.2) and Step 3 (Section 2.2.2.4).

Write a use case document for the use case `Update Order Status`. The use case is to allow a customer to check the status of the computer order.

Is the name of the use case reflecting its functionality? Should it be changed to a different name?

E6   *OnLine Shopping* – refer to Step 9 (Section 2.2.4.3).

In Figure 2.29 the class `Customer` is not associated directly with the classes `Payment`, `Invoice`, and `ConfiguredComputer`. Should it be associated? If so, modify the diagram. Explain.

E7   *OnLine Shopping* – refer to Step 11 (Section 2.2.4.5).

Figure 2.31 is a relatively simple example illustrating generalization. What complications might arise if there are differences required between the information on invoices for `StandardComputer` sales and `ConfiguredComputer` sales? For example, there might be additional charges depending on the modifications required for `ConfiguredComputer` systems and a discount for bulk purchases of `StandardComputer` systems.

Modify the diagram to reflect such complications. Explain briefly.

E8   *OnLine Shopping* – refer (for a pattern) to Step 13 (Section 2.2.5.1) and to Step 6 (Section 2.2.3.2).

Draw a sequence diagram for the activity `Display Purchase Form` (Figure 2.26).

E9   *OnLine Shopping* – refer to a solution to Exercise E8 above.

Add operations to the classes denoted by the objects in the Sequence Diagram.

E10   *OnLine Shopping* – refer to Step 16 (Section 2.2.6.1).

The statechart diagram in Figure 2.37 conforms to the restriction that only one partial payment is allowed. Suppose that this is not the case and more partial payments are allowed. Modify the diagram accordingly.

Provide two solutions. One for the situation in which partial payments are a priori designated as partial. The second for the situation in which the system has to calculate if a payment is partial or in full.

Chapter

3

Requirements Determination

Requirements determination is about social, communication and managerial skills. This is the least technical phase of system development but, if not done thoroughly, the consequences are more serious than in other phases. The downstream costs of not capturing, omitting or misinterpreting customer requirements may prove unsustainable later in the process.

This chapter introduces a broad spectrum of issues in requirements determination. The first half of the chapter is concerned with the methods of requirements elicitation, negotiation and validation as well as with the principles of requirements management. The latter includes the issues of traceability and change management – the topic that we will discuss in more depth in Chapter 10.

The second half of the chapter introduces basic graphical modeling techniques for describing a business model relevant to an organization and to a targeted application domain. The structure of a requirements document is also discussed.

3.1 Principles of requirements determination

Requirements determination is the first phase in the system development lifecycle. The system to be developed is determined by the *system planning* activities (Section 1.2). The purpose of requirements determination is to provide a narrative definition of functional and other requirements that the stakeholders expect to hold in the implemented and deployed system.

Requirements define expected services of the system (*service statements*) and constraints that the system must obey (*constraint statements*). The service statements can be grouped into those that describe the scope of the system, the necessary business functions (*function requirements*) and the required data structures (*data requirements*). The constraint statements can be classified according to different categories of restrictions imposed on the system, such as the required system's 'look and feel,' performance, security, etc.

Requirements need to be obtained from customers (users and system owners). This is a *requirements elicitation* activity conducted by a business (or system) analyst. There are many techniques that can be employed, starting from traditional interviews of customers and culminating (if necessary) in building a software prototype through which to discover more requirements.

The collected requirements must be subjected to careful analysis to eliminate duplications and contradictions. This invariably leads to *requirements reviews and re-negotiations* with the customers.

Once acceptable to customers, the requirements are defined, classified, numbered, and prioritized in the *requirements document*. The document is structured according to a *template* chosen in the organization for documenting requirements.

Although the requirements document is largely a narrative document, a high-level diagrammatic *business model* is likely to be included. The business model will normally consist of a *system scope model*, *business use case model* and a *business class model*.

Customer requirements are a moving target. To handle volatile requirements we need to be able to manage change. *Requirements management* includes activities such as estimating the impact of the change on other requirements and on the rest of the system.

3.2 Requirements elicitation

A *business analyst* through consultation discovers the system requirements. The consultation involves *customers* and *experts* in the problem domain. In some cases, the business analyst has sufficient domain experience and the help of a domain expert may not be required. A `Business Analyst` is then a kind of `Domain Expert`, as modeled with a generalization relationship in Figure 3.1. (Bear in mind, however, that Figure 3.1 is not a use case model – the use case notation has only been used for its convenience.)

FIGURE 3.1
Influences during requirements determination.

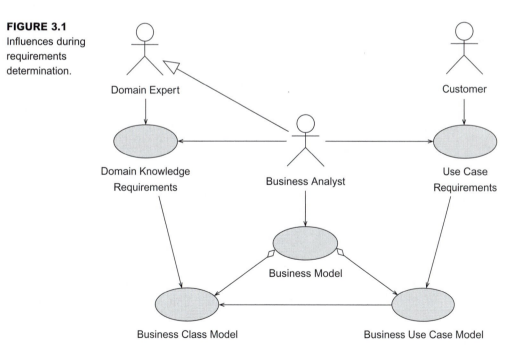

Requirements elicited from domain experts constitute the domain knowledge. They capture widely acknowledged time-independent business rules applicable to most organizations and systems. Requirements elicited from customers are expressed in use case scenarios. They go beyond the basic domain knowledge and capture the unique character of the organization – the way the business is done here and now or how it should be done.

The task of a business analyst is to combine the two sets of requirements into a business model. As shown in Figure 3.1, the Business Model contains a Business Class Model and Business Use Case Model. The Business Class Model is a high-level class diagram that identifies and relates together *business objects*. The Business Use Case Model is a high-level use case diagram that identifies major functional building blocks in the system.

In general, domain classes (business objects) do not have to be driven from use cases (cp. Rumbaugh, 1994). In practice, however, a Business Class Model should be validated against the Business Use Case Model. The validation is likely to lead to some adjustments or extensions in the Business Class Model.

Following Hoffer *et al.* (1996), we distinguish traditional and modern methods of fact finding and information gathering.

3.2.1 Traditional methods of requirements elicitation

Traditional methods of requirements elicitation include interviews, questionnaires, observation, and study of business documents. These are simple and cost-effective methods.

The effectiveness of traditional methods is inversely proportional to the *risk* of the project. The high risk implies that the system is difficult to implement – even the high-level requirements are not quite clear. In such projects the traditional methods are unlikely to suffice.

3.2.1.1 *Interviewing customers and domain experts*

Interviews are a primary technique of fact finding and information gathering. Most interviews are conducted with customers. Interviews with customers elicit mostly 'use case' requirements (Figure 3.1). Domain experts can also be interviewed, if the business analyst does not have sufficient domain knowledge.

Interviews with domain experts are frequently a simple knowledge transfer process – a learning exercise for the business analyst. Interviews with customers are more complex (Kotonya and Sommerville, 1998; Sommerville and Sawyer, 1997).

Customers may have only a vague picture of their requirements. They may be unwilling to cooperate or be unable to express their requirements in understandable terms. They may also demand requirements that exceed the project budget or which are not implementable. Finally, it is likely that requirements of different customers may be in conflict.

There are two basic kinds of interview: structured (formal) and unstructured (informal). A *structured interview* is prepared in advance, has a clear agenda and many questions are pre-determined. Some questions may be *open-ended* (for which possible responses cannot be anticipated), others may be *closed-ended* (with the answer to be picked from a range of provided answers).

Structured interviews need to be supplemented with *unstructured interviews*. Unstructured interviews are more like informal meetings, with no pre-determined questions or anticipated objectives. The purpose of an unstructured interview is to encourage the customer to speak his/her mind and in the process lead to requirements that the business analyst would not have expected and would not, therefore, ask questions about.

Both structured and unstructured interviews must provide some starting point and context for discussion. This may be a short written document or e-mail sent to the interviewee prior to the meeting explaining the interviewer's objective or posing some questions.

Three kinds of question should, in general, be avoided (cp. Whitten and Bentley, 1998):

■ *Opinionated questions*, in which the interviewer expresses (directly or indirectly) his/her opinion on the issue ('do we have to do things the way we do them?').

■ *Biased questions*, similar to opinionated, except that the interviewer's opinion is clearly biased ('you are not going to do this, are you?').

■ *Imposing questions*, which assume the answer in the question ('you do things this way, don't you?').

There are many factors to a successful interview but perhaps the most important are the interviewer's *communication and interpersonal* skills. While the interviewer asks questions and maintains control, it is equally important to listen carefully and be patient so that the interviewee is at ease. To maintain good interpersonal rapport and to obtain good feedback, a memorandum summarizing the interview should be sent to the interviewee within a day or two.

3.2.1.2 *Questionnaires*

Questionnaires are an efficient way of gathering information from many customers. Questionnaires are normally used in addition to interviews, not in lieu of them. An exception may be a low risk project with well-understood objectives. In such a project the passive nature and lesser depth of a questionnaire may suffice.

In general, questionnaires are less productive than interviews because no clarification can be sought to the questions or to possible responses. Questionnaires are passive – this is both an advantage and disadvantage. It is an advantage because the respondent has time to consider the responses and can remain anonymous. It is a disadvantage because the respondent does not have an easy opportunity to clarify the questions.

A questionnaire should be designed for ease of question answering. In particular, open-ended questions should be avoided – most questions should be closed-ended. *Closed-ended questions* can take three forms (Whitten and Bentley, 1998):

■ *Multiple-choice questions*, where the respondent must pick one or more answers from the set of answers provided. An additional commentary from the respondent may also be allowed.

- *Rating questions*, where the respondent has to express his/her opinion about a statement. Possible ratings can be: strongly agree, agree, neutral, disagree, strongly agree, and don't know.

- *Ranking questions*, where the provided answers should be ranked with sequential numbers, percentage values, or similar ordering means.

A well-designed, easy to answer, questionnaire will encourage the respondents to return the completed document promptly. However, when evaluating the questionnaire results, the business analyst should consider possible distortions due to the fact that people who did not respond would have been likely to provide different responses (cp. Hoffer *et al.*, 1996).

3.2.1.3 *Observation*

There are situations when the business analyst finds it difficult to obtain complete information through interviews and questionnaires. The customer may be unable to convey the information effectively or may have only fragmented knowledge of a complete business process. In such cases, *observation* may be an effective fact-finding technique. After all, the best way of learning how to tie a tie is by observing the process.

Observation can take two forms:

- *Passive observation*, where the business analyst observes business activities without interruption or direct involvement. In some cases, video cameras may be used for even less intrusive observation.

- *Active observation*, where the business analyst participates in the activities and becomes effectively part of the team.

To be representative, observations should be carried out for a prolonged period of time, at different time intervals, and at different workloads (pick times). The main difficulty with observation is that people tend to behave differently when they are watched. In particular, they tend to work according to formal rules and procedures. This distorts the reality by hiding any work shortcuts – positive or negative. We ought to remember that 'work to rule' is an effective form of industrial action.

3.2.1.4 *Study of documents and software systems*

The *study of documents and software systems* is an invaluable technique for finding both use case requirements and domain knowledge requirements (see Section 3.2). The technique is always used, although it may only target the selective aspects of the system.

Use case requirements are discovered through studies of existing organizational documents and system forms/reports (if a computerized solution for the current system exists, as is typically the case in large organizations). One of the most valuable insights into use case requirements is the record (if one exists) of defects and change requests for an existing system.

Organizational documents to study include: business forms (completed, if possible), work procedures, job descriptions, policy manuals, business plans, organizational charts, inter-office correspondence, minutes of meetings, accounting records, external correspondence, customer complaints, etc.

System forms and reports to study include: computer screens and reports together with the associated documentation – system operational manuals, user documentation, technical documentation, system analysis and design models, etc.

Domain knowledge requirements are discovered through researching business domain journals and reference books. The studies of proprietary software packages, such as Enterprise Resource Planning Systems (ERPS), can also provide a wealth of domain knowledge. Hence, visits to libraries and software vendors are a part of the requirements elicitation process (of course, the Internet allows many such 'visits' to be accomplished without leaving the office).

3.2.2 Modern methods of requirements elicitation

Modern methods of requirements elicitation include the use of software prototypes, Joint Application Development (JAD), and Rapid Application Development (RAD). They offer better insights into the requirements, but at a higher cost and effort. The long-term payoff, however, may be very rewarding.

Modern methods are typically employed when the *risk* of the project is high. The factors for high project risks are many. They include unclear objectives, undocumented procedures, unstable requirements, eroded user expertise, inexperienced developers, insufficient user commitment, etc.

3.2.2.1 *Prototyping*

Prototyping is the most frequently used method of modern requirements elicitation. Software prototypes are constructed to visualize the system, or just part of it, to the customers in order to obtain their feedback.

A *prototype* is a demonstration system – a 'quick and dirty' working model of the solution that presents a graphical user interface (GUI) and simulates the system behavior for various user events. The information content of GUI screens is hard-coded in the prototype program rather than obtained dynamically from the database.

The complexity (and the growing customer expectations) of modern GUIs makes prototyping an indispensable element in software development. The feasibility and usefulness of the system can be estimated through prototypes well before real implementation is undertaken.

In general, a system prototype is a very effective way of eliciting requirements difficult to obtain from customers through other means. This is frequently the case with systems that are to deliver new business functionality. This is also the case with conflicting requirements or when communication problems exist between customers and developers.

There are two kinds of prototype (cp. Kotonya and Sommerville, 1998):

■ The *'throw-away' prototype*, which is to be discarded when the requirements elicitation is completed. The 'throw-away' prototype targets the requirements determination phase of the lifecycle. It typically concentrates on the least-understood requirements.

■ The *evolutionary prototype*, which is retained after requirements elicitation and used to produce the final product. The evolutionary prototype targets the speed of product delivery. It typically concentrates on well-understood requirements so that the first version of the product can be delivered quickly (though with incomplete functionality).

An additional argument in favor of the 'throw-away' prototype is that it avoids the risk of retaining 'quick and dirty' or otherwise inefficient solutions in the final product. However, the power and flexibility of contemporary software production tools have weakened that argument. There is no reason why in a well-managed project inefficient prototype solutions cannot be eradicated.

3.2.2.2 *Joint Application Development (JAD)*

Joint Application Development (JAD) is what the name implies – a joint application development in one or more workshops that bring together all stakeholders (customers and developers) (Wood and Silver, 1995). Although we include JAD within modern methods of requirements elicitation, the technique was introduced (by IBM) in the late 1970s.

There are many JAD brands and there are many consulting firms that offer the service of organizing and running a JAD session. A JAD meeting can take a few hours, a few days or even a couple of weeks. The number of participants should not exceed 25 to 30. The meeting's participants are (cp. Hoffer *et al.*, 1996; Whitten and Bentley, 1998):

■ *Leader* – the person who conducts and moderates the meeting. This person has excellent communication skills, is not a stakeholder in the project (apart from being a JAD Leader), has a good knowledge of the business domain (but not necessarily good software development knowledge).

■ *Scribe* – the person who records the JAD session on computer. This person should have touch-typing skills and should possess strong knowledge of software development. The scribe can use CASE tools to document the session and to develop initial solution models.

■ *Customers* (*users and managers*) – these are the main participants who communicate and discuss requirements, take decisions, approve project objectives, etc.

■ *Developers* – business analysts and other members of the development team. They listen rather than speak – they are at the meeting to find facts and gather information, not to dominate the process.

JAD capitalizes on group dynamics. The 'group synergy' is likely to produce better solutions to problems. Groups increase productivity, learn faster, make more educated judgments, eliminate more errors, take riskier decisions (this may be a negative though!), focus participants' attention to most important issues, integrate people, etc. When conducted according to the rules, JAD sessions tend to deliver surprisingly good outcomes. But be warned, '. . . Ford Motor Co. in the 1950s experienced a marketing disaster with the Edsel – a car designed by a committee.' (Wood and Silver, 1995, p. 176.)

3.2.2.3 *Rapid Application Development (RAD)*

A *Rapid Application Development* (RAD) is more than a requirements elicitation method, it is an approach to software development as a whole (Hoffer *et al.*, 1996). As the name suggests, the RAD aims at delivering system solutions fast. Technical excellence is secondary to the speed of delivery.

According to Wood and Silver (1995), the RAD combines five techniques:

- *Evolutionary prototyping* (Section 3.2.2.1).
- *CASE tools* with code generation and round-trip engineering between the design models and the code.
- *Specialists with Advanced Tools* (SWAT) – the RAD development team. The best analysts, designers, and programmers that the organization can get. The team works under a strict time regime and is co-located with the users.
- *Interactive JAD* – a JAD session (Section 3.2.2.2) during which the scribe is replaced by the SWAT team with CASE tools.
- *Timeboxing* – a project management method that imposes a fixed time period (timebox) on the SWAT team to complete the project. The method forbids 'scope creep'; if the project is running late, the scope of the solution is trimmed down to allow the project to complete in time.

The RAD approach may be an attractive proposition for many projects, in particular smaller projects which are not in the organization's core business area and which do not, therefore, set the agenda for other development projects. Fast solutions are unlikely to be optimal or sustainable for core business areas. Problems associated with RAD include:

1. inconsistent GUI designs;
2. specialized rather than generic solutions to facilitate software reuse;
3. deficient documentation;
4. software that is difficult to maintain and scale up, etc.

3.3 Requirements negotiation and validation

Requirements elicited from customers may overlap or conflict. Some requirements may be ambiguous or unrealistic. Other requirements may remain undiscovered. For these reasons, requirements need to be negotiated and validated before they find their way into the requirements document.

In reality, *requirements negotiation and validation* is done in parallel with *requirements elicitation*. As requirements are elicited, they are subjected to a certain degree of scrutiny. This is naturally so with all modern techniques of requirements elicitation that involve so-called *group dynamics*. Nevertheless, once the elicited requirements are put together, they still need to undergo careful negotiation and validation.

Requirements negotiation and validation cannot be disassociated from the process of writing up a requirements document. *Requirements negotiation* is typically based on a draft of the document. The requirements listed in the document draft are negotiated and modified, if necessary. Spurious requirements are removed. Newly discovered requirements are added.

Requirements validation requires a more complete version of the requirements document, with all requirements clearly identified and classified. Stakeholders read the document and conduct formal review meetings. *Reviews* are frequently structured into so-called *walkthroughs* or *inspections*. Reviews are a form of *testing* (Section 10.1.1).

3.3.1 Out of scope requirements

The choice of IT projects and, therefore, the systems to be implemented (and the broad scope of them) are determined during the *system planning* activities (Section 1.2). However, the detailed interdependencies between the systems can only be uncovered during the *requirements analysis* phase. It is the task of requirements analysis to determine the *system boundary* (*system scope*) so that 'scope creep' can be addressed early in the process.

To be able to decide if any particular requirement is within or outside the system scope, a reference model, against which to take such a decision, is needed. Historically, such a reference model has been provided by a *context diagram* – the top-level diagram of the popular structured modeling technique called Data Flow Diagrams (DFD). Although DFDs have been superseded in UML by the use case diagrams, the context diagram is still a superior method of establishing the system boundary (Section 3.5.1).

However, there may be other reasons why a requirement can be classified as being outside the scope (cp. Sommerville and Sawyer, 1997). For example, a requirement may be too difficult to implement in the computerized system and it is left to a human process. Or the requirement may have a low priority and be excluded from the first version of the system. A requirement may also be implemented in the hardware or other external device, and be beyond the control of the software system.

3.3.2 Requirements dependency matrix

Assuming that all requirements are clearly identified and numbered (Section 3.4.1), a *requirements dependency matrix* (or *interaction matrix*) can be constructed (cp. Sommerville and Sawyer, 1997; Kotonya and Sommerville, 1997). The matrix lists requirement identifiers in sorted order in the row and column headings, as shown in Figure 3.2.

FIGURE 3.2
Requirements
dependency
matrix.

Requirement	R1	R2	R3	R4
R1	X	X	X	X
R2	Conflict	X	X	X
R3			X	X
R4		Overlap	Overlap	X

The right upper part of the matrix (above and including the diagonal) is not used. The remaining cells indicate whether or not any two requirements overlap, are in conflict, or are independent (empty cells). *Conflicting requirements* should be discussed with customers and reformulated where possible to alleviate conflicts (and the record of the conflict, visible to subsequent development, should be kept). *Overlapping requirements* should also be restated to eliminate overlaps.

The requirements dependency matrix is a simple but effective technique for finding conflicts and overlaps when the number of requirements is relatively small. When this is not the case then the technique may still be used if requirements are grouped into categories (Section 3.4.1) and then compared separately in each category.

3.3.3 Requirements risks and priorities

Once conflicts and overlaps in requirements have been resolved and a revised set of requirements is produced, they need to undergo a risk analysis and prioritization. A *risk analysis* identifies requirements that are likely to cause development difficulties. A *prioritization* is needed to allow for easy re-scoping of the project when faced with delays.

Requirements may be 'risky' due to a variety of factors. Typical kinds of *risk* are (cp. Sommerville and Sawyer, 1997):

■ *Technical risk*, when a requirement is technically difficult to implement.

■ *Performance risk*, when a requirement – when implemented – can adversely affect the response time of the system.

■ *Security risk*, when a requirement – when implemented – can expose the system to security breaches.

■ *Database integrity risk*, when a requirement cannot be easily validated and can cause data inconsistency.

■ *Development process risk*, when a requirement requires the use of unconventional development methods unfamiliar to developers (e.g. formal specification methods).

■ *Political risk*, when a requirement may prove difficult to fulfill for internal political reasons.

■ *Legal risk*, when a requirement may fall foul of current laws or anticipated changes to the law.

■ *Volatility risk*, when a requirement is likely to keep changing or evolving during the development process.

Ideally, requirements *priorities* are first obtained from individual customers in a requirements elicitation process. They are then negotiated in meetings and modified again when the risk factors are attached to them.

To eliminate ambiguity and facilitate priority assignment, the number of priority classifications should be small. Three to five different priorities are usual. They can be named: 'high', 'medium', 'low', 'not sure'. An alternative list might be: 'essential', 'useful', 'hardly matters', 'to be decided'.

3.4 Requirements management

Requirements have to be managed. *Requirements management* is really a part of an overall project management. It is concerned with three main issues:

1. Identifying, classifying, organizing and documenting the requirements.
2. Requirements changes (i.e. with processes that set out how inevitable changes to requirements are proposed, negotiated, validated and documented).
3. Requirements traceability (i.e. with processes that maintain dependency relationships between requirements and other system artifacts as well as between the requirements themselves) (ref. Chapter 10).

3.4.1 Requirements identification and classification

Requirements are described in *natural language statements*, such as:

■ 'The system shall schedule the next phone call to a customer upon telemarketer's request.'
■ 'The system shall automatically dial the scheduled phone number and simultaneously display on the telemarketer's screen customer information including: phone number, customer number, customer name.'
■ 'Upon successful connection, the system shall display an introductory text that the telemarketer would communicate to the customer to establish conversation.'

A typical system would consist of hundreds or thousands of requirements statements like those above. To properly manage such large numbers of requirements, they have to be numbered with some *identification scheme*. The scheme may include a *classification* of requirements into more manageable groups.

There are several techniques of identifying and classifying requirements (Kotonya and Sommerville, 1998):

■ *Unique identifier* – usually a sequential number assigned manually or generated by a CASE tool's database (i.e. the database (or *repository*) where the CASE tool stores the analysis and design artifacts).

■ *Sequential number within document hierarchy* – assigned with consideration to the requirement's position within the requirements document (e.g. the seventh requirement in the third section of the second chapter would be numbered 2.3.7).

■ *Sequential number within requirement's category* – assigned in addition to a mnemonic name that identifies the category of the requirement (where the categories of requirements can be: function requirement, data requirement, performance requirement, security requirement, etc.).

Each identification method has its pros and cons. The most flexible and least error-prone is the *database generated unique identifier*. Databases have built-in capability of generating unique identifiers for every new record of data under a concurrent multi-user access to data.

Some databases can additionally support the maintenance of multiple versions of the same record (by extending the unique identifier value with the version number). Finally, databases can maintain *referential integrity* links between the modeling artifacts, including requirements, and can therefore provide necessary support for requirements change management and traceability.

3.4.2 Requirements hierarchies

Requirements can be hierarchically structured in *parent–child relationships*. Parent–child relationships are similar to *composition relationships* (Section 2.1.4). A parent requirement is composed of child requirements. A child requirement is effectively a sub-requirement of the parent requirement.

Hierarchical relationships introduce an additional level of requirements classification. This may or may not be directly reflected in identification numbers (by using the dot notation). Hence, the requirement numbered 4.9 would be the ninth child of the parent identified by number four.

The following is a set of hierarchical requirements:

1. 'The system shall schedule the next phone call to a customer upon telemarketer's request.'
   1.1 'The system shall activate `Next Call` push button upon entry to `Telemarketing Control` form or when the previous call has terminated.'
   1.2 'The system shall remove the call from the top of the queue of scheduled calls and make it the current call.'
   1.3 etc.

Hierarchies of requirements allow defining requirements that are at different *levels of abstraction*. This is consistent with the overall modeling principle of systematically adding details to models when moving to the lower level of abstraction. As a result, high-level models can be constructed for parent requirements and lower-level models can be linked to child requirements.

3.4.3 Change management

Requirements change. A requirement may change, be removed, or a new requirement may be added, at any phase of the development lifecycle. Change is not a kick in the teeth, unmanaged change is.

The more advanced the development, the more costly the change is. In fact, the *downstream cost* of putting the project back on track after change will always grow and will frequently grow exponentially. Changing a requirement just created and not linked to other requirements is a straightforward editing exercise. Changing the same requirement after it has been implemented in software may be prohibitively costly.

A change may be linked to a human error, but is frequently caused by internal policy changes or external factors, such as competitive forces, global markets, or technology advances. Whatever the reason, strong management policies are needed to document *change requests*, to assess a *change impact*, and to effect the changes.

Because changes to requirements are costly, a formal *business case* must be made for each change request. A valid change, not dealt with previously, is assessed for technical feasibility, the impact on the rest of the project, and the cost. Once approved, the change is incorporated into relevant models and implemented in software.

Change management involves tracking of large amounts of interlinked information over long periods of time. Without tool support, change management is doomed. Ideally, the requirements changes should be stored and tracked by a *software configuration management tool* used by developers to handle versions of models and programs across the development lifecycle. A good CASE tool should either have its own configuration management capability or be linked to a stand-alone configuration management tool.

3.4.4 Requirements traceability

Requirements traceability is just a part, albeit a critically important part, of the *change management*. A requirements traceability module of change management maintains traceability relationships to track changes from/to a requirement throughout the development lifecycle.

Consider the requirement: 'The system shall schedule the next phone call to a customer upon the telemarketer's request.' This requirement could then be modeled in a sequence diagram, activated from the GUI by an action button labeled 'Next Call', and programmed in a database trigger. If a traceability relationship exists between all these elements, a change to any element will make the relationship open again to discussion – the trace becomes *suspect* (to use one tool's parlance).

A traceability relationship can cut across many models in successive lifecycle phases. Only adjacent traceability links can be directly modified. For example, if an element A is traced to an element B, and B traced to C, then change at either endpoint of the relationship will need to be done in two steps: by modifying link A–B, and B–C. (Chapter 10 explains traceability and change management in detail.)

3.5 Requirements business model

The *requirements determination* phase captures requirements and defines them (predominantly) as natural language statements. A formal modeling of requirements using UML is conducted afterwards in the *requirements specification* phase. Nevertheless, a high-level visual representation of gathered requirements – called *requirements business modeling* – is routinely undertaken during requirements determination.

As a minimum, high-level visual models are needed to determine the system scope, to identify principal use cases, and to establish the most essential business classes. Figure 3.3 shows the dependencies between these three models of the requirements determination phase and the models of the remaining lifecycle phases.

The leading role of use case diagrams in the lifecycle is indicated in Figure 3.3 by recognizing that the test cases, user documentation, and project plans are all derived from the use case models. Apart from that, use case diagrams and class models are used concurrently and drive each other in successive development iterations. The design and implementation are also intertwined and can feed back to the requirements specification models.

3.5.1 System scope model

Perhaps the main concern in system development is the *scope creep* due to ever changing requirements. While some changes to requirements are unavoidable, we have to ensure that the requested changes do not go beyond the accepted scope of the project.

FIGURE 3.3
Business models
in the lifecycle.

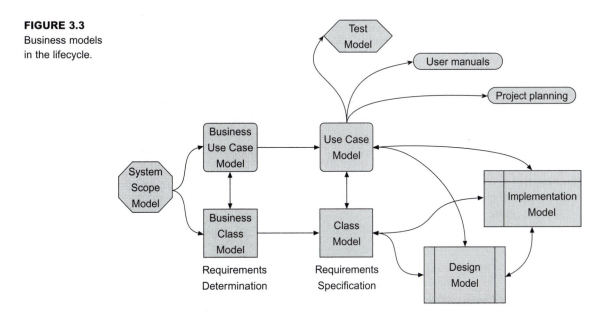

The question is: 'How do we define the scope of the system?' Answering this question is not straightforward because any system is only a part of a larger environment – a part of a set of systems that together constitute that environment. The systems collaborate by exchanging information and by invoking services of each other. Hence, the above question could be interpreted as: 'Should we implement the requirements or is the requested functionality a responsibility of another system?'

To be able to answer the scope questions, we need to know the *context* in which our system operates. We need to know the *external entities* – other systems, organizations, people, machines, etc. that expect some services from us or provide services to us. In business systems, those services translate to information – to *data flows*.

The system scope, therefore, can be determined through identification of external entities and input/output data flows between the external entities and our system. Our system obtains the input information and does necessary *processing* to produce the output information. Any requirement that cannot be supported by the system's internal processing is outside the scope.

UML does not provide a good visual model to define the scope of the system. Therefore, the old-fashioned *context diagram* of DFDs (Section 3.3.1) is frequently used for the task. Figure 3.4 shows the context diagram for the telemarketing application.

3.5.1.1 *Example for system scope modeling*

Example 3.1 (Telemarketing)

Consider the problem statement for Telemarketing (Section 2.3.4) and construct a context diagram for it. Additionally, reflect on the following observations:

1. The campaigns are planned on recommendations from the society trustees who decide on worthy and timely charitable causes. The campaigns have to be approved by the local government. The design and planning of campaigns is supported by a separate `Campaign Database` application system.

2. There is also a separate `Supporter Database` that stores and maintains information about all supporters – past and present. This database is used to select supporters to be contacted in a particular campaign. The selected *segment* of supporters is made available to telemarketing activities for the campaign.

3. Orders from supporters for lottery tickets are recorded during telemarketing for perusal by the `Order Processing` system. An order processing system maintains the status of orders in the supporter database.

A context diagram that you may be coming up with as a solution to this example is shown in Figure 3.4. The 'bubble' in the center of the diagram represents our system. The rectangles

FIGURE 3.4
System scope
model – context
diagram
(Telemarketing).

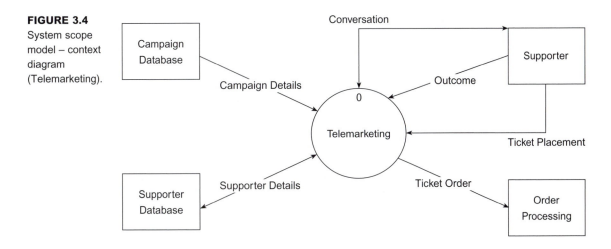

around it designate external entities. The arrows depict data flows. The detailed information content of data flows is not visible on the diagram – the content of data flows is defined separately and stored in the CASE tool's repository.

The `Telemarketing` system obtains information about the current campaign from the external entity `Campaign Database`. This information includes the number and prices of tickets, lottery winning prizes, the campaign duration, etc.

Similarly, `Telemarketing` obtains supporter details from `Supporter Database`. During a telemarketing call, new information about a supporter may emerge (for instance, that the supporter intends to change their phone number). `Supporter Database` needs to be updated accordingly – hence, the data flow `Supporter Details` is bi-directional.

The main activity is between `Telemarketing` and `Supporter`. The data flow `Conversation` contains information that is exchanged during the telephone conversation. A supporter's reply to the telemarketer's offer to buy lottery tickets is transferred along the data flow `Outcome`. A separate data flow called `Ticket Placement` is used to record details about tickets ordered by a supporter.

Further processing of ticket orders is outside the scope of our system. The data flow `Ticket Order` is forwarded to the external entity `Order Processing`. We can assume that after orders are entered, other external entities can handle payments from supporters, ticket mail-outs, prize draws, etc. These are not our concern as long as the current status of orders, payments, etc. are available to us from the external entities `Campaign Database` and `Supporter Database`.

3.5.2 Business use case model

A *business use case model* (Kruchten, 1999) is a use case model at a high level of abstraction (Section 2.2.2). A business use case model identifies high-level business processes – *business use cases.* A business use case corresponds to what is sometimes called a *system feature.* (System features are identified in a *vision document.* If a vision document is present then it may be used as a replacement for the business use case model.)

The focus of a business use case diagram is the *architecture* of business processes. The diagram provides a bird's eye view of desired system behavior. The narrative description for each *business use case* is brief, business-oriented, and focusing on the main flow of activities. A business use case model is not adequate for communicating to *developers* exactly what the system should do.

Business use cases are turned into *use cases* in the requirements specification phase. It is in that phase that the detailed use cases are identified, the narrative descriptions are extended to include sub-processes and alternative processes, some GUI screens are mocked up, and the relationships between use cases are established.

Actors in a business use case diagram are different from *external entities* in the context diagram. The difference is in the way the actors interact with the system. Actors are active. They are in control. They instigate use cases by sending *events* to them. Use cases are event-driven. The communication lines between actors and use cases are not data flows. The communication lines represent the flow of events from actors and the flow of responses from use cases.

There is an interesting dichotomy with regard to actors. *Actors can be both external and internal to a system.* They are *external* because they interact with the system from the outside. They are *internal* because the system may maintain information about the actors so that it can knowingly interact with the 'external' actors. The system specification must describe, as a model, the system and its environment. The environment contains actors. The system may itself keep information about the actors. Hence, the specification holds two models related to actors – a model of the actor and a model of what the system records about the actor.

3.5.2.1 Example for business use case modeling

Example 3.2 (Telemarketing)

Consider the problem statement and the context diagram for Telemarketing (Sections 2.3.4 and 3.5.1.1) and construct a business use case diagram.

A possible business use case diagram is presented in Figure 3.5. There are two actors: Telemarketer and Supporter. Telemarketer requests the system that the phone call to a supporter be scheduled and dialed up. Upon successful connection, Supporter is involved as an actor. The business use case Schedule Phone Conversation (which includes here the establishment of the connection) becomes a piece of externally visible functionality of value to both actors.

FIGURE 3.5
Business use
case model
(Telemarketing).

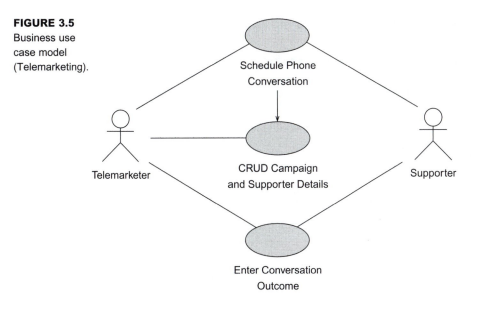

During a conversation, `Telemarketer` may need to access and modify campaign and supporter details. This functionality is captured in the business use case `CRUD Campaign and Supporter Details`. (CRUD is a popular acronym that stands for the four main operations on data: Create, Read, Update, Delete.)

Finally, the business use case `Enter Conversation Outcome` serves the purpose of entering the successful or unsuccessful results of the telemarketing action. This use case delivers an identifiable value to both actors.

The omission of a relationship between the use cases `CRUD Campaign and Supporter Details` and `Enter Conversation Outcome` is arbitrary. In general, all relationships between use cases can be suppressed to avoid cluttering and overcrowding of the diagram. Use cases tend to have some sort of communication with most other use cases and the inclusion of all relationships defeats the purpose.

3.5.3 Business class model

A *business class model* is a *class model*. Just as with the business use case model, the difference lies in the level of abstraction. A business class model identifies main 'business objects' in the system – the business data structures that underpin and drive the system.

A business class model is presented at a high level of abstraction. At that level, we are less interested in the attribute content of classes – class names and a brief description may suffice.

Interestingly enough, it is frequently the case that *actors* of a business use case model are represented *as classes* in the business class model. This is consistent with our observation that actors are frequently both external and internal to the system (Section 3.5.2).

3.5.3.1 Example for business class modeling

Example 3.3 (Telemarketing)

Consider the problem statement, the context diagram and the business use case diagram for Telemarketing (Sections 2.3.4, 3.5.1.1 and 3.5.2.1) and construct a business class diagram. The following hints may be of assistance:

1. The emphasis in the system is on call scheduling. The call scheduling itself is a procedural computation, i.e. the solution to it is strongly algorithmic in nature. Nevertheless, the scheduled call queues and the outcomes of calls must be stored in some data structure.

2. As discussed above, information about actors may need to be stored in classes.

A first-cut business class model is shown in Figure 3.6. The diagram contains six classes; two of them (`Supporter` and `Telemarketer`) are derived from the actors of the business use case model. The call scheduling algorithm obtains a phone number and other information from the class `Supporter` and schedules the call to one of the currently available `Telemarketers`. The algorithm will ultimately be implemented in the system's database in the form of a *stored procedure* (Section 9.1.2.1).

FIGURE 3.6
Business
class model
(Telemarketing).

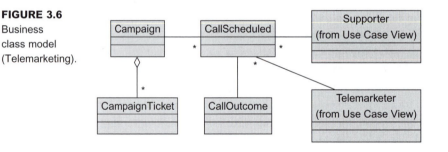

The class `CallScheduled` contains the current queue of calls, including those that are currently active. Call outcomes are recorded in `CallOutcome` as well as propagated to other affected classes, such as `CampaignTicket` or `Supporter`.

The class `Campaign` contains `CampaignTickets` and it can have many `Call-Scheduled`. Similarly, `Supporter` and `Telemarketer` may have many `CallScheduled`. The association between `CallScheduled` and `CallOutcome` is one-to-one.

3.6 Requirements document

The *requirements document* is a tangible outcome of the requirements determination phase. Most organizations produce a requirements document according to a pre-defined template. The *template* defines the structure (table of contents) and the style of the document.

The main body of a requirements document consists of requirements statements. As discussed in Section 3.1, the requirements can be grouped into *service statements* (frequently called *functional requirements*) and *constraint statements*. The service statements can be further classified into *function requirements* and *data requirements*. (In the literature, the term 'functional requirements' is used interchangeably in the broad or narrow sense. When used in the narrow sense, it corresponds to what we call function requirements.)

Apart from the requirements *per se*, the requirements document has to address *project issues*. Normally, the project issues are discussed at the beginning of the document and again at the end of the document. In the introductory part of the document, the project's business context is discussed, including the project's purpose, stakeholders, and main constraints. Towards the end of the document, all other project issues are raised, including schedule, budget, risks, documentation, etc.

3.6.1 Document templates

Templates for requirements documents are widely available from textbooks, standards organizations (IEEE, ANSI, etc.), web pages of consulting firms, vendors of software engineering tools, etc. In due course, each organization should develop its own standard that fits its organizational practices, culture, expected readership, types of systems, etc.

A requirements document template defines the structure of the document and gives detailed guidelines of what to write in each section of the document. The guidelines may include the content matters, motivation, examples, and additional considerations (cp. Robertson and Robertson, 2000).

Figure 3.7 shows a typical table of contents for requirements document. The explanations for the content are discussed in the following sections.

3.6.2 Project preliminaries

The project preliminaries part of the document predominantly targets managers and decision makers who are unlikely to study the whole document in detail. The *purpose and scope* of the project needs to be explained clearly at the beginning of the document, followed by the business context.

The requirements document has to make a *business case* for the system. In particular, any *system planning* efforts (Section 1.2) that established the need for the system have to be referred to. The requirements document should explain how the proposed system would contribute to the organization's business objectives and goals.

Stakeholders (Section 1.1.2) of the system have to be identified. It is important that the *customer* is not just an impersonal department or office – people's names should be listed. At the end of the day, a person will decide whether the delivered software product is acceptable.

FIGURE 3.7
Requirements
document – table
of contents.

Requirements Document
Table of Contents

1. **Project Preliminaries**
   1.1 Purpose and Scope of the Product
   1.2 Business Context
   1.3 Stakeholders
   1.4 Ideas for Solutions
   1.5 Document Overview
2. **System Services**
   2.1 The Scope of the System
   2.2 Function Requirements
   2.3 Data Requirements
3. **System Constraints**
   3.1 Interface Requirements
   3.2 Performance Requirements
   3.3 Security Requirements
   3.4 Operational Requirements
   3.5 Political and Legal Requirements
   3.6 Other Constraints
4. **Project Matters**
   4.1 Open Issues
   4.2 Preliminary Schedule
   4.3 Preliminary Budget

Appendices
   Glossary
   Business Documents and Forms
   References

Although a requirements document should be as far away from the technical solutions as possible, it is still important to brainstorm *ideas for the solution* early in the development lifecycle. Any off-the-shelf solutions are of special interest. It always makes good business sense to buy a product rather than develop it from scratch.

The requirements document should provide a list of existing software packages and components that ought to be further investigated as potential solutions. Note that taking up an off-the-shelf solution varies the development processes but it does not dispense with the requirements analysis and system design!

Finally, it is a good idea to include an *overview* of the rest *of the document* in the project preliminaries section. This may entice a busy reader to study other parts of the document and it will facilitate understanding of the document content. The overview should also explain the analysis and design methodology embraced by the developers.

3.6.3 System services

The main part of the requirements document is dedicated to the definition of *system services* (Sections 1.3.1 and 3.1). This part is likely to account for more than half of the entire document. This is also just about the only part of the document that may contain high-level models for the solution – *requirements business models* (Section 3.5).

The *scope of the system* can be modeled with a *context diagram* (Section 3.5.1). In explaining the context diagram, the boundaries for the proposed project must be clearly defined. Without this definition, the project will not be able to stand up to the demands of scope creep.

Function requirements can be modeled with a *business use case diagram* (Section 3.5.2). However, the diagram will only provide a high-level embracement for the detailed listing of function requirements. As discussed in Section 3.4, each requirement has to be identified, classified and defined.

Data requirements can be modeled with a *business class diagram* (Section 3.5.3). As with function requirements, the business class diagram is not a complete definition of business data structures. Each business class needs to be further explained. The attribute content of classes ought to be described. Identifying attributes of classes must be determined. Otherwise, it is not possible to properly explain associations.

3.6.4 System constraints

System services define *what* the system must accomplish. *System constraints* (Sections 1.3.1 and 3.1) describe *how* the system is constrained when accomplishing its services. System constraints are set with regard to:

■ Interface requirements.
■ Performance requirements.
■ Security requirements.
■ Operational requirements.
■ Political and legal requirements, etc.

Interface requirements define how the product interfaces with the users. In the requirements document we only define the 'look and feel' of the GUI. Initial design (screen painting) of the GUI will be conducted during *requirements specification* and later during *system design*.

Depending on the application domain, *performance requirements* can become quite central to the success of the project. In a narrow sense, they specify the speed (the system's *response times*) at which various tasks have to be accomplished. In a broader sense, performance requirements include other constraints – with regard to the system's reliability, availability, throughput, etc.

Security requirements describe users' access privileges to the information under the system's control. Users can be given restricted access to data and/or restricted rights to execute certain operations on data.

Operational requirements determine the hardware/software environment, if known, in which the system will operate. These requirements may make an impact on other aspects of the project, such as user training and system maintenance.

Political requirements and *legal requirements* are frequently assumed rather than explicitly stated in the requirements document. This can be a very costly mistake. Unless these requirements are brought out in the open, the product may be difficult or impossible to deploy for political or legal reasons.

Other categories of *constraints* are also possible. For example, some systems may place extra demands on the ease of the system's use (*usability requirements*) or on the ease of system maintenance (*maintainability requirements*).

The importance of watertight definitions for system constraints cannot be overstated. There are numerous examples of failed projects due to omitted or misinterpreted system constraints. The issue is as sensitive with regard to the customers as it is with regard to the developers. Unscrupulous or desperate developers can play the system constraints card to their advantage in an effort to evade their responsibilities.

3.6.5 Project matters

The final part of the requirements document addresses other project matters. An important section in this part is called *Open Issues*. In here, we specify any issues that can affect the success of the project, but have not been discussed under other headings in the document. This may include an expected growth in importance of some requirements that are currently out of scope. This may also include any potential problems or malpractices that the deployment of the system can trigger.

A *preliminary schedule* for major tasks on the project needs to be developed (Section 1.3.8). This should include the preliminary allocation of human and other resources. A project management software tool can be used to produce standard planning charts, such as PERT or Gantt charts (Maciaszek, 1990).

As a direct upshot of the schedule, the *preliminary budget* can be provided. The project cost can be expressed as a range, rather than a figure. If the requirements are well documented, one of the estimating methods to assess the cost (e.g. *function point analysis*) can be used.

3.6.6 Appendices

Appendices contain other useful information for requirements understanding. The main inclusion here is a glossary. The *glossary* defines terms, acronyms and abbreviations used in the requirements document. The importance of a good glossary cannot be overestimated. Terminology misinterpretations can be very damaging.

One of the frequently overlooked aspects of the requirements document is that the business domain it defines can be quite well understood through the study of *documents and forms* used in workflow processes. Whenever possible, completed business forms should be included – empty forms do not convey the same level of insight.

References provide citations to documents referenced or used in the preparation of the requirements document. These may include books and other published sources of information, but – even more importantly – minutes of meetings, memoranda and internal documents should also be cited.

Summary

In this chapter we have taken a comprehensive look at requirements determination. The determination of requirements precedes their specification. The determination is about discovering requirements and documenting them in a mostly narrative requirements document. The requirements specification – discussed in the next chapter – provides more formal models of requirements.

Requirements elicitation follows two lines of discovery – from the domain knowledge and from the use cases. These two lines of investigation complement each other and lead to the determination of a business model for the system to be developed.

There are various *methods of requirements elicitation*: interviewing customers and domain experts, questionnaires, observation, study of documents and software systems, prototyping, JAD and RAD.

Requirements elicited from customers may overlap and conflict. It is a business analyst's job to resolve these overlaps and conflicts through *requirements negotiation and validation*. To do this job properly, the business analyst ought to construct a *requirements dependency matrix* and to assign *risks* and *priorities* to the requirements.

Large projects have to *manage* large volumes of requirements. It is essential in such projects that the requirement statements are *identified and classified*. *Requirements hierarchies* can then be defined. Such steps ensure proper *requirements traceability* in the next project stages as well as proper handling of *change requests*.

Even though the requirements determination does not include formal system modeling, a basic *requirements business model* may be constructed. The business model can result in three generic diagrams – the context diagram, the business use case diagram, and the business class diagram.

A document that results from the requirements determination – the *requirements document* – begins with a high-level description of the *project preliminaries* (mostly for the benefit of a managerial readership). The main parts of the document describe *system services* and *system constraints*. The final part handles other project matters, including the *schedule* and the *budget* details.

Review questions

R1   During requirements elicitation we try to reconcile domain knowledge requirements and use case requirements. Explain the difference between these two kinds of requirement. Should one of them take precedence over the other in the requirements determination process? Give reasons.

R2   During interviews it is recommended that questions which are opinionated, biased or imposing are avoided. Can you think about the situations where such questions may be necessary for the benefit of the project?

R3   What is prototyping? How is it useful for requirements determination?

R4   What is JAD? What are the main advantages of JAD in comparison with other requirements determination methods?

R5   What is scope creep? How can it be addressed during requirements determination?

R6   List and define requirements risks.

R7   Why should the requirements be numbered?

R8   What is a suspect trace?

R9   How are actors in a business use case diagram different from external entities in a context diagram?

R10   Describe a typical structure (table of contents) of a requirements document.

Exercise questions

Problem statement (Advertising Expenditure Measurement)

Consider the problem statement for an Advertising Expenditure Measurement (AEM) business:

1. The AEM organization collects data on advertising from various media outlets: television and radio stations, newspapers, magazines, as well as cinema, outdoor and Internet advertisers.

2. This data provides two areas of reporting to the AEM clients. A client may request a report that the advertisements they paid for appeared as they were supposed to (this is called campaign monitoring). A client can also request a report outlining their competitive advertising position in their specific industry (this is called expenditure reporting). The expenditure reports capture the expenditures achieved by an advertiser or an advertised product by various criteria (time, geographical regions, media, etc.).

3. The expenditure reporting is the core business of AEM. In fact, any AEM client (not just an advertising client) can purchase expenditure reports – in the form of custom-designed reporting software or as hard copies. The AEM's customer base comprises individual advertisers, advertising agencies, media companies, media buying consultancies, as well as sales and marketing executives, media planners, buyers, etc.

4. The AEM has contractual arrangements with many media outlets to regularly receive from them electronic log files with information pertaining to the advertising content of these outlets. The log information is transferred to the AEM database and it is then subjected to a careful verification – partly automatic and partly manual. The task of verification is to

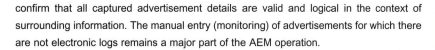

confirm that all captured advertisement details are valid and logical in the context of surrounding information. The manual entry (monitoring) of advertisements for which there are not electronic logs remains a major part of the AEM operation.

5. Once entered and verified, the advertisements undergo valorization – the process of assigning an expenditure estimate to an advertisement.

E1   *Advertising Expenditure Measurement* – refer to the problem statement above.

Draw a context diagram for the AEM system. Explain the model.

E2   *Advertising Expenditure Measurement* – refer to the problem statement above.

Draw a business use case diagram for the AEM system. Explain the model.

E3   *Advertising Expenditure Measurement* – refer to the problem statement above.

Draw a business class diagram for the AEM system. Explain the model.

Chapter

4

Requirements Specification

The requirements need to be specified in graphical and other formal models. Many models are necessary to specify the system completely. The UML offers a plethora of integrated modeling techniques to assist a system analyst in this job. The process is iterative and incremental. The use of CASE tools is essential for successful modeling.

The requirements specification produces three categories of models: state models, behavior models, and state change models. Each category offers a few modeling techniques to work with. This chapter explains and exemplifies all major UML modeling techniques.

Even though we start with the state models followed by the behavior models and the state change models, this is not a reflection on the sequence in which the modeling is conducted. Many models are developed in parallel and feed from each other. This is particularly true for the two principal models – the class model and the use case model.

4.1 Principles of requirements specification

Requirements specification is concerned with rigorous *modeling* of customer requirements defined during *requirements determination*. Only the desired services of the system (*service statements*) are considered (Section 3.1). The *constraint statements* are not developed further in the specification phase, although they can be modified as a result of a normal *iteration* cycle.

The requirements specification takes the narrative customer requirements as input and constructs specification models as output. The models (Section 2.2) provide a more formal definition for various aspects (views) of the system. The two main categories of customer requirements are considered: *function requirements* and *data requirements*.

An outcome of the specification phase is an extended ('elaborated') *requirements document* (Section 3.6). The new document is frequently called a *specifications document* (or specs in the jargon). The structure of the original document is not changed, but the content is significantly extended in the chapters that define customer requirements. Eventually, the specifications document replaces the requirements document for the purposes of the design and implementation (in practice, the extended document is likely to be still called a requirements document).

Specification models can be classified into three groups:

1. State models.

2. Behavior models.

3. State change models.

State models 'elaborate' data requirements. *Behavior* models provide detailed specifications for function requirements. *State change* models span the two kinds of requirement. They explain how functions cause data changes.

The models are presented in diagrams of a *Visual Modeling Language* – UML in our case. Normally, a diagram serves one of the three modeling purposes – the state, the behavior, or the state change. A notable exception is a class diagram that specifies all three aspects – the state and the behavior of objects, and indirectly the changes of object states.

Each diagram emphasizes a particular aspect (*view*) of the system. Together, the diagrams allow the developers and users to look at the proposed solution from a variety of perspectives, highlighting some aspects and suppressing others. No one diagram gives a complete definition of the system. The system can only be understood from the intertwined set of diagrams.

As with the interpretation of completed models, the construction of the diagrams is not a sequential process of building one diagram after the other. The diagrams are developed in parallel and the details are added in successive iterations. Unless a strict development process is imposed on the developers, the decision as to which models constitute the driving force is very much up to the personal preferences of analysts. Two most important models, use case diagrams and class diagrams, should normally be constructed in parallel – feeding ideas to each other.

The depth and the detail of specifications increase with each development iteration. Many advanced properties of model objects are expressed textually, rather than graphically. Some properties define the *design* of a model object, not the *analysis*. Some other properties may be specific to a CASE tool.

4.2 State specifications

The *state* of an object is determined by the values of its attributes and associations. For example, a state of a `BankAccount` object may be 'overdrawn' when the value of the attribute `balance` is negative. Since object states are determined from the data structures, the models of data structures are called *state specifications*.

State specifications provide a *static view* on the system (hence, state modeling is sometimes called static modeling). The main task here is to define *classes* in an application domain, their *attributes* and *relationships* with other classes. *Operations* of classes are normally left out at first. They will be derived from the models of *behavior specifications*.

In a typical situation, we first identify *entity classes*, i.e. classes that define the application domain and will have *persistent* presence in the database for the system. Such classes are sometimes called '*business objects*.' Classes that service system events (*control classes*) and classes that represent the GUI (*view* or *boundary classes*) are not established until the behavioral characteristics of the system are known.

4.2.1 Modeling classes

The class model is the cornerstone of object-oriented system development. Classes set the foundation upon which the state and the behavior of the system are observable. Unfortunately, classes are chronically difficult to find and the properties of classes are not always obvious. No two analysts will come up with the identical set of classes and their properties, for the same nontrivial application domain. Although the class models may be different, the eventual outcome and user satisfaction may be equally good (or equally bad).

Class modeling is not a deterministic process. There is no recipe for how to find and define good classes. The process is highly *iterative* and *incremental*. Paramount to successful class design is the analyst's:

1. knowledge of class modeling;

2. understanding of the application domain;

3. experience with similar and successful designs;

4. ability to think forward and predict the consequences;

5. willingness to revise the model to eliminate imperfections, etc.

The last point is related to the use of CASE tools. Large-scale application of CASE technology may hinder the system development in immature organizations (Section 1.1.4.2). However, the use of CASE tools for *personal productivity* is always warranted.

4.2.1.1 Discovering classes

No two analysts will come up with the identical class models for the same application domain, and no two analysts will use the same thinking processes when discovering the classes. The literature is full of suggested approaches to *class discovery*. Analysts may even initially follow one of these approaches but the successive iterations will almost certainly involve unconventional and rather arbitrary mechanisms.

Bahrami (1999) goes over the main points of the four most popular approaches for identifying classes:

1. Noun phrase approach.

2. Common class patterns approach.

3. Use case driven approach.

4. CRC (class–responsibility–collaborators) approach.

Bahrami (1999) attributes each approach to the published work but – in our opinion – only the last approach has an indisputable origin. Next, we summarize these approaches and then give examples that use a *mixed approach*.

4.2.1.1.1 Noun phrase approach

The *noun phrase* approach advises that an analyst read the statements in the requirements document looking for noun phrases. Every noun is considered a *candidate class*. The list of the candidate classes is then divided into three groups:

1. relevant classes;

2. fuzzy classes;

3. irrelevant classes.

Irrelevant classes are those that are outside of the problem domain. We cannot formulate a statement of purpose for them. Experienced practitioners are likely not to include irrelevant classes in the original list of candidate classes. This way, the formal step of identifying and eliminating irrelevant classes is avoided.

Relevant classes are those that manifestly belong to the problem domain. The nouns representing the names of these classes appear frequently in the requirements document. Additionally, we can confirm the significance and purpose of these classes from our general knowledge of the application domain and from the investigation of similar systems, textbooks, documents, and proprietary software packages.

Fuzzy classes are those that we cannot confidently and unanimously classify as relevant. They provide the greatest challenge. We need to analyze them further and to either include them in the list of relevant classes or to exclude them as irrelevant. The eventual classification of these classes to one or the other group will make a difference between a good class model and a bad one.

The noun phrase approach assumes that the requirements document is complete and correct. In reality, this is rarely true. Even if this were the case, a tedious search through large volumes of text might not necessarily lead to a comprehensive and accurate outcome.

4.2.1.1.2 Common class patterns approach

The *common class patterns* approach derives candidate classes from the generic classification theory of objects. *Classification theory* is a part of science concerned with partitioning the world of objects into useful groups so that we can reason about them better.

Bahrami (1999) lists the following groups (patterns) for finding candidate classes:

- *Concept* class. A concept is a notion that a large community of people share and agree on. Without concepts people are not able to communicate effectively, or even communicate to any satisfactory degree. For example, `Reservation` is a concept class in an airline reservation system.

- *Events* class. An event is something that does not take time relative to our time scale. For example, `Arrival` is an event class in an airline reservation system.

- *Organization* class. Organization is any kind of purposeful grouping or collection of things. For example, `TravelAgency` is a class in an airline reservation system.

- *People* class. 'People' is understood here as a role that a person plays in the system, rather than as a physical person. For example, `Passenger` is a class in an airline reservation system.

- *Places* class. Places are physical locations relevant to the information system. `TravelOffice` is such a class in an airline reservation system.

Rumbaugh *et al.* (1999) propose a different classification scheme:

- *Physical* class (e.g. `Airplane`).

- *Business* class (e.g. `Reservation`).

- *Logical* class (e.g. `FlightTimetable`).

- *Application* class (e.g. `ReservationTransaction`).

- *Computer* class (e.g. `Index`).

- *Behavioral* class (e.g. `ReservationCancellation`).

The common class patterns approach provides useful guidance, but it does not offer a systematic process whereby a reliable and complete set of classes can be discovered. This approach may be successfully used to determine the initial set of classes or to verify if some classes (derived by other means) should be there or perhaps must not be there. However, the common class patterns approach is too loosely bound to specific user requirements to offer a comprehensive solution.

A particular danger associated with the common class patterns approach relates to possibilities for misinterpretation of class names. For example, what does an `Arrival` mean? Does it mean arrival on the runway (landing time), arrival at the terminal (disembarkation time), arrival at baggage reclaim (luggage clearance time), etc.? Similarly, the word `Reservation` in the context of a North American Indian environment has an entirely separate meaning to the one understood here.

4.2.1.1.3 Use case driven approach

The *use case driven* approach is emphasized, if not recommended, by UML (by the Rational Unified Process (RUP), to be precise). The graphical model of use cases is supplemented with narrative descriptions and with sequence or collaboration diagrams for individual use cases (Section 2.2 and later in this chapter). These additional descriptions and diagrams define steps (and objects) needed for each use case to occur. From this information, we can generalize to discover candidate classes.

The use case driven approach has a bottom-up flavor. Once the use cases are known and the *interaction view* of the system is at least partly defined in sequence diagrams, the objects used in these diagrams lead to the discovery of classes.

In reality, the approach bears some similarity with the noun phrase approach. The common ground lies in the fact that the use cases specify the requirements. Both approaches study the statements in the requirements document to discover candidate classes. Whether these statements are narrative or graphical is secondary. In any case, at this stage in the lifecycle, most use cases will only be described in text, with no interaction diagrams.

The use case driven approach suffers from similar deficiencies as the noun phrase approach. Being a bottom-up approach, it relies for its accuracy on the completeness and correctness of the use case models. It can even lead to undesirable imbalance in iterative and incremental software development, in which the use case models have to be completed before the class models can be built. For all means and purposes, this leads to a *function-driven* approach (OO proponents prefer to call it *problem-driven*).

4.2.1.1.4 CRC approach

The *CRC* (class–responsibility–collaborators) approach is more than a technique for class discovery – it is an attractive way of interpreting, understanding and teaching about objects. Rebecca Wirfs-Brock and her colleagues (Wirfs-Brock and Wilkerson, 1989; Wirfs-Brock *et al.*, 1990) have popularized the CRC approach.

The CRC approach involves brainstorming sessions made easy by the use of specially prepared cards. The cards have three compartments: the *class name* is written in the upper compartment, the class *responsibilities* are listed in the left compartment and the *collaborators* are listed in the right compartment. Responsibilities are the services (operations) that the class is prepared to perform on behalf of other classes. Many responsibilities to be fulfilled require collaboration (services) of other classes. Such classes are listed as collaborators.

The CRC approach is an animated process during which the developers 'play cards' – they fill the cards with the class names and assign responsibilities and collaborators while 'executing' a processing scenario (e.g. a use case scenario). Whenever services are needed and the existing classes do not cover them, a new class is created, and it is assigned appropriate responsibilities and collaborators. If a class becomes 'too busy,' it is divided into a number of smaller classes.

Unlike other approaches, the CRC approach identifies classes from the analysis of messages passing between objects to fulfill the processing tasks. The emphasis is placed on the uniform distribution of intelligence in the system and some classes may be derived from such a technical need, rather than discovered as 'business objects' as such. In this sense, CRC may be more suitable for the verification of classes already discovered by other methods. CRC is also useful for the determination of class properties (as implied by the class responsibilities and collaborators).

4.2.1.1.5 Mixed approach

In practice, the process of class discovery is likely to be guided by different approaches at different times. Frequently, the elements of all four approaches explained above are involved. The analysts' overall knowledge, experience and intuition are also contributing factors. The process is neither top-down nor bottom-up; it is middle-out. We call such a process of class discovery the *mixed approach*.

One possible scenario is as follows. The initial set of classes may be discovered from the generic knowledge and experience of analysts. The common class patterns approach can provide additional guidance. Other classes may be added from the analysis of high-level descriptions of the problem domain using the noun phrase approach. If use case diagrams are available, then the use case driven approach can be used to add new and verify existing classes. Finally, the CRC approach will allow brainstorming the list of classes discovered so far.

4.2.1.1.6 Guidelines for discovering classes

The following is an imperfect list of *guidelines* or rules of thumb that the analysts should follow when selecting candidate classes. Recall again that we are concerned here only with the *entity classes*:

1. Each class must have a clear *statement of purpose* in the system.

2. Each class is a template description for a *set of objects*. *Singleton* classes – for which we can only imagine a single object – are very unlikely among 'business objects.' Such classes usually constitute a 'common knowledge' to the application and will be hard-coded in the application programs. As an example, if the system is designed for a single organization, the existence of the Organization class is not warranted.

3. Each class (i.e. entity class) must house a *set of attributes*. It is a good idea to determine identifying attribute(s) (*keys*) to help us reason about the class cardinality (i.e. an expected number of objects of that class in the database). Remember, however, that a class does not need to have a user-defined key. *Object identifiers* (OIDs) identify objects of classes (Section 2.1.1.3).

4. Each class should be distinguished from an *attribute*. Whether a concept is a class or attribute depends on the application domain. Color of a car is normally perceived as an attribute of the class Car. However, in a paint factory Color is definitely a class with its own attributes (brightness, saturation, transparency, etc.).

5. Each class houses a *set of operations*. However, at this stage we are not concerned with the identification of operations. The operations in the *interface* of the class (the services that the class provides in the system) are implied from the statement of purpose (Point 1).

4.2.1.1.7 Examples for class discovery

Example 4.1 (University Enrolment)

Consider the following requirements for the University Enrolment system and identify the candidate classes:

1. Each university degree has a number of compulsory courses and a number of elective courses.

2. Each course is at a given level and has a credit-point value.

3. A course can be a part of any number of degrees.

4. Each degree specifies a minimum total credit points value required for degree completion (e.g. BSc (Computing and Information Systems) requires 68 credit points including compulsory courses).

5. Students may combine course offerings into programs of study suited to their individual needs and leading to the degree in which a student is enrolled.

Let us analyze the requirements in order to discover candidate classes. In the first statement, the relevant classes are `Degree` and `Course`. These two classes conform to the five guidelines listed earlier. We cannot be sure yet if and how the class `Course` can be specialized into classes `CompulsoryCourse` and `ElectiveCourse`. It is clear, for example, that a course is compulsory or elective with respect to a degree. It is possible that the distinction between compulsory and elective courses can be captured by an association or even by an attribute of a class. Hence, `CompulsoryCourse` and `ElectiveCourse` are considered fuzzy classes.

The second statement identifies only attributes of the class `Course`, namely `course_level` and `credit_point_value`. The third statement characterizes an association between classes `Course` and `Degree`. The fourth statement introduces `min_total_credit_points` as an attribute of class `Degree`.

The last statement allows us to discover three more classes: `Student`, `CourseOffering` and `StudyProgram`. The first two are undoubtedly relevant classes, but `StudyProgram` may yet turn out to be an association between `Student` and `CourseOffering`. For that reason, `StudyProgram` is classified as a fuzzy class. This discussion is reflected in Table 4.1.

Example 4.2 (Video Store)

Consider the following requirements for the Video Store system and identify the candidate classes:

1. The video store keeps in stock an extensive library of current and popular movie titles. A particular movie may be held on video tapes or disks.

2. Video tapes are in either 'Beta' or 'VHS' format. Video disks are in 'DVD' format.

3. Each movie has a particular rental period (expressed in days), with a rental charge for that period.

4. The video store must be able to answer immediately any inquiries about a movie's stock availability and how many tapes and/or disks are available for rental (the current condition of each tape and disk must be known and recorded).

TABLE 4.1 Candidate classes (University Enrolment).

Relevant classes	Fuzzy classes
Course	CompulsoryCourse
Degree	ElectiveCourse
Student	StudyProgram
CourseOffering	

The first statement has a few nouns but only some of them can be turned into candidate classes. The video store is not a class because the whole system is about it (there would only be one object of that class in the database – the so-called *singleton class*). Similarly, the notions of stock and library are too generic to be considered classes, at least at this stage. The relevant classes seem to be MovieTitle, VideoTape, and VideoDisk.

The second statement introduces additional *specialization* on video tapes and disks. We can propose three new classes: BetaTape, VHSTape, and DVDDisk. However, as there is only one kind of video disk, we may not need to retain both VideoDisk and DVDDisk in the final model. Which one to retain will depend on the final level of specialization applied to video tapes and disks. Note that we are not sure yet if BetaTape and VHSTape will have any differentiating attributes (apart from the fact that one is Beta and the other is VHS).

The third statement says that each movie title has rental conditions associated with it. However, it is not clear what is understood by 'movie' – movie title or movie medium (tape or disk)? We will need to clarify this requirement with the customers. In the meantime, we may want to declare RentalConditions to be a fuzzy class, rather than to store information about rental period and rental charge in the movie title or movie medium class.

The last statement reassures us that BetaTape, VHSTape, and DVDDisk (or VideoDisk) are relevant classes. We need to store information about the current condition of each tape and disk. However, the attributes such as video_condition or number_currently_available can be generically declared in a higher-level abstract class (let us call it VideoMedium) and inherited by the concrete subclasses (such as VHSTape). This discussion is reflected in Table 4.2.

TABLE 4.2 Candidate classes (Video Store).

Relevant classes	Fuzzy classes
MovieTitle	RentalConditions
VideoMedium	
VideoTape	
VideoDisk (or DVDDisk)	
BetaTape	
VHSTape	

Example 4.3 (Contact Management)

Consider the following requirements for the Contact Management system and identify the candidate classes:

1. The system supports the function of 'keeping in touch' with our current and prospective customer base so as to be responsive to their needs and to win new contracts for our products.

2. The system stores the names, phone numbers, postal and courier addresses, etc. of organizations and our contact persons in these organizations.

3. The system allows our employees to schedule tasks and events that need to be carried with regard to relevant contact persons. Employees schedule the tasks and events for other employees or for themselves.

4. A task is a group of events that take place to achieve a result. The result may be to convert a prospective customer to a customer, to organize product delivery, or to solve customer's problem. Typical types of events are: phone call, visit, sending a fax, arranging for training, etc.

The first statement contains the notions of customer, contract and product. Our generic knowledge and experience tells us that these are typical classes. However, contract and product are not the concepts within the scope of the Contact Management system and should be refuted.

Customer is a relevant class, but we may prefer to call it Contact on the understanding that not all contacts are our current customers. The distinction between a current and prospective customer may or may not warrant the introduction of classes: CurrentCustomer and ProspectiveCustomer. As we are not sure, we will declare these two classes fuzzy.

The second statement sheds new light on the discussion above. We need to distinguish between a contact organization and a contact person. Customer does not seem to be a good name for the class. After all, Customer implies only a current customer and the name can embody both organization and contact person. Our new proposal is to name the classes: Organization, Contact (meaning a contact person), CurrentOrg (i.e. an organization that is our current customer) and ProspectiveOrg (i.e. an organization that is our prospective customer).

In the second statement, a few attributes of classes are mentioned. However, postal and courier addresses are composite attributes and they apply to both classes: Organization and Contact. As such, PostalAddress and CourierAddress are legitimate fuzzy classes.

The third statement introduces three relevant classes: Employee, Task and Event. The statement explains the scheduling activity.

The last statement further clarifies the meaning and relationships between the classes, but it does not implicate any new classes.

TABLE 4.3 Candidate classes (Contact Management).

Relevant classes	Fuzzy classes
Organization	CurrentOrg
Contact	ProspectiveOrg
Employee	PostalAddress
Task	CourierAddress
Event	

4.2.1.2 Specifying classes

Once the list of candidate classes is known, they should be further specified by placing them on a class diagram and by defining the class properties. Some properties can be entered and displayed inside graphical icons representing classes in class diagrams. Many other properties in the class specification have only textual representation. CASE tools provide easy editing capabilities to enter or modify such information through dialog windows with tabbed pages, or similar techniques.

As explained at the beginning of this chapter, we specify classes at a particular level of abstraction. More advanced modeling capabilities of UML are not used – they are discussed in Chapter 5 and later.

4.2.1.2.1 Naming classes

Each class has to be given a *name*. In some CASE tools a *code* for the class, possibly different from the name, may also be assigned. The code would conform to the naming conventions demanded by a target programming language or database system. The code, not the name, is used for the generation of software code from the design models.

In passing, we have adopted a particular convention for class names. The convention is that a class name *begins with a capital letter*. For compound names, the first letter of *each word is capitalized* (rather than separated by an underscore or hyphen). This is only a recommended convention, but it has a reasonable following among developers. (In Section 6.1.3.2, we will recommend to add a single-letter prefix to each class to identify the software layer to which the class belongs).

The name of the class should be a *singular noun* (e.g. Course) or an adjective and a singular noun (e.g. CompulsoryCourse), whenever possible. It is clear that a class is a template for many objects and using plural nouns would not add any new information. At times, a singular noun does not capture the true intention of the class. In such situations, using plural nouns is acceptable (e.g. RentalConditions in Example 4.2).

A class name should be *meaningful*. It should capture the true nature of the class. It should be drawn from the *users' vocabulary* (not from the developers' jargon).

It is better to use a longer name than to make the name too cryptic. We believe that names longer than *thirty characters* are unwieldy (and some programming environments may not accept them, if the CASE tool is working with the class names, instead of the class codes). Longer descriptive names are also possible, in addition to class names and codes.

4.2.1.2.2 Discovering and specifying class attributes

The graphical icon representing a class consists of three compartments (class name, attributes, operations) (Section 2.1.2). The specification of class attributes belongs to *state specifications* and it is discussed here. The specification of class operations is discussed later in this chapter under the heading of *behavior specifications* (Section 4.3).

Attributes are discovered in parallel with the discovery of classes. Identification of attributes is a side effect of class determination. This does not mean that attribute discovery is a straightforward activity. On the contrary, it is a demanding and highly iterative process.

In the initial specification models, we define only attributes that are essential to understanding the *states* in which objects of that class can be. Other attributes may be temporarily ignored (but the analyst must make sure that the existence of the ignored information is not lost by failure to record it in the future). It is unlikely that all class attributes will be mentioned in the requirements document, but it is important not to include the attributes that are not implied by requirements. More attributes can be added in subsequent iterations.

Our recommended convention for attribute names is to use *small letters*. Words in a compound name are separated by an *underscore*.

4.2.1.2.3 Examples for class specifications

Example 4.4 (University Enrolment)

Refer to Example 4.1 and consider the following additional requirements from the requirements document:

1. A student's choice of courses may be restricted by timetable clashes and by limitations on the number of students who can be enrolled in the current course offering.

2. A student's proposed program of study is entered in the online enrolment system. The system checks the program's consistency and reports any problems. The problems need to be resolved with the help of an academic adviser. The final program of study is subject to academic approval by the delegate of the head of division and it is then forwarded to the registrar.

The first statement mentions timetable clashes but we are not sure how to model this issue. It is possible that we are talking here about a use case that procedurally determines timetable clashes. The second part of the same statement can be modeled by adding `enrolment_quota` attribute to class `CourseOffering`. It is also clear now that `CourseOffering` should have attributes `year` and `semester`.

The second statement reinforces the need for `StudyProgram` class. We can see that `StudyProgram` combines a number of course offerings currently on offer. Therefore, `StudyProgram` should also have attributes `year` and `semester`.

The closer analysis of fuzzy classes `CompulsoryCourse` and `ElectiveCourse` leads to the observation that a course is compulsory or elective *with relation to* the degree. The same course may be compulsory with relation to one degree, elective with regard to another degree, and it may not be allowed towards some other degrees. If so, `CompulsoryCourse` and `ElectiveCourse` are not classes in their own rights. (Note that we are not entering here into the realm of modeling with generalization (Section 2.1.5) – generalization modeling is discussed in Section 4.2.4.)

Figure 4.1 represents a class model conforming to the discussion so far. Additionally, we used symbols (*stereotypes*) <<PK>> and <<CK>> to mean a primary key and a candidate key, respectively (Section 8.4.1.2). These are unique identifiers of objects in the classes concerned. Data types for attributes have been specified as well.

The classes `StudyProgram` and `CourseOffering` do not have identifying attributes. They will be added to these classes when the associations among classes are discovered (Sections 2.1.3 and 4.2.2).

Example 4.5 (Video Store)

Refer to Example 4.2. Let us assume that we have now clarified requirement 3 about the rental conditions. The additional requirements are as follows:

1. The rental charge differs depending on the video medium: tape or disk (but it is the same for the two categories of tape: Beta and VHS).

2. Although the DVD disk is the only format of video disks currently kept in the store, the users want the system to extend easily to other disk formats in the future.

3. The employees of the video store tend to remember the codes of the most popular movies. They frequently use a movie code, instead of movie title, to identify the movie. This is a useful practice because the same movie title may have more than one release by different directors.

The first statement explains that rental conditions are different for `VideoTape` and `VideoDisk` containing the same movie. It makes sense, therefore, to have `RentalConditions` as a separate class (to be associated with `VideoTape` and `VideoDisk` classes).

FIGURE 4.1
Class
specifications
(University
Enrolment).

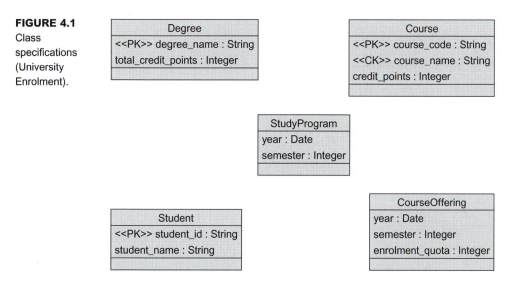

The second statement implies the need for both `VideoDisk` and `DVDDisk` classes to co-exist. A generalization hierarchy rooted at `VideoMedium` is now quite obvious, but we delay the discussion of generalization relationships until Section 4.2.4.

The third statement adds `movie_code` (as the key attribute) and `director` to the class `MovieTitle`. Other attributes are as discussed in Example 4.2.

Figure 4.2 shows the class model for the Video Store application as per the discussion in Examples 4.2 and 4.5. `MovieTitle.is_in_stock` is a *derived* attribute. `VideoMedium.percentage_excellent_condition` is a *class-scope* (*static*) attribute (Section 2.1.6). This attribute will contain the percentage of `VideoMedium` objects with the value of the attribute `video_condition = "excellent"`. Although not shown in the diagram, a class-scope operation (named, for example, `$computePercentageExcellentCondition`) would need to be associated with that attribute to compute its current value on demand.

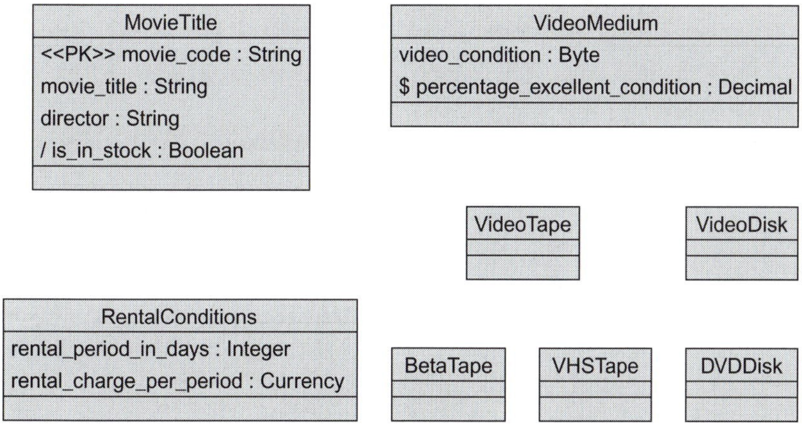

FIGURE 4.2
Class
specifications
(Video Store).

Example 4.6 (Contact Management)

Refer to Example 4.3 and consider the following additional information:

1. A customer is considered current if there exists a contract with that customer for delivery of our products or services. Contract management is, however, outside the scope of our system.

2. The system allows producing various reports on our contacts based on postal and courier addresses (e.g. find all customers by post code).

3. Date and time of the task creation is recorded. The 'money value' expected from the task completion might also be stored.

4. Events for the employee will be displayed on the employee's screen in the calendar-like pages (one day per page). The priority of each event (low, medium or high) is visually distinguished on the screen.

5. Not all events have a 'due time' associated with them – some are 'untimed' (they can be performed any time during the day for which they were scheduled).

6. The creation time of an event cannot be changed, but the due time can.

7. On event's completion, the completion date and time is recorded.

8. The system also stores identifications of employees who created tasks and events, who are scheduled to do the event ('due employee'), and who completed the event.

The analysis of the first statement tells us that the notion of the current customer is derived from the association between `Organization` and `Contract`. The association may be quite dynamic. Hence, the classes `CurrentOrg` and `ProspectiveOrg` are not viable. Moreover, our system is not involved in contract management and is not responsible for the maintenance of class `Contract`. The best we can do is to model the solution by a derived attribute `Organization.is_current` to be modified as necessary by the contract management subsystem.

The second statement provides the reason for having two address classes: `PostalAddress` and `CourierAddress`.

The remaining statements provide additional information about the attribute content for the classes. There are also some hints about association relationships and integrity constraints (to be discussed later).

The class specification for Contact Management is presented in Figure 4.3. No relationships are modeled yet. Hence, for example, the eighth statement that relates employees to tasks and events is not reflected in the model.

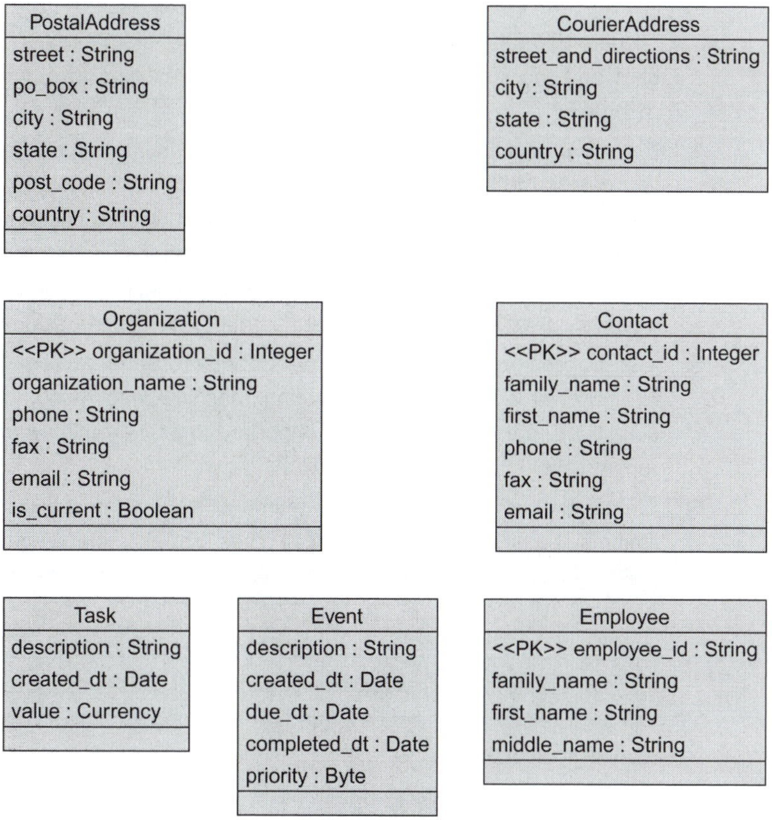

FIGURE 4.3
Class specifications (Contact Management).

PostalAddress
street : String
po_box : String
city : String
state : String
post_code : String
country : String

CourierAddress
street_and_directions : String
city : String
state : String
country : String

Organization
<<PK>> organization_id : Integer
organization_name : String
phone : String
fax : String
email : String
is_current : Boolean

Contact
<<PK>> contact_id : Integer
family_name : String
first_name : String
phone : String
fax : String
email : String

Task
description : String
created_dt : Date
value : Currency

Event
description : String
created_dt : Date
due_dt : Date
completed_dt : Date
priority : Byte

Employee
<<PK>> employee_id : String
family_name : String
first_name : String
middle_name : String

Example 4.7 (Telemarketing)

Refer to Section 2.3.4 (Problem statement 4) and to Section 3.5 that presented the requirements business model for the Telemarketing application. In particular, consider the business class diagram in Figure 3.6 (Section 3.5.3.1). Take into consideration the following additional information.

1. A campaign has a title that is generally used for referring to it. It has also a unique code for internal reference. Each campaign runs over a fixed period of time. Soon after the campaign is closed, the prizes are drawn and the holders of winning tickets are advised.

2. All tickets are numbered. The numbers are unique across all tickets in a campaign. The total number of tickets in a campaign, number of tickets sold so far, and the current status of each ticket are known (e.g. available, ordered, paid for, prize winner).

3. To determine the performance of the society's telemarketers, the duration of calls and the successful call outcomes (i.e. resulting in ordered tickets) are recorded.

4. Extensive information about supporters is maintained. Apart from normal contact details (address, phone number, etc.), this information includes historical details such as the first and most recent dates when a supporter had participated in a campaign along with the number of campaigns in which they participated. Any known supporter's preferences and constraints (such as unwelcome times to call or the usual credit card used in ticket purchases) are also kept.

5. The processing of telemarketing calls needs to be prioritized. Calls which are unanswered or where an answering machine was found, need to be rescheduled to try again later. It is important to alternate times when attempting repeat calls.

6. We can try calling over and over again until a call attempt limit is reached. The limit may be different for different call types. For example, a normal 'solicitation' call may have different limit than a call to remind a supporter of an outstanding payment.

7. The possible outcomes of calls are categorized to facilitate data entry by telemarketers. Typical outcomes are: success (i.e. tickets ordered), no success, call back later, no answer, engaged, answering machine, fax machine, wrong number, disconnected.

From the first statement we can derive a few attributes in the class `Campaign`. `Campaign` contains `campaign_code` (primary key), `campaign_title`, `date_start` and `date_closed`.

The last sentence in Statement 1 refers to campaign prizes. A closer look should convince us that `Prize` is a class on its own – it is drawn, it has a winner, and it must have other properties not explicitly stated, such as description, value and ranking within other campaigns' prizes.

We add `Prize` to the class model together with the attributes `prize_descr`, `prize_value`, and `prize_ranking`. We observe that the date on which prizes are drawn is the same for all prizes in a campaign. We add the attribute `date_drawn` to the class `Campaign`. A winner of the prize is a supporter. We can capture this fact later on in an association between `Prize` and `Supporter`.

Statement 2 says that each ticket has a number, but the number is not unique across all tickets (it is only unique within a campaign). We add the attribute `ticket_number` but we don't make it a primary key within `CampaignTicket`. Two other attributes in `CampaignTicket` are `ticket_value` and `ticket_status`. The total number of tickets and the number of sold tickets are attributes of `Campaign` (`num_tickets` and `num_tickets_sold`).

Statement 3 uncovers a few challenging issues. What data structures do we need to compute telemarketers' performance? To start with we need to come up with some measures by which the performance can be expressed. One possibility is that we compute an average number of calls per hour and an average number of successful calls per hour. We can then calculate a performance indicator by dividing successful calls by the number of calls. We add the attributes `average_per_hour` and `success_per_hour` to the class `Telemarketer`.

To calculate telemarketers' performance indicators we need to store the duration of each call. The placeholder for this information is the class `CallOutcome`. We add the attributes `start_time` and `end_time` to that class. We assume that each call outcome will be linked to a telemarketer by an association.

Statement 4 results in attributes to be included in the class `Supporter`. The attributes are `supporter_id` (primary key), `supporter_name`, `phone_number`, `mailing_address`, `date_first`, `date_last`, `campaign_count`, `preferred_hours`, `credit_card_attributes`. Some of these attributes (`mailing_address`, `preferred_hours`) are complex enough to expect that they will have to be converted to additional classes later in the development process. We store them as attributes for now.

Statement 5 refers to the class `CallScheduled`. We add to it the attributes `phone_number`, `priority` and `attempt_number`. We are not quite sure how to support the requirement that successive calls should be made at different times of day. This is obviously the responsibility of the scheduling algorithm, but a support in data structures will be necessary. Fortunately, some light on this issue is provided in the next statement.

Statement 6 results in a new class `CallType`. The class contains attributes `type_descr`, `call_attempt_limit`, and also `alternate_hours`. The latter is a complex data structure, similar to `preferred_hours` in `Supporter`, and it will eventually end up as a separate class.

The last statement categorizes call outcomes. This is a direct hint that a class `OutcomeType` is needed. Possible outcome types can be stored in attribute `outcome_type_descr`. It is not clear what other attributes can be included in `OutcomeType`, but we are convinced that they will emerge with the study of detailed requirements. One such attribute could be `follow_up_action` to hold information about a typical next step for each outcome type.

Figure 4.4 is a class model that concludes the discussion above. The associations already established in the business class model (Figure 3.6) are retained. No new associations have been added.

4.2.2 Modeling associations

Associations connect objects in the system. They facilitate collaboration between objects. Without associations, the objects can only be related at run time if they share the same attributes or know (by other means, such as global variables) the object identity values of other objects.

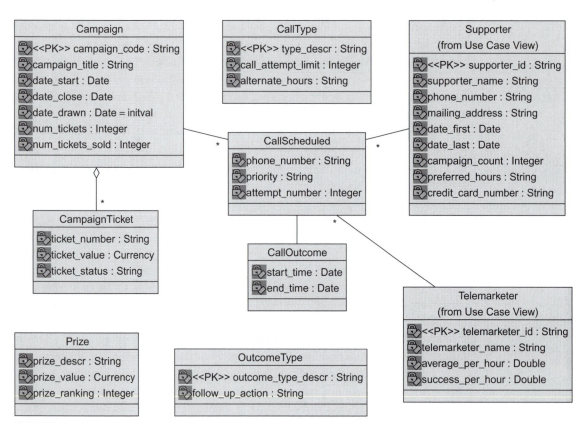

FIGURE 4.4 Class specifications (Telemarketing).

Associations are the most essential kind of relationships in the model, in particular in the model of persistent 'business objects'. Associations support the execution of use cases and, therefore, they tie together the state and behavior specifications.

4.2.2.1 Discovering associations

Finding main associations is a side effect of discovering classes. When defining classes, the analyst takes a decision about the class attributes, and some of these attributes are associations to other classes. Attributes can have primitive data types or they can be typed as other classes, thus establishing relationships to other classes. In essence, any attribute with a *non-primitive data type* should be modeled as an association (or aggregation) to a class representing that data type.

Doing the 'dry-run' of use cases can discover the remaining associations. Collaboration paths between the classes, necessary for a use case execution, are determined. Associations should normally support these collaboration paths.

Each *ternary association* should be replaced with a cycle of binary associations. Ternary associations introduce the risk of semantic misinterpretations.

Occasionally, a *cycle of associations* does not have to commute (be closed) to fully express the underlying semantics (Maciaszek, 1990). That is, at least one of the associations in the cycle can be *derived*. Such an association is redundant in the semantic sense and should be eliminated (a good semantic model should be non-redundant). It is possible, and indeed likely, that many derived associations will, nevertheless, be included in the design model (e.g. for efficiency reasons).

4.2.2.2 Specifying associations

The specification of associations involves:

1. naming them;

2. naming the association roles;

3. determining the association multiplicity (Section 2.1.3.2).

The naming rules should follow the convention for attribute names – lower case letters, words separated by the underscore (Section 4.2.1.2.2).

If only one association connects two classes, the specification of association name and association *rolenames* (Section 2.1.2.1.1) between these classes is optional. A CASE tool would internally distinguish each association through system-provided identification names.

Rolenames can be used to explain more complicated associations, in particular *self associations* (*recursive* associations that relate objects of the same class). If provided, the rolenames should be chosen with the understanding that in the design models they will become attributes in classes on the opposite end of an association.

The *multiplicities* should be specified for both ends (roles) of an association. If unclear, the lower and upper multiplicity bounds can be omitted at this stage.

4.2.2.3 Example for association specifications

Example 4.8 (Contact Management)

Refer to Examples 4.3 and 4.6. The requirements in these examples let us discover and specify associations on classes in the Contact Management system.

The association model for Contact Management is presented in Figure 4.5. To demonstrate the flexibility of association modeling, the use of association names and rolenames is unsystematic.

The multiplicity of all associations between `PostalAddress` and `CourierAddress` on one hand and `Organization` and `Contact` on the other is 'zero or one'. Let us explain using the association between `Organization` and `PostalAddress`.

FIGURE 4.5
Association
specifications
(Contact
Management).

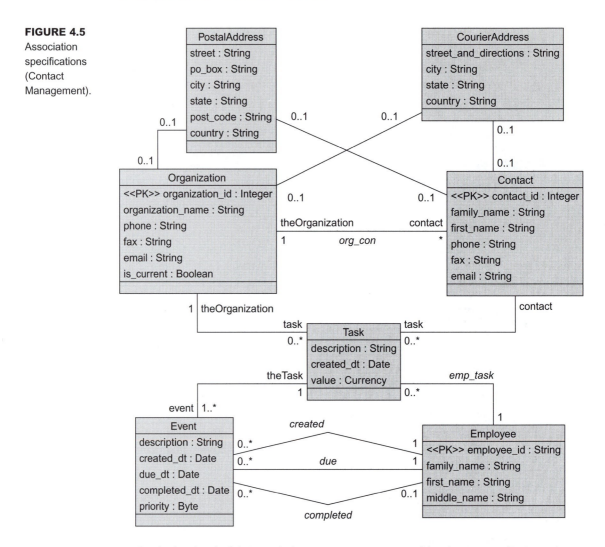

On the 'one' end of the association, an `Organization` object is connected to a maximum one `PostalAddress` object, but only if the postal address of the organization is known. On the opposite end of the association, a particular `PostalAddress` object relates to an `Organization` object *or* to a `Contact` object. Hence, the multiplicity must be 'zero or one' to obey this constraint. (Even so, the constraint itself should be separately documented using the constraint modeling support of UML (Section 5.1.2).)

The association between `Organization` and `Contact` demonstrates the use of both the association names and the rolenames. The rolenames will be converted to attribute names in the Contact Management implementation model. The implementation model will contain attributes: `Organization.contact` and `Contact.theOrganization`. The prefix 'the' signifies the exactly 'one' multiplicity of the role `theOrganization`. The multiplicity of the role `contact` is 'many' (lower and upper bounds are not determined).

The multiplicity of the role `contact`, between `Task` and `Contact`, is unspecified. The requirements have not explained if a task must be directly linked to a contact. If so, we are still not sure if it can be linked to more than one contact.

Finally, there are three associations between `Event` and `Employee`. These associations determine which employee created the event, which is due to perform it, and which will eventually complete it. At the time of event creation, the employee who is going to complete that event is unknown (so the multiplicity on the employee end of association `completed` is 'zero or one').

4.2.3 Modeling aggregation and composition relationships

Aggregation, and its stronger form – *composition*, carries the 'whole–part' semantics between a composite (superset) class and a component (subset) class (Section 2.1.4). In UML, aggregation is treated as a constrained form of association. This is a gross underestimation of the modeling significance of aggregation. Suffice to say that aggregation, along with generalization, is the most important technique for reusing functionality in object-oriented systems.

The modeling power of UML would be greatly facilitated if the language supported the four possible semantics for aggregation (Maciaszek *et al.*, 1996b):

1. 'ExclusiveOwns' aggregation.
2. 'Owns' aggregation.
3. 'Has' aggregation.
4. 'Member' aggregation.

The *ExclusiveOwns* aggregation states that:

■ component classes are *existence-dependent* on their composite class (hence, deleting a composite object propagates down so that the related component objects are also deleted);

■ aggregation is *transitive* (if object $C1$ is part of $B1$, and $B1$ is part of $A1$, then $C1$ is part of $A1$);

■ aggregation is *asymmetric* (*irreflexive*) (if $B1$ is part of $A1$, then $A1$ is not part of $B1$);

■ aggregation is *fixed* (if $B1$ is part of $A1$, then it can never be part of Ai ($i \neq 1$)).

The *Owns* aggregation supports the first three properties of an *ExclusiveOwns* aggregation, that is:

■ existence-dependency;

■ transitivity;

■ asymmetricity.

The *Has* aggregation is semantically weaker than the *Owns* aggregation. The *Has* aggregation supports:

- transitivity;

- asymmetricity.

The *Member* aggregation has a property of a purposeful grouping of independent objects – a grouping that does not make assumptions with regard to existence-dependency, transitivity, asymmetricity or the fixed property. It is an abstraction whereby a collection of component members is considered as a higher-level composite object. A component object in a Member aggregation can at the same time belong to more than one composite object (hence, the *multiplicity* of a Member aggregation can be *many-to-many*).

Although *aggregation* has been recognized as a fundamental modeling concept for at least as long as *generalization* (Smith and Smith, 1977), it has only been given marginal attention in object-oriented analysis and design (with the exception of the 'perfect match' application domains, such as multimedia systems). Fortunately, this trend may be reversed in the future because of the contributions and insights from the methodologists working on *design patterns*. This is evident, for example, in the treatment of aggregation (composition) in the seminal book by Gamma *et al.* (1995).

4.2.3.1 *Discovering aggregations and compositions*

Aggregations are discovered in parallel with the discovery of associations. If an association exhibits one or more of the four semantic properties discussed above, then it can be modeled as an aggregation.

The litmus test is to use phrases '*has*' and '*is-part-of* ' when explaining the relationship. In the top-down explanation, the phrase is 'has' (e.g. Book 'has' Chapter). In the bottom-up interpretation, the phrase is 'is-part-of' (e.g. Chapter 'is-part-of' Book). If the relationship is read aloud with these phrases and the sentence does not make sense in English, then the relationship is *not* an aggregation.

From a structural point of view, aggregation frequently relates together a large number of classes whereas an association is meaningless beyond the binary degree (ref. Section 2.1.3.1). When we need to relate more than two classes together, a *Member* aggregation may be an excellent modeling proposition.

4.2.3.2 *Specifying aggregations and compositions*

UML provides only limited support for aggregation. A strong form of aggregation in UML is called *composition*. In composition, the composite object may physically contain the part objects ('by value' semantics). A part object can only belong to one composite object. The UML *composition* corresponds (more or less) to our *ExclusiveOwns* and *Owns* aggregations.

A weak form of aggregation in UML is simply called *aggregation*. It has 'by reference' semantics – the composite object does not physically contain the part objects. The same part object can have many aggregation or association links in the model. Loosely speaking, the UML *aggregation* corresponds to our *Has* and *Member* aggregations.

The *solid diamond* in UML represents a composition. The *hollow diamond* is used to define an aggregation. The rest of the aggregation specification is consistent with the association notation.

4.2.3.3 *Example for aggregation and composition specifications*

Example 4.9 (University Enrolment)

Refer to Examples 4.1 and 4.5. Consider the following additional requirements:

1. The student's academic record should be available on demand. The record should include information about the grades obtained by the student in each course that the student enrolled in (and has not withdrawn without penalty, i.e. within the first three weeks from the beginning of the semester).

2. Each course has one academic in charge of a course, but additional academics may also teach in it. There may be a different academic in charge of a course each semester and there may be different academics for each course each semester.

Figure 4.6 demonstrates a class model that emphasizes aggregation relationships. `Student` 'has' `AcademicRecord` is a UML composition ('by value' semantics). Each `AcademicRecord` object is physically embedded in one `Student` object. Despite the existence of the association `takes`, `AcademicRecord` includes attribute `course_code`.

FIGURE 4.6
Aggregation specifications (University Enrolment).

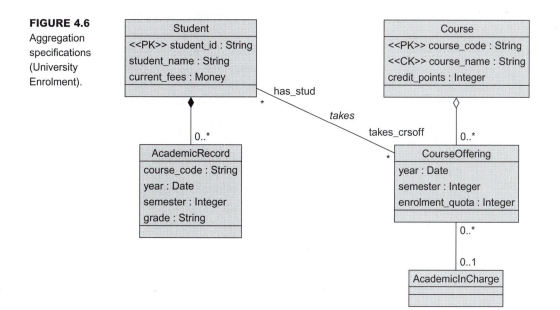

This is necessary because the association `takes` will be implemented by the attribute `takes_crsoff` in `Student` typed as a *collection*, e.g. `Set[CourseOffering]`. The attribute `takes_crsoff` is independent from the information in the embedded `AcademicRecord` object, although it ultimately links `Student` to `Course`.

`Course` 'has' `CourseOffering` is a UML aggregation ('by reference' semantics). Each `CourseOffering` object is only logically contained in one `Course` object. `CourseOffering` can also participate in other aggregations and/or associations (e.g. with `Student` and `AcademicInCharge`).

4.2.4 Modeling generalization relationships

Common *features* (attributes and operations) of one or more classes can be abstracted into a more generic class. This is known as *generalization*. The generalization relationship connects a generic class (*superclass*) with more specific classes (*subclasses*). The generalization permits *inheritance* (*reuse*) of the superclass features by the subclasses. In a conventional object-oriented system, inheritance applies to classes, not to objects (types are inherited, not values).

Apart from *inheritance*, generalization has two objectives (Rumbaugh *et al.*, 1999):

1. Substitutability.
2. Polymorphism.

Under the *substitutability* principle, a subclass object is a legal value for a superclass variable. For example, if a variable is declared to hold `Fruit` objects, then an `Apple` object is a legal value.

Under the *polymorphism* principle, the same operation can have different implementations in different classes. A calling object can invoke an operation without knowing or caring which implementation of the operation will execute. The called object knows to what class it belongs and executes its own implementation.

Polymorphism works best when it is used hand-in-hand with inheritance. It is frequent that a polymorphic operation in the superclass is declared but no implementation is provided. That is, an operation is given a *signature* (the name and the list of formal arguments) but an implementation must be provided in each subclass. Such an *operation* is *abstract*.

Abstract operation should not be confused with *abstract class*. The latter is a class that does not have any direct instance objects (but its subclasses may have instance objects). There may be no instances of `Vegetable`. The only direct instances are the objects of classes `Potato`, `Carrot`, etc.

In reality, a class with an abstract operation is abstract. A concrete class, such as `Apple`, cannot have abstract operations (Hoffer *et al.*, 1999). While abstract operations are captured in *behavior specifications*, abstract classes are the domains of *state specifications*.

4.2.4.1 *Discovering generalizations*

An analyst observes many superclasses/subclasses when an initial list of classes is determined. Many other generalizations are detected when defining associations. Different associations (even from the same class) may need to be connected to a class at a different level of generalization/specialization. For example, class `Course` may be associated with a `Student` (Student *takes* Course) and it may be connected to a `TeachingAssistant` (TeachingAssistant *teaches* Course). Further analysis can show that `TeachingAssistant` is a subclass of `Student`.

The litmus test for generalization is in using the phrases '*can-be*' and '*is-a-kind-of*' when explaining the relationship. In the top-down explanation, the phrase is 'can-be' (e.g. `Student` 'can-be' a `TeachingAssistant`). In the bottom-up interpretation, the phrase is 'is-a-kind-of' (e.g. `TeachingAssistant` 'is-a-kind-of' `Student`). Note that if a `TeachingAssistant` is also a kind of `Teacher` then we have established *multiple inheritance*.

4.2.4.2 *Specifying generalizations*

A generalization relationship between classes shows that one class shares the structure and behavior defined in one or more other classes. Generalization is represented in UML by a solid line with an *arrowhead* pointing to the superclass.

A complete specification of generalization includes a number of powerful options. For example, one can further define a generalization relationship by specifying its *access*, identifying whether the class grants *rights* to another class, deciding what to do in a *multiple inheritance* situation, etc. These issues are discussed in Chapter 5.

4.2.4.3 *Example for generalization specifications*

Example 4.10 (Video Store)

Refer to Examples 4.2 and 4.5. The classes identified in Figure 4.2 (Example 4.5) imply a generalization hierarchy rooted at the class `VideoMedium`. So far, however, we have not modeled any state and/or behavior differences between different kinds of `VideoMedium`.

Let us assume that the Video Store needs to know if a `VideoTape` is a brand new tape or it was already taped over (this can be captured by an attribute `is_taped_over`). Let us assume also that the storage capacity of a `VideoDisk` allows holding multiple versions of the same movie, each in a different language or with different endings.

Our task is to extend the model in Figure 4.2 to include relationships between classes, and in particular to specify generalization relationships.

Figure 4.7 is an extended class model for Video Store. The generalization hierarchy states that `VideoMedium` 'can-be' `VideoTape` or `VideoDisk`. `VideoTape` 'can-be' `BetaTape` or `VHSTape`. `VideoDisk` 'can-be' `DVDDisk` (currently, `VideoDisk` 'must-be' `DVDDisk`, but we assume that new subclasses of `VideoDisk` are possible in the future).

FIGURE 4.7
Generalization
specifications
(Video Store).

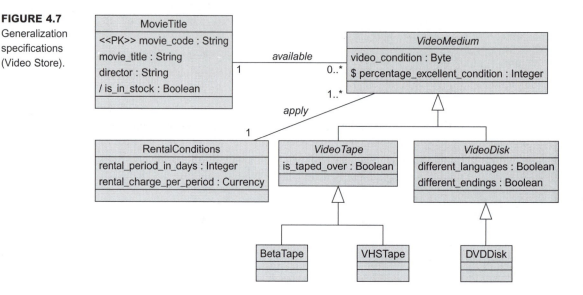

VideoMedium, VideoTape and VideoDisk are *abstract classes* (shown by italicizing their names). Abstract classes do not instantiate objects. VideoMedium objects are instantiated by the classes BetaTape, VHSTape and DVDDisk. Hence, for example, the association available would in reality connect a MovieTitle object to one or more concrete objects of the class VideoMedium (i.e. to BetaTape, VHSTape and/or DVDDisk objects).

The same is true for the association apply. However, in case of the association apply, we can see inefficiency in the model. We know from the Video Store requirements that rental conditions are different for video tapes and different for video disks of the same movie. But all tapes of the same movie and all disks of the same movie have the same rental conditions. This suggests that a RentalConditions object would better be associated with concrete objects of classes VideoTape and VideoDisk. For now, we will put up with this inefficiency.

4.2.5 Modeling objects

Modeling is concerned with definitions of systems. A model is not an executable system and, therefore, it does not show instance objects. In any case, the number of objects in the system is enormous and representing them graphically is impossible. Nevertheless, when modeling classes, we frequently imagine objects and discuss difficult scenarios using examples of objects.

4.2.5.1 *Specifying objects*

UML provides a graphical representation for an *object* (Section 2.1.1.1). We can draw object diagrams to illustrate complex relationships between classes or to demonstrate changes to objects over time. Object models can be used to illustrate and examine how objects will collaborate during an execution of the system.

FIGURE 4.8
Object diagram
for (University
Enrolment).

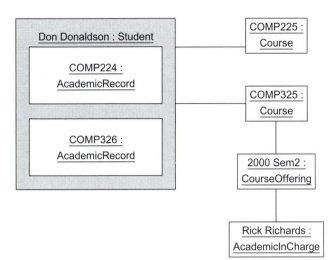

4.2.5.2 Example for object specifications

 Example 4.11 (University Enrolment)

Our task in this example is to show a few objects representing the classes from the class model in Figure 4.6 (Example 4.9).

Figure 4.8 is an object diagram corresponding to the class model in Figure 4.6. It shows that the `Student` object (Don Donaldson) physically contains two `AcademicRecord` objects (for courses COMP224 and COMP326). Don is currently enrolled in two courses: COMP225 and COMP325. One offering of COMP325 was given in year 2000 in semester 2. Rick Richards was the academic in charge of that offering.

4.3 Behavior specifications

Behavior of the system, as it appears to an outside user, is depicted in *use cases* (Section 2.2.2). Use case models can be developed at different levels of abstraction. They can apply to the system as a whole in order to specify the main functional units in the application under development. They can also be used to capture the behavior of a UML *package*, a part of the package or even a *class* within the package.

During *analysis*, use cases capture the system requirements by focusing on *what* the system does or should do. During *design*, use case views can be used to specify the behavior of the system as it is to be implemented.

The behavior entailed by a use case requires that computations are performed and that objects interact to execute a use case. *Computations* can be modeled with activity diagrams.

Interactions of objects can be specified with sequence diagrams or collaboration diagrams. (We will only use sequence diagrams in this chapter. collaboration diagrams will be used in the design chapters (Section 6.2).)

Behavior specifications provide an *operational view* of the system. The main task here is to define *use cases* in the application domain and to determine which *classes* are involved in the execution of these use cases. We identify class *operations* and the *message passing* between the objects. Although object interactions trigger changes to object states, in behavior specifications we define an *operational view on a frozen state* of the system. Changes in object states are explicitly depicted in *state change specifications*.

Use case models should be developed iteratively and concurrently with class models. The classes determined in state specifications will be further elaborated and the most important operations will be identified. We recall, however, that state specifications define only *entity classes* ('business objects'). As behavior modeling proceeds, two other layers of classes will be revealed:

1. classes that service user events and represent business processes (*control classes*);
2. classes that represent GUI (*boundary classes*) (Section 5.2.4).

4.3.1 Modeling use cases

Use case modeling is tightly integrated with requirements determination (see Chapter 3). Textual requirements in the requirements document need to be traced down to use cases in the specifications document. If use cases drive the rest of the development process then the process is *problem-driven* (Section 4.2.1.1.3).

Like class modeling, use case modeling is inherently *iterative* and *incremental*. The initial use case diagram can be determined from the top-level requirements. This could be a *business use case model* (Section 3.5.2). Further refinements should be driven by more detailed requirements. If user requirements change during the development lifecycle, those changes are first made in the requirements document and then in the use case model. Changes to use cases are then traced down to the other models (Hoffer *et al.*, 1999; Rational, 2000).

4.3.1.1 *Discovering use cases*

When discovering use cases, the analyst must ensure that they adhere to the essential features of the use case concept. A use case represents (Hoffer *et al.*, 1999; Kruchten, 1999; Quatrani, 2000; Rumbaugh *et al.*, 1999):

1. a *complete* piece of functionality (including the *main flow* of logic, any variations on it (*subflows*), and any exceptional conditions (*alternative flows*));
2. a piece of *externally visible* functionality (not an internal function);
3. an *orthogonal* piece of functionality (use cases can share objects during executions but the execution of each use case is independent of the others);

4. a piece of functionality *initiated by an actor* (but once initiated, the use case can interact with other actors) – it is possible, however, for an actor to be only on the receiving end of a use case initiated (perhaps indirectly) by another actor;

5. a piece of functionality that delivers an identifiable *value to an actor* (and that value is achieved in a single use case).

Use cases are discovered from the analysis of:

1. requirements identified in the requirements document;

2. actors and their purpose in the system.

Requirements management issues were discussed in Section 3.4. We recall that requirements are typed. For discovery of use cases we are only interested in *function requirements*.

Use cases can be determined from the analysis of tasks performed by actors. Jacobson (1992) suggests asking a range of questions about actors. Answers to these questions can result in the identification of use cases. The questions are:

■ What are the main tasks performed by each actor?

■ Will an actor access or modify information in the system?

■ Will an actor inform the system about any changes in other systems?

■ Should an actor be informed about unexpected changes in the system?

In analysis, use cases address identifiable needs of actors. In some way, these are *actor use cases*. Since use cases determine major functional building blocks for a system, then there is also a need to identify *system use cases*. System use cases extract commonality from actor use cases and allow developing generic solutions applicable (via inheritance) to a range of actor use cases. The 'actor' of the system use case is the designer/programmer, not the user. System use cases are identified in the design phase.

4.3.1.2 *Specifying use cases*

The use case specification includes graphical presentation of actors, use cases, and four kinds of relationships (Fowler, 1999; Rumbaugh *et al.*, 1999):

1. Association.

2. Include.

3. Extend.

4. Use case generalization.

The *association* relationship establishes the communication path between an actor and a use case. The *include* and *extend* relationships are stereotyped by the words: «include» and «extend». The *generalization* relationship allows a specialized use case to change any aspect of the base use case.

The «include» relationship allows factoring out the common behavior in the included use case. (This replaces the common application of the earlier UML concept of the «uses» relationship.) The «extend» relationship provides a controlled form of extending the behavior of a use case by activating another use case at specific extension points. The «include» relationship differs from the «extend» relationship in that the 'included' use case is necessary for the completion of the 'activating' use case.

In practice, the projects can get easily into trouble by putting too much effort into discovering relationships between use cases and determining which relationships apply for specific pairs of use cases. In addition, high-level use cases tend to be so intertwined that relationship links can dominate and obscure the diagram, shifting emphasis from proper identification of use cases to relationships between use cases.

4.3.1.3 *Example for use case specifications*

Example 4.12 (University Enrolment)

Refer to the Problem statement for the University Enrolment system in Section 2.3.1 and to the requirements defined in Examples 4.1 and 4.4 in Section 4.2.1. Our task is to determine use cases from the analysis of function requirements.

Figure 4.9 shows a high-level use case diagram for University Enrolment. The model contains four actors and four use cases. Each use case is initiated by an actor and is a complete, externally visible and orthogonal piece of functionality. All actors, except Student, are the *initiating* actors. Student obtains examination results and enrolment instructions before the program of study for the next semester (term) can be entered and validated.

The use case Provide Examination Results *may* «extend» the use case Provide Enrolment Instructions. The former does not always extend the latter use case. For example, for new students, the examination results are not known. This is why we modeled the relationship with «extend» stereotype, not «include».

The «include» relationship was established from the use case Enter Program of Study to the use case Validate Program of Study. The «include» relationship signifies that the former use case always includes the latter. Whenever the program of study is entered, it is validated for timetable clashes, special approvals, etc.

Example 4.13 (Contact Management)

Refer to the Problem statement for the Contact Management system in Section 2.3.3 and to the requirements defined in Examples 4.3 and 4.6 in Section 4.2.1. Our task is to determine use cases from the analysis of function requirements.

FIGURE 4.9
Use case
diagram
(University
Enrolment).

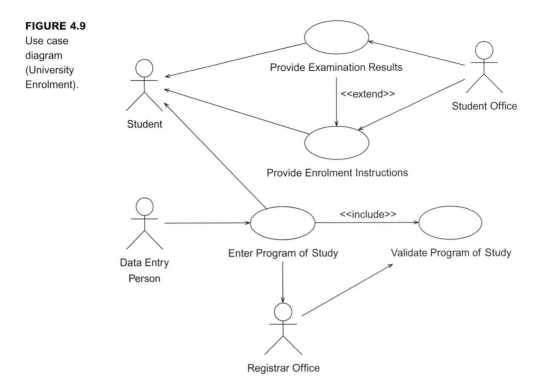

There are three actors and five use cases in the use case diagram for Contact Management (Figure 4.10). An interesting aspect of the model is that actors are related by generalization relationships. `Customer Services Manager` 'is-kind-of' `Customer Services Employee` who in turn 'is-kind-of' `Employee`. The generalization hierarchy improves the expressiveness of the diagram. Any event performed by an `Employee` can also be performed by `Customer Services Employee` or `Customer Services Manager`. Consequently, `Customer Services Manager` is implicitly associated with (and can initiate) every use case.

The use case `Create Task` «includes» `Schedule Event` because of the requirement that the task cannot be created without scheduling the first event. The «extend» relationships signify the fact that the completion of an event can trigger changes to the organization or contact details.

Example 4.14 (Video Store)

Refer to the Problem statement for the Video Store system in Section 2.3.2 and to the requirements defined in Examples 4.2 and 4.5 in Section 4.2.1. Our task is to determine use cases from the analysis of function requirements.

For one of the use cases, write narrative specifications with the following headings: summary, actors, preconditions, description, exceptions, and postconditions.

FIGURE 4.10
Use case
diagram (Contact
Management).

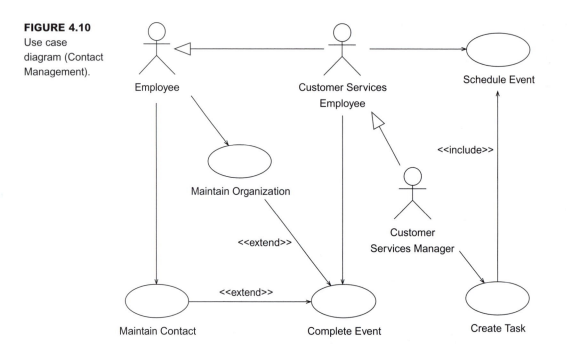

There are six use cases and only two actors in the use case diagram for Video Store (Figure 4.11). Secondary actors, such as Customer or Supplier, are not shown. These actors do not initiate any use cases. The actor Employee initiates all use cases. The relationship between actors Scanning Device and Employee is a *dependency*, stereotyped by the analyst with the phrase «depends on».

FIGURE 4.11
Use case
diagram (Video
Store).

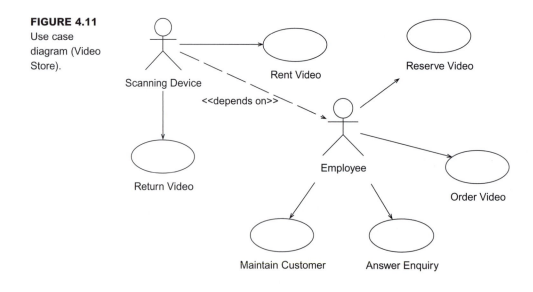

Table 4.4 illustrates that the graphical representation of use cases is but one aspect of the complete use case model. Each use case in the diagram has to be further documented in the CASE tool repository. In particular, a narrative description is necessary. Table 4.4 uses one popular structure for the narrative specification of use cases (Section 2.2.2.4).

TABLE 4.4 Narrative specification for use case 'Rent Video' (Video Store).

Use case	Rent Video
Brief description	A customer wishes to rent a video tape or disk that is picked from the store's shelves or that has been previously reserved by the customer. Provided the customer has a non-delinquent account, the tape is rented out once the payment has been received. If the tape is not returned in a timely fashion, an overdue notice is mailed to the customer.
Actors	Employee, Scanning device.
Preconditions	Video tape or disk is available to be hired. Customer has a membership card. Scanner devices work correctly. Employee at the front desk knows how to use the system.
Main flow	A customer may ask an employee about video availability (including a reserved video) or may pick a tape or disk from the shelves. The video and the membership card are scanned and any delinquent or overdue details are brought up for the employee to query the customer about. If the customer does not have a delinquent rating, then he/she can hire up to a maximum of eight videos. However, if the rating of the customer is 'unreliable' then a deposit of one rental period for each tape or disk is requested. Once the amount payable is received, the stock is updated and the tapes and disks are handed out to the customer together with the rental receipt. The customer pays by cash, credit card or electronic transfer. Each rental record stores (under the customer's account) the check-out and due-in dates together with the identification of the employee. A separate rental record is created for each video hired. The use case will generate an overdue notice to the customer if a video has not been returned within two days of the due date, and a second notice after another two days (and at that time the customer is noted as 'delinquent').
Alternative flows	A customer does not have a membership card. In this case, the 'Maintain Customer' use case may be activated to issue a new card. An attempt to rent too many videos. No videos can be rented because of the customer's delinquent rating. The video medium or membership card cannot be scanned because of damage to them. The electronic transfer or credit card payment is refused.
Postconditions	Videos are rented out and the database is updated accordingly.

Example 4.15 (Telemarketing)

Refer to the Problem statement for the Telemarketing system in Section 2.3.4 and to the requirements defined in Examples 3.1, 3.2 and 3.3 and in Example 4.7. Our task is to determine use cases from the analysis of function requirements.

The solution in Figure 4.12 consists of a number of use cases. The actors directly communicate with three use cases: Schedule and Make Next Call, Record Call Outcome, and Display Call Details. The latter can in turn be extended to Display Campaign Details, Display Supporter History and Display Prize Details. The use case Update Supporter extends Display Supporter History. Record Ticket Order and Schedule Callback can extend Record Call Outcome. It is assumed that

FIGURE 4.12
Use case diagram (Telemarketing).

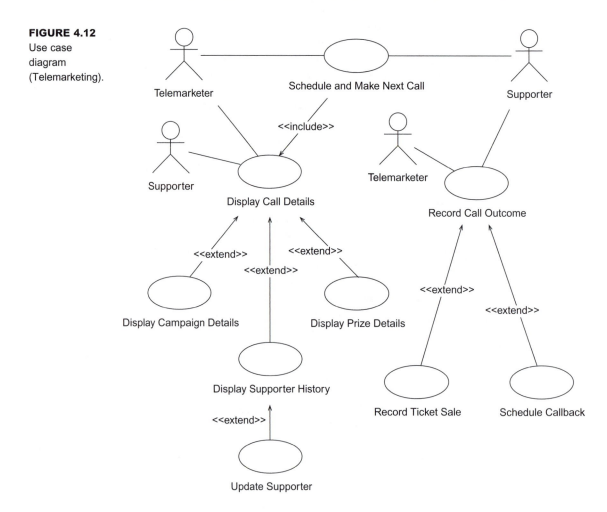

the actors can indirectly communicate with the extension use cases, but no explicit communication links are drawn to those use cases.

4.3.2 Modeling activities

Activity diagrams are a late addition to UML (Section 2.2.3). Like traditional *flow charts* and *structure charts* popularized in the structured methods for procedural program design, activity diagrams represent the flow of logic in object-oriented programs (albeit at a high level of abstraction). The difference lies in the possibility of representing a *concurrent control* in activity diagrams, in addition to the *sequential control*.

The activity models are extensively used in the *design*. However, they also provide a great technique to express computations or workflows at the level of abstraction applied in the *analysis*. Activity graphs can be used to show varying levels of detail of a computation.

Activity models can be particularly useful to define the flow of *activities* in the execution of a use case. Since the activity models do not show the *objects* that perform the activities, an activity graph can be constructed even if the class model is not developed or is underdeveloped. Eventually, each activity will be defined by one or more operations in one or more collaborating classes. The detailed design for such collaboration is likely to be modeled in a collaboration diagram (Section 6.2.2).

4.3.2.1 Discovering activities

Each use case can be modeled by one or more activity graphs. An event from an actor that initiates a use case is the same event that triggers the execution of the activity graph. The execution proceeds from one *activity state* to the next. An activity state completes when its computation is completed. External event-based interruptions, that would cause the activity state to complete, are allowed only in exceptional situations. If they are expected to be frequent then a statechart diagram should be used instead.

Activities are best discovered from the analysis of sentences in the *narrative specifications* of use cases (Table 4.4). Any phrases with verbs are candidate activities. The description of alternative flows introduces branches or forks in the activity graph. They result in an exceptional (unexpected) activity state. Concurrent threads are also possible.

4.3.2.2 Specifying activities

Once the activity states are discovered, the specification of activities is a relatively straightforward process of connecting them by *transition lines*. Concurrent threads are initiated (*forked*) and *rejoined* with *synchronization bars*. Alternative threads are created (*branched*) and *merged* with *branch diamonds*.

External events are not normally expected on activity graphs. However, the graphical techniques exist if the external events must be included. Similarly, the graphical notation exists for object flow states to represent an object that is an input or output of an activity.

4.3.2.3 *Example for activity specifications*

📁 **Example 4.16 (Video Store)**

Refer to Example 4.14 and in particular to the narrative specification for use case 'Rent Video' (Table 4.4). Our task is to design an activity diagram for 'Rent Video'.

Figure 4.13 is the activity diagram for the 'Rent Video' use case. Not surprisingly, the diagram reflects the narrative specification for the use case (Table 4.4). The processing begins when either a customer card or video medium is scanned. These two activities are considered independent from each other (shown by the use of a fork).

The activity `Verify Customer` checks the customer history and the computation proceeds after evaluating the branch conditions. If a customer is delinquent then 'Rent Video'

FIGURE 4.13
Activity diagram for use case 'Rent Video' (Video Store).

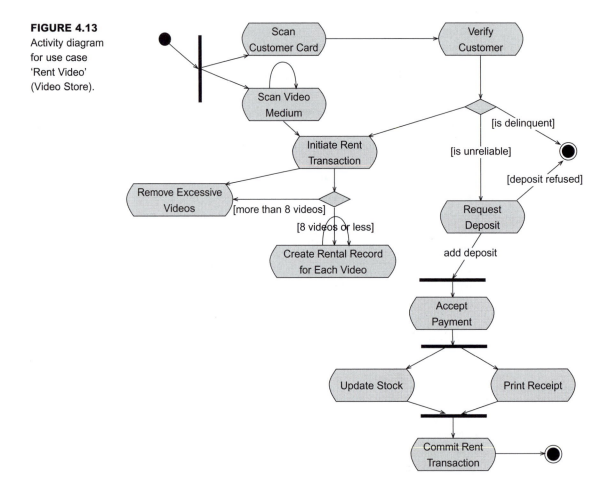

terminates. If a customer is unreliable then we will request a deposit before concluding the transaction. If a customer has a good record then the activity `Initiate Rent Transaction` fires.

The second branch condition ensures that no more than eight videos are rented out to a single customer. After the payment is accepted, another fork allows for a concurrent execution of the activities `Update Stock` and `Print Receipt`. These concurrent threads are joined, before the activity `Commit Rent Transaction` fires and the entire processing terminates.

4.3.3 Modeling interactions

Sequence diagrams and collaboration diagrams are two kinds of interaction diagram. They show patterns of *interactions* among objects necessary to accomplish a use case, an operation or other behavioral component.

Sequence diagrams show an exchange of messages between objects arranged in a time sequence. Collaboration diagrams emphasize the relationships between objects along which the messages are exchanged. We find the sequence diagrams more useful in analysis and the collaboration diagrams in design.

Because interaction models refer to objects, they require that at least the first iteration of state modeling has been completed and major classes of objects have been identified. Although interactions affect states of objects, the interaction diagrams do not explicitly model state changes in objects. This is the domain of state change specifications and the statechart diagrams (Sections 2.2.6 and 4.4).

Interaction diagrams can be used to determine *operations* (methods) in classes (Sections 2.2.5 and 4.3.4). Any message to an object in an interaction diagram must be serviced by some method in that object's class.

4.3.3.1 *Discovering message sequences*

The discovery of message sequences follows on from activity models. *Activities* in an activity diagram are mapped to *messages* in a sequence diagram. If the abstraction levels used in the construction of the activity model and the sequence model are similar, then the mapping between activities and messages is quite straightforward.

4.3.3.2 *Specifying message sequences*

When specifying messages, it is advantageous to distinguish between a message that is a signal and a message that is a call (Rumbaugh *et al.*, 1999). A *signal* denotes an asynchronous inter-object communication. The sender can continue executing immediately after sending the signal message. A *call* signifies a synchronous invocation of an operation with the provision for the return of control to the sender. The return message can return some values to the caller or it can simply acknowledge that the operation has been successfully accomplished. In the latter case, we can elect not to show the return message on the sequence diagram.

4.3.3.3 *Example for sequence specifications*

Example 4.17 (University Enrolment)

Refer to Examples 4.9 and 4.12 and to the use case 'Enter Program of Study' in Figure 4.9. Our task is to construct a sequence diagram for this use case.

We are not concerned here with the verification of an entered program of study. Another use case ('Validate Program of Study') handles the verification of pre-requisites, timetable clashes, special approvals, etc. Our task is only to check whether the course on which the student wants to register is offered in the next semester and if it is still open (there are places available).

Figure 4.14 shows the sequence diagram for the above scenario. The actor Data Entry Person initiates the use case by sending the request message to an object of the *boundary* class ProgramEntryWindow to add a student (identified by argument std) to a course (argument crs) in a semester (argument sem).

An object of the class ProgramEntryWindow validates with aStudent object if the student is eligible to enroll (e.g. if the student paid the fees). The output argument s_check will return value 'yes' or 'no' to :ProgramEntryWindow. If 'no' is returned, the enrolment cannot proceed and the object :ProgramEntryWindow sends a *self message* to itself to destroy itself (a *destructor* operation). The *condition* notation in square brackets informs about the optionality of the operation destroy.

(Using a self message to indicate object destruction is a notational shortcut. In reality, an instance object cannot destroy itself. The destroy message must be sent to the class object. Also, UML has a special notation for object destruction – a large **X** placed on the object lifeline at the point at which the object is destroyed.)

If aStudent can be enrolled then we need to find out if aCourse is still open. To service this request, the object aCourse must query its current aCourseOffering object (identified by following the aggregation link from Course to CourseOffering (Figure 4.6)). If there are no places available in the current aCourseOffering object, the enrolment cannot proceed and the object :ProgramEntryWindow again sends a *self message* to itself to destroy itself.

If the enrolment can go ahead, the object :ProgramEntryWindow requests aStudent to add aCourseOffering to itself and it then requests that aCourseOffering adds aStudent to itself. The sequence of the two operations from :ProgramEntryWindow can be reversed as long as the program ensures the referential integrity between aCourseOffering and aStudent (i.e. if a student is enrolled in a course offering then the course offering must have that student in its list of students).

FIGURE 4.14

Sequence diagram for use case 'Enter Program of Study' (University Enrolment).

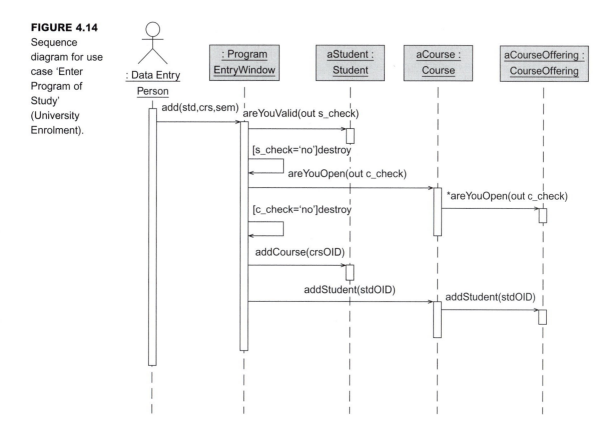

Note that if database software is involved in storing the Student and CourseOffering objects then the object :ProgramEntryWindow would send only one of those two messages, i.e. either addCourse or addStudent. Once aStudent is added to aCourseOffering, the database software would take the responsibility of maintaining referential integrity and would fix the aStudent link to the aCourseOffering, and vice versa.

Note also that the actual arguments included in addCourse and addStudent messages are OID objects containing the OID values (*handles*) to aStudent object or aCourseOffering object, respectively. These OID values have been determined when :ProgramEntryWindow accessed aStudent and aCourse objects with areYouValid and areYouOpen messages.

4.3.4 Modeling public interfaces

A *public interface* of a class is determined by the set of *operations* that the class offers as a service to other classes in the system. Such operations are declared with public visibility. It is only through the public interfaces that objects can collaborate to execute use cases.

Public interfaces are first determined towards the end of the analysis phase when the state and behavior specifications are largely defined. In analysis, we only define the *signature* of each public operation (operation name, list of formal arguments, return type). In design, we will provide a definition for the algorithm of a *method* that implements the operation.

4.3.4.1 Discovering class operations

Class operations are best discovered from sequence diagrams. Every *message* in a sequence model, other than a return value, must be serviced by an *operation* in the destination object (Section 2.2.5.2). If the sequence models are fully developed, the determination of public operations is an automatic task.

In practice, however, the sequence diagrams – even if developed for all use cases – might not provide sufficient detail to permit discovery of all public operations. In addition, sequence diagrams might not be available for operations that cross use case boundaries (for instance, where a business transaction spans more than one use case).

For these reasons, supplementary methods for operation discovery can be helpful. One such method comes from the observation that objects are responsible for their own destiny and, therefore, they must support four primitive operations:

1. create;
2. read;
3. update;
4. delete.

These are known as *CRUD operations* (Section 3.5.2.1). The CRUD operations allow other objects to send messages to an object to request:

1. a new object instance;
2. access to the state of an object;
3. modification of the state of an object;
4. that an object destroys itself.

4.3.4.2 Specifying class operations

At this stage of the lifecycle, a class diagram needs to be modified to include *operation signatures*. The scope of operations may also be determined. By default, the *instance scope* is assumed (the operation applies to *instance objects*). The *class (static) scope* must be declared explicitly (the '$' sign in front of an operation name). The class scope states that the operation applies to the *class object* (Section 2.1.6).

Other properties of operations, such as concurrency, polymorphic behavior and algorithm specification, will be specified later during design.

4.3.4.3 *Example for operation specifications*

Example 4.18 (University Enrolment)

Refer to Examples 4.9 and 4.17 and to the classes `Course` and `CourseOffering` in Figure 4.6. Objects of these two classes have been used in the sequence diagram in Figure 4.14.

Our task is to derive operations from the sequence diagram and add them to the classes `Course` and `CourseOffering`.

The operations specified in the extended class model in Figure 4.15 are obtained directly from the sequence diagram in Figure 4.14. The icons in front of attributes signify that the attributes have the *private* scope. The icons in front of operations inform that they are *public*.

FIGURE 4.15
Class operation specifications (University Enrolment).

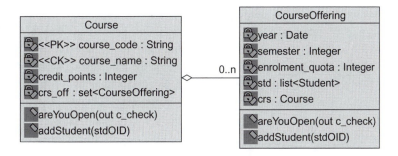

The operations are `Course.areYouOpen`, `CourseOffering.areYouOpen`, `Course.addStudent` and `CourseOffering.addStudent`. We assume that `Course` obtains its lists of students by accessing its component objects of the class `CourseOffering`.

Although relationship attributes are not normally shown in the analysis models (they are implicit in relationship links), we included three relationship attributes that are needed by the operations. These are: `Course.crs_off`, `CourseOffering.std`, and `CourseOffering.crs`. Note that `crs_off` and `std` have *parameterized types*; they are *collections* (`set` and `list`) of objects.

4.4 State change specifications

The state of an object at a point in time is determined by the values of its attributes, including relationship attributes. State specifications define the class attributes (among other issues). Behavior specifications define the class operations, some of which have *side effects* (i.e. they alter the state of an object). However, to understand how an object can change its state over time, we need a more targeted view of the system. Such a view is provided by the state change specifications.

The importance of state change specifications varies between application domains. The modeling of state changes in business applications is much less critical than in engineering and real-time applications. Many *engineering and real-time applications* are all about state changes. In modeling such systems, we have to concentrate on state changes from day one: What happens if the temperature is too high? What if the valve is not closed? What if the container is full? etc.

In this textbook, we are predominantly concerned with *business applications* where state changes are less frequent. Therefore, the modeling of state changes is typically done towards the end of the analysis (and then continued with much greater depth in the design). Many of the state change specifications define *exceptional conditions* in the system. It is natural that the exceptions to the normal behavior of the system are modeled after the normal behavior is specified.

4.4.1 Modeling object states

The modeling of object states is done with statechart diagrams. A state graph (state machine) is a graph of states and transitions. State models are built for each class that exhibits interesting *dynamic behavior*. Not all classes in the class diagram will be in this category.

Statechart diagrams can also be used to describe the dynamic behavior of other modeling elements, for example use cases, collaborations or operations. This is, however, infrequent and some CASE tools may not support such functionality.

4.4.1.1 *Discovering object states*

The process of discovery of object states is based on the analysis of the attribute content in a class and determinating which of these attributes are of special interest to use cases. Not all attributes determine state changes.

For example, the modification of a phone number by a customer does not change the state of the Customer object. The customer still has the phone; the number of the phone is not relevant. But the deletion of the phone number may be a state change of interest to some use cases. The customer is not reachable by phone any more.

Similarly, the change of the phone number that includes a change of area code may be an interesting state change indicating a customer has moved to another geographical location and this change might need to be noted and modeled in a statechart diagram.

4.4.1.2 *Specifying object states*

The basic UML notation for statechart specifications has been explained in Section 2.2.6. To use this notation successfully, an analyst must understand how different concepts inter-relate, which combinations of concepts are unnatural or not allowed, and what notational shortcuts are possible. It is also likely that a CASE tool will introduce some restrictions, but perhaps also some interesting extensions.

A state transition fires when a certain event occurs *or* a certain condition is satisfied. This means, for example, that a transition line does not have to be labeled with an *event name*. A *condition* itself (written in square brackets) will fire the transition whenever an *activity* in the state is completed and the condition evaluates to true.

In a typical situation, a transition is triggered by a signal event or a call event. A *signal event* establishes an explicit, asynchronous one-way communication between two objects. A *call event* establishes a synchronous communication in which the caller waits for a response. Two other kinds of event are: *change event*, and *time event*. In particular, time events that fire transitions based on the absolute or relative notion of time are very useful in some models.

Another consideration in statechart modeling relates to the possibility of specifying entry actions inside a state icon or on an incoming transition. Similarly, exit actions can be placed inside state icons or on outgoing transitions. Although the semantics is not affected, the choice of which technique to use can influence the readability of the model (see Rumbaugh *et al.*, 1991).

4.4.1.3 *Example for statechart specifications*

Example 4.19 (Video Store)

Refer to the class `MovieTitle` in Example 4.9 (Figure 4.7). Our task is to specify a statechart diagram for `MovieTitle`.

The statechart for `MovieTitle` is given in Figure 4.16. The diagram demonstrates different ways in which transitions can be specified. The transitions between the states `Available` and `Not in Stock` specify parameterized event names together with action names and guarded conditions. On the other hand, the transition from the state `Reserved` to `Not Reserved` lacks an explicit trigger event. It is triggered by the completion of activity in the state `Reserved`, provided that the condition `[no more reserved]` is true.

Summary

This has been the nuts and bolts chapter in the textbook – UML in action. The case studies introduced in Chapter 2 provided the illustrative material. All frequently used UML models have been put to the task. The motto of the chapter could be: there are no black-or-white, zero–one, true–false solutions in IS analysis models. For every problem there are many potential solutions. The trick is to arrive at a solution that will satisfy the customer requirements and that will work.

■ State specifications describe the IS world from the *static* perspective of *classes*, their *attribute* content and their *relationships*. There are many methods of *class discovery* but none of them offers a single 'cookbook recipe.' A mix of methods that suits the analyst's knowledge and

FIGURE 4.16
Statechart
diagram for class
'MovieTitle'
(Video Store).

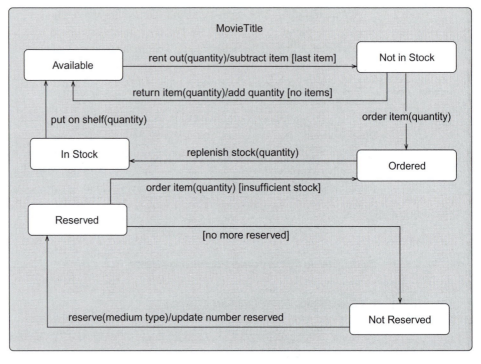

experience is a practical answer to the class discovery. Classes are specified in UML *class diagrams*. The diagrams visualize classes and three kinds of relationship between them: *associations*, *aggregations* and *generalizations*.

■ Behavioral specifications describe the IS world from the *operational* perspective (in order not to use the overloaded term – the *functional* perspective). The driving force for behavioral specifications, and, indeed, for the requirements analysis and system design in general, are *use cases*. The *use case diagrams* provide only simple visualization – the real power of use cases is in their *narrative specifications*. Other behavioral diagrams are derived from use case models. They include *activity diagrams*, *interactions diagrams*, and the addition of *operations* to classes.

■ State change specifications describe the IS world from the *dynamic* perspective. The objects are bombarded by events and some of these events cause changes to objects' *states*. *Statechart diagrams* allow modeling of state changes.

📖 Review questions

R1 Discuss how function and data requirements identified in the requirements determination phase relate to state, behavior and state change models of the requirements specification phase.

R2 Explain pros and cons of using CASE tools for requirements specification.

R3   Explain the main differences in the four approaches to class discovery.

R4   Discuss and contrast the processes associated with the discovery and specification of class attributes and class operations. Would you model attributes and operations in parallel or separately? Why?

R5   Refer to the class model in Figure 4.7 (Example 4.10). Explain why `MovieTitle.is_in_stock` is modeled as a *derived* attribute, and `VideoMedium.percentage_excellent_condition` as a *static* attribute.

R6   Ternary and derived associations are not desirable in the analysis models. Why? Give examples.

R7   Refer to the class model in Figure 4.5 (Example 4.8). Consider the top part of the model defining classes and associations between `PostalAddress`, `CourierAddress`, `Organization` and `Contact`. Think about the different ways of modeling the same requirements. Can the model be made more flexible to accommodate potential changes to the requirements? What are the pros and cons of different solutions?

R8   Give an example for each of the four kinds of aggregation: ExclusiveOwns, Owns, Has and Member.

R9   Refer to the class model in Figure 4.6 (Example 4.9). How would the semantics of the model change, if the class `AcademicRecord` were modeled as an 'association as a class' linked to the association `takes`?

R10   Inheritance without polymorphism is possible but not terribly useful. Why? Give an example.

R11   What UML models are useful for behavior specifications? Explain their individual strengths and how they interrelate to define the behavior of the system.

R12   Explain how use cases differ from business functions or business transactions.

R13   Give an example of an «include» relationship and an «extend» relationship between use cases. What is the main difference?

R14   Give an example of a class with few attributes. Discuss which attributes can trigger a state transition and which attributes are indifferent to state changes.

Exercise questions

Additional requirements (University Enrolment)

Consider the following additional requirements for University Enrolment:

1.   The University is organized into Divisions. The Divisions divide into Departments. Academics work for a single Department.

2.   Most degrees are managed by one Division, but some are managed jointly by two or more divisions.

3. New students receive their acceptance form and enrolment instructions by mail. Continuing students, who are eligible to re-enroll, receive (also by mail) enrolment instructions together with the notification of their examination results.

4. Enrolment instructions include the class timetable for the course offerings.

5. During the enrolment, the students may consult an academic adviser in their Division of registration on the formulation of a program of study.

6. Students are not restricted to studying only courses offered by their Division of registration and may at any time change their Division of registration (by completing a change of program form available from the Student Office).

7. To take certain courses, a student must first pass the prerequisite courses with the required grade (i.e. a straight pass may not be sufficient). A student who has not passed a course satisfactorily may attempt to do the same course again. Special approvals by the delegate of the Head of the relevant Division are needed to enroll in a course for the third time or when requesting waivers of prerequisites.

8. Students are classified as part time if they are enrolled for the year in course offerings carrying a combined total of fewer than 18 credit points.

9. A special permission needs to be obtained to enroll in a program of course offerings carrying a combined total of more than 14 credit points in a given semester.

10. Each course has one academic in charge of the course, but additional academics may be involved as well. There may be a different academic in charge of a course each semester and there may be different academics for each course each semester.

Additional requirements (Video Store)

Consider the following additional requirements for Video Store:

1. Tapes/disks returned late induce a payment equal to an extra rental period. Each movie medium has a unique identification number.

2. The movies are ordered from suppliers who are generally able to supply tapes/disks within one week. Typically, several movies are ordered in a single order to a supplier.

3. Reservations are accepted for a movie that is on order and/or because all copies of a particular movie are rented out. Reservations are also accepted for movies that are neither in store nor on order, but a customer is then asked for a deposit of one rental period.

4. Customers can make many reservations, but a separate reservation request is prepared for each movie reserved. A reservation may be canceled due to the lack of response from a customer, more precisely one week from the date the customer was contacted

that the movie was available for rental. If a deposit has been paid it is then credited to the customer's account.

5. The database stores usual information about suppliers and customers, i.e. addresses, phone numbers, etc. Each order to a supplier identifies the ordered movies, tape/disk formats, and quantities, and also an expected delivery date, purchase price, applicable discounts, etc.

6. When a tape is returned by a customer or is delivered from a supplier, reservations are first satisfied. This involves contacting the customer who made the reservation. In order to ensure that reservations are properly handled, both the 'reserved movie has arrived' contact with the customer and the subsequent rental to the customer are related back to the reservation. These steps ensure that reservations are properly carried through.

7. A customer can borrow many tapes or disks but each borrowed video medium constitutes separate rental record. For each rental, the check-out, due-in and return dates and times are recorded. The rental record is later updated to indicate that the video has been returned and the final payment (or reimbursement) has been made. The clerk who authorizes the rental is also recorded. Details about a customer and rentals are kept for a year to enable the customer rating to be easily determined. Old rental details are kept for auditing purposes for the year.

8. All transactions are made by cash, electronic money transfer or credit cards. Customers are required to pay the rental charges when tapes/disks are checked out.

9. When a tape/disk is returned late (or it cannot be returned for whatever reason), a payment is taken either from the customer's account or directly from the customer.

10. If a tape/disk is overdue by more than two days, an Overdue Notice is sent to the customer. Once two Overdue Notices on a single tape/disk have been sent, the customer is noted to be delinquent and the next rental is subject to management removing the delinquent rating.

E1   *University Enrolment* – refer to the additional requirements above and to Example 4.1 (Section 4.2.1.1.7).

What new classes can be derived from the extended requirements?

E2   *Video Store* – refer to the additional requirements above and to Example 4.2 (Section 4.2.1.1.7).

What new classes can be derived from the extended requirements?

E3   *University Enrolment* – refer to the additional requirements above, to Exercise E1, and to Example 4.9 (Section 4.2.3.3).

Extend the class model of Figure 4.6 (Example 4.9) to include the extended requirements. Show classes and relationships.

E4 *Video Store* – refer to the additional requirements above, to Exercise E2, and to Example 4.10 (Section 4.2.4.3).

Extend the class model of Figure 4.7 (Example 4.10) to include the extended requirements. Show classes and relationships.

E5 *University Enrolment* – refer to the additional requirements above and to Example 4.12 (Section 4.3.1.3).

Extend the use case model of Figure 4.9 (Example 4.12) to include the extended requirements.

E6 *Video Store* – refer to the additional requirements above and to Example 4.14 (Section 4.3.1.3).

Study the narrative specification for the use case `Rent Video` in Table 4.4 (Example 4.14). Ignore the last paragraph in the Main Flow section of the table (this paragraph refers rather to the use case `Maintain Customer`). Develop a separate use case diagram to depict *child* use cases for Rent Video.

E7 *University Enrolment* – refer to the additional requirements above and to Example 4.17 (Section 4.3.3.3).

Extend the sequence diagram of Figure 4.14 (Example 4.17) to include the checking of prerequisites – a student will only be added to the course if he/she passed the prerequisite courses.

E8 *University Enrolment* – refer to Example 4.18 (Section 4.3.4.3) and to the solution of Exercise E7 above.

Use the extended sequence diagram to add operations to relevant classes, including to the two classes in Figure 4.15 (Example 4.18).

E9 *Contact Management* – refer to Example 4.8 (Section 4.2.2.3).

Develop a statechart diagram for the class `Event`.

E10 *Telemarketing* – refer to Example 4.7 (Section 4.2.1.2.3).

Add missing class associations in Figure 4.4. Determine multiplicity of each association.

E11 *Contact Management* – refer to Example 4.8 (Section 4.2.2.3).

Consider the classes `Organization`, `Contact`, `PostalAddress` and `CourierAddress`. As an extension to the model in Figure 4.5, allow for a hierarchical structure to organizations, i.e. an organization can consist of smaller organizations. Improve the class model by using generalization and at the same time extend it to capture the hierarchy of organizations.

Chapter 5

Advanced Analysis

The previous chapter has painted a rosy picture of visual object-oriented modeling. The examples were undemanding, the visual modeling language was simple and attractive to use, the dependencies between models were apparent. We used the modeling techniques indiscriminately and we paid little attention to alternative solutions.

The realities of software development are more complex. And there are no simple solutions to complex problems, as we observed at the very beginning of this textbook. Objects provide the current technology to solving complex problems. As such, objects need to provide the technical depth corresponding to the level of complexity they address.

This chapter is a critical appraisal of the object technology and its suitability for solving complex problems. We introduce advanced concepts in class modeling, class layering, inheritance, and delegation. Throughout, we compare, pass judgments, give opinions, and suggest alternative solutions. Because of its technical character, many topics discussed in this chapter extend directly into system design. This is consistent with the ubiquitous nature of UML and the iterative and incremental process of object-oriented software development.

5.1 Advanced class modeling

The analysis modeling concepts discussed so far are sufficient to produce complete analysis models, but at a level of abstraction that does not exhaust all possible details permissible in analysis modeling (i.e. details that do not yet reveal the hardware/software solution but enrich the semantics of the model). UML includes notations for a number of additional concepts that we only alluded to in passing or that we have not addressed at all.

The additional modeling concepts include stereotypes, constraints, derived information, visibility, qualified associations, association class, parameterized class, and a few more. These concepts are optional. Many models may be acceptable without them. When used, they have to be applied with care and precision so that any future reader of the model can understand the intention of the writer without misgivings.

5.1.1 Stereotypes

A *stereotype* extends an existing UML modeling element. It varies the semantics of an existing element. It is not a new model element *per se*. It does not change the structure of UML – it

FIGURE 5.1
Icons and labels
for stereotypes.

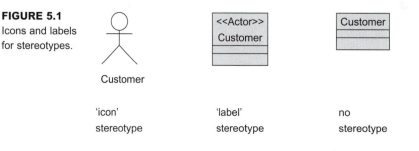

Customer

'icon'
stereotype

'label'
stereotype

no
stereotype

enriches only the meaning of an existing notation. It allows extending and customizing the method. The possible uses of stereotypes are diverse.

Typically, stereotypes are *labeled* in the models with a name within matched guillemets (quotation symbols in French), such as «global», «PK», «include». An *iconic* presentation of stereotypes is also possible.

Some popular stereotypes are built-in – they are pre-defined in UML. The built-in stereotypes are likely to have icons readily available in a CASE tool. Most CASE tools provide a possibility to create new icons at the analyst's will. Figure 5.1 gives an example for a class stereotyped with an icon, with a label, and with no stereotype.

The restriction that a stereotype extends the semantics but not the structure of UML is quite insignificant. The bottom line in any object-oriented system is that *everything* in it *is an object* – a class is an object, and attribute is an object, a method is an object, etc. Hence, by stereotyping a class we can in effect create a new modeling element that introduces a new category of objects.

For example, in Sections 7.6.1 and 9.2.1, we show how stereotypes can be used to create new modeling techniques – window navigation diagrams and program navigation diagrams. When used that way, stereotypes extend UML for a particular purpose. That purpose has frequently to do with design modeling, rather than analysis modeling. The design models conform to an implementation platform. They must, therefore, work with modeling elements properly representing that platform.

A purposeful set of stereotypes to address a design modeling issue is called a *profile*. Future UML standards may include profiles for popular design targets, such as databases or CORBA (Common Object Request Broker Architecture).

5.1.2 Constraints

Stereotypes are frequently confused with constraints. Indeed, the distinction between these two concepts is blurred at times. A *stereotype* is frequently used to introduce a new *constraint* to the model – something meaningful to the modeler but not directly supported as a constraint in UML.

Any modeling element can have an associated constraint or can be stereotyped. Only simple constraints are shown in a model diagram. They are shown as text in curly brackets (or as a *note* symbol – see Section 5.1.3) and they are graphically and semantically bound to a modeling element. More elaborate constraints (too long to be shown on a graphical model) are stored in a CASE repository, typically as a word-processing document.

Example 5.1 (Telemarketing)

Refer to Example 4.7 (Section 4.2.1.2.3). Recall a part of Requirement 2 in Example 4.7 stating: 'All tickets are numbered. The numbers are unique across all tickets in a campaign.'

In the solution to Example 4.7 (Figure 4.4), we could not capture the above constraint (short of including `campaign_code` (with `ticket_number`) in `CampaignTicket` as a part of a composite primary key).

Our task is to model the constraint on the class diagram.

Figure 5.2 represents a simple extension to the class model to show the constraint. The constraint is *bound* to the class `CampaignTicket`. In any reports produced by the CASE tool, the constraint will be listed along with other properties of the class.

FIGURE 5.2
Constraint
for a class
(Telemarketing).

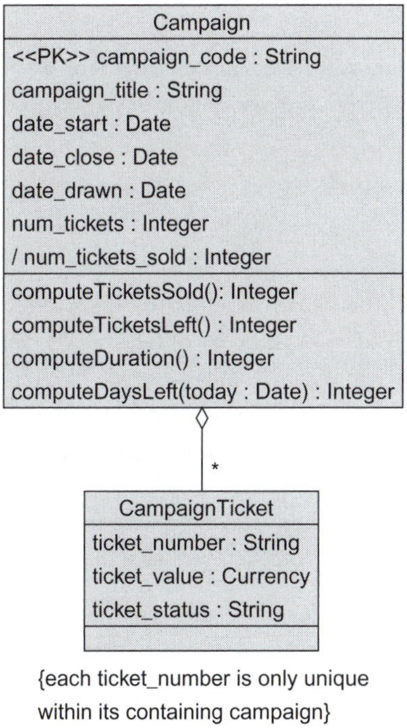

Campaign
<<PK>> campaign_code : String
campaign_title : String
date_start : Date
date_close : Date
date_drawn : Date
num_tickets : Integer
/ num_tickets_sold : Integer
computeTicketsSold(): Integer
computeTicketsLeft() : Integer
computeDuration() : Integer
computeDaysLeft(today : Date) : Integer

*

CampaignTicket
ticket_number : String
ticket_value : Currency
ticket_status : String

{each ticket_number is only unique
within its containing campaign}

FIGURE 5.3
Constraint on
associations
(Contact
Management).

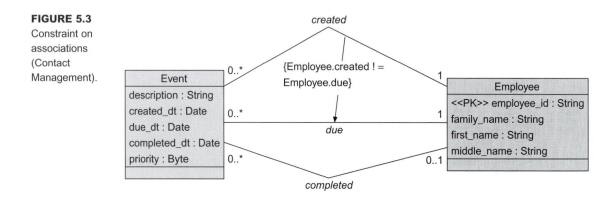

> ### Example 5.2 (Contact Management)
>
> Refer to Example 4.8 (Section 4.2.2.3). Assume that a new requirement has been discovered that the system does not handle: scheduling of events by employees to themselves. This means that an employee who created an event must not be the same as the employee who is due to perform that event.
>
> Extend a relevant part of the class model (Figure 4.5), to include the new requirement.

The solution to this example (Figure 5.3) results in a constraint on association lines. This is shown as a dashed dependency arrow from the association `created` to the association `due`. The constraint is *bound* to the arrow.

5.1.3 Notes and tags

When the constraint text is long or when a constraint is to be expressed on three or more graphical symbols, the UML concept of *note* can be used. Graphically, 'a note is a dog-eared rectangle with its upper-right corner bent over' (Rumbaugh *et al.*, 1999, p. 359).

The note symbol can contain text to express a constraint, but – in general – it can contain any information whatsoever. To ensure that the note is a constraint, it should be additionally stereotyped with the keyword «constraint».

Like notes, *tags* represent arbitrary textual information in the model, possibly a constraint. Like constraints, tags are written inside curly brackets and take the form

`tag = value`, e.g.:
`{analyst = Les, status = 2`[nd]` iteration}`.

Like stereotypes and constraints, few tags are predefined in UML. A typical use of tags is in providing project management information.

FIGURE 5.4
Constraint note and tag (Contact Management).

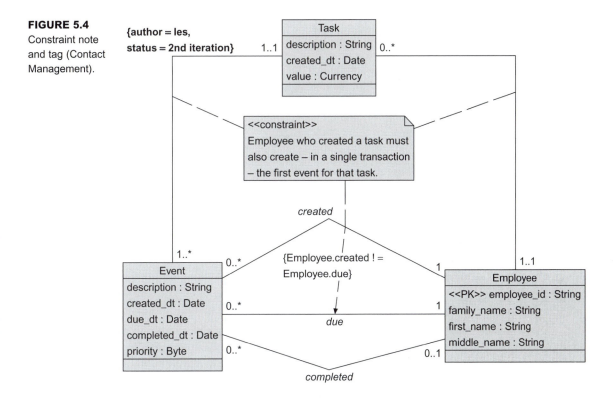

Example 5.3 (Contact Management)

Refer to Example 4.8 (Section 4.2.2.3) and to Example 5.2 above. Assume that a new requirement has been discovered: that an employee who created a task must also create – in the same transaction – the first event for that task.

Extend a relevant part of the class model (Figures 4.5 and 5.3), to include the new requirement. Use a note constraint. Also, show on the diagram that the analyst is Les and the diagram is in its second iteration.

Figure 5.4 shows the extended model. The project information is given in a tag in the left upper corner. A note was used to express the constraint on three associations. The note is stereotyped with the keyword «constraint» to confirm that the note is a constraint.

5.1.4 Visibility and encapsulation

Concepts of *visibility*, and the related notion of *encapsulation*, were initially explained in Sections 2.1.2.1.2 and 2.1.2.2.2. However, we only distinguished public and private visibility of attributes and operations. The third kind of UML pre-defined visibility – *protected* – has not been discussed.

FIGURE 5.5
Visibility notation in a CASE tool.

Visibility
🔒 private
🔑 protected
◇ public
🔒 private()
🔑 protected()
◇ public()

Similarly, we have not discussed various subtle influences between visibility and *inheritance*. Neither have we discussed a popular and convenient (some would say undesirable) technique of breaching an object's encapsulation with a *friend* operation.

The standard UML notation for visibility are the signs + (for public), # (for protected), and − (for private). The signs are placed in front of a property name. CASE tools frequently replace this rather dull notation. Figure 5.5 is an example of a more attractive notation.

5.1.4.1 Protected visibility

Having the *private properties* (attributes and operations) of a base class only accessible to objects of the base class is not always convenient. There are many situations in which objects of a derived class (a subclass of the base class) should be allowed to access the private properties of the base class.

Consider a class hierarchy where Person is the base class and Employee is a derived class. If Joe is an object of Employee, then − by definition of generalization − Joe must have access to (at least some) properties of Person (e.g. to the attribute date_of_birth).

In order to allow a derived class to have free access to properties of its base class, these (otherwise private) properties need to be defined in the base class as *protected*. (Recall from Section 2.1.2.1.2 that visibility applies between classes. If Betty is another object of Employee, she can access any property of Joe, whether public, protected or private.)

Such a scenario is true in most popular object-oriented programming environments, as exemplified by C++ and Java (Fowler and Scott, 2000). UML is not specific on this issue. It simply states: 'Visibility is part of the relationship between an element and the container that holds it. The container may be a package, a class, or some other namespace.' (Rumbaugh *et al.*, 1999, p. 497.)

Example 5.4 (Telemarketing)

Refer to Problem statement 4 (Section 2.3.4) and to Example 4.7 (Section 4.2.1.2.3). Problem statement 4 contains the following observation: 'The schemes include special *bonus campaigns* to reward supporters for bulk buying, for attracting new contributors, etc.' This observation has not been modeled yet.

Suppose that one of the bonus campaigns involves 'ticket books.' If a supporter buys the whole book of tickets, an extra ticket from the parent campaign is given free of charge.

Our task is to:

- Update the class model to include the class BonusCampaign.

- Change the visibility of attributes in Campaign (Figure 5.2) so that they can be visible to BonusCampaign with the exception of date_start. Make campaign_code and campaign_title visible to other classes in the model.

- Add the following operations to the class Campaign: computeTicketsSold, computeTicketsLeft, computeDuration, computeDaysLeft.

- Observe that the outside classes need not be interested in computeTicketsSold. They need only to know computeTicketsLeft. Also, computeDuration is only used by the operation Campaign.computeDaysLeft.

- The class BonusCampaign stores the attribute ticket_book_size and provides an access operation to it called bookSize.

Figure 5.6 shows a class model corresponding to the explanations above. The stereotype «protected» on the generalization line is explained in the next section. The operation computeDuration is private in Campaign. The operation computeTicketsSold is protected in Campaign. The remaining two operations in Campaign are public. The operation bookSize is specific to BonusCampaign and it is public.

5.1.4.2 *Visibility of inherited class properties*

As acknowledged by UML, the *visibility* applies to objects at various levels of granularity. By usual understanding, the visibility applies to *primitive objects* – attributes and operations. But, visibility can also be specified with regard to other 'containers'. This creates a whole tangle of overriding rules.

Consider, for example, a popular situation where the visibility is defined in the inheritance hierarchy at the level of the base class *and* at the level of properties of the base class. Let's say, a class B is a subclass of class A. The class A contains the mixture of attributes and operations – some public, others private, yet others protected. The question is: 'What is the visibility of inherited properties in the class B?'

An answer to this question depends on the visibility level given to the base class A when declaring it in the derived class B. The base class could have been defined public (class B: public A), or protected (class B: protected A), or private (class B: private A).

A typical resolution to the above scenario is as follows (Horton, 1997):

FIGURE 5.6
Visibility of class
properties
(Telemarketing).

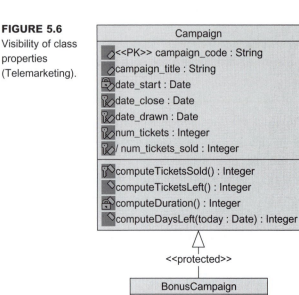

The **private** properties (attributes and operations) of the base class A are not visible to the class B objects, no matter how the base class A is defined in B.

■ If the base class A is defined as **public**, the visibility of inherited properties does not change in the derived class B (**public** are still public and **protected** are still protected).

■ If the base class A is defined as **protected**, the visibility of inherited **public** properties changes in the derived class B to **protected**.

■ If the base class A is defined as **private**, the visibility of inherited **public** and **protected** properties changes in the derived class B to **private**.

 Example 5.5 (Telemarketing)

Refer to Example 5.4 above. Assume that the stereotype «**protected**» on the generalization line means that Campaign is defined in BonusCampaign as **protected**:

`class BonusCampaign: protected Campaign`

Explain the visibility level of inherited class properties in the class BonusCampaign.

If the base class is defined as protected then its public properties will change to protected in the derived class. The protected properties will remain protected. The private properties will not be accessible to the derived class (they never are).

Figures 5.7 and 5.8 represent CASE repository windows that show, respectively, the attributes and operations of BonusCampaign after inheritance has taken effect. To be

FIGURE 5.7
Inherited
attributes in
`BonusCampaign`
(Telemarketing).

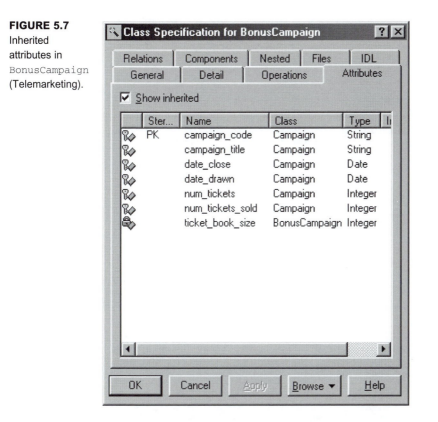

precise, the class in Figures 5.7 and 5.8 should also contain the attribute `date_start` and the operation `computeDuration()` inherited from `Campaign`. These properties should be modeled as `private` in `BonusCampaign`. (Note that `private` properties of the base class remain `private` to the base and are inaccessible to operations of the derived class. However, the definition of a `private` property is inherited in the usual way.)

5.1.4.3 *Friend*

There may be circumstances in which a function (or even an entire class) should be given direct access to the properties of another class, independently of the visibility levels of these properties. Such a situation arises when two classes are intertwined and operations in one class depend on properties of another class. A typical example may be with two classes `Book` and `BookShelf` and an operation in `Book` called `putOnBookShelf`.

One solution to solve situations like the one above is to declare the operation `putOnBookShelf` a *friend* within the class `BookShelf` – something like: `friend void Book::putOnBookShelf()`.

A friend can be another class or an operation of another class. Friendship is not reciprocal. A class that makes another class a friend may not be a friend of that class.

A friend (operation or class) is declared *within* the class that grants the friendship. However, a friend operation is not a property of the class, so the visibility attributes do not apply. This

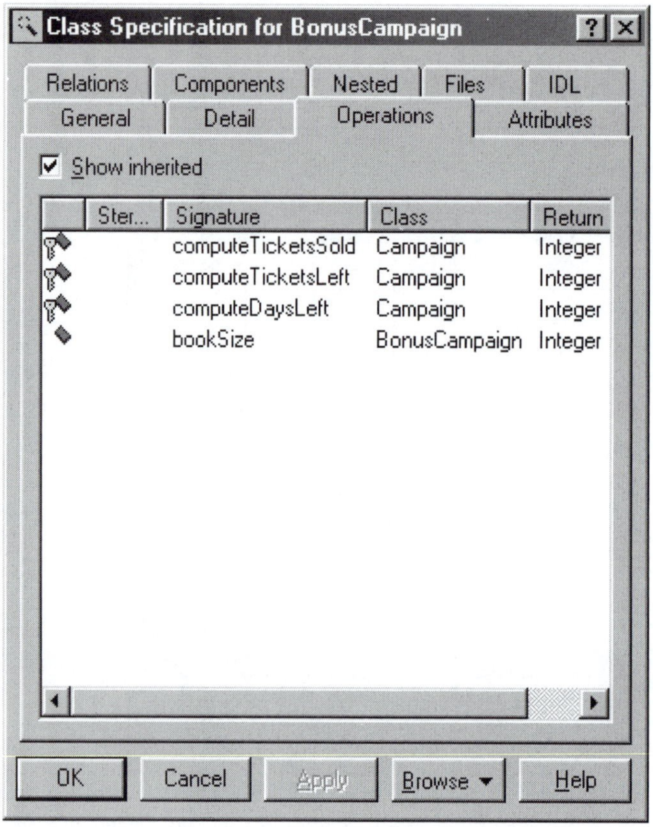

FIGURE 5.8 Inherited operations in `BonusCampaign` (Telemarketing).

also means that in the definition of a friend we cannot reference attributes of the class just by their names – they each have to be qualified by the class name (just as if a friend was a normal external operation).

In UML, a friendship is shown as a dashed *dependency relationship* from a friend class or operation to the class that granted the friendship. The stereotype «`friend`» is bound to the dependency arrow. Admittedly, the UML notation does not fully recognize and support the friend's semantics.

Example 5.6 (Telemarketing)

Refer to Example 4.7 (Section 4.2.1.2.3). Consider the relationship between the classes `Campaign` and `CallScheduled`.

Objects of the class `CallScheduled` are very active and they need special privileges when executing their operations. In particular, they contain an operation called `getTicketsLeft` that establishes if there are any tickets left so that

> a supporter's order can be satisfied. It is important that this operation has direct access to the properties of Campaign (such as num_tickets and num_tickets_sold).
>
> Our task is to declare the operation getTicketsLeft and make it a friend of Campaign.

The UML solution to our example is shown in Figure 5.9. The operation getTickets-Left is shown within CallScheduled. We remind you that in a programming language used for the implementation, getTicketsLeft will be declared a friend within Campaign (because Campaign decides who is its friend), and then fully defined in CallScheduled.

The *dependency relationship* captures the fact that Campaign granted some friendship status to CallScheduled. The notation is not explicit on whether the friendship is for the entire class or for some operations of the class (and for which operations).

5.1.5 Derived information

Derived information is a kind of constraint that applies (most frequently) to an attribute or an association. The derived information is computed from other model elements. Strictly speaking, the derived information is redundant – it can be computed as needed.

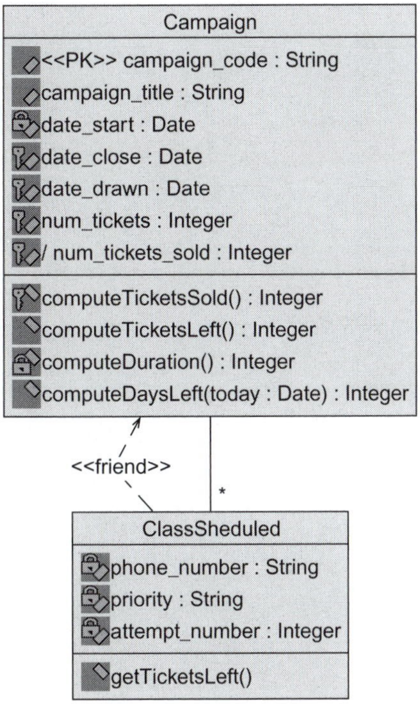

FIGURE 5.9
Friend
(Telemarketing).

Campaign

◇<<PK>> campaign_code : String
◇campaign_title : String
◇date_start : Date
◇date_close : Date
◇date_drawn : Date
◇num_tickets : Integer
◇/ num_tickets_sold : Integer

computeTicketsSold() : Integer
computeTicketsLeft() : Integer
computeDuration() : Integer
computeDaysLeft(today : Date) : Integer

<<friend>>

*

ClassSheduled

phone_number : String
priority : String
attempt_number : Integer

getTicketsLeft()

Although derived information does not enrich the semantics of an *analysis model*, it can make the model more readable (because the fact that something can be computed is explicit in the model). The decision to show or not to show the derived information in an analysis model is quite arbitrary, as long as it is taken consistently across the entire model.

The knowledge of derived information is more important in *design models* where optimization of access to information needs to be considered. In design models, a decision may also be taken if some derived information is to be stored (after the derivation) or is to be dynamically computed every time it is needed. This is not a new feature – it was known in old-style network databases under the terms of *actual* (i.e. stored) and *virtual* data.

The UML notation for derived information is a slash (/) in front of the name of the derived attribute or association.

5.1.5.1 Derived attribute

Although without explanation, we used derived attributes in passing in a couple of example diagrams. For instance, num_tickets_sold in Figure 5.2 is a derived attribute. An extended diagram for that figure is shown in Figure 5.10 below.

The value of the attribute num_tickets_sold is computed by the operation computeTicketsSold. The operation follows the aggregation links to tickets in a campaign and checks each ticket_status. If ticket_status is 'sold' then it is added

FIGURE 5.10
Derived attribute
(Telemarketing).

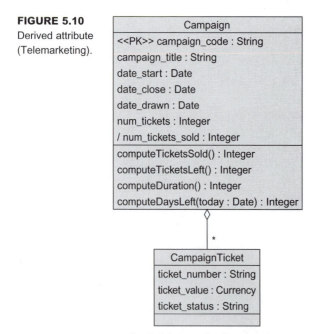

{each ticket_number is only unique
within its containing campaign}

to the count of sold tickets. When all tickets are processed, the current value of `num_tickets_sold` has been derived.

5.1.5.2 *Derived association*

The derived association is a more controversial topic. In a typical scenario, a derived association happens between three classes already connected by two associations and with no third association that would close the loop. The third association is frequently needed for the model to be semantically correct (this is known as the *loop commutativity*). When not explicitly modeled, the third association can be derived from the other two associations.

Example 5.7 (OnLine Shopping)

Refer to the OnLine Shopping tutorial in Chapter 2 and to the class diagram in Figure 2.32 (Section 2.2.4.6). Consider a part of the model with classes `Customer`, `Order` and `Invoice`.

Is it possible to introduce a derived association to the model? If so, add it to the diagram.

Yes, it is possible to add a derived association between classes `Customer` and `Invoice`. It is called `/CustInv` in Figure 5.11 below. The association is derived due to a slightly unusual business rule that the association multiplicity between `Order` and `Invoice` is one-to-one.

FIGURE 5.11
Derived
association
(Telemarketing).

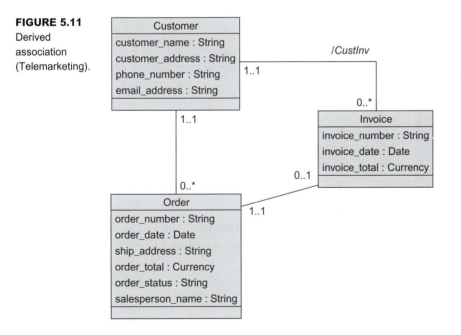

The derived association has not introduced any new information. We could always assign a customer to an invoice by finding out a single order for each invoice, and then a single customer for each order.

5.1.6 Qualified association

The concept of a *qualified association* is a tough and controversial proposition. Some modelers like it; others hate it. Arguably, one can construct complete and sufficiently expressive class models without qualified associations. However, if qualified associations are used, they should be used consistently across the board.

A qualified association has an attribute compartment (a *qualifier*) on one end of a binary association (an association can be qualified on both ends but this is rare). The compartment contains one or more attributes that can serve as an index key for traversing the association from the *qualified class* via the qualifier to the *target class* on the opposite association end.

For example, an association between `Flight` and `Passenger` is many-to-many. However, when the class `Flight` is qualified by attributes `seat_number` and `departure`, the multiplicity is reduced to one-to-one (Figure 5.12). The composite index key introduced by the qualifier (`flight_number` + `seat_number` + `departure`) can only be linked to zero or one `Passenger` object.

FIGURE 5.12
Qualified
association.

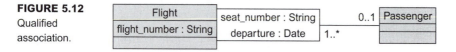

In the forward traversal, the association multiplicity represents a number of target objects related by the composite key (qualified object + qualifier value). In the reverse traversal, the multiplicity describes a number of objects identified by the composite key (qualified object + qualifier value) and related to each target object (Rumbaugh *et al.*, 1999).

The uniqueness introduced by a qualifier is frequently important semantic information that cannot be captured efficiently by other means (such as constraints or an inclusion of additional attributes in the target class). In general, it is not desirable to duplicate a qualifier attribute in the target class.

Example 5.8 (OnLine Shopping)

Refer to the OnLine Shopping tutorial in Chapter 2 and to the class diagram in Figure 2.32 (Section 2.2.4.6). Consider a part of the model with classes `Order` and `Computer`.

Change the association between `Order` and `Computer` to a qualified association to explicitly capture the constraint: 'a single order item per computer on order.'

FIGURE 5.13
Qualified
association
(OnLine
Shopping).

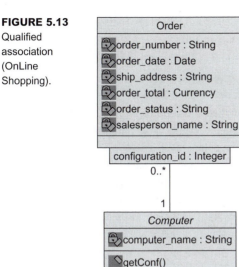

Recall that a computer is ordered after being configured by a customer. A unique number can identify each such configuration. A standard configuration can also be granted a unique configuration number. Hence, `configuration_number` is a qualifier for `Order`. The composite key (`order_number` + `configuration_number`) links to a single `Computer` object (Figure 5.13).

5.1.7 Association class versus reified class

In Section 2.1.3.4 we explained and exemplified an *association class* – an association that is also a class. An association class is typically used if there is a many-to-many association between two classes and each association instance (a *link*) has its own attribute values. To be able to store these attribute values we need a class – an association class.

Simple as it seems, the concept of association class carries a tricky constraint. Consider an association class *C* between the classes *A* and *B*. The constraint is that there can only be one instance of *C* for each pair of linked instances of *A* and *B*.

If such a constraint is not acceptable then the modeler has to *reify* the association by replacing the class *C* with an ordinary class *D* (Rumbaugh *et al.*, 1999). The *reified class D* would have two binary associations to *A* and *B*. The class *D* is independent of classes *A* and *B*. Each instance of *D* has its own identity so that multiple instances of it can be created to link to the same instances of *A* and *B*, if required.

5.1.7.1 Example statement for employee database

To explain the difference between an association class and a reified class we need a targeted example. The example relates to the recording of current and previous salaries of employees.

Indeed, the distinction between an association class and reified class arises most frequently in the context of modeling temporal (historical) information.

Example statement (Employee Database)

Each employee in an organization is assigned a unique `emp_id`. The name of the employee is maintained and consists of the last name, first name and middle initial.

Each employee is employed at a certain salary level. There is a salary range for each level, i.e. the minimum and maximum salary. The salary ranges for a level never change. If there is a need to change the minimum or maximum salary, a new salary level is created. The start and end dates, for each salary level, are also kept.

Previous salaries of each employee are kept, including the start date and finish date at each level. Any changes of the employee's salary within the same level are also recorded.

5.1.7.2 Model with association class

Objects of an association class – like objects of any ordinary class – are assigned their OIDs when instantiated (Section 2.1.1.3). Apart from system-generated OIDs, objects can also be identified by their attribute values. In case of an association class, an object takes its identity from the attributes that designate the associated classes (Section 2.1.2.1.1). Other attribute values do not contribute to an object's identification.

Example 5.9 (Employee Database)

Refer to the Employee Database Example statement above. Draw a class model for it. Use an association class.

The Example statement creates a number of challenges. We know that we need to have a class to store employee details (`Employee`) and a class to store information about salary levels (`SalaryLevel`). The challenge is in modeling historical and current assignments of salaries to employees. At first it may seem natural to use an association class `SalaryHistoryAssociation`.

Figure 5.14 presents a class model with the association class `SalaryHistoryAssociation`. The solution is deficient. Objects of `SalaryHistoryAssociation` derive their identity from the composite key created from the references to the primary keys of classes `Employee` and `SalaryLevel` (i.e. `emp_id` and `level_id`).

No two `SalaryHistoryAssociation` objects can have the same composite key (the same links to `Employee` and `SalaryLevel`). This also means that the design in Figure 5.14

FIGURE 5.14
Inadequate use
of association
class (Employee
Database).

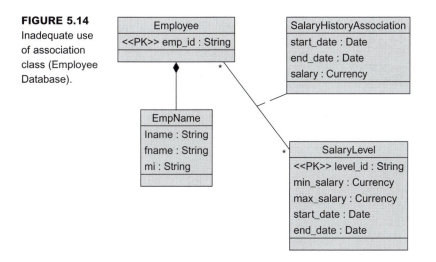

will not accommodate the requirement that 'any changes of the employee's salary within the same level are also recorded.' The solution in Figure 5.14 cannot be sustained – a better model is needed.

5.1.7.3 Model with reified class

An association class cannot have duplicates among its object references to the associated classes. A reified class is independent from the associated classes and does not place such a restriction. The primary key of a reified class does not use attributes that designate related classes.

Example 5.10 (Employee Database)

Refer to the Employee Database Example statement (Section 5.1.7.1). Draw a class model for it. Use a reified class.

Figure 5.15 demonstrates a class model that uses the reified class `SalaryHistoryReified`. The class does not have an explicitly marked primary key. We can guess, however, that the key will consist of `emp_id` and `seq_num`. The attribute `seq_num` stores the sequential number of salary changes for an employee. Every object of `SalaryHistoryReified` belongs to a single `Employee` object and is linked to a single `SalaryLevel` object. The model can now capture employee's salary changes within the same salary level.

Note that the model in Figure 5.15 would need to be further improved. In particular, it is most likely that the assumption that 'the salary ranges for a level never change' would need to be relaxed.

FIGURE 5.15
Better solution
with reified class
(Employee
Database).

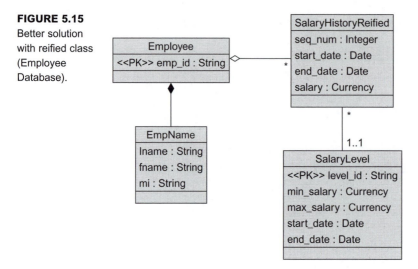

5.2 Class layers

Software developers know that the difficulty of producing a small system cannot be compared with the difficulty of delivering a large-scale solution. A small object system is often easy to understand, implement and deploy. A large object solution is dominated by complex *networks* of objects responding to random events that invoke a mesh of interrelated operations (methods). Without a clear architectural design and rigorous processes, large software projects are likely to fail.

A well-known cognitive psychology principle – *the 7 ± 2 rule* – states that the short-term memory of a human brain can *simultaneously* handle up to nine (7 + 2) things (graphical elements, ideas, concepts, etc.). The lower bound of five (7 − 2) indicates that fewer than five things constitute a trivial problem.

The rules of cognitive psychology do not change the fact that we have to produce large systems, and large systems are complex. Much of this complexity is human-generated, rather than essential (Section 1.1.1).

The main culprit is the system modeling that allows for unrestricted communication between objects. Objects, in such systems, form *networks* – webs of cross-referenced objects. Message passing follows the references. Down-calls and up-calls are possible. In networks, the number of communication paths between objects grows exponentially with the addition of new objects. As noted by Szyperski '. . . object references introduce linkage across arbitrary abstraction domains. Proper layering of system architectures thus lies somewhere between the challenging and impossible.' (Szyperski, 1998, p. 57.)

Successful systems are organized in hierarchies – the network structures are restricted and carefully controlled. *Hierarchies* reduce the complexity from exponential to polynomial. They introduce layers of objects and constrain intercommunication between layers. In a typical hierarchy, only objects in adjacent layers communicate directly. The complexity is hidden and divided in separate layers.

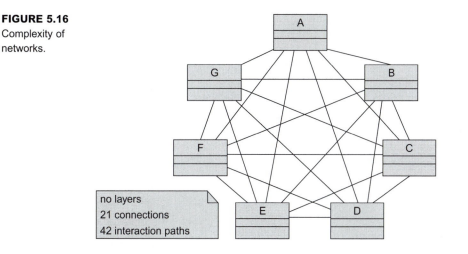

FIGURE 5.16
Complexity of networks.

no layers
21 connections
42 interaction paths

5.2.1 Complexity of networks

To talk about the *complexity* of object systems we need to agree on a measurement. How do we measure complexity? Complexity has different kinds and shapes. A simple, but very illustrative, measurement is the number of connections between classes. We define a *connection* as the existence of a persistent or transient link between classes (Section 2.1.1.3).

Each connection would typically allow for a both-directional interaction between classes, i.e. from *A* to *B* and *B* to *A*. Figure 5.16 illustrates the complexity of a network of seven classes. There are $n(n-1)/2$ possible connections between *n* classes. This formula, applied to seven classes, gives us 21 connections (and 42 interaction paths).

Note that we measure the complexity with regard to the number of classes, not objects. In programs, the objects – not the classes – send messages to other objects, of the same or different class. This introduces additional difficulty to the programmer responsible for delivering the application logic and managing the program's variables and other data structures. The main challenge, however, is not an individual program's complexity but the complexity of the entire system of programs.

An object can only send a message to another object if there is a persistent or transient link between them. The transient links are resolved within a single program invocation and, therefore, they do not add to the complexity of the whole system. The persistent links, on the other hand, exist only if there is a connection (e.g. association) defined in the class model. The classes can be shared and reused across many programs.

5.2.2 Complexity of hierarchies

The solution to complexity control lies in reducing the network structures through grouping of classes into *class hierarchies*. This way, classes can form naturally into layers that emphasize a

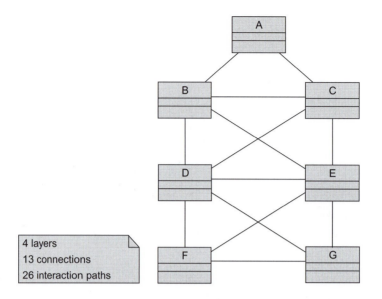

FIGURE 5.17
Complexity of
hierarchies.

hierarchical decomposition between layers while allowing for network-like interactions within the layers.

The hierarchical layering offers reductions in complexity by restricting the number of potential interaction paths between classes. The reduction is achieved by stratifying classes into layers and allowing only for direct class interactions within a layer and between adjacent layers.

Figure 5.17 shows the complexity of a seven-class hierarchy when the classes are grouped into four layers. In comparison with the network structure in Figure 5.16, the complexity is reduced from 42 to 26 interaction paths.

The example in Figure 5.17 is contrived to correspond to the four layers of our *B C D E* approach discussed in Section 6.1.3.2. In a hierarchical structure with a large number of classes the number of *inter-layer connections* may be troublesome. To reduce the complexity of inter-layer connections, the inter-layer communication may be channeled through a few dedicated *mediator classes*. This would further reduce the overall system's complexity.

5.2.3 Package

UML provides a notion of *package* to represent a group of classes (or other modeling elements, e.g. use cases) (Rumbaugh *et al.*, 1999). Packages serve to partition the logical model of an application program. They are clusters of highly related classes that are themselves cohesive, but are loosely coupled relative to other such clusters (Lakos, 1996).

Packages can be *nested*. This allows decomposing large systems into subsystems, modules, etc. For example, a package stereotyped as «system» could contain packages stereotyped as «subsystem». An outer package has access to any classes directly contained in its nested packages.

FIGURE 5.18
Packages and
dependencies.

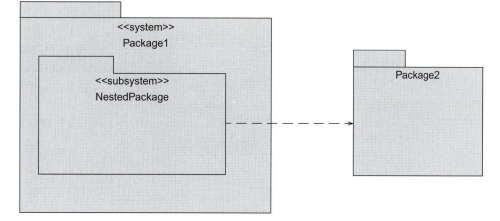

A class can only be owned by one package. This does not inhibit the class from appearing in other packages or from communicating with classes in other packages. By declaring a class within a package to be private, protected, or public, we can control the communication and dependencies between classes in different packages (Section 5.1.4).

5.2.3.1 Package notation

A package is shown as a folder icon (Figure 5.18). A nested package is drawn inside its outer package. Each package would have its own class diagram defining all classes owned by the package.

Packages can be related with two kinds of relationships: *generalization* and *dependency*. The relationship in Figure 5.18 is a dependency. It states that NestedPackage depends on Package2. The exact nature of dependency is not specified except for saying that changes to Package2 may require changes in NestedPackage. Probably the most frequent dependency between packages is due to a class in one package sending a message to a class in another package.

UML specifies a number of different categories of the dependency relationship (e.g. a *usage* dependency, *access* dependency, *visibility* dependency). We found that determining the category of dependency is not particularly helpful in the analysis diagrams. The true nature of each dependency needs to be entered as a descriptive constraint in the CASE repository for use in the design models.

Note that a generalization between packages implies also a dependency. The dependency is from a subtype package to the supertype package. Changes in the supertype package affect the subtype package.

5.2.3.2 Package diagram

The concept of a package diagram as such does not exist in UML, but it is nevertheless a convenient term to use. Packages are created in a class diagram or in a use case diagram. In the first case, a package diagram models a state view of the system. In the second case, a behavioral

FIGURE 5.19
Packages
(University
Enrolment).

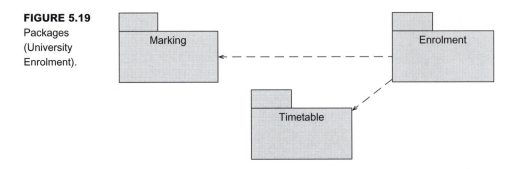

view of the system. Once created, the assignment of classes (or use cases) to a package is provided in a separate class diagram (or use case diagram).

Without doubt, a package diagram for a state view describes the main architectural framework for the system. A behavioral package diagram serves only as a description for a high-level functional structure (Conallen, 2000). The state package diagram assists in managing the size and complexity of the system. It is also essential as an access and configuration management mechanism to permit collaboration between developers.

Example 5.10 (University Enrolment)

A closer look at the University Enrolment application reveals that the system has to be 'aware' of the class timetable and of the students' grades in order to validate the enrolment of students to classes.

We do not know if 'timetabling' and 'marking' exist as separate software modules into which our enrolment system can be plugged. If not, the enrolment system will have to include such modules.

Our task in this example is to provide a package model for University Enrolment.

Figure 5.19 shows the three packages and dependency relationships between them. `Enrolment` depends on `Marking` and `Timetable`.

5.2.4 BCE approach

The *Boundary–Control–Entity* (BCE) is an approach to object modeling based on a three-way factoring of classes. The BCE approach corresponds loosely to a well-known *Model–View–Controller* (MVC) approach (Collins, 1995; Buschmann *et al.,* 1996; Olsen, 1998). UML predefines three stereotypes on a class: boundary, control and entity (Rumbaugh *et al.,* 1999). Hence, the acronym BCE is our preference.

A *boundary class* describes objects that represent the interface between an actor and the system. It captures a portion of the system's state and presents it to the user in the form of a

FIGURE 5.20
Object
connections
in the BCE
package
hierarchy.

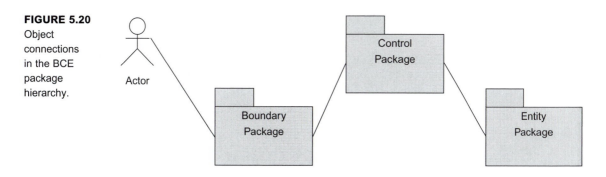

visual display or a sound effect. Boundary objects often *persist* beyond a single execution of the program.

A *control class* describes objects that intercept user input events and control the execution of a business process. A control class represents actions and activities of a use case. Control objects frequently do not persist beyond the program's execution.

An *entity class* describes objects that represent the semantics of entities in an application domain. It corresponds to a data structure in the system's database. Entity objects always persist beyond the program's execution and participate in many use cases.

As shown in Figure 5.20, in a well-designed hierarchy of packages, an actor can interact only with objects in BoundaryPackage, objects in EntityPackage can interact only with objects of ControlPackage, and objects in ControlPackage can interact with any object (see Conallen, 2000).

Boundary classes correspond to the classes present in the GUI design. Boundary objects are dependent on Entity objects (via some Control objects). An Entity object broadcasts changes to its state so that the Boundary object can update the GUI display. A region of the boundary (screen) that is temporarily out of sync with its entity is said to be *damaged*.

Control objects handle the interactions between user-generated events and the affected Entity and Boundary objects. In particular, each Boundary object that permits interaction would have an associated Control object. Because of this, some architectures (e.g. Microsoft Foundation Classes (MFC)) combine the two functions into a single class.

The BCE approach is 'the way of thinking' that reflects good software engineering practice. As such, it should be a part of any object application development method, whether or not enforced by the underlying implementation platform.

The main advantage of BCE is in grouping classes into hierarchical layers. This improves the model's understandability and reduces its complexity. It also reduces the risk of creating classes that do too much; *monster classes* that take control over the entire system functionality. In a good object-oriented design, the intelligence of the system is uniformly distributed across all classes.

An additional advantage of the BCE approach is its alignment with the *three-tier client/server* model that separates data management (Entity) from presentation (Boundary) via the application logic middle-tier (Control).

We emphasize, however, that the `EntityPackage` describes the entity classes in the client program memory, not in the server database. The server database is likely not to even be object-oriented, but relational. The persistent business objects are then stored as records of relational tables. To handle the mapping from the entity classes to a relational storage, and to hold other relevant information about the database structures, a separate layer of classes is required. This layer can be called the `DatabasePackage` (Section 6.1.3.2).

5.3 Advanced generalization and inheritance modeling

There are three main kinds of relationship between classes: association, aggregation and generalization. A careful reader would have noticed that we have devalued the usefulness of generalization in analysis models. *Generalization* is a useful and powerful concept but it can also create many problems due to the intricate mechanisms of *inheritance*, in particular in large software projects.

The terms of generalization and inheritance are related but not the same. It is important to know the difference. The price for imprecision is a resulting lack of understanding – frequently evident in the literature. Indeed, unless the difference is acknowledged, it is easy to engage in irrational and groundless discussions about the pros and cons of generalization and inheritance.

Generalization is a semantic relationship between classes. It states that the *interface* of the subclass must include all (public and protected) properties of the superclass. *Inheritance* is 'the mechanism by which more specific elements incorporate structure and behavior defined by more general elements' (Rumbaugh *et al.*, 1999).

5.3.1 Generalization and substitutability

From a semantic modeling perspective, *generalization* introduces additional classes, categorizes them into generic and more specific classes and establishes superclass–subclass relationships in the model. Although generalization introduces new classes, it can reduce the overall number of *association* and *aggregation* relationships in the model.

Based on the desired semantics, an association or aggregation from a class can link to the most generic class in the generalization hierarchy (see the class diagrams in Figures 2.31 and 4.7). Since a subclass can be *substituted* for its generic class, the objects of the subclass have all association and aggregation relationships of the superclass. This allows capturing the same model semantics with the smaller number of association/aggregation relationships. In a good model, the trade-off between the depth of generalization and the consequent reduction in association/aggregation relationships is properly balanced.

When used considerately, generalization improves the expressiveness, understandability and abstraction of system models. The benefits of generalization arise from the *substitutability* principle – a subclass object can be used in place of a superclass object in any part of the code where the superclass object is accessed. However, and unfortunately, the inheritance mechanism may be used in a way that defeats the benefits of the substitutability principle.

5.3.2 Inheritance versus encapsulation

Encapsulation demands that an object's attributes are only accessible through the operations in the object's interface. If enforced, the encapsulation leads to a high level of data independence so that future changes to encapsulated data structures do not necessitate modification of existing programs. But is this notion of encapsulation enforceable in applications?

The reality is that encapsulation is orthogonal to inheritance and query capabilities and it has to be traded-off against these two features. In practice, it is impossible to declare all data as private.

The *inheritance* compromises encapsulation by allowing subclasses to directly access *protected attributes*. Computations spanning objects belonging to different classes may require that different classes be *friends* of each other, thus further infringing encapsulation. Occasionally, *static attributes*, global to all objects of the class, have to be used. And, one has to realize that encapsulation refers to the notion of the class, not the object – in most object programming environments (with the exception of Smalltalk) an object cannot hide anything from another object of the same class.

Finally, users accessing databases by means of SQL or an SQL-like *ad-hoc query language* raise justified expectations that they want to refer directly to attributes in the queries, rather than to be forced to work with some data access methods that make query formulations more difficult and more error-prone. This requirement is particularly strong in data warehouse applications with OnLine Analytical Processing (OLAP) queries.

Applications should be designed so that they achieve the desired level of encapsulation, balanced against inheritance, ad-hoc querying, and computational requirements.

5.3.3 Interface inheritance

When generalization is used with the aim of substitutability then it is synonymous with the notion of *interface inheritance* (*subtyping, type inheritance*). This is a 'harmless' form of inheritance. A subclass inherits attribute types and operation signatures (operation names plus formal arguments). A subclass is said to *support* a superclass interface. The implementation of inherited operations is deferred until later.

The *interfaces* are normally declared through an *abstract class*. We can say – with one proviso – that an interface is an abstract class. The proviso is that an abstract class can provide partial implementations for some operations whereas a pure interface defers the definition of all operations.

FIGURE 5.21
Interface
inheritance.

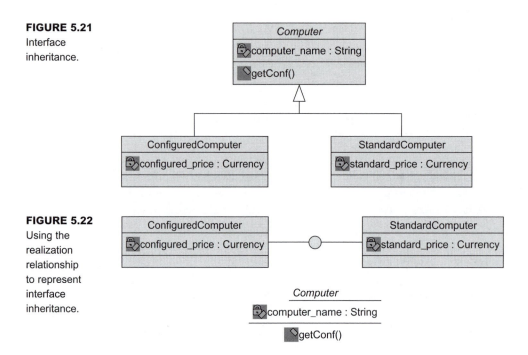

FIGURE 5.22
Using the
realization
relationship
to represent
interface
inheritance.

Figure 5.21 is an excerpt from the class model for Telemarketing that demonstrates the interface inheritance. `Computer` is an abstract class. No objects of that class can be instantiated. The operation `getConf()` has two different implementations – one in `ConfiguredComputer`, the other in `StandardComputer`.

Figure 5.22 is an alternative way of representing the interface inheritance using a 'lollypop' symbol to indicate the supported interface. The 'lollypop' relationship from a subclass (concrete class) to an abstract class is formally called the *realization relationship*.

5.3.4 Implementation inheritance

As we observed in the previous section, generalization can be used to imply *substitutability* and it is then realized by an *interface inheritance*. However, generalization can also be used (deliberately or not) to imply *code reuse* and it is then realized by an *implementation inheritance*. This is a very powerful, sometimes dangerously powerful, interpretation of generalization. It is also the 'default' interpretation of generalization.

Implementation inheritance – called also *subclassing, code inheritance* or *class inheritance* – combines the superclass properties in the subclasses and allows *overriding* them with new implementations, when necessary. *Overriding* can mean the inclusion (call) of a superclass method in the subclass method and extending it with new functionality. It can also mean a complete replacement of the superclass method by the subclass method. Implementation inheritance allows sharing of property descriptions, *code reuse*, and *polymorphism*.

When modeling with generalization we have to be clear which kind of inheritance is implied. Interface inheritance is safe to use as it only involves the inheritance of contract fragments – operation signatures. Implementation inheritance involves the inheritance of code – the inheritance of implementation fragments (Szyperski, 1998; Harmon and Watson, 1998). If not carefully controlled and restrained, implementation inheritance can bring more harm than good. The pros and cons of implementation inheritance are discussed next.

5.3.4.1 *Proper use of implementation inheritance – extension inheritance*

UML is quite specific about the alignment of inheritance with generalization and the proper use of implementation inheritance (Rumbaugh *et al.*, 1999). The only proper use of inheritance is as an incremental definition of a class. A subclass has more properties (attributes and/or methods) than its superclass. A subclass *is-a-kind-of* superclass. This is known also as an *extension inheritance*.

The example in Figure 2.17 (repeated here for convenience as Figure 5.23) represents an extension inheritance. Any Employee object *is-a-kind-of* Person object. This does not mean that an Employee object is simultaneously the instance of two classes: Person and Employee (see the discussion about multiple classification in Section 2.1.5.2.2). An Employee object is the instance of the class Employee.

Person in Figure 5.23 is not an abstract class. There will be some Person objects that are just that (i.e. that are not an Employee).

In extension inheritance, the *overriding* of properties should be used with care. It should only be allowed to make properties more specific (e.g. to constrain values or to make implementations of operations more efficient), not to change the meaning of a property. If overriding changed the meaning of a property then a subclass object could no longer be substituted for the superclass object.

FIGURE 5.23
Extension
inheritance.

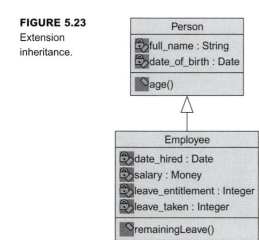

FIGURE 5.24
Restriction
inheritance.

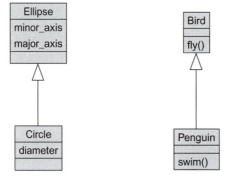

5.3.4.2 Problematic use of implementation inheritance – restriction inheritance

In extension inheritance, the definition of a subclass is extended with new properties. But it is also possible to use inheritance as a restriction mechanism whereby some of the inherited properties are suppressed (overridden) in the subclass. Such inheritance is called *restriction inheritance* (Rumbaugh *et al.*, 1991).

Figure 5.24 demonstrates two examples of restriction inheritance. Because the inheritance cannot be selectively stopped, the class `Circle` would inherit `minor_axis` and `major_axis` from `Ellipse` and would have to replace them with the attribute `diameter`. Similarly, `Penguin` would inherit the flying capability (the operation `fly`) from `Bird` and would have to replace it with the operation `swim` (perhaps flying under a negative altitude could make up for swimming).

Restriction inheritance is problematic. From a generalization point of view, a subclass does not include all properties of the superclass. A superclass object can still be substituted by a subclass object provided that whoever is using the object is aware of the overridden (suppressed) properties.

In restriction inheritance, the properties of one class are used (by inheritance) to implement another class. If overriding is not extensive, restriction inheritance can be of benefit. In general, however, restriction inheritance gives rise to maintenance problems.

5.3.4.3 Improper use of implementation inheritance – convenience inheritance

Inheritance that is not an extension or restriction inheritance is 'bad news' in system modeling. Such an inheritance can occur when two or more classes have similar implementations, but there is no taxonomic relationship between the concepts represented by the classes. One class is selected arbitrarily as an ancestor of the others. This is called *convenience inheritance* (Maciaszek *et al.*, 1996a; Rumbaugh *et al.*, 1991).

Figure 5.25 provides two examples of convenience inheritance. The class `LineSegment` is defined as a subclass of the class `Point`. Clearly, a line segment is not a point and therefore

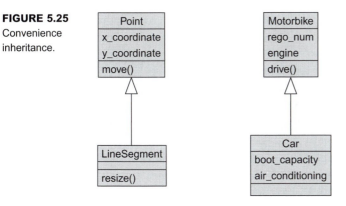

FIGURE 5.25
Convenience
inheritance.

the generalization as defined earlier does not apply. However, inheritance can be used. Indeed, for the class `Point` we can define attributes like `x_coordinate` and `y_coordinate` and an operation `Move`. The class `LineSegment` would inherit these properties and would define an additional operation `Resize`. The operation `Move` needs to be overridden. Similarly, in the second example, `Car` inherits properties of `Bike` and adds some new ones.

Convenience inheritance is improper. It is semantically incorrect. It leads to extensive overriding. The substitution principle is normally invalid because the objects are not of a similar type (`LineSegment` is not a `Point`; `Car` is not a `Motorbike`).

In practice, and regrettably, developers use convenience inheritance often because many object programming environments encourage indiscriminate use of implementation inheritance. Many languages are equipped with a myriad of tools for 'power programming' with inheritance while support for other object features (most notably aggregation) is missing.

5.3.4.4 *The evils of implementation inheritance*

The previous discussion does not mean that if we forbid convenience inheritance then we are fine. Implementation inheritance is a risky business by many standards. If not properly controlled and managed, inheritance can be overused and abused and can create the problems that it is supposed to be solving in the first place. This is particularly true in the development of large systems with hundreds of classes and thousands of objects, with dynamically changing states of objects, and with evolving class structures (such as in typical business applications).

The main risk factors are related to the following troublesome concepts (Szyperski, 1998):

- Fragile base class
- Overriding and callbacks
- Multiple implementation inheritance

5.3.4.4.1 Fragile base class

The *fragile base class* (superclass) problem is about making the subclasses valid and operational while allowing the evolution of the *implementation* of their superclass (or superclasses, if the multiple inheritance applies). This is a serious problem in any case, but particularly when we consider that the superclasses may be obtained from external sources outside the control of the system development team.

Consider a situation that the superclasses from which your application inherits form part of an operating system, a database system or a GUI interface. If you buy an object database system for your application development, you really buy a class library to implement typical database functions, such as object persistence, transaction management, concurrency, recovery, etc. If your classes inherit from that class library, the impact of new versions of the object database system on your application is unpredictable (and certainly so if no precautions are taken when designing the inheritance model for the application).

The problem of the fragile base class is difficult to harness short of declaring the public interfaces immutable or, at least, short of avoiding the implementation inheritance from the superclasses outside our control. Changes to the implementation of a superclass (for which we might not even have the source code) will have a largely unpredictable effect on the subclasses in the application system. This is true even if the superclass interface remains unchanged. The situation can be further aggravated if the changes also affect interfaces. Some examples are (Szyperski, 1998):

- Changing the signature of a method.
- Splitting the method into two or more new methods.
- Joining existing methods into a larger method.

The bottom line is that to harness the fragile base class problem the developers designing a superclass should know beforehand how people are going to be reusing that superclass now and in the future. This is, of course, impossible without a crystal ball. As a bumper sticker joke says, 'madness is inherited, you get it from your children' (Gray, 1994). In Section 5.4, we will discuss some alternative object development methods that are not based on inheritance yet deliver the expected object functionality.

5.3.4.4.2 Overriding and callbacks

Implementation inheritance allows for selective overriding of inherited code. There are five techniques in which a subclass method can reuse code from its superclass:

1. The subclass can inherit the method interface and implementation and introduce no changes to the implementation.
2. The subclass can inherit the code and include it (call it) in its own method with the same signature.
3. The subclass can inherit the code and then completely override it with a new implementation with the same signature.
4. The subclass can inherit code that is empty (i.e. the method declaration is empty) and then provide the implementation for the method.
5. The subclass can inherit the method interface only (i.e. the interface inheritance) and then provide the implementation for the method.

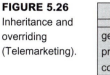

FIGURE 5.26
Inheritance and
overriding
(Telemarketing).

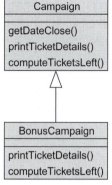

From the five reuse techniques, the first two are the most troublesome when the base class evolves. The third one shows contempt for inheritance. The last two techniques are special cases – the fourth case is trivial, the fifth does not involve implementation inheritance.

Example 5.11 (Telemarketing)

Refer to the Telemarketing application and to Example 5.4 (Section 5.1.4.1) in particular. Modify the generalization relationship between `Campaign` and `BonusCampaign` to include operations that exemplify the first three reuse techniques listed above.

Figure 5.26 shows a special version of the generalization relationship between `Campaign` and `BonusCampaign` to demonstrate the three reuse techniques. The corresponding operations are: `getDateClose`, `printTicketDetails`, and `computeTicketsLeft`.

The implementation of the operation `getDateClose()` will be inherited by `BonusCampaign` and reused as is (this is the first technique in the above list).

Two remaining operations are overridden in `BonusCampaign`. This is modeled by duplicating the operations' names in `BonusCampaign`. We assume that the operation `printTicketDetails` represents the second technique. That is `BonusCampaign.printTicketDetails()` calls the inherited `Campaign.printTicketDetails()` to print, say, the total number of tickets in the campaign. It then prints specific information about the bonus tickets, such as the number of ticket books and book sizes.

We assume further that the operation `computeTicketsLeft()` represents the third reuse technique. `BonusCampaign.computeTicketsLeft()` inherits (because it has to) from `Campaign.computeTicketsLeft()` and it then completely overrides the inherited code.

Example 5.11 demonstrates how overriding contributes to the fragile base class problem. It also demonstrates that implementation inheritance introduces network-like communication paths which we argued were unsustainable in large systems (Section 5.2). Message passing with implementation inheritance is all over the place. Apart from simple *down-calls* that follow the inheritance direction, *callbacks* (*up-calls*) are made (Section 6.2.2.8).

As observed by Szyperski (1998, p. 104): 'In conjunction with observable state, this leads to re-entrance semantics close to that of concurrent systems. Arbitrary call graphs formed by interacting webs of objects abolish the classical layering and make re-entrance the norm.'

To give justice to inheritance, callbacks are possible whenever there is a reference between objects. To quote Szyperski (1998, p. 57) again: 'With object reference . . . every method invocation is potentially an up-call, every method potentially a callback.' Inheritance only adds to the trouble, but it does add considerably.

5.3.4.4.3   Multiple implementation inheritance

We introduced multiple inheritance in Section 2.1.5.2.1, but we did not make the distinction there between *multiple interface inheritance* (multiple supertyping) and *multiple implementation inheritance* (multiple superclassing). Multiple interface inheritance allows for merging of interface contracts. Multiple implementation inheritance permits merging of implementation fragments.

Multiple implementation inheritance does not really introduce a new 'evil' of implementation inheritance. It rather exaggerates the problems caused by the fragile base class, overriding, and callbacks. Apart from the need to stop inheritance of any duplicate implementation fragments (if two or more superclasses define the same operation), it may also force renaming of operations whenever duplicate names are coincidental (and should really mean separate operations).

In this context, it is worthwhile remembering the inherent growth of complexity due to multiple inheritance – the growth that results from the lack of support in object systems for *multiple classification* (Section 2.1.5.2.2). Any orthogonal inheritance branches rooted at a single superclass have to be joined lower in the inheritance tree by specially created 'join' classes (see Section 2.1.5.2.2 for an example).

5.4   Advanced aggregation and delegation modeling

Aggregation is the third technique of linking classes in analysis models (Section 2.1.4). Compared with the other two techniques (conventional association and generalization), aggregation has been given the least attention. Yet, aggregation is the most powerful technique we know to manage the complexity of large systems through the allocation of classes to hierarchical layers of abstraction.

Aggregation (and its stronger variation – *composition*) is a containment relationship. A *composite class* contains one or more *component classes*. The component classes are elements of their composite class (albeit elements that have their own existence). Although aggregation has been considered a fundamental modeling concept for at least as long as generalization, it has only been given marginal attention in object application development (with the exception of the 'perfect match' application domains, such as multimedia systems).

In programming environments (including most object databases), aggregation is implemented in the same way as conventional associations – by acquiring references between composite and component objects. Although the compile-time structure of aggregation is the same as for association, the run-time behavior is different. The semantics of aggregation is stronger and it is (unfortunately) the programmer's responsibility to ensure that the run-time structures obey this semantics.

5.4.1 Putting more semantics into aggregation

While the current programming environments ignore aggregation, the object application development methods incorporate aggregation as a modeling option, but give it the least emphasis. Also (or as a consequence of the lack of support in programming environments), the object application development methods do not strive to enforce a rigorous semantic interpretation of the aggregation construct, frequently treating it as just a special form of association.

As discussed in Section 4.2.3, four possible semantics for aggregation can be distinguished (Maciaszek *et al.*, 1996b):

1. 'ExclusiveOwns' aggregation.

2. 'Owns' aggregation.

3. 'Has' aggregation.

4. 'Member' aggregation.

UML recognizes only two semantics of aggregation, namely *aggregation* (reference semantics) and *composition* (value semantics) (Section 2.1.4). We will now show how the existing UML notation can be used to represent the four different kinds of aggregation identified above.

5.4.1.1 The 'ExclusiveOwns' aggregation

The *ExclusiveOwns* aggregation in UML can be represented by a *composition* stereotyped with the keyword «ExclusiveOwns» and constrained additionally with the keyword *frozen* (Fowler and Scott, 2000). The *frozen* constraint applies to a component class. It states that an object of the component class cannot be *reconnected* (over its lifetime) to another composite object. A component object can possibly be deleted altogether but it cannot be switched to another owner.

Figure 5.27 shows two examples for the *ExclusiveOwns* aggregation. The left-hand example is modeled with UML value semantics (a filled diamond), the right-hand with UML reference semantics (a hollow diamond).

A Chapter object is a part of at most one CopyrightedBook. Once incorporated (by value) in a composite object, it cannot be reconnected to another CopyrightedBook object. The connection is frozen.

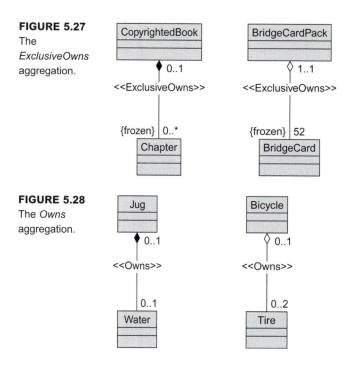

FIGURE 5.27
The *ExclusiveOwns* aggregation.

FIGURE 5.28
The *Owns* aggregation.

A `BridgeCardPack` contains exactly fifty-two cards. The UML reference semantics is used to model the ownership. Any `BridgeCard` object belongs to precisely one `BridgeCardPack` and cannot be reconnected to another pack of cards.

5.4.1.2 The 'Owns' aggregation

Like the *ExclusiveOwns* aggregation, the *Owns* aggregation can be expressed in UML with a composition's value semantics (a filled diamond) or an aggregation's reference semantics (a hollow diamond). At any point in time a component object belongs to at most one composite object but it can be *reconnected* to another composite object. When a composite object is deleted, its component objects are also deleted.

Figure 5.28 demonstrates two examples of the *Owns* aggregation. A `Water` object can be reconnected from one `Jug` to another. Similarly a `Tire` object can be switched from one `Bicycle` to another. Because of the existence dependency, destruction of a `Jug` or a `Bicycle` propagates down to their component objects.

5.4.1.3 The 'Has' aggregation

The *Has* aggregation would normally be modeled in UML using the aggregation's reference semantics (a hollow diamond). There is no existence dependency in a *Has* aggregation – the deletion of a composite object does not automatically propagate down to the component objects. The Has aggregation is only characterized by transitivity and asymmetricity.

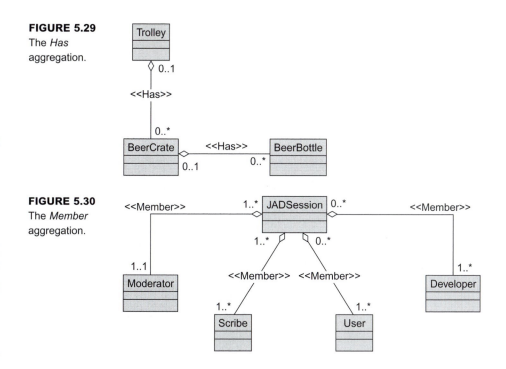

FIGURE 5.29
The *Has* aggregation.

FIGURE 5.30
The *Member* aggregation.

An example of a Has aggregation is shown in Figure 5.29. If a `Trolley` object has a number of `BeerCrate` objects and a `BeerCrate` object contains a number of `BeerBottle` objects, then the `Trolley` object has these `BeerBottle` objects (*transitivity*). If a `Trolley` has a `BeerCrate` then a `BeerCrate` cannot have a `Trolley` (*asymmetricity*).

5.4.1.4 The 'Member' aggregation

The *Member* aggregation allows for *many-to-many multiplicity* of the relationship. No special assumptions are made about the existence-dependency, transitivity, asymmetricity or the frozen property. If needed, any of these four properties can be expressed as a UML constraint. Because of the many-to-many multiplicity, the *Member* aggregation can only be modeled in UML using the aggregation's reference semantics (a hollow diamond).

Figure 5.30 demonstrates four Member aggregation relationships. A `JADSession` (Section 3.2.2.2) object consists of one moderator and one or many scribes, users, and developers. Each of the component objects can participate in more than one `JADSession` object.

5.4.2 Aggregation as alternative to generalization

Generalization is a superclass–subclass relationship. Aggregation is more like a superset–subset relationship. Notwithstanding this difference, a generalization can be repres-ented as an aggregation.

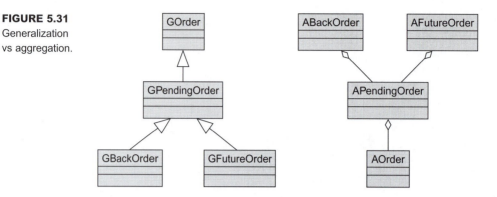

FIGURE 5.31
Generalization
vs aggregation.

Consider Figure 5.31. Customer orders that are not filled can be pending some further action. The pending order can be a back order that is to be filled once sufficient stock is available. The pending order is a future order if it is to be filled at a later date, as specified by the customer.

The left-hand side model is a generalization for customer orders. The class GOrder can be a GPendingOrder. The GPendingOrder can be a GBackOrder or GFutureOrder. Inheritance ensures sharing of attributes and operations down the generalization tree.

A similar semantics can be modeled with the aggregation shown at the right-hand side in Figure 5.31. The classes ABackOrder and AFutureOrder include the attributes and operations of the class APendingOrder, which in turn incorporates the class AOrder.

Although the two models in Figure 5.31 capture similar semantics, there are differences. The main one derives from the observation that the generalization model is based on the notion of class, whereas the aggregation model is really centered on the notion of object.

A particular GBackOrder object is also an object of GPendingOrder and GOrder. There is one *object identifier* (OID) for the GBackOrder. On the other hand, a particular ABackOrder object is built up of three separate objects each with its own object identifier – the ABackOrder itself, the contained APendingOrder object and then the contained AOrder object.

Generalization uses *inheritance* to implement its semantics. Aggregation uses *delegation* to reuse the implementation of the component objects. This is discussed next.

5.4.2.1   *Delegation and prototypical systems*

The computational model of inheritance is based on the notion of a class. However, it is possible to base the computational model on the notion of an object. An object-centered computational model structures objects in aggregation hierarchies. Whenever a composite object (*outer object*) cannot complete a task by itself it can call on the methods in one of its component objects (*inner objects*) – this is called *delegation*.

In delegation-based approaches, the functionality of the system is implemented by including (*cloning*) the functionality of existing objects in the newly required functionality. The existing objects are treated as *prototypes* for the creation of new objects. The idea is to search for the functionality in existing objects (*inner objects*) and then to implement the desired functionality in an *outer object*. The outer object asks for the services of inner objects as required. Systems constructed this way from existing prototypical objects are called *prototypical systems*.

An object may have a *delegation relationship* to any other identifiable and visible object in the system (Lee and Tepfenhart, 1997). When an outer object receives a message and cannot complete the service by itself, it will delegate the execution of that service to an inner object. The inner object, if necessary, may forward the message to any of its own inner objects.

The inner object's interfaces may or may not be visible to objects other than the outer object. The four kinds of aggregation identified in Section 5.4.1 can be used for controlling the level of visibility of inner objects. For example, an outer object may expose the inner objects' interfaces as its own in weaker forms of aggregation (such as in a typical *Has* or *Member* aggregation). In stronger forms of aggregation, an outer object may hide its inner objects' interfaces from the outside world (thus introducing a level of *encapsulation*).

5.4.2.2 *Delegation versus inheritance*

It can be shown that a delegation can model the inheritance and vice versa. This means that the same system functionality can be delivered with inheritance or with delegation. The consensus on this issue was first reached at a conference in Orlando, Florida in 1987 and it is known as the Treaty of Orlando (Stein *et al.*, 1989).

In passing, we discussed the evils of implementation inheritance. A pressing question arises if the delegation avoids the disadvantages of the implementation inheritance. The answer to this question is not straightforward (Szyperski, 1998).

From the *reuse* point of view, the delegation comes very close to inheritance. An outer object reuses the implementation of the inner object. The difference is that – in the inheritance case – the control is always returned to the object that receives the original message (request for service) after the service is accomplished.

In the delegation case, once the control has been passed from an outer to an inner object, it stays there. Any self-recursion has to be explicitly planned and designed into the delegation. In the implementation inheritance, the self-recursion always happens – it is unplanned and patched in (Szyperski, 1998). The *fragile base class problem* is but one undesired consequence of the unplanned/patched reuse.

The other potential advantage of delegation is that the sharing and reuse can be determined dynamically at run time. In inheritance-based systems, the sharing and reuse is normally determined statically when the object is created. The trade-off is between the safety and execution speed of the *anticipatory sharing* of inheritance, and the flexibility of the *unanticipatory sharing* of delegation.

An argument in favor of delegation is that the unanticipatory sharing is more natural and closer to the way people learn (Lee and Tepfenhart, 1997). Objects are naturally combined to form larger solutions and can evolve in unanticipated ways. The next section provides another viewpoint on the same issue.

5.4.3 Aggregation and holons – some cerebral ammunition

In Maciaszek *et al.* (1996a) and (1996b), to restrain complexity of object models, we proposed a new approach for describing software architectures based upon Arthur Koestler's interpretation of the structure of natural systems (Koestler, 1967; Koestler, 1978). The central concept is the idea of '*holons*', which are interpreted as objects that are both parts and wholes. More precisely, they are considered as self-regulating entities that exhibit both the interdependent properties of parts and the independent properties of wholes.

Living systems are hierarchically organized. Structurally, they are *aggregations* of semi-autonomous units that display both the independent properties of wholes and interdependent properties of parts. As Arthur Koestler would put it, they are aggregations of holons, from the Greek word *holos*, meaning *whole*, with the suffix changed to *on* to suggest a particle or part (as in proton or neutron) (Koestler, 1967).

Parts and wholes in the absolute sense do not exist in living organisms or even in social systems. Holons are hierarchically layered according to complexity, e.g. in a biological organism we can discern a hierarchy of atoms, molecules, organelles, cells, tissues, organs, and organ systems. Such hierarchies of holons are called *holocracies*.

Each holocracy layer hides its complexity from the layer above. *Looking downward*, a holon is something complete and unique, a whole. *Looking upward*, a holon is an elementary component, a part. Each holocracy layer contains many holons, e.g. atoms (hydrogen, carbon, oxygen, etc.), cells (nerve muscles, blood cells, etc.).

Looking inward, a holon provides services to other holons. *Looking outward*, a holon requests services of other holons. Holocracies are open-ended. There is no absolute 'leaf' holon or 'apex' holon, except those identified as such for our interpretative convenience. Because of this characteristic, complex systems can evolve from simple systems.

Individual holons are therefore represented by four characteristics:

1. Its internal charter (interactions between them can form unique patterns).

2. A self-assertive aggregation of subordinate holons.

3. An integrative tendency with regard to superior holons.

4. Relationships with their peer holons.

Successful systems are arranged in holocracies that hide complexity in successively lower layers, whilst providing greater levels of abstraction within the higher layers of their structures. This concept matches the semantics of aggregation.

Aggregation provides for the separation of concerns – it allows each class to remain encapsulated and to focus on a specific behavior (collaborations and services) of the class in a way that is unbound by the implementation of its parent classes (as it is in generalization). At the same time, aggregation allows for free movements between the stratified layers at run time.

The balance between integration and self-assertion of objects (holons) is achieved by the requirement that aggregation objects must 'respect each others' interfaces' (Gamma *et al.*,

1995). Encapsulation is not broken because objects communicate only through their interfaces. The evolution of the system is facilitated because the object communication is not hard-coded in the implementation through mechanisms similar to inheritance.

Structurally, aggregation can model large quantities of objects by grouping them in various sets and establishing whole–part relationships between them. Functionally, aggregation allows for objects (holons) to look 'upward' and 'downward.'

However, aggregation is not able to model the necessary interoperability between peer holons so that they can look 'inward' and 'outward.' This structural and functional gap can be successfully filled by the generalization and association relationships.

In our recommended approach, aggregation provides a 'vertical' solution and generalization a 'horizontal' solution to object application development. The aggregation becomes a dominant modeling concept that determines the overall framework of the system. This framework could be further formalized by providing a set of design patterns (Gamma *et al.*, 1995) specifically supporting the holon approach and utilizing the four kinds of aggregation. We hope that the above discussion provides some cerebral ammunition for the reader's own pursuits.

Summary

In this chapter we have completed our discussion of requirements analysis. The object technology support for a large-scale system development was scrutinized. The chapter was technically difficult but it offered insights into the object technology not easily found in books on systems analysis and design. Many of these insights revealed important weaknesses and downsides of object technology.

Stereotypes are the main extensibility technique of UML. They allow modeling beyond the pre-defined UML features. Because of the inventive nature of this chapter, stereotypes were used extensively. Stereotypes must not be confused with UML *constraints*, *notes*, and *tags*.

The public and private *visibility*, discussed in the previous chapters, gives only a basic support for the important notion of *encapsulation*. *Protected visibility* permits control of encapsulation within the inheritance structures. *Class-level visibility* (as opposed to the visibility of individual attributes and operations) is another important concept related to inheritance. The *friend* notion allows us to 'break' the encapsulation to handle special situations.

UML offers a number of additional modeling concepts to improve the expressiveness of class models. They include *derived attributes*, *derived associations*, and *qualified associations*. One of the most intriguing aspects of class modeling is the choice between an *association class* and a *reified class*.

Modern software systems are very complex. It is important that the modeling solutions simplify and reduce this inherent complexity wherever possible. Perhaps the most important mechanism for handling software complexity is the *hierarchical layering* of system architectures. Proper structuring of classes in *packages*, organized according to the BCE *approach*, is an important architectural objective.

The concept of *generalization and inheritance* is a double-edged sword in system modeling. On one hand, it facilitates software reuse and improves the expressiveness, understandability and abstraction of system models. On the other hand, it has the potential of self-destroying all these benefits if not used properly.

The concept of *aggregation and delegation* is an important modeling alternative to generalization and inheritance. *Delegation and prototypical systems* have an additional benefit of backing the hierarchical architectural structures. The *holon* abstraction provides an interesting insight into the way complex systems should be constructed.

Review questions

R1 What is a profile in UML? Give an example.

R2 At times, a class is only allowed to instantiate immutable objects, i.e. objects that cannot change after instantiation. How can such a requirement be modeled in UML?

R3 Explain the difference between a constraint and a note.

R4 Is encapsulation the same as visibility? Explain.

R5 The visibility of inherited properties in a derived class depends on the visibility level given to the base class in the declaration of that derived class. What is this visibility if the base class is declared as private? What are the consequences to the rest of the model? Give an example.

R6 The concept of a friend applies to a class or an operation. Explain the difference. Give an example (other than in this textbook) where the use of a friend could be desirable.

R7 What are the modeling benefits of derived information?

R8 When should a reified class replace an association class? Give an example (other than in this textbook).

R9 What is the complexity of a network of nine classes (measured as the number of possible connections between these classes)? Draw a hierarchy with four layers for these nine classes. What complexity reduction can be achieved in a four-layer hierarchy?

R10 Suppose that a class model for a banking application contains a class called InterestCalculation. What BCE package does that class belong to? Explain.

R11 What is the substitutability principle? Explain.

R12 Explain the difference between the interface inheritance and implementation inheritance.

R13 What is the fragile base class problem? What are the main reasons for fragile base classes?

R14 Explain the difference between the *ExclusiveOwns* and *Owns* aggregation. What is the modeling advantage gained by distinguishing between these two kinds of aggregation?

R15 Compare inheritance and delegation. What are the similarities? What are the differences?

Exercise questions

E1   Refer to Figure 2.13 (Section 2.1.3.2). Suppose that a teacher who manages a course offering must also teach that course offering.

Modify the diagram in Figure 2.13 to capture the above fact.

E2   Refer to Figures 2.17 (Section 2.1.5) and 2.18 (Section 2.1.5.1). Combine the two figures into a single class model.

Design the visibility into the class model. Explain.

What would be the visibility of inherited attributes in the class `Employee` and the class `Manager`? Explain.

E3   *University Enrolment* – refer to Example 4.9 (Section 4.2.3.3).

Is it possible to introduce derived information to the model in Figure 4.6? If so, modify the diagram.

E4   Refer to Figure 2.15 (Section 2.1.3.4). Suppose that the system has to monitor students' assessments in multiple course offerings of the same course. This is because of the constraint that a student can only fail the same course three times (the fourth enrolment is not permitted).

Extend the diagram in Figure 2.15 to model the above constraint. Use a reified class. Model and/or explain any assumptions.

E5   *Advertising Expenditure Measurement* – refer to the Problem statement in the Exercise questions at the end of Chapter 3.

Draw a package diagram for the AEM system. Explain any assumptions.

E6   *Video Store* – refer to Example 4.10 (Section 4.2.4.3).

Redraw the diagram in Figure 4.7 using realization relationships.

E7   *Video Store* – refer to Example 4.10 (Section 4.2.4.3).

Redraw the diagram in Figure 4.7 using aggregation in place of generalization. Explain the pros and cons of the new model.

6

Underpinnings of System Design

This chapter is a direct continuation of the ideas and topics discussed in the previous chapter. The difference is that the subject matter is now discussed from the design perspective. Issues that were less relevant in analysis, such as the technical details of object collaborations, are now explained in depth.

The system design encompasses two major issues: the architectural design and the detailed design. The architectural design involves the layered organization of classes and packages, the assignment of processes to computing facilities, reuse and component management. The detailed design addresses the collaboration models required for the realization of the system functionality captured in use cases.

Following the book principle adopted in Chapter 2, the underpinnings of system design are exemplified as soon as the concepts are explained. The explanations are put together in a guided design tutorial for the OnLine Shopping application that continues from the analysis tutorial in Chapter 2.

6.1 Software architecture

The design is a low-level model of a system's architecture and its internal workings. The *design* is done in terms of the software/hardware platform on which the system is going to be implemented. In an iterative and incremental software development, the analysis models are continually 'elaborated' with technical details. Once the technical details include software/hardware considerations, an analysis model becomes a design model.

The distinction between the analysis and design is not clear-cut. One can talk about deeply technical issues without relating to specific software/hardware solutions. In this sense, much of the discussion in Chapter 5 could be classified as the design rather than analysis.

The description of a system in terms of its modules is called an *architectural design*. The architectural design includes decisions about the solution strategies for the client and for the server components of the system.

The description of the internal workings of each module (use case) is called a *detailed design*. The detailed design develops complete algorithms and data structures for each module. These algorithms and data structures are tailored to all (reinforcing and obtrusive) constraints of the underlying implementation platform.

6.1.1 Distributed architecture

The architectural design is concerned with the selection of a *solution strategy* and with the *modularization* of the system. The solution strategy needs to resolve the client and server issues as well as any middleware needed to 'glue' the client and the server. The decision on the basic building blocks (modules) is only partly dependent on a chosen solution strategy.

The client and server are logical concepts (Bochenski, 1994). The *client* is a computing process that makes requests of the server process. The *server* is a computing process that services the client requests. Normally, the client and the server processes run on different computers but it is perfectly possible to implement a client/server system on a single machine.

In a typical scenario, the *client process* is responsible for controlling the display of information on the user's screen and for handling user's events. The *server process* is any computer node with a database of which data may be requested by a client process.

The *client/server* (C/S) architecture can be extended to represent an arbitrary distributed system. Any computer node with a database can be a client in some business transactions and a server in other transactions. Connecting such nodes by a communication network gives rise to a *distributed processing system architecture*, as shown in Figure 6.1.

In a distributed processing system the client can access any number of servers. However, the client may be allowed to access only one server at a time. This means that in a single request it may not be possible to combine data from two or more database servers. If this is possible then the architecture supports a *distributed database system*.

FIGURE 6.1
Distributed processing system architecture.

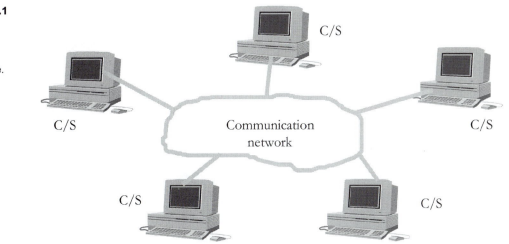

6.1.2 Three-tier architecture

In Section 5.2.4 we explained the BCE (boundary–control–entity) approach. We also stated there that the BCE approach is nicely aligned with *three-tier architecture* in which a separate application logic middle-tier (control) is introduced between the client (boundary) and the server (entity).

As with the client and server processes, the *application process* is a logical concept that may or may not be supported by separate hardware. The application logic can equally well run on a client or a server node, i.e. it can be compiled into the client or the server process and implemented as a Dynamic Link Library (DLL), Application Programming Interface (API), Remote Procedure Calls (RPC), etc. (Next, 1996).

When the application logic is compiled into the client then we talk about the *thick client architecture* ('a client on steroids'). When it is compiled into the server, then we talk about the *thin client architecture* ('a skinny client'). Intermediate architectures, in which application logic is partly compiled into the client and partly into the server, are also possible.

The application logic can also be deployed on a separate computing node, as shown in Figure 6.2. This is the 'purest' three-tier architecture. Its best characteristics are good flexibility, growth, user independence, availability, and a low upgrade cost. However, such an architecture might have a high initial cost and it may suffer from some performance problems (Umar, 1997).

6.1.3 Programming databases

Independently of where the application logic resides, the program (client) interacts with the database (server) to obtain information for display and user's manipulation. But modern databases can be programmed as well. We say that those modern databases are *active*.

FIGURE 6.2
Three-tier
architecture.

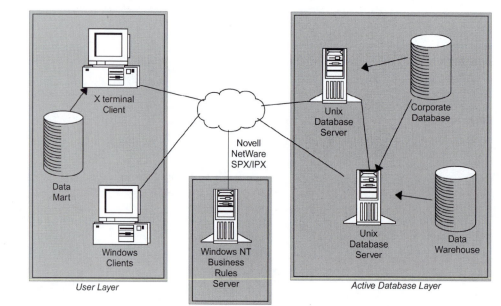

A database program is called a *stored procedure*. A stored procedure is stored in the database itself (it is *persistent*). It can be invoked from a client program (or from another stored procedure) by a normal procedure/function call statement.

A special kind of the stored procedure – called a *trigger* – cannot be explicitly called. A trigger fires automatically on an attempt to change the content of the database. Triggers are used to implement enterprise-wide business rules that have to be enforced in the way that is independent from the client programs (or stored procedures). Triggers enforce integrity and consistency of the database. They do not allow individual applications to break the database-imposed business rules.

6.1.3.1   Application–database interaction

We need to decide which parts of the system should be programmed into the client and which into the database. The 'programmable' parts to consider include:

- User interface.
- Presentation logic.
- Application function.
- Integrity logic.
- Data access.

The *user interface* part of a program knows how to display information on a particular GUI, such as the Microsoft Windows GUI, Unix Motif GUI, Macintosh GUI. The *presentation logic* is responsible for handling the GUI objects (forms, menus, action buttons, etc.) as required by the application function.

The *application function* contains the main logic of the program. It captures what the application does. It is the glue that puts the client and the database together. From the perspective of the BCE approach (Section 5.2.4) the application function is implemented in the classes of the *control package*.

The *integrity logic* is responsible for enterprise-wide business rules. These are the rules that apply across all application programs, i.e. all programs have to conform to them. The *data access* knows how to access persistent data on the disk.

Figure 6.3 shows a typical scenario. The user interface and presentation logic belong to the client. The data access and integrity logic (triggers) are the responsibility of the database. The application function is frequently programmed (as SQL queries) into the client during the early development phase, but it is moved to the database (as stored procedures) for the final deployment of the software product.

6.1.3.2   BCED approach

The *Boundary–Control–Entity–Database* (BCED) approach is an extension of the BCE approach (Section 5.2.4). It effectively separates the EntityPackage from the classes responsible for

FIGURE 6.3
Application–
database
interaction.

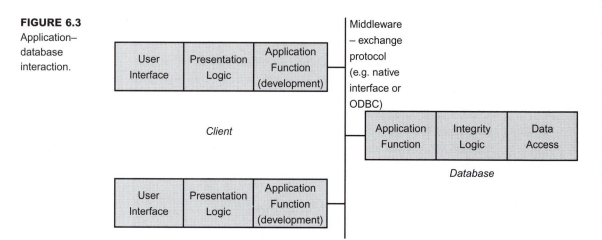

extracting the data from the database. Those classes are placed in the `DatabasePackage` (Figure 6.4). (The `DatabasePackage` is really a `DatabaseInterfacePackage` but we prefer to stick to short labels. Calling the package an `InterfacePackage` is not a good option in any case because of the many meanings of the notion of interface.)

The `EntityPackage` still provides 'an executing model of the business' (Fowler, 1997). It stores and buffers data obtained by the program from the database or other data sources. It effectively requests two services from the `DatabasePackage`, namely `loadMe(anObject)` with the database data and `saveMe(anObject)` to the database (Fowler, 1997). These services are likely to be implemented in the `DatabasePackage` classes named `DatabaseReader` and `DatabaseUpdater`, or similar names.

The `DatabasePackage` provides a level of indirection between the application and database. The application logic (`ControlPackage`) is now separated from the changes to data sources. Any changes to database structures and to protocols to retrieve data from the database are effected in the classes of `DatabasePackage`. Storing and buffering of data (in `EntityPackage`) for the application function remains the same as far as the `ControlPackage` is concerned.

FIGURE 6.4
BCED layers.

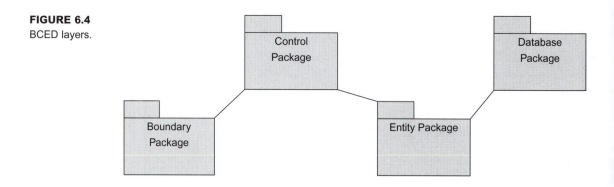

In reality, the classes in `DatabasePackage` perform a range of other services. The additional services may be to open and close connections with the database, instruct the database when to commit or rollback a transaction, determine run-time parameters for the database configuration, handle the user authorization, extract and store the meta-data information about database objects (such as tables, columns, views, stored procedures, indexes, etc.).

The separation of concerns introduced by the BCED approach can be 'imposed' on the system designers and programmers through a simple technique of prefixing class names. Since each class can only belong to one package, it can be named with a single letter prefix (B, C, E or D). For example, the class labeled `B_TreeBrowseView` belongs to the `BoundaryPackage` and the class `D_DatabaseUpdater` to the `DatabasePackage`.

6.1.3.3 System software

A solution strategy for an *object-oriented client* will typically evolve around software environments with GUI building tools. A decision here is likely also to involve the database connectivity considerations, such as:

- a *native database interface* as provided by many 4GLs (e.g. PowerBuilder, Developer 2000, Delphi); or

- an *ODBC* or *JDBC* driver to a database (as in e.g. Visual C++, Power J++).

A solution strategy for a *server* will determine the database technology. Because 'the data stays for ever but applications come and go' (Bob Epstein of Sybase (quoted from memory)), a solution strategy for a server is likely to significantly influence the client strategy. Frequently, client development environments provided by a database vendor are chosen.

The server strategies include:

- a *relational database* (e.g. Sybase, Oracle, Informix); or

- an *object-relational database* (e.g. Oracle8, Informix/Illustra, UniSQL); or

- an *object database* (e.g. ObjectStore, Versant, Objectivity/DB).

Currently these three database technologies do not compete; they excel at different issues and address the needs of different application domains. As a result, the decision on a database model should be based on the current and expected application needs.

6.1.4 Reuse strategy

UML defines reuse as 'the use of pre-existing artifact' (Rumbaugh *et al.*, 1999). In passing, we discussed the object-oriented *techniques for software reuse*, such as inheritance and delegation. In this section, we address the *strategies of software reuse*. It turns out that the strategies imply also the *granularity* at which the reuse is done. The *granularity of reuse* can be:

- the class;

- the component; or

- the solution idea.

Associated with the granularity, there are three corresponding strategies for reuse (Coad *et al.*, 1995; Gamma *et al.*, 1995):

1. Toolkits (class libraries).

2. Frameworks.

3. Analysis and design patterns.

6.1.4.1 Toolkit reuse

A *toolkit* emphasizes *code reuse* at a class level. In this kind of reuse the programmer 'fills the gaps' in the program by making calls to *concrete classes* in some library of classes. The main body of the program is not reused – it is written by the programmer.

There are two kinds (levels) of toolkit (Page-Jones, 2000):

1. Foundation toolkits.

2. Architecture toolkits.

The *foundation classes* are widely provided by object programming environments. They include classes to implement primitive data types (such as `String`), structured data types (such as `Date`), and collections (such as `Set`, `List` or `Index`).

The *architecture classes* are normally available as part of a system software, such as an operating system, database software, or GUI interface software. For example, when we buy an object database system what we really get is an architecture toolkit that implements the expected functionalities of the system such as the persistency, transactions, and concurrency.

6.1.4.2 Framework reuse

A *framework* emphasizes *design reuse* at a component level (components are discussed next in Section 6.1.5). As opposed to toolkit reuse, a framework provides the skeleton of the program. The programmer then 'fills the gaps' in this skeleton (customizes it) by writing the code that the framework needs to call. Apart from concrete classes (for the framework itself), a framework provides a large volume of abstract classes to be implemented (customized) by the programmer.

A framework is customizable application software. The best examples of frameworks are ERPS (Enterprise Resource Planning Systems) such as SAP, PeopleSoft, Baan or J.D. Edwards. The reuse in those systems, however, is not based on pure object-oriented techniques.

Object-oriented frameworks for IS development are proposed within distributed component technologies such as CORBA, DCOM and EJB (Section 1.1.1). They are known as *'business objects'* – 'shippable' products to meet specific business or application needs. For example, a business object could be an accounting framework with customizable classes such as `Invoice` or `Customer`.

While frameworks are an attractive reuse proposition, they also have a number of drawbacks. Perhaps the most significant one is that the generic 'lowest common denominator' solutions that they deliver are suboptimal or even obsolete. As a result, they do not give a competitive advantage to their adopters and can create a maintenance burden when chasing state-of-the-art solutions.

6.1.4.3   *Pattern reuse*

Patterns emphasize the *approach reuse* by providing ideas and examples for object *collaborations* that are known to represent good development practices leading to understandable and scalable solutions (collaborations are discussed in Section 6.2). Patterns can apply to the analysis or design phase of the development lifecycle (hence, *analysis patterns* and *design patterns*).

A pattern is a documented solution that has been shown to work well in a number of situations. These situations are identified and can be used as an index entry for the development seeking a solution to the problem. Any known disadvantages or side effects of a pattern are listed to allow the developer to take a knowledgeable decision.

Pattern reuse is largely conceptual though many design patterns contain sample code for the programmer's reuse. The scope of a *design pattern* (e.g. Gamma *et al.*, 1995) is that of the collaboration (Section 6.2) – typically larger than a class but smaller than a component. The scope of an *analysis pattern* (e.g. Fowler, 1997) depends on the level of modeling abstraction at which the pattern applies.

6.1.5   Component

The *component* is a physical part of the system, a piece of implementation, a software program (Booch *et al.*, 1999; Lakos, 1996; Rumbaugh *et al.*, 1999; Szyperski, 1998). Components are typically perceived as binary executable (EXE) parts of the system. But the component can also be a part of the system that is not directly executable (e.g. a source code file, data file, DLL (Dynamic Link Library), or database stored procedure).

UML currently defines five standard stereotypes for components (Booch *et al.*, 1999):

1. *Executable* (i.e. a directly executable module).
2. *Library* (i.e. a static or dynamic object library module).
3. *Table* (i.e. a database table).
4. *File* (i.e. a source code or data document).
5. *Document* (i.e. a human-readable document).

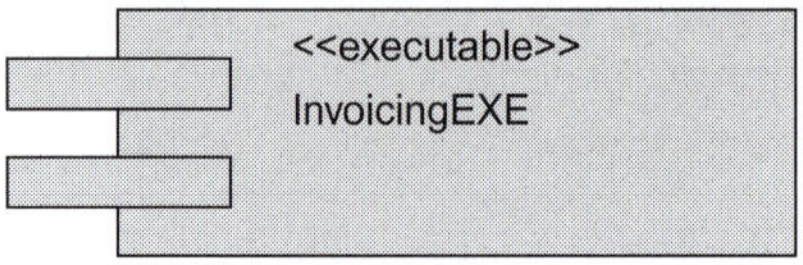

FIGURE 6.5
Component
notation.

The characteristics of a component are (Rumbaugh *et al.*, 1999; Szyperski, 1998):

■ A unit of independent deployment (never deployed partially).

■ A unit of third-party composition (i.e. sufficiently documented and self-contained to be 'plugged into' other components by a third-party).

■ That it has no persistent state (i.e. cannot be distinguished from copies of its own; in any given application, there will be at most one copy of a particular component).

■ That it is a replaceable part of a system, i.e. it can be replaced by another component that conforms to the same interface.

■ That it fulfills a clear function and is logically and physically cohesive.

■ That it may be nested in other components.

6.1.5.1 Component notation

A component is rendered graphically as a rectangle with two smaller rectangles on its left side. A unique name for the component is written inside the large rectangle. A dependency relationship can be specified between any two components.

Figure 6.5 shows the component InvoicingEXE. The component is stereotyped as an executable.

6.1.5.2 Component diagram

A component diagram shows components and how they relate to each other. Components can be related by *dependency relationships*. A dependent component requires the services of the component pointed to by the dependency relationship. Components can also be related to each other by the *composition relationship*, i.e. a component can contain another component.

Figure 6.6 shows three components. The component InvoicingEXE depends on the other two components. The nature of these dependencies is not specified because the interfaces of components are not revealed.

UML allows the modeling of component interfaces with the 'lollypop' notation (Section 5.3.3). If a dependency between components is negotiated through interfaces, then another component that realizes the same set of interfaces can replace a component.

FIGURE 6.6
Component
diagram.

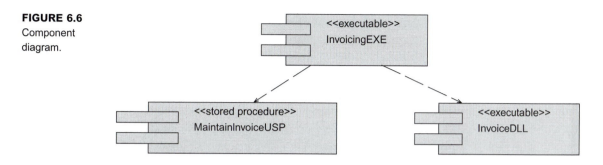

6.1.5.3 Component versus package

The *package* is a logical part of the system (Section 5.2.3). At the logical level, every class belongs to a single package. At the physical level, every class is implemented by at least one component and it is possible that a component implements only one class. Abstract classes defining interfaces are frequently implemented by more than one component.

Packages are typically larger architectural units than components. They tend to group classes in a *horizontal* way – by static proximity of classes in the application domain. *Components* are *vertical* groups of classes with behavioral proximity – they may come from different domains but they contribute to a single piece of business activity, perhaps a use case.

The above orthogonality of packages and components makes it difficult to establish dependencies between them. A frequent situation is that a logical package depends on a few physical components.

Example 6.1 (University Enrolment)

Refer to the packages identified in Example 5.10 (Section 5.2.3.2). Consider the `Timetable` package. Assume that the package will be implemented as a C++ program that embodies the logic of allocation of university rooms to classes. The program accesses a database for room and class information. Two stored procedures will be implemented to provide that service to the program.

Draw a component diagram that demonstrates the dependencies between the package and the necessary components.

Figure 6.7 shows the component model. Three components are identified: `RoomAllocEXE`, `RoomUSP` and `ClassUSP`. The package `Timetable` depends on these components.

6.1.5.4 Component versus class and interface

Like classes, the components realize interfaces. The difference is twofold. First, a component is a physical abstraction deployed on some computer node. A class represents a logical thing that has to be implemented by a component to act as a physical abstraction.

FIGURE 6.7
Package versus
component
(University
Enrolment).

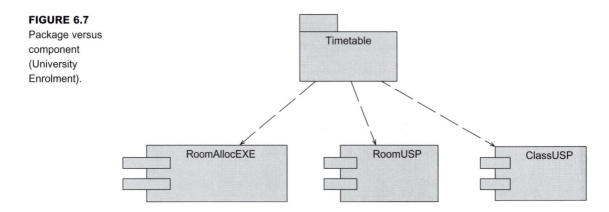

Second, a component reveals only some interfaces of the classes that it contains. Many other interfaces are encapsulated by the component – they are only used internally by collaborating classes and are not visible to other components.

The interface that a component realizes may be implemented in a separate class. Such a class is called a *dominant class* (Rumbaugh *et al.*, 1999). Since the dominant class represents the interface of the component, any object inside the component is reachable from the dominant class via composition links. 'A dominant class subsumes the interface of the component' (Rumbaugh *et al.*, 1999, p. 219).

Example 6.2 (University Enrolment)

Refer to the three components in Example 6.1 (Section 6.1.1.3.3). Assume that the component RoomAllocEXE initiates allocation of rooms to courses by providing the component ClassUSP with the class identification. To this aim, ClassUSP realizes the interface called Allocate.

The component ClassUSP does the rest of the job by requesting the room details from the component RoomUSP. To provide that service, RoomUSP implements the interface called Reserve.

Figure 6.8 demonstrates the component diagram corresponding to the requirements above.

6.1.6 Deployment

In UML, a three-tier architecture (like in Figure 6.2) or any other architecture for the system is rendered as a deployment diagram. In fact, the diagram in Figure 6.2 is a legal UML deployment diagram in which the computational resources are represented as special icons.

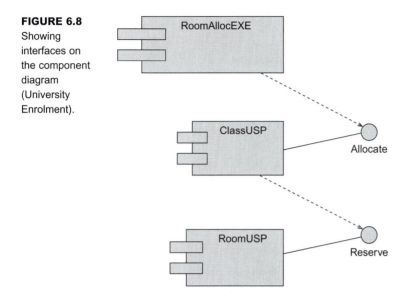

The computational resource (a run-time physical object) is called a *node*. As a minimum, the node has a memory and some computing capability (e.g. the X terminal client in Figure 6.2). The node can also be a database server, likely an active (i.e. programmable) server.

6.1.6.1 *Node notation*

In UML, a *node* is rendered graphically as a cube. The cube can be stereotyped. The stereotyped cube can be an icon. Every node is given a unique name (a textual string).

Figure 6.9 shows the node `CorporateDatabaseServer`. The stereotype «Sybase» informs that the node is located on a Sybase DBMS (Database Management System) platform.

6.1.6.2 *Deployment diagram*

A deployment diagram shows nodes and how they relate to each other. Nodes can be related by *connection relationships*. A connection relationship can be named to indicate the network protocol used (if applicable) or to characterize the connection in some other way. In general,

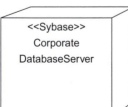

FIGURE 6.10
Deployment
diagram.

a connection relationship is an association and it can be modeled with typical association properties, such as the degree, multiplicity, roles, etc. (Section 2.1.3).

Figure 6.10 shows two nodes in a deployment diagram. The connection relationship `download_nightly` says that the node `DataWarehouseServer` (running on the Sybase IQ software) is downloading data every night from the transactional database node `CorporateDatabaseServer`.

6.1.6.3 *Node versus component*

Nodes are locations on which the components run. Nodes execute components. Components are deployed on a node. A node together with its components is sometimes called a *distribution unit* (Booch *et al.*, 1999).

Figure 6.11 shows a node called `CorporateDatabaseServer`. The node runs two stored procedures which are represented as components: `CustomerUSP` and `InvoiceUSP`.

Figure 6.12 is an alternative way of modeling the 'containment' of components in a node. This notation can be extended so that the entire component diagram can be placed on a deployment diagram (Fowler and Scott, 2000).

FIGURE 6.11
Node and its
components.

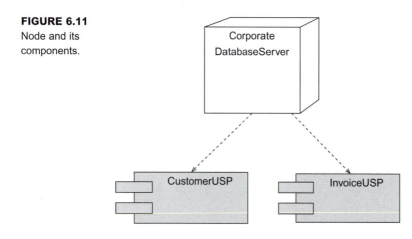

FIGURE 6.12
Node and its
components.

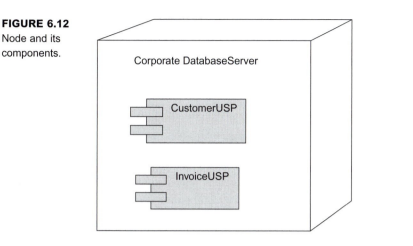

6.2 Collaboration

The architectural design makes an impact on the detailed design in that it determines the target hardware/software platform that the detailed design must conform to. Apart from that, the detailed design is a direct continuation from the analysis. The objective is to turn the analysis models into detailed design documents from which the programmers can implement the system.

In analysis, we simplify the models by abstracting away the details that interfere with the presentation of a particular viewpoint on the system. In design, we tend to do exactly opposite. We take one architectural part of the system at a time and add technical details to the models or create brand new design models at a low level of abstraction.

In passing, we used the term *collaboration* freely to refer to sets of objects collaborating to perform a task (Sections 2.1.1.2 and 2.1.2.2.1). UML uses the term collaboration with the same intent and associates to it specific modeling methods. In particular, collaborations are used in UML to specify the *realization* of use cases and operations (Booch *et al.*, 1999; Rumbaugh *et al.*, 1999).

6.2.1 Collaboration notation

Not surprisingly, the notation for *collaboration* is similar to that for use case. The collaboration is rendered as an ellipse with dashed borders.

Figure 6.13 demonstrates two collaborations: Browse Student List and Add Student to Course Offering. The two collaborations realize (via the *realization relationships*) the use case Enter Program of Study.

Note that a CASE tool can substitute explicit modeling of realization relationships as in Figure 6.13 with hyperlinks between the use case and collaboration models (Booch *et al.*,

FIGURE 6.13
Collaboration
notation.

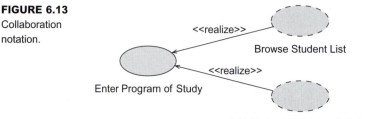

1999). In other words, one or more UML diagrams, linked internally by a CASE tool to their use case, can represent each collaboration model. The designer can navigate between a use case and its collaboration models without utilizing any realization relationships.

6.2.2 Collaboration diagram

The collaboration diagram is one kind of UML interaction model (Section 2.2.5). The other kind is the sequence diagram (Section 2.2.5.3). We prefer to use sequence diagrams in analysis and collaboration diagrams in design (see Section 6.2.3 for a comparison of these two kinds of interaction models).

The collaboration diagram in Figure 6.14 corresponds to the sequence diagram in Figure 2.33 (Section 2.2.5.1). The sequence numbers capture the temporal sequence of messages. The sequence numbers are optional. In complex algorithms it is difficult to assign a meaningful temporal sequence to messages and additional models (such as activity diagrams or a pseudocode) may be necessary to express temporal sequences.

Note that object names in a collaboration diagram are really the *roles* that the objects play in a collaboration. The UML notation is:

FIGURE 6.14
Collaboration
diagram for
'Display Current
Configuration'
(OnLine
Shopping).

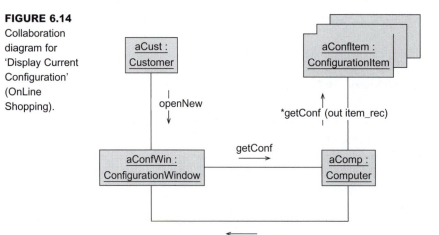

FIGURE 6.15
Alternative
message
notations.

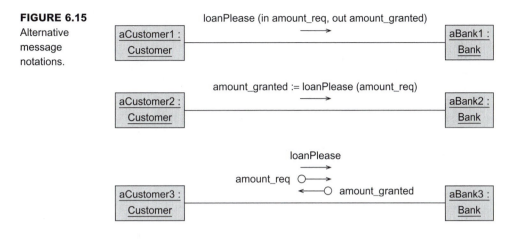

rolename:classname

To be accurate, a role is not an object. In UML, a role is a 'classifier' that represents any object that may appear in different instances of the collaboration. Also, the same object may play different roles in successive collaborations. In general, the rolename may be omitted but the colon in front of the class name must be included to distinguish it from an ordinary class (Rumbaugh *et al.*, 1999).

6.2.2.1 Message notation

The structure of a message corresponds to the *signature* of the target method (Section 2.1.2.2). To successfully send a message, the sender object has to provide (Page-Jones, 2000):

■ An *OID value* (the handle) for the target object. This is normally stored in one of the sender's attributes (*variables*, from the programming perspective).

■ The name of the *operation* (*method*) in the target object.

■ Optionally, the actual input and output (return) *arguments* to substitute for the corresponding formal arguments in the method.

Figure 6.15 presents alternative UML notations for the message definition. The top notation maps directly to the method's signature (the keyword in can be omitted for conciseness). The middle notation uses a return value and an assignment statement in lieu of an output argument. The bottom notation replaces the input and output arguments with directional data tokens.

6.2.2.2 Message structure

In the sender's code, the messages in Figure 6.15 would include a variable containing an OID value of the target object. The variable would correspond to the name of the target object on the diagram, e.g.:

```
aBank1.loanPlease(in amount_req, out amount_granted)
```

Note the arrangement – the object first, the operation second (Page-Jones, 2000). The arrangement emphasizes the object-oriented thinking that stresses object collaborations instead of procedure calls. It points also to the possible polymorphic nature of messages where the same operation (`loanPlease`) can have different implementations in different classes (objects of which are pointed to by the OID value in the variable `aBank1`).

Message arguments in Figure 6.15 are data tokens. This is acceptable in popular object-oriented environments but it falls foul of pure object-oriented thinking. In a pure implementation, the message arguments would be OID variables (*object handles*) (Page-Jones, 2000). Everything we touch in a pure object-oriented system is an object!

Assume for a while that the arguments in the message `loanPlease` are objects of the class `Money`. If so, the values of `amount_req` and `amount_granted` would be OID values (pointers) to memory cells holding the dollar amounts for these two arguments. If this is hard to understand then consider that the class of an argument may be any user-defined class, such as `Employee` or `BankAccount`, not just a primitive class such as `Money` or `Integer`. It should be easier to understand now why a message argument is an OID handle to an object.

6.2.2.3 *Types of message*

A message can be sent to a class object (Section 2.1.6) or to an instance object. Typical messages sent to a class object are *constructors* (to create new instance objects) and *destructors* (to destroy existing instance objects). Other types of messages (to both class and instance objects) can be classified into three groups (the alternative names in brackets come from Page-Jones (2000)):

■ Read messages (interrogative, present-oriented messages).

■ Update messages (informative, past-oriented messages).

■ Collaborative messages (imperative, future-oriented messages).

A *read message* requests that a target object provides some information, possibly values of its private attributes. It is 'present-oriented' because it asks for current information. An example could be:

```
aBank1.openingHours(in weekday, out hours)
```

An *update message* requests that a target object updates itself based on the information provided in the message. It is 'past-oriented' because it updates the object with the information that is already known to the sender. An example could be:

```
aCustomer1.newCreditRating
            (in credit_rating, effective_date)
```

A *collaborative message* requests that a target object assists in executing a requested action that contributes to the collaboration. It is 'future-oriented' because it requests the object to carry out an action on behalf of the sender as part of a larger task to be completed in the immediate future. The message `loanPlease` is an example of a collaborative message. To complete the request, `aBank1` may request further collaboration from other objects.

```
aBank1.loanPlease(in amount_req, out amount_granted)
```

6.2.2.4 Overriding versus overloading

When designing interaction models we have to recognize that a method name can be overridden or overloaded. These two terms are not the same.

Method *overriding* was explained in Section 5.3.4.4.2. The overriding constitutes the basis for polymorphism. It means that there exist several methods with the same name in different classes. A different implementation of the same method would execute depending on the class of the target object.

Method *overloading* also means that there exist several methods with the same name but in the same class. For example, apart from the previously defined method `loanPlease`, we may have another `loanPlease` method in the class `Bank`. This second `loanPlease` method would include an additional argument specifying the minimum loan amount that a customer is prepared to take, as shown below:

```
aBank1.loanPlease(in amount_req, minimum_amount,
          out amount_granted)
```

The method `loanPlease` is now overloaded. Which one of the overloaded methods executes would depend on the signature of the message. It follows that the determination of message signatures is important during the design phase.

6.2.2.5 Iteration messages and templates

An *iteration message* is sent repeatedly to many objects of the class – it iterates over many objects. UML uses an *iteration marker* – an asterisk in front of the message label – to signify iteration (Section 2.2.5.1).

The objects over which an iteration message iterates are known as *collections*. The collection can be a set, a list (unordered set) or an array of objects. In a collaboration diagram, a collection is shown as a stack of objects (Figure 6.14 in Section 6.2.2).

In the object-oriented sense, a collection (set, list, etc.) is itself a class. Indeed, many object-oriented programming environments provide classes named `Set`, `List`, `FixedArray`, `VarryingArray`, `BtreeIndex`, etc. A collection class can then be used to contain objects of a user-defined class. A typical use of collection classes is in implementing links of association or aggregation relationships with multiplicity 'many' (Section 2.1.3.2).

Consider Figure 6.14 and the iteration message `*getConf(out item_rec)` from `aComp` to `aConfItem`. The message iterates over a collection of `ConfigurationItem` objects. However, the collaboration diagram does not reveal how the collection is implemented. This information can be derived from the class diagram.

FIGURE 6.16

Aggregation relationship with roles.

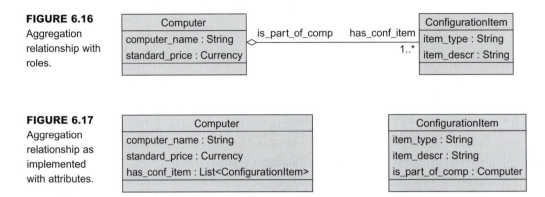

FIGURE 6.17

Aggregation relationship as implemented with attributes.

Figure 6.16 is the class diagram showing the aggregation relationship between the classes `Computer` and `ConfigurationItem`. Note that the role names will eventually be implemented as attributes of the classes. Figure 6.17 represents an implementation-level class diagram with role names converted to attribute names.

As seen in Figure 6.17, the type of attribute `has_conf_item` is `List<ConfigurationItem>`. The class `ConfigurationItem` is the parameter for the collection class `List`. In general, `List` can replace its formal parameter with other classes. We say that the type of `has_conf_item` is a *template* – a *parameterized type*.

The definition of the template is essential for understanding the scope of an iteration message. The message `*getConf(out item_rec)` will iterate over the `List` of `ConfigurationItem` objects. The list constitutes a current value of the attribute `has_conf_item`. To be precise, the list contains OID values (handles) to all `ConfigurationItem` objects included in a particular `Computer` object.

6.2.2.6 *Self messages*

An object can send a message to itself. A *self message* signifies a local call invocation – one method calls another method in the same object. The name 'self message' is borrowed from Smalltalk. The corresponding C++ and Java term is a *this* object. A self/this object is a constant (not a variable) that holds an object's OID (Page-Jones, 2000).

A self message may happen in a sequence of collaborative messages (Section 6.2.2.3) which act on the same class before releasing the control to another class. It will also happen if the control returns to a sender and the next message invokes a method in the sender (the sender and the target are the same object).

Figure 6.18 provides an example of two self messages (`currentLeave` and `longServiceLeave`) activated as a result of the request to calculate the employee's `leaveEntitlement`.

A self object can – in some rare situations – be passed as an argument in a message, i.e.:

```
messagename(self)
```

FIGURE 6.18
Self messages.

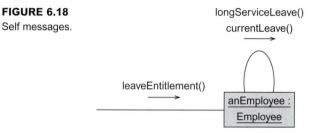

Sending the OID of the sender to the target object is normally not necessary in a *synchronous message* (during which a sender must wait for the return of control from the target before finishing execution). The return of execution control is automatic, at least in all major object-oriented programming environments.

6.2.2.7 *Asynchronous messages*

In an *asynchronous message*, a sender object does not have to wait for the target object to finish its work before continuing execution in another thread of control. Asynchronous message passing assumes multiple threads of control (*concurrency*) in the program.

UML uses a half arrow notation to signify an asynchronous message. The object me in Figure 6.19 spawns two threads of control by sending two asynchronous messages to objects myCoffeeMaker and myRadio.

Asynchronous message passing is frequent in engineering and real-time applications. Typical business applications, executing business transactions, rely mostly on synchronous message passing.

6.2.2.8 *Callbacks*

Callbacks were previously mentioned in the context of inheritance (Section 5.3.4.4.2). A *callback* is an up-call back to the sender. A typical use of callbacks is in *asynchronous message passing* where the sender (*subscriber*) requests the target (*listener*) that it needs to be informed about the completion of an action. The target has to send an asynchronous message back to the sender.

FIGURE 6.19
Asynchronous message passing.

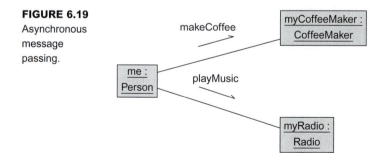

FIGURE 6.20
Callback in
asynchronous
message
passing.

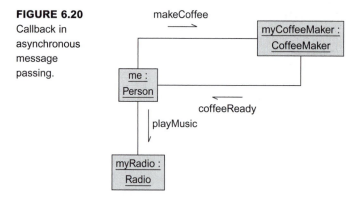

Figure 6.20 extends the collaboration diagram in Figure 6.19 with a callback from myCoffeeMaker to me. After all I am waiting for coffee and I do not mind being interrupted once the coffee is ready.

Callbacks are a handy device but they are inherently difficult to program. For callbacks to properly do the job, the listener has to somehow observe the state and the state changes in the subscriber before the callback is sent. Sending the message coffeeReady to me when I am already on the way out will not do much good!

6.2.3 Sequence diagram versus collaboration diagram

Collaboration and sequence diagrams are equivalent in the sense that they can be automatically converted from one to the other. They do, however, emphasize some different aspects of object interaction (and those differing aspects can be sometimes lost in the conversions).

A sequence diagram puts the emphasis on the time sequence of messages between objects. The sequence diagrams are awkward and imprecise in representing alternative message paths – something that the activity diagrams excel in. They are also cumbersome in representing larger collaborations with many objects (although a careful arrangement of object lifelines can frequently improve the readability by a whole factor).

A collaboration diagram can explicitly show static relationships between objects along which the messages can flow. As a result, collaboration diagrams provide for a better precision when visualizing such things as a polymorphic message. The layout of collaboration diagrams permits showing more objects on the same graphical area. The messages can be fully specified and annotated.

We prefer to use sequence diagrams in the analysis models and collaboration diagrams in the design models. Both diagrams can be supplemented with activity diagrams. An activity diagram can be drawn at the level of abstraction corresponding to that of the related sequence or collaboration diagram.

6.2.4 Realization of use cases

Collaborations are to design what use cases are to analysis. If use cases drive the analysis then collaborations drive the design activities. Use cases are *realized* by collaborations. Because of different levels of abstraction, each use case is realized by a number of collaborations.

The collaboration has a structural and behavioral part. The *structural part* represents the static aspect of collaboration. It is represented by a subset of class diagram corresponding to the scope of collaboration. The class diagram is *elaborated* (in comparison with its analysis version) with the implementation details. In particular, the signatures of class operations are identified.

The *behavioral part* represents the dynamics that shows how the static elements collaborate. The behavioral part is modeled as *interactions* (Section 2.2.5). Apart from the sequence diagrams (Section 2.2.5.3), the collaboration diagrams are frequently used for the behavioral specification of collaborations. In practice, the structural and behavioral aspects of the collaboration are likely to be developed concurrently.

6.2.4.1 Structural aspect of collaboration

Example 6.3 (University Enrolment)

Refer to Example 4.9 (Section 4.2.3.3) and to Example 4.17 (Section 4.3.3.3). We consider the use case 'Enter Program of Study'. The use case handles enrolment of students in course offerings.

For the purpose of this example, we assume that the use case checks (before a student can be enrolled) if the student paid the fees and if the student satisfies the prerequisites.

Our task is to extend the class diagram in Figure 4.6 (Example 4.9) to model the structural aspect of the collaboration necessary for the described scenario.

To solve the problem we need to consider any additional classes and additional attributes and operations in classes necessary to support the collaboration. We need to elaborate the class diagram produced during analysis. The sequence diagram for the use case developed during analysis provides guidance (Figure 4.14, Section 4.3.3.3).

As shown in Figure 6.21, a few classes are added to the class diagram. The boundary class `ProgramEntryWindow` is obtained from the sequence diagram in Figure 4.14. The class `PrereqCourse` is needed to establish a many-to-many prerequisite relationship between courses. The class `Grade` is added for completeness but it is not going to be used by the use case under consideration. Past grades of students are kept in `AcademicRecord`. `Grade` contains the marks and grades that a student achieves in course offerings currently taken.

FIGURE 6.21

Structural aspect of collaboration (University Enrolment).

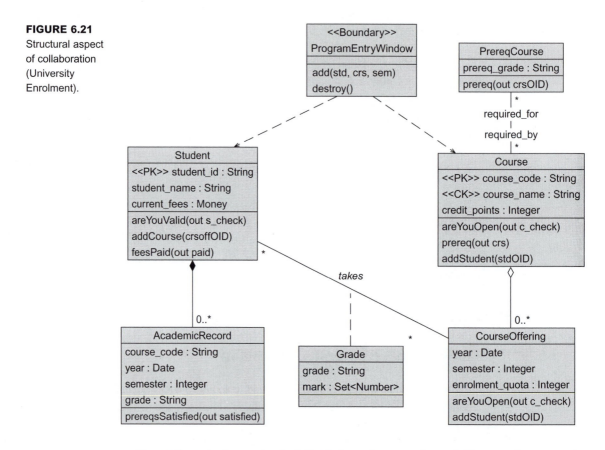

The attributes in the previously defined classes have not changed. The new classes contain attributes that should be self-explanatory. The main additions in the elaborated class diagram are the operation definitions. The operations are directly derived from the collaboration diagram for the behavioral aspect of the collaboration (see the next section).

6.2.4.2 Behavioral aspect of collaboration

Example 6.4 (University Enrolment)

Refer to Example 4.9 (Section 4.2.3.3) and to Example 4.17 (Section 4.3.3.3). Our task is to create a collaboration diagram for the behavioral aspect of the collaboration as specified in Example 4.9. The collaboration diagram should be an elaboration of the sequence diagram in Figure 4.14 (Example 4.17).

Figure 6.22 is the solution for the example. In comparison with the sequence diagram (Figure 4.14), two objects are added: `anAcademicRecord` and `aPrereqCourse`. These

FIGURE 6.22
Behavioral
aspect of
collaboration
(University
Enrolment).

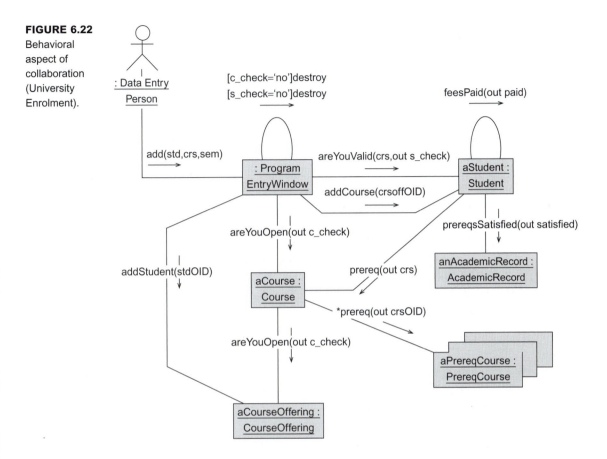

objects are needed to handle checking of student's fees and prerequisites before the student can be registered in a `CourseOffering`.

6.2.5 Realization of operations

Collaborations can also be used to model realizations of more complex operations (Booch *et al.*, 1999). Both structural and behavioral aspects of collaboration can be used for that purpose.

Only complex operations that require the collaboration of a number of objects should be modeled as collaborations. Simpler operations – confined to one or two classes – are better modeled with activity diagrams, in particular if they are algorithmically intensive. The same principle applies to simpler operations that are components of a complex operation modeled as collaboration.

Finally, the most straightforward operations can be modeled with *pseudocode* or can be directly implemented in code. The code that realizes such operation can still be included in the UML model as a note or an attached document.

📁 **Example 6.5 (University Enrolment)**

Refer to Examples 4.18 (Section 4.3.4.3), 6.3 (Section 6.2.4.1), and 6.4 (Section 6.2.4.2). Consider the message `addStudent(stdOID)` in Figure 6.22 (Example 6.4).

Our task is to design an activity diagram to realize the operation `CourseOffering.addStudent`. The operation would add a student to the attribute `CourseOffering.std`. The attribute is typed as a *template* `list<Student>` (Figure 4.15, Example 4.18).

Before the student is added to the course offering, the system performs a check to find out whether the course offering is still open. This is necessary even though the same check was performed just prior to issuing the event `addStudent(stdOID)` (Figure 6.22). In a highly-concurrent database system, the status of course offering (open or closed) could have changed in the meantime.

Once the student has been added to `:CourseOffering`, our algorithm has to fix the opposite link in `:Student`. The object `:Student` has to be updated to point back to `:CourseOffering`.

Figure 6.23 is the solution for the example. The scope of the activity diagram is the class `CourseOffering` except for the need to communicate with the class `Student` to maintain the referential integrity between the links.

The *event* (message) `addStudent` activates the *activity* (method) `addStudent`. The internal message `areYouOpen` activates the method `areYouOpen`. The activity `areYouOpen` checks the enrolment quota against the number of students already enrolled to arrive at the decision. The checks are done by internal *do actions*.

If the decision is negative, the *state* of the object `CourseOffering` will become `Closed`. Otherwise it will be `Open`. The execution of the activity diagram would terminate if in the `Closed` state.

If in the `Open` state, the activity `addStudent` continues. The *action* `add stdOID to CourseOffering.std` results in the new state `Student Added`. When in that state, another action `add crsoffOID to Student.crsoff` invokes the activity `Student.setCrsOff`.

The last activity identifies a new method to be included in the class `Student` (Figure 6.21). It also identifies the need for the attribute in `Student` called `crsoff` of type `list<Course>`.

6.3 Guided tutorial in design modeling

In Chapter 2, we presented a guided tutorial for the OnLine Shopping application. The purpose of that tutorial was to guide the reader through the basic concepts of analysis by using

FIGURE 6.23
Activity diagram
to model the
realization of
operation
(University
Enrolment).

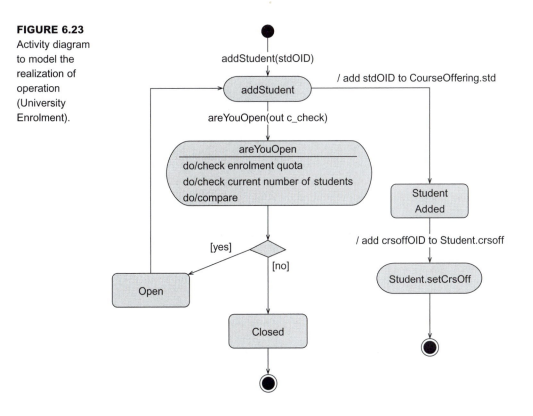

a case study. In this chapter we extend the same guided tutorial to put together the *basic design* concepts.

The objective of the tutorial is twofold. First, we *reinforce the new concepts* (introduced in Chapters 5 and 6) by using them in a single application domain. We address both the architectural issues (package, component, node) and the detailed design issues (collaborations). Second, we *elaborate the analysis models* developed in Section 2.2. That is, we add design details and extend existing models to effectively turn them into design documents, albeit still at relatively high abstraction level.

The scope of the tutorial is limited to the concepts introduced so far in the textbook. The detailed design of the user interface (Chapter 7), database (Chapter 8) and program logic (Chapter 9) is not considered.

6.3.1 Package design

In Section 5.2.3, we remarked that packages could group together classes or other modeling elements, most commonly – use cases. When used *in the analysis*, packages are typically applied to identify main clusters of use cases. *In the design*, packages are used in their most characteristic way – to cluster classes. Consequently, we distinguish between:

- Use case packages, and
- Class packages.

Package models are only warranted in structuring *larger systems*. Small systems may be understood and managed with no packages identified. The use cases may provide sufficient level of modularization in such systems. Occasionally, packages are created as 'architectural placeholders' to accommodate expected growth in the system scope or to acknowledge that the initial set of use cases and classes would grow as the development continues and the detailed design progresses.

Class packages in particular evolve during design as the *boundary, control* and *database classes* are added to the class models (we remind the reader that the class diagrams constructed in analysis identify and relate *entity classes* – other kinds of class are not really addressed until the design). Accordingly, a class package model takes a dominant role in the design. A *use case package* model is unlikely to be used beyond early design stages because the class package model effectively replaces it.

6.3.1.1 Use case packages

Design tutorial: Step 1 (OnLine Shopping)

Refer to the OnLine Shopping tutorial (Section 2.2). Consider the use case diagram in Figure 2.24 (Section 2.2.2.3). A closer look at the specifications for OnLine Shopping lead us to an observation that the use case model is not complete.

When studying and documenting the use cases already identified, we would certainly discover more use cases. New use cases may be *extensions* or *inclusions* of existing use cases (Section 4.3.1.2) or they may signify the use cases overlooked in the initial requirements analysis.

Either way, we assume that new use cases could add significantly to the complexity of the system and we, therefore, would like to structure the existing use cases into packages. The packages would be our 'functional placeholders' for the allocation of the existing and new packages.

In this example, we construct a use case package diagram to contain existing use cases and to accommodate the future growth.

Our solution to the example is presented in Figure 6.24. Five packages are identified and the use cases (Figure 2.24) assigned to them. The dependency relationships between packages are also shown.

Perhaps not surprisingly, the packages in Figure 6.24 tag along the sequence of doing business in OnLine Shopping. They reflect the order in which a customer that shops for a computer uses the browser's web pages and forms.

FIGURE 6.24
Use case
packages
(OnLine
Shopping).

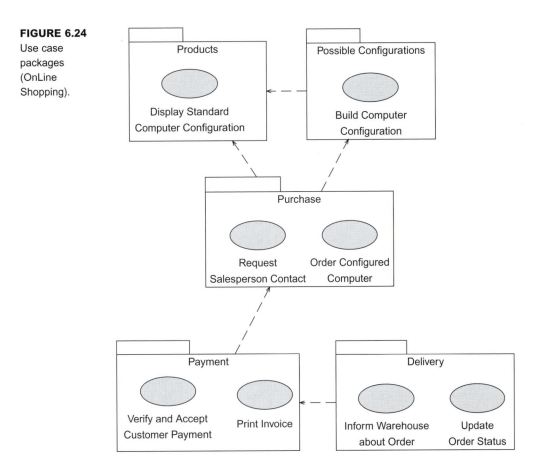

6.3.1.2 *Class packages*

Design tutorial: Step 2 (OnLine Shopping)

Refer to the OnLine Shopping tutorial (Section 2.2). Naturally enough, most classes that we defined in Section 2.2 represented *persistent database objects* ('business objects'). A more complete model for the system would require that *application program classes* be identified. This can be done during the collaboration design later in this tutorial.

Even though we do not have application program classes yet, we can speculate about packages that would group classes into coherent units according to the BCED approach (Section 6.1.3.2). Our task in this example is to think about possible packages in OnLine Shopping and the main dependencies between them.

The best way to attack the example is to 'impersonate the system' and imagine what needs to be done to accept a customer's order for a configured computer. The most obvious observation is that the system handles two separate functions: the computer configuration and order entry. These two functions require separate GUI windows. In the tutorial, we identified only two *boundary classes* but we can be certain that each function would demand a range of GUI objects. Hence, we can create two packages: `ConfigurationGUI` and `OrderGUI`.

On the 'business side' of the class spectrum, we identified a range of classes in the class diagram (Figure 2.31). These *persistent database classes* can be naturally grouped in three *entity packages*: `Customers`, `Computers`, and `Orders` (the latter would also include the classes `Invoice` and `Payment`).

Still missing are packages that glue the boundary and entity classes together, i.e. control packages. We need packages that contain *control classes* concerned with the execution of the application logic. We need a package to sensibly configure computers and calculate configuration prices. Let us call such a package `ConfigureProcess`. We also need a package responsible for entering and recording orders – an `OrderPlacement` package.

The three *entity packages* (`Customers`, `Computers`, and `Orders`) represent the in-memory run-time structure for persistent database classes. They provide a transient representation of otherwise persistent classes stored in a database. At any point of the program's execution, the objects of entity classes contain only a fraction of the database content. They also provide an object-oriented image of data structures, which are typically stored in non-object-oriented database structures, namely as relational tables. Consequently, there is a need for classes that establish an interface from entity classes to the database – there is a need for one or more *database packages*.

The main database package can be called `CRUD` – create–read–update–delete package (Section 4.3.4.1). The `CRUD` package mediates between the entity classes and the database tables whenever the application needs to access or modify the database content.

The `CRUD` package depends on two other database packages called `Connection` and `Schema`. Classes in the `Connection` package are responsible for the handling of connections, authorizations and transactions. The `Schema` package contains the current information about the database schema objects – tables, columns, stored procedures, etc. The application can instantiate the `Schema` objects when it starts so that it can validate that the database objects exist in the database before actually attempting to access the database (e.g. before a stored procedure is called, the application can verify, using an in-memory schema object, that the stored procedure still exists).

Figure 6.25 shows the packages as identified above. It shows also the main dependencies. The dependencies are initial and arguable. Without knowing all classes and communication links between them, the dependencies between packages are speculative. The main principle is that the boundary packages depend on the control packages, which in turn depend on the entity packages. Finally, the entity packages depend on the database packages.

Note that dependencies between packages are *not transitive* (Fowler and Scott, 2000). For example, in Figure 6.25 a change within the package `Customers` may necessitate changes in `ConfigureProcess` and `OrderPlacement`, but not in `ConfigurationGUI` and

FIGURE 6.25
Class packages (OnLine Shopping).

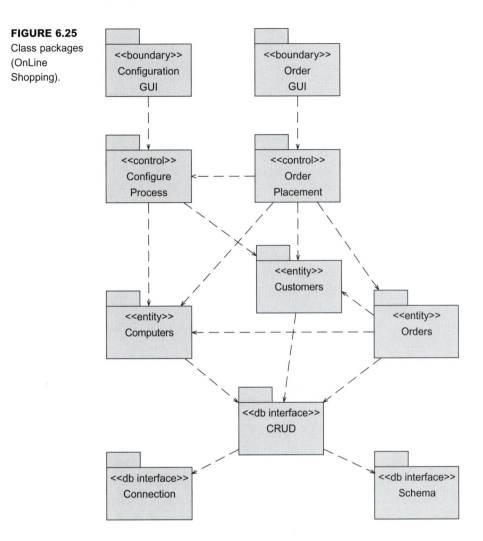

OrderGUI. Non-transitivity is of course necessary to achieve the (expected) complexity reduction in hierarchical or semi-hierarchical structures (Section 5.2.2).

Cycles in the dependency structure are another complexity factor. As a principle, cycles should be avoided (Lakos, 1996). In practice, cycles are sometimes very difficult to eliminate, in particular between packages at the same hierarchical layer (Fowler and Scott, 2000).

6.3.2 Component design

Components are physical parts of the system. The component design, therefore, cannot be separated from the implementation platform. OnLine Shopping is a web application with a database server. Other aspects of the implementation platform have not been determined.

The component design demands that the implementation platform is known. As we do not intend to advocate specific solutions or software vendors in this textbook, we will speculate on a possible implementation platform at a reasonably high level of generality.

6.3.2.1 *Implementing web applications*

'A Web application is a Web system that allows its users to execute business logic with a web browser.' (Conallen, 2000, p. 10.) The *business logic* can reside on the server and/or on the client. A *web application* is therefore a kind of C/S system (Section 6.1.1) with a web site.

An Internet client *browser* renders *web pages* on a computer screen. A *web server* delivers the web pages to the browser. Web page documents can be *static* (unmodifiable) or *dynamic*. A web page document can be a *form* that a user fills in. *Frames* can be used by the application to divide the screen's 'real estate' so that the user can view multiple web pages at the same time.

A web application can include an *application server* (Section 6.1.2) to manage the application logic and to monitor the application state. In applications like OnLine Shopping the state monitoring is an important system activity to keep track of actions of online customers, e.g. of computer configurations that they requested. A customer may decide to purchase a particular configuration at any point during an *online session* and the system must link the purchase order to the configuration.

A typical technique to monitor state is to store a *cookie* in the browser – a short string of characters that represents the state of an online user. Because the number of online users to be monitored by the web or application server is arbitrarily large, a *session timeout* may be imposed on the online user's activity. If the user is not active for 15 minutes (the typical timeout), the server disconnects from the client. The cookie itself may or may not be removed from the client machine.

Scripts and applets are used to make the *client page* dynamic. A *script* (e.g. written in JavaScript) is a program interpreted by the browser. An *applet* is a compiled component that executes in the browser's context but it has only limited access to other resources of the client computer (for security reasons).

A web page can also have scripts executed by the server. Such a page is called a *server page*. A server page has access to all resources of the database server. Server pages manage client sessions, place cookies on the browser and build client pages (i.e. build page documents from the server's business objects and send them back to the client).

Standard *data access libraries* are used to allow the scripts in the server pages to access the database. Typical enabling technologies include ODBC (Open Database Connectivity), JDBC (Java Database Connectivity), RDO (Remote Data Objects) and ActiveX Data Objects (ADO). In a situation where an organization standardizes on a particular database management system, low-level function calls to DBLib (Database Library) allow more direct access to the database.

The enabling technology for the *web server* is likely to be scripted HTML (HyperText Markup Language) pages – ASP (Active Server Pages) or JSP (Java Server Pages). The enabling technology for *web pages* can be client scripts (JavaScript or VBScript), XML (eXtensible Markup Language) documents, Java applets, JavaBean or ActiveX controls.

Clients use HTTP (Hypertext Transfer Protocol) to obtain web pages from the web server. The page may be scripted or it may contain compiled and directly executable DLL (Dynamic Link Library) modules, e.g. ISAPI (Internet Server Application Programming Interface), NSAPI (Netscape Server Application Programming Interface), CGI (Common Gateway Interface) or Java servlets (Conallen, 2000).

The *cookie* serves as a primitive mechanism for maintaining connection between the client and the server in what is otherwise a *connectionless Internet* system. More sophisticated mechanisms for connecting clients and servers turn the Internet into a *distributed object system*. In a distributed object system, objects are uniquely identified with OIDs (Section 2.1.1.3) and they communicate by obtaining each other's OIDs. The principal mechanisms are CORBA, DCOM and EJB (Section 1.1.1). In these technologies, objects can communicate without using HTTP (Hypertext Transfer Protocol) or going through a web server (Conallen, 2000).

6.3.2.2 *Component diagram*

Design tutorial: Step 3 (OnLine Shopping)

Refer to the discussion in Section 6.3.2.1 above and propose a component diagram for OnLine Shopping. Consider that a component is a cohesive functional unit with clear interfaces so that it becomes a replaceable part of the system. Since the implementation platform for OnLine Shopping is not specified, the identification of smaller components (such as libraries, stored procedures, etc.) is not possible at this stage.

One way of addressing this tutorial step is to consider the typical sequence of access to web pages by an online customer wishing to purchase a computer. The guidelines can be obtained from the analysis of use cases (Section 2.2.1) and use case packages (Section 6.3.1.1).

The first web page that an online customer would visit is the vendor's page that lists product categories (such as servers, desktops, portables), highlights latest offers and discounts, and provides links to web pages that list the products and give short descriptions of each product. The short descriptions include prices for standard product configurations. This part of the system is concerned with advertising the products to an online shopper. It is a cohesive unit of functionality that could constitute the component called `ProductList`.

The customer's next step would be to ask for technical specifications for a chosen product. This includes a visual display of the product from different angles. This is a stand-alone web page and a good candidate for the next component called `ProductDisplay`.

Assuming that the previous web pages attracted the customer to a product, different configurations for the product may be requested to satisfy the customer's special needs and budget. This would be done through dynamic web pages where configurations can be interactively built and displayed complete with a configured price. This is another good candidate for a component. Let us call it `Configuration`.

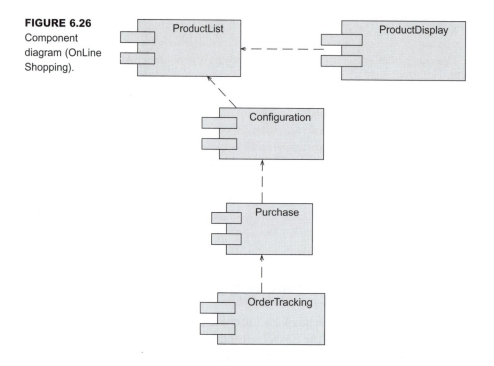

FIGURE 6.26
Component
diagram (OnLine
Shopping).

The customer who decides to buy a product is presented with the purchase order form. The details to be entered include the name and address for shipment and invoice. The payment method is also chosen and the relevant details submitted via some secure transfer protocol. This is the fourth component – `Purchase`.

The last component that we identify in this tutorial has to do with the order fulfillment and tracking. From the customer's perspective, this provides for the possibility of viewing the status of the order on a web page (after the customer number and the order number are entered). This component can be called `OrderTracking`.

The five components identified in the above discussion are shown in Figure 6.26. It is interesting to note the resemblance of this diagram to use case packages in Figure 6.24. This is not surprising because the use case packages and components are functional units with clear boundaries. Use case packages are logical units of functionality – they do not make an impact on the way the system is eventually built and they do not even need to be constructed if the system is simple. Components are physical tangible units of independent deployment – they have to be carefully designed and implemented even for small systems.

6.3.3 Deployment design

The connectionless nature of the Internet (Section 6.3.2.1) makes the *deployment* of a web application significantly more difficult than the deployment of a C/S database application. To start with, the web server has to be set up as the routing point between all client browsers and the database.

If the session management cannot be satisfactorily solved with the *cookie* technology then *distributed objects* need to be engaged. Deploying distributed objects would require a separate architectural element – an application server – to be placed between the web server and the database server.

The deployment design must address security issues. Secure transfer and encryption protocols make additional deployment demands. Careful planning is also needed with regard to network loads, Internet connections, backups, etc.

6.3.3.1 Deploying web applications

The deployment architecture capable of supporting more sophisticated web applications includes four tiers of computing nodes:

1. Client with browser.

2. Web server.

3. Application server.

4. Database server.

The browser of the *client node* can be used to display static or dynamic pages. Scripted pages and applets can be downloaded and run within the browser. Additional functionality can be supplied to the client's browser with objects such as ActiveX controls or JavaBeans. Running application code on the client but outside the browser may satisfy other GUI requirements.

The *web server* handles page requests from the browser and dynamically generates pages and code for execution and display on the client. The web server also deals with the customization and parameterization of the session with the user.

The *application server* is indispensable when distributed objects are involved in the implementation. It manages the business logic. The business components publish their interfaces to other nodes via component interfaces such as CORBA, DCOM or EJB.

The business components encapsulate persistent data stored in a database, probably a relational database. They communicate with the *database server* via database connectivity protocols such as JDBC or ODBC. The database node provides for a scalable storage of data and multi-user access to it.

6.3.3.2 Deployment diagram

Design tutorial: Step 4 (OnLine Shopping)

Refer to the discussion in Section 6.3.3.1 above and propose a deployment diagram for OnLine Shopping. In particular consider if there is a need in OnLine Shopping for an application server.

FIGURE 6.27
Deployment
diagram (OnLine
Shopping).

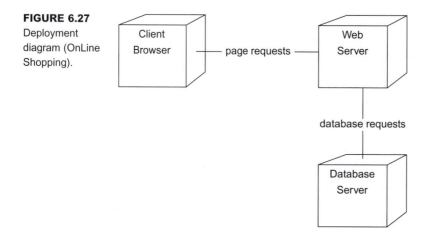

As shown in Figure 6.27, the OnLine Shopping application can be deployed without a separate application server. The web server would execute the code in the server pages. The potential advantage of an application server is that the application components they house can be reused by other web applications to invoke the same business logic. However, OnLine Shopping is a stand-alone system and no other web applications to take advantage of its business logic could be identified.

6.3.4 Collaboration design

As explained at the beginning of this chapter, system design divides into the architectural design and the detailed design. The design of packages, components and nodes belongs to the *architectural design*. The *detailed design* concentrates on collaborations (Section 6.2).

Collaborations define the realization of use cases and the realization of more intricate operations (simple operations do not have to be modeled as collaborations). The design of collaborations leads invariably to the *elaboration* (modifications and extensions) of existing class diagrams and to the production of new collaboration diagrams (or the elaboration of existing sequence diagrams). Other kinds of diagram, in particular statechart diagrams, may also need to be developed or elaborated.

6.3.4.1 *Elaborating use cases*

An important spin-off (or even a prerequisite) of collaboration design is the need to *elaborate use cases*. The use cases documented during requirements analysis are unlikely to contain sufficient level of detail for designing collaborations. The use case specifications have to be elaborated into the design documents. New design-level use case specifications must include the system-level demands while still maintaining the actors' perspective.

If the requirements management (Section 3.4) was laidback in analysis, now there is the last opportunity to get more formal and disciplined. The requirements should be carefully classified and numbered. To ensure the proper change and traceability management, the requirements should be stored in a CASE tool repository. (The significance of requirements management goes far beyond the requirements analysis and the early design phases. This is discussed in Chapter 10.)

6.3.4.1.1 Numbering and structuring requirements

Requirements need to be numbered (Section 3.4.1) and structured (Section 3.4.2). Both activities can best be accomplished with the assistance of a CASE tool. Attempts to track changes to requirements manually are destined to fail. With a CASE tool, renumbering and restructuring of requirements is easy.

Figure 6.28 shows a part of a use case specification document with numbered requirements. The requirements are numbered using the Dewey decimal system with the prefix UC (Use Case). The prefix is helpful when a use case document contains more than one type of requirement. Note that the requirements are enclosed in square brackets, are underlined and displayed in green (trust us on the color issue).

FIGURE 6.28
Excerpt from a use case document managed by a CASE tool.

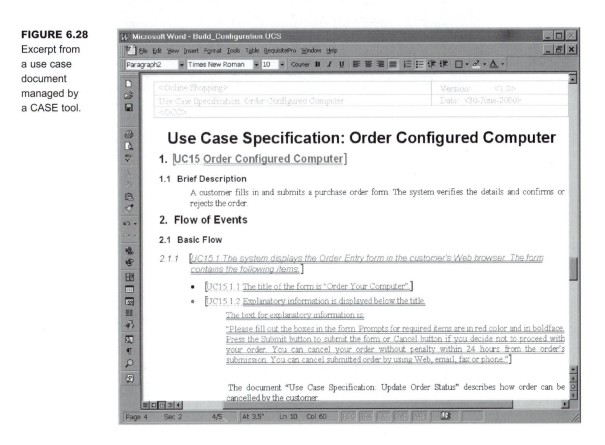

FIGURE 6.29
Requirements
management in a
CASE tool.

RequisitePro Views - [UC: Attribute Matrix]

File   View   Requirement   Window   Help

Requirements:	Property	Affect
⊟ UC15: Order Configured Computer	Name	False
⊟ UC15.1: The system displays the Order Entry form in the customer's...	Basic Flo	False
UC15.1.1: The title of the form is "Order Your Computer".	Basic Flo	False
UC15.1.2: Explanatory information is displayed below the title.The text...	Basic Flo	False
⊟ UC15.1.3: Shipment items.	Basic Flo	False
UC15.1.3.1: The required shipment items are: name, country, city,...	Basic Flo	False
UC15.1.3.2: The optional shipment items are: suburb, state, post code.	Basic Flo	False
⊟ UC15.1.4: Contact details other than provided in shipment items.	Basic Flo	False
UC15.1.4.1: Preferred means of contact: email, phone, fax, post mail,...	Basic Flo	False
UC15.1.4.2: The required contact detail is one of the following items:...	Basic Flo	False
UC15.1.4.3: The optional contact details are: two of the three contact...	Basic Flo	False
UC15.1.5: Invoice address if different than provided in shipment items.	Basic Flo	False
⊟ UC15.1.6: Payment method.	Basic Flo	False
UC15.1.6.1: The customer can choose to pay by check or credit card.	Basic Flo	False
UC15.1.6.2: For check payment, the system provides details to whom...	Basic Flo	False
UC15.1.6.3: For credit card payment, the system displays items to be...	Basic Flo	False
UC15.1.7: The name of the salesperson representative, if known to the	Basic Flo	False

UC15.1.6.3. For credit card payment, the system displays items to be filled in by the customer.

Ready   128 requirements

Once entered into a CASE repository, the requirements can be viewed and modified by other tools supported by the CASE toolkit. Figure 6.29 demonstrates one such display in which the hierarchy of requirements is emphasized. The designer can use this display to modify any requirement or to attach various attributes to them.

6.3.4.1.2   Use case design document

Design tutorial: Step 5 (OnLine Shopping)

Refer to the use case analysis document for OnLine Shopping in Section 2.2.2.4 (Table 2.2). The document is for the use case 'Order Configured Computer'. The document is not sufficient for designing a collaboration from it.

The purpose of this tutorial step is to elaborate the use case document into a design-level use case specification. The elaborated document is to be organized as in Figure 6.28. In fact, Figures 6.28 and 6.29 reveal a part of the solution to this tutorial step.

The text proper of the use case design document is shown below. Note that the document can be printed differently to the format presented here. For example, the display and printing of use case numbers can be suppressed.

Use Case Specification: Order Configured Computer

1. [UC15 Order Configured Computer]

1.1 Brief Description

A customer fills in and submits a purchase order form. The system verifies the details and confirms or rejects the order.

2. Flow of Events

2.1 Basic Flow

2.1.1 [UC15.1 The system displays the Order Entry form in the customer's Web browser. The form contains the following items.]

- [UC15.1.1 The title of the form is 'Order Your Computer'.]

- [UC15.1.2 Explanatory information is displayed below the title.

  The text for explanatory information is:

  'Please fill out the boxes in the form. Prompts for required items are in red color and in boldface. Press the Submit button to submit the form or Cancel button if you decide not to proceed with your order. You can cancel your order without penalty within 24 hours from the order's submission. You can cancel the submitted order by using Web, email, fax or phone.']

  The document 'Use Case Specification: Update Order Status' describes how an order can be cancelled by the customer.

- [UC15.1.3 Shipment items.]

  [UC15.1.3.1 The required shipment items are: name, country, city, street, courier directions.]

  [UC15.1.3.2 The optional shipment items are: suburb, state, post code.]

- [UC15.1.4 Contact details other than provided in shipment items.]

[UC15.1.4.1 Preferred means of contact: email, phone, fax, post mail, courier mail.]

[UC15.1.4.2 The required contact detail is one of the following items: email, phone, fax.]

[UC15.1.4.3 The optional contact details are: two of the three contact items listed as required, postal address (if different to provided in shipment items).]

- [UC15.1.5 Invoice address if different than provided in shipment items.]

- [UC15.1.6 Payment method.]

  [UC15.1.6.1 The customer can choose to pay by check or credit card.]

  [UC15.1.6.2 For check payment, the system provides details to whom the check should be paid and to what address it should be mailed. It also informs the customer that it takes three days to clear the check once received.]

  [UC15.1.6.3 For credit card payment, the system displays items to be filled in by the customer. The items are: the picklist of acceptable credit cards, credit card number, credit card expiry date.]

- [UC15.1.7 The name of the salesperson representative, if known to the customer from previous dealings.]

- [UC15.1.8 Two action buttons: Submit and Cancel.]

2.1.2 **[UC15.2 The system prompts the customer to enter order details by placing the cursor on the first editable field (the Name item).] [UC15.3 The system allows entering information in any order]**

- [UC15.4 If the customer does not submit or cancel the form within 15 minutes, the alternative flow 'Customer Inactive' executes.]

2.1.3 **[UC15.5 If the customer presses the Submit button and all required information has been provided, the order form is submitted to the Web server. The Web server communicates with the Database server to store the order in the database.] [UC15.6 The Database server assigns a unique order number and a customer account number to the purchase order.]**

- [UC15.7 If Database server is unable to create and store the order, the alternative flow 'Database Exception' executes.]

- [UC15.8 If the customer submits order form with incomplete information, the alternative flow 'Incomplete Information' executes.]

2.1.4 [UC15.9 If the customer provided email address as the preferred means of communication, the system emails to the customer the order and customer numbers, together with all order details, as the confirmation of the order's receipt. The use case terminates.] [UC15.10 Otherwise, the order details will be mailed to the customer and the use case terminates as well.]

2.1.5 [UC15.11 If the customer presses the `Cancel` button, the alternative flow 'Cancel' executes.]

2.2 *Alternative Flows*

2.2.1 Customer inactive

[UC15.4.1 If the customer is inactive for more than 15 minutes, the system terminates the connection with the browser. The use case terminates.]

2.2.2 Database exception

[UC15.7.1 If the database raises an exception, the system interprets it and informs the customer about the nature of the error. If the customer has disconnected, the system emails the error message to the customer and to a salesperson. The use case terminates.] If the customer is not reachable by Internet or email, the salesperson needs to contact the customer by other means.

2.2.3 Incomplete information

[UC15.8.1 If the customer has not filled in all required items, the system invites the customer to provide missing information. The list of missing items is displayed. The use case continues.]

2.2.4 Cancel

[UC15.11.1 If the customer presses the `Cancel` button, the form fields are cleared. The use case continues.]

3. Pre-Conditions

3.1 The customer points the Internet browser to the system's Web page. The page displays details of the configured computer together with its price. The customer presses the `Purchase` button.

3.2 The customer presses the `Purchase` button within 15 minutes from requesting the last computer configuration to be built and displayed in the browser's page.

4. Post-Conditions

4.1 If the customer's order submission is successful, the purchase order is recorded in the system's database. Otherwise, the system's state is unchanged.

6.3.4.2 *Structure of collaboration*

The class diagram developed during analysis identifies *persistent database classes*. *Application program classes* cannot really be determined before the design starts. Consequently, a class diagram that defines the structure of any collaboration needs to be developed almost from scratch. Collaboration classes are designed to adhere to the enabling technology chosen for the application (Section 6.3.2.1).

A *web page* can contain the scripts executed on the server or interpreted on the client by the browser, or both. The collaboration design for web pages is a challenge. The enabling technology may not properly support the object-oriented view of the world. In some cases, the entire application may be driven by a single web page loaded with objects and applets.

In more complex web applications, it should be possible to separate the client pages from the server pages. From the perspective of the BCED approach (Sections 6.1.3.2 and 6.3.1.2), HTML-formatted *client pages* correspond to *boundary classes*. *Server pages* can have associations with client pages on one hand and with other web server resources on the other hand. Server pages correspond to *control classes* in the BCED hierarchy (Conallen, 2000).

Design tutorial: Step 6 (OnLine Shopping)

Refer to the use case design document for 'Order Configured Computer' in Section 6.3.4.1.2. Based on the flow of events in that document, we would like to design the structural aspect of collaboration that realizes the 'Order Configured Computer' use case.

Even for such a simple use case, the detailed design of collaboration is beyond the scope of this tutorial. Several simplifications are made. There is no need to handle all the details of the order form structure and layout (see Chapter 7). Similarly, at the other end of the spectrum, there is no need to resolve the interfaces between the application and the database (i.e. we are not concerned here in the retrieval and storage of information in the database) (see Chapter 8).

The *BCED approach* applies (Section 6.3.1.2). All proposed classes should be assigned the prefix b, c, e, or d to signify their associations to an appropriate BCED package layer. The classes should also be stereotyped with one of the following stereotypes: «client page», «form», «server page», «entity», «db interface».

FIGURE 6.30
Structural
collaboration for
use case 'Order
Configured
Computer'
(OnLine
Shopping).

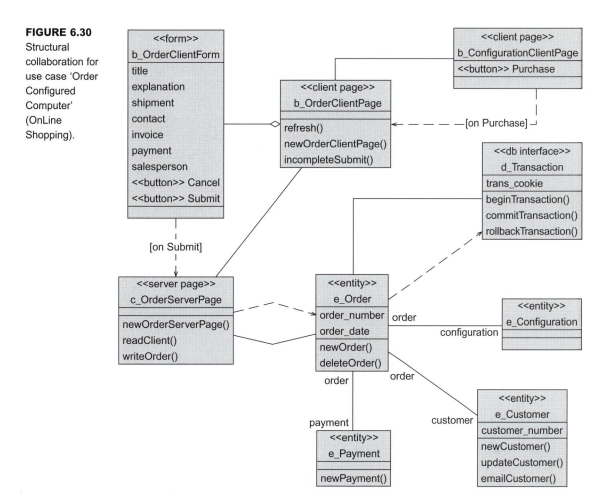

Any *association and aggregation relationships* between classes are to be identified. Also, *instantiation relationships* are to be shown to signify the flow of messages to instantiate objects (instantiation relationships are drawn in UML with arrowed dotted lines from the sender of a message to the class that is requested to instantiate the new object). If an object is instantiated as a result of a user event (e.g. a user pressing an action button), the event can be shown on the instantiation line.

Figure 6.30 is the class diagram that represents structural collaboration for the use case 'Order Configured Computer'. Because the use case is only part of the application and to model the pre- and post-conditions of the use case, two classes from another use case ('Build Computer Configuration') are shown and linked. These two classes are: b_ConfigurationClientPage and e_Configuration.

Note that [on Purchase] event activated from b_ConfigurationClientPage sets the scene for the use case. The class b_OrderClientPage is responsible for handling the content of b_OrderClientForm. The form is a collection of input fields on the screen that accept the input from the user. Once the form is filled in, it is submitted to a server page (c_OrderServerPage) for processing.

The four «entity» objects (e_Order, e_Configuration, e_Payment, and e_Customer) store the current order information independently of the web pages. Remember, however, that these are only *memory objects* – the persistent storage of an order in the database is outside the scope of this tutorial.

Associated with the collaboration is a d_Transaction object instantiated by c_OrderServerPage once the order is submitted. Although not shown explicitly on the diagram, the class d_Transaction would communicate with the database to ensure that the order transaction is properly committed to the database. This class is also the application mechanism for managing the client state – it instigates placing and removing cookies from the client.

6.3.4.3 *Behavior of collaboration*

Design tutorial: Step 7 (OnLine Shopping)

Refer to the use case design document for 'Order Configured Computer' in Section 6.3.4.1.2 and to the previous tutorial step (Section 6.3.4.2). Based on the flow of events in the use case document and availability of classes in Figure 6.30, we would like to design the behavioral aspect of collaboration for the use case.

Figure 6.31 is a collaboration diagram that represents the behavioral collaboration for the use case 'Order Configured Computer'. The diagram expresses the functional use case requirements. The collaboration starts when the first use case pre-condition is satisfied and the customer presses the Purchase button. This is modeled on the diagram as the message [on Purchase] newOrderClientPage.

An object of the class b_OrderClientPage services the message [on Purchase] newOrderClientPage. This HTML-formatted client page contains a «form» object of the class b_OrderClientForm (Figure 6.30). The attributes of this class represent the input fields on the form, including two action buttons: Cancel and Submit.

Once the client page displays the form in the browser's screen (UC15.1), the customer can enter the order information (UC15.2 and UC15.3). The Cancel action (UC15.11.1) is serviced by b_OrderClientPage (the refresh method). The Submit action when the customer has not filled in all required items (UC15.8.1) is also serviced by b_OrderClientPage (the incompleteOrder method).

FIGURE 6.31

Behavioral collaboration for use case 'Order Configured Computer' (OnLine Shopping).

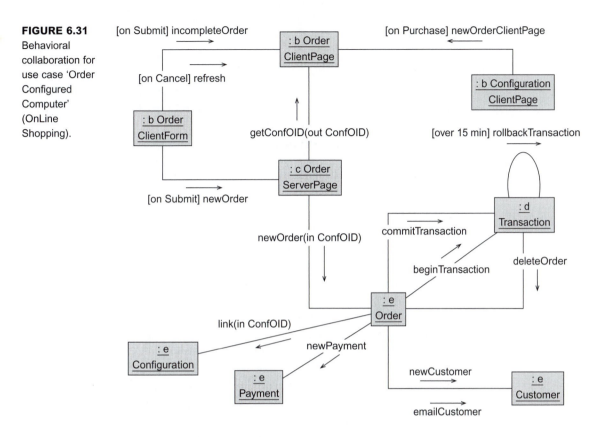

When the customer presses the Submit button and all required information has been provided (UC15.5), the class c_OrderServerPage takes control. It creates entity objects e_Order, e_Customer, e_Payment, and e_Configuration. The first three entity objects store the order form items entered by the customer.

The e_Configuration entity object has been instantiated before by another use case ('Build Computer Configuration'). It is now linked to e_Order after c_OrderServerPage obtained its OID from the link attribute in b_OrderClientPage (there is an association defined between b_OrderClientPage and b_ConfigurationClientPage).

Once e_Order is instantiated, the business transaction begins. To this aim a new d_Transaction object is created. It manages the client state, including cookie-driven timeouts. If the transaction commits, e_Order requests e_Customer to confirm the order receipt to the customer by e-mail (UC15.9).

If the cookie expires (UC15.4) or the database returns an error (UC15.7.1), the method rollbackTransaction requests that e_Order deletes itself and d_Transaction releases itself to the operating system. The customer would need to re-enter order form information to continue. The communication between d_Transaction and the database server is not modeled in the diagram.

Summary

This chapter has opened the discussion about the system design by presenting the system design underpinnings. The discussion followed on from the previous chapter on advanced requirements analysis. The two main (and distinctive) aspects of the design – the architectural design and the detailed design – were explained.

Typical IS applications are based on the *client/server* architectural principle. Specific C/S solutions include *distributed processing systems* and *distributed database systems*. *Three-tier systems* extend the basic C/S architecture by extracting an application logic into a separate logical and/ or physical layer.

The architectural decisions make an impact on the design of interfaces between an application and the database. The BCE hierarchy of packages (introduced in Chapter 5) has to be extended with a database interface package to constitute a *BCED hierarchy*.

Reuse is a major design consideration affecting the architectural as well as the detailed design issues. The choices are between a *toolkit reuse*, *framework reuse*, and *pattern reuse*. The choices are not exclusive – a mix of reuse strategies is recommended. The reuse from external sources has to be aligned with the internal design of packages, *components*, classes and interfaces. The computational resources are eventually represented as *deployment* diagrams.

The detailed design concentrates on *collaborations*. A collaboration specifies the realization of a use case or an operation. A collaboration models the message passing between objects. Issues to consider include overriding, overloading, iteration, templates, self messages, asynchronous messages, and callbacks. *Structural* aspects of collaboration are modeled in class diagrams; *behavioral* aspects in collaboration diagrams.

The chapter concluded with a *guided tutorial* in design modeling – a continuation of the analysis tutorial from Chapter 2 (utilizing the OnLine Shopping application). The tutorial illustrated the use of the UML design techniques – the design of packages, components, deployment and collaborations.

Review questions

R1 Explain the difference between a distributed processing system and a distributed database system.

R2 What is a three-tier architecture? What are its advantages and disadvantages?

R3 What do we mean by an active database?

R4 What is the purpose of the database package in the BCED approach?

R5 Compare the toolkit and the framework reuse.

R6 How are components and packages related to each other?

R7 What is a dominant class?

R8 What is a connection relationship?

R9 What is a realization relationship in a collaboration? Give an example (other than from this textbook).

R10 What are the alternative means of representing message arguments on collaboration diagrams?

R11 What are the main message types (apart from constructors and destructors)?

R12 What is the difference between overriding and overloading?

R13 How are iteration messages related to collections?

R14 A sender of a message may or may not send its OID to the target object. Does this statement apply to asynchronous messages? Explain.

R15 Which UML diagram is used for designing the structural aspect of collaboration? Explain its suitability for this task.

R16 Which UML diagrams can be used for designing the behavioral aspect of collaboration? Compare their suitability for this task.

R17 Compare the applicability of the use case packages and the class packages in the analysis and design phases of the system development lifecycle.

Exercise questions

Additional requirements (Video Store)

Consider the following additional requirements for Video Store (repeated here from the end of Chapter 2 for convenience):

1. Tapes/disks returned late induce a payment equal to an extra rental period. Each movie medium has a unique identification number.

2. The movies are ordered from suppliers who are generally able to supply tapes/disks within one week. Typically, several movies are ordered in a single order to a supplier.

3. Reservations are accepted for a movie that is on order and/or because all copies of a particular movie are rented out. Reservations are also accepted for movies that are neither in store nor on order, but a customer is then asked for a deposit of one rental period.

4. Customers can make many reservations, but a separate reservation request is prepared for each movie reserved. A reservation may be canceled due to the lack of response from a customer, more precisely one week from the date the customer was contacted that the movie was available for rental. If a deposit has been paid it is then credited to the customer's account.

5. The database stores the usual information about suppliers and customers, i.e. addresses, phone numbers, etc. Each order to a supplier identifies the ordered movies, tape/disk formats, and quantities, and also an expected delivery date, purchase price, applicable discounts, etc.

6. When a tape is returned by a customer or is delivered from a supplier, reservations are first satisfied. This involves contacting the customer who made the reservation. In order to ensure that reservations are properly handled, both the 'reserved movie has arrived' contact with customer, and the subsequent rental to the customer are related back to the reservation. These steps ensure that reservations are properly carried through.

7. In a single rental transaction, a customer can borrow many tapes or disks. For each rental, the check-out, due-in and return dates and times are recorded. The rental record is later updated to indicate that the video has been returned and the final payment (or reimbursement) has been made. The clerk who authorizes the rental is also recorded. Details about a customer and rentals are kept for a year to enable the customer rating to be determined easily. Old rental details are kept for auditing purposes for the year.

8. All transactions are made by cash, electronic money transfer or credit cards. Customers are required to pay the rental charges when tapes/disks are checked out.

9. When a tape/disk is returned late (or it cannot be returned for whatever reason), a payment is taken either from the customer's account or directly from the customer.

10. If a tape/disk is overdue by more than two days, an Overdue Notice is sent to the customer. Once two Overdue Notices on a single tape or disk have been sent, the customer is noted to be delinquent and the next rental is subject to management removing the delinquent rating.

E1 *Video Store* – refer to the additional requirements above and to Example 4.14 (Section 4.3.1.3). For assistance, refer also to the solutions to the Video Store exercises at the end of Chapter 4.

Design a structural collaboration diagram for the realization of the 'Reserve Video' use case.

E2 *Video Store* – refer to the additional requirements above and to Example 4.14 (Section 4.3.1.3). For assistance, refer also to the solutions to the Video Store exercises at the end of Chapter 4.

Design a behavioral collaboration diagram for the realization of the 'Reserve Video' use case.

E3 *Video Store* – refer to the additional requirements above and to Example 4.14 (Section 4.3.1.3). For assistance, refer also to the solutions to the Video Store exercises at the end of Chapter 4.

Design a structural collaboration diagram for the realization of the 'Return Video' use case.

E4 *Video Store* – refer to the additional requirements above and to Example 4.14 (Section 4.3.1.3). For assistance, refer also to the solutions to the Video Store exercises at the end of Chapter 4.

Design a behavioral collaboration diagram for the realization of the 'Return Video' use case.

E5 *Video Store* – refer to the additional requirements above and to Example 4.14 (Section 4.3.1.3). For assistance, refer also to the solutions to the Video Store exercises at the end of Chapter 4.

Design a structural collaboration diagram for the realization of the 'Order Video' use case.

E6   *Video Store* – refer to the additional requirements above and to Example 4.14 (Section 4.3.1.3). For assistance, refer also to the solutions to the Video Store exercises at the end of Chapter 4.

Design a behavioral collaboration diagram for the realization of the 'Order Video' use case.

E7   *Video Store* – refer to the additional requirements above and to Example 4.14 (Section 4.3.1.3). For assistance, refer also to the solutions to the Video Store exercises at the end of Chapter 4.

Design a structural collaboration diagram for the realization of the 'Maintain Customer' use case.

E8   *Video Store* – refer to the additional requirements above and to Example 4.14 (Section 4.3.1.3). For assistance, refer also to the solutions to the Video Store exercises at the end of Chapter 4.

Design a behavioral collaboration diagram for the realization of the 'Maintain Customer' use case.

E9   *Video Store* – refer to Example 4.16 (Section 4.3.2.3). Consider the activity `Update Stock` in Figure 4.13. For assistance, refer also to the solutions to the Video Store exercises at the end of Chapter 4.

Draw an activity diagram for the realization of the operation `Update Stock`.

Chapter 7

User Interface Design

The days when the screens were dumb and green and the keyboard the only input device are gone. Today the screens are intelligent and colorful and the user is equipped with the mouse (not to mention the voice and touch) to control the program's execution. Of course, the program can still be designed to disallow illegal or unauthorized events but the shift of control from the algorithm to the user has changed the way the GUI systems are designed and implemented.

The development of user interfaces begins with early sketches of GUI windows in the requirements analysis phase. These sketches are used for requirements gathering, in storyboarding sessions with the customers, for prototyping, and for inclusion in the use case documents. During the design, the GUI windows for the application are developed to conform to the underlying GUI presentation software and to the peculiarities and constraints of the chosen programming environment. This is the subject of this chapter.

7.1 Interface design as a multidisciplinary activity

The GUI (Graphical User Interface) design is a *multidisciplinary activity*. It requires the multidisciplinary skills of a *team* – a single person is unlikely to have the knowledge demanded by the multifaceted considerations of GUI design. A good GUI design requires the combined skills of a graphic artist, requirements analyst, system designer, programmer, technology expert, social and behavioral scientist, and perhaps a few other professions depending on the nature of the system.

A typical process of GUI design for IS applications begins with *use cases*. The *analyst* describing the flow of events for a use case has some visual image of GUI to support the human–computer interaction. In some cases, the analyst may choose to insert graphical depictions for user interfaces in the use case document. The complex human–computer interactions cannot be adequately described in prose alone. Occasionally, the process of gathering and negotiating customer requirements necessitates the production of GUI sketches.

The *designer* involved in specifying collaborations for realization of use cases must have a clear visual image of GUI screens. If the analyst has not done this before, the designer will be the first person to produce depictions for user interfaces. The designer's depictions must conform to the underlying GUI technology – windowing and widget toolkits, Internet browsers, etc. A *technology expert* may need to be consulted to successfully exploit technological features.

Before collaboration designs are passed on to programmers for implementation, a 'user-friendly' prototype of GUI screens needs to be constructed. This task should engage *graphic artists* and *social and behavioral scientists*. Together they can offer a GUI that is attractive and usable.

The *programmer's* task is not just to blindly implement the screens but also to suggest changes motivated by the programming environment. In some cases, the changes may be improvements. In other cases, the changes may worsen the design due to the programming or performance restrictions.

The above short discussion makes it clear that the GUI design is a very comprehensive task. Separate books have been written to emphasize different aspects of the GUI design (e.g. Constantine and Lockwood, 1999; Galitz, 1996; Fowler, 1998; Olsen, 1998; Ruble, 1997; Windows, 2000). In this chapter, we concentrate on what the system *designer* must know to *collaboratively design* a successful interface.

7.2 From interface prototype to implementation

The central issue in GUI design is that the *user is in control* (with the proviso that the system, not the user, controls the system integrity, safety and security). A modern object-oriented program is *event-driven*. Objects respond to events (messages). The internal communication between objects is triggered by external user-activated events.

The GUI 'look and feel' sells the software product to the customer. A GUI prototype can serve the double purpose of evaluating the 'feel' of the GUI screen and conveying its functions. The real 'look' of the screen is delivered in the implementation phase.

Example 7.1 (Contact Management)

Refer to the Problem statement for Contact Management (Section 2.3.3) and to the successive examples for Contact Management in Chapter 4. In particular, consider the design of the class `Organization` in Example 4.8 (Section 4.2.2.3).

The purpose of this example is to demonstrate the change that a GUI screen for Organization can undergo from an initial prototype to the final implementation. We assume that the underlying GUI technology is Microsoft Windows.

A GUI prototype for Organization is presented in Figure 7.1. Its main purpose is to visualize data and control objects in the window. The feedback obtained from the users and the ideas of the GUI development team will change the window's 'look' and possibly also its 'feel.'

Figure 7.2 shows the possible implementation of the Organization window as a dialog box. As can be seen, the programmer opted for the tabbed pages in the implemented window and

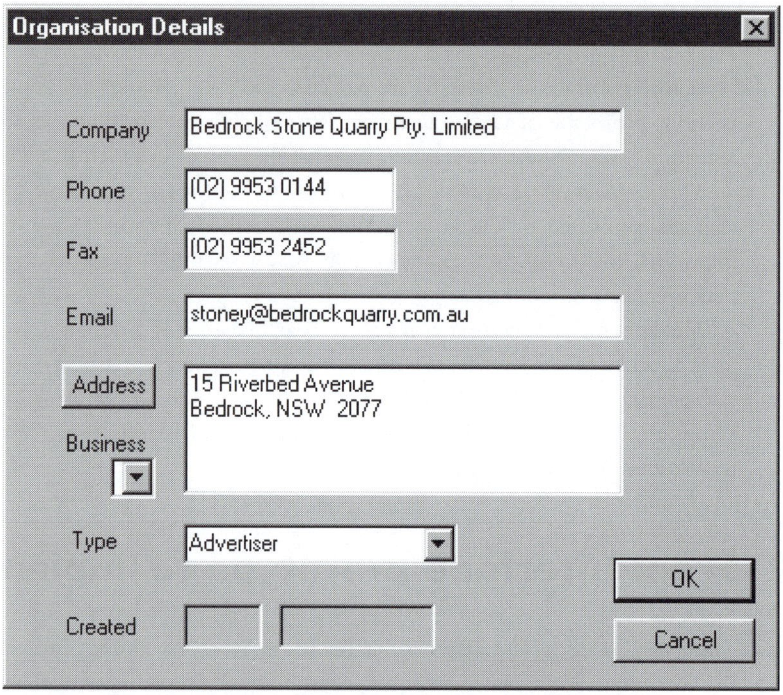

FIGURE 7.1
Window
prototype for
the class
Organization
(Contact
Management)
(courtesy of
ACNielsen AdEx,
Sydney,
Australia).

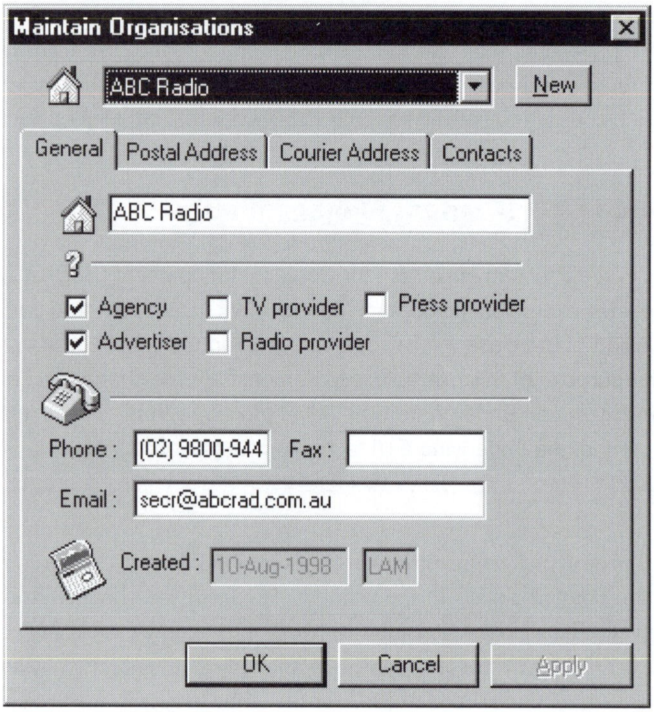

FIGURE 7.2
Implemented
window for
the class
Organization
(Contact
Management)
(courtesy of
ACNielsen AdEx,
Sydney,
Australia).

a number of other 'look-and-feel' changes have been made to conform to the Microsoft Windows GUI design principles.

7.3 Guidelines for user-centered interface design

The GUI design centers on the user. Associated with this observation is a range of guidelines to software developers. The guidelines are published by the manufacturers of GUI interfaces (e.g. Windows, 2000). They are also discussed in many books (e.g. Galitz, 1996; Ruble, 1997).

The *GUI guidelines* constitute the foundations on which the developer builds. They should be at the back of the developer's mind in all GUI design decisions. Some of the guidelines sound like aged pieces of the ubiquitous wisdom; others have been motivated by the modern GUI technology.

7.3.1 User in control

The *user in control* is the principal GUI guideline. This could be better called the *user's perception of control*. Some call it the *no mothering* principle – the program should not act like your mother; do things for you (Treisman, 1994). The underlying meaning is that the user initiates actions and if, as a result, the program takes control then the user obtains a necessary *feedback* (an hourglass, wait indicator, or similar).

Figure 7.3 demonstrates a typical flow of control in a human–computer interaction. A user event (a menu action, mouse click, screen cursor movement, etc.) can open a GUI window or invoke a program – typically, a 4GL-SQL program in IS applications. The program temporarily takes control from the user.

The program execution can return the control back to the same or another window. Alternatively, it can call another 4GL-SQL module or can invoke an external routine. In some cases, the program can in fact do things for the user. This may happen, for example, when the program needs to do a computation that is normally associated with an explicit user's event or if the program moves the cursor to another field on the screen and the event of leaving the original field has an exit processing associated with it.

7.3.2 Consistency

Consistency is arguably the second most important guideline of good interface design. Consistency really means the adherence to standards and the usual way of doing things. There are at least two dimensions to consistency:

- Conformance to the GUI vendor's standards;
- Conformance to the naming, coding and other GUI-related standards developed internally by the organization.

FIGURE 7.3
GUI program
flow of control.

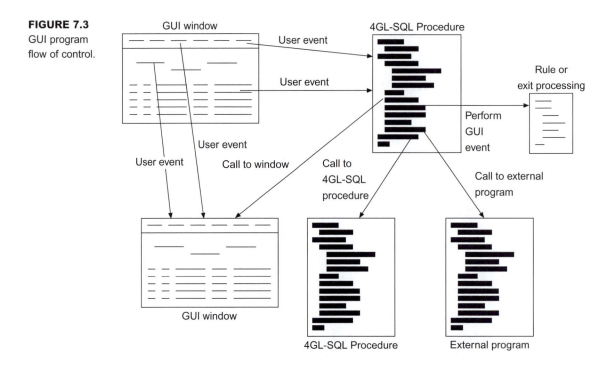

Both dimensions are important and the second (over which the developers have influence) must not contradict the first. If an application is developed for Windows then the Windows 'look-and-feel' must be delivered. On a Macintosh, replacing the celebrated apple menu by a 'kangaroo menu,' as the author of this book once attempted, is not a good idea either!

A GUI developer must not be too creative and innovative in the interface design. Being so will erode the confidence and ability of the users. The users should be presented with a familiar and predictable environment. As Treisman (1994) observed, imagine what a car designer would do to the car driving community if new cars were released with the accelerator and brake pedals swapped around!

Conformance to naming, coding, abbreviations and other internal standards cannot be underestimated either. This includes the naming and coding of the menus, action buttons, screen fields, etc. It also includes any standards for the placement of objects on the screen and consistent use of other GUI elements across all internally developed applications.

7.3.3 Personalization and customization

Personalization and customization are two related guidelines. GUI personalization is simply customization for personal use whereas customization – as we understand it here – is an administrative task of tailoring the software to different groups of users.

An example of personalization is when a user reorders and resizes columns in a row browse (grid) display and saves these changes as his/her personal preference. Next time the program is activated, the personal preferences are taken into account.

An example of customization is when the program can operate differently for novice and advanced users. For instance, the novice users may be offered an explicit help and extra warning messages for user events perceived to be dangerous.

In many cases, the distinction between personalization and customization is blurred or negligible. Changing menu items, creating new menus, etc. are cases in point. If done for personal use, it is personalization. If done by a system administrator for the user community at large, it is customization.

7.3.4 Forgiveness

A good interface should allow the users to experiment and make mistakes in a forgiving way. *Forgiveness* encourages an explorable interface because the user is allowed to take erroneous routes but can be 'rolled back' to the starting point if necessary. Forgiveness implies a multi-level *undo* operation.

This is easily said, difficult to implement. The implementation of forgiveness into the interface is a particular challenge in multi-user database applications. The user who withdrew (and spent) money from the bank account cannot possibly undo this operation! He/she can only rectify the problem by depositing the money back into the account in another transaction. Whether or not a forgiving interface should be warning the user of the consequences of cash withdrawal is a debatable issue (and the one that relates to the personalization guideline).

7.3.5 Feedback

The *feedback* guideline is a spin-off of the first guideline – the user in control. To be in control implies knowledge of what's going on when the control is temporarily with the program. The developer should build into the system visual and/or audio cues for every user event.

In most cases, an hourglass or a wait indicator is sufficient feedback to show that the program is doing something. For those parts of the application that may experience occasional performance problems, a more vivid form of feedback may be necessary (such as the display of an explanatory message). Either way, the developer must never assume that the application performs so quickly that the feedback is unnecessary. Any surge in application workload will prove the developer painfully wrong.

7.3.6 Aesthetics and usability

Aesthetics are about the system's visual appeal. *Usability* is about the ease, simplicity, efficiency, reliability, and productivity in using the interface. Ultimately, both are about *user satisfaction*.

This is where the GUI developer needs the assistance of a graphic artist and a social and behavioral expert.

There are many golden rules for an aesthetic and usable design (Galitz, 1996; Constantine and Lockwood, 1999). The issues to consider include the fixation and movement of the human eye, the use of colors, the sense of balance and symmetry, the alignment and spacing of elements, the sense of proportion, the grouping of related elements, etc.

The guideline of aesthetics and usability turns the GUI developer into an artist. It is good to remember in this context that 'simple is beautiful'. In fact, *simplicity* is frequently considered as yet another GUI guideline, strongly related to the aesthetics and usability guideline. Simplicity in complex applications is best achieved by the 'divide and conquer' approach – the progressive disclosure of information so that it is shown only when needed, possibly in separate windows.

7.4 Interface windows

There are two main aspects of GUI design – the design of windows and the design of windows' input and editing controls. Both depend on the underlying GUI environment. In the following discussion we concentrate on the Microsoft Windows environment (Windows, 2000).

A typical Windows application consists of a single main application window, the *primary window*. The primary window is supported by a set of pop-up windows, the *secondary windows*. The secondary windows support the user's activities in the primary window. Many activities supported by secondary windows are the CRUD (create, read, update and delete) operations on the database.

7.4.1 Primary window

A *primary window* has a border (frame). The frame contains a title bar (caption bar) for the window, a menu bar, toolbars, a status bar, and the window's viewable and modifiable content. Horizontal and vertical scroll bars are used to scroll through the content, if required.

The window's viewable and modifiable content can be organized into panes. Panes permit seeing and manipulating different but related information content. Figure 7.4 demonstrates a primary window that displayed after a successful login to an application. The pane on the left contains an application map in the Windows Explorer style (the close button in the right upper corner of the pane informs the user that the pane can be dismissed, if so desired). The commentary explains the well-known Windows terminology.

A typical distinguishing feature of a primary window is the existence of the menu bar and toolbar. The toolbar contains action icons for most frequently used menu items. The toolbar icons duplicate these menu items. They provide for a quick way of executing frequent actions.

FIGURE 7.4
Primary window
(courtesy of
ACNielsen AdEx,
Sydney,
Australia).

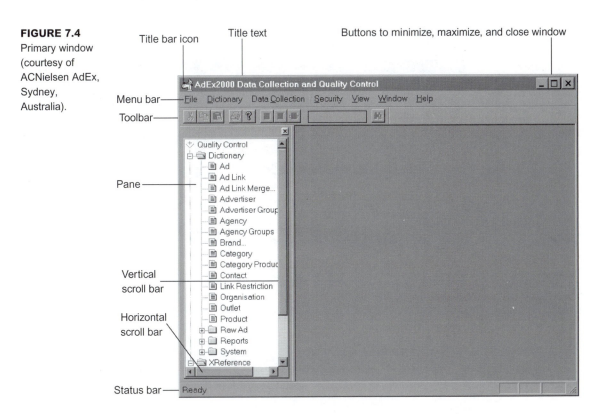

Example 7.2 (Contact Management)

Refer to the Problem statement for Contact Management (Section 2.3.3) and to the successive examples for Contact Management in Chapter 4. The users require that the Contact Management application be modeled on the functionality of the Calendar window in Microsoft Outlook (Figure 7.5).

The primary window should display the activities scheduled for the day for the employee who is using the system. The Calendar control can display past and future activities. The events scheduled for a particular time of the day (*timed events*) are to be displayed as in the Microsoft Outlook left pane. However, there is also a requirement to show and handle *untimed*, *outstanding* (due in the past), and *completed* events.

Our task in this example is to design a primary window for Contact Management that conforms to the above requirements.

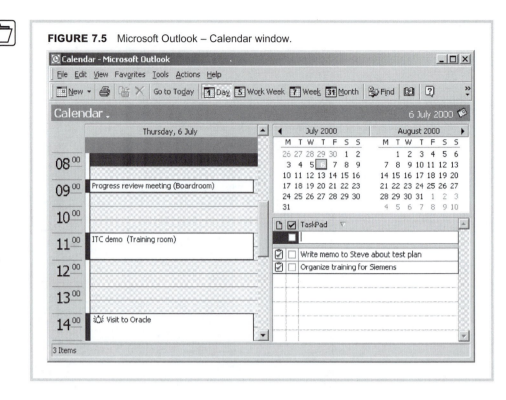

FIGURE 7.5 Microsoft Outlook – Calendar window.

Figure 7.6 shows the primary window in Contact Management. The Calendar control is designed as a detachable 'floating' window to conserve space. It can be closed if so desired. For each event in the left-hand pane, the event's short description and either an organization or contact name is shown. For some events, additional information may be shown as well, e.g. the organization's or contact's phone number, a fax number or address. Although not clearly visible in this book's black-and-white print, color is used in the left pane to signify the priority assigned to the event (high – in red, normal – in black, and low – in blue).

The right-hand pane serves three purposes. It displays three kinds of event. *Completed* events are removed from the left-hand pane and placed at the top of the right-hand pane. The text is in blue type and crossed out. The main reason why a completed event is not altogether removed from the display is that the completed event may need to be 'uncompleted' (perhaps we prematurely thought that the job was done but found out later that it was not quite done).

The *outstanding* events are listed in the right pane. They are in red. Finally, the *untimed* events are shown in black and listed at the bottom of right pane. The left-hand side column in the pane is designed with color-blind users in mind. The icons there signify the three kinds of event possible in the right pane.

FIGURE 7.6
Primary window
in Contact
Management
(courtesy of
ACNielsen AdEx,
Sydney,
Australia).

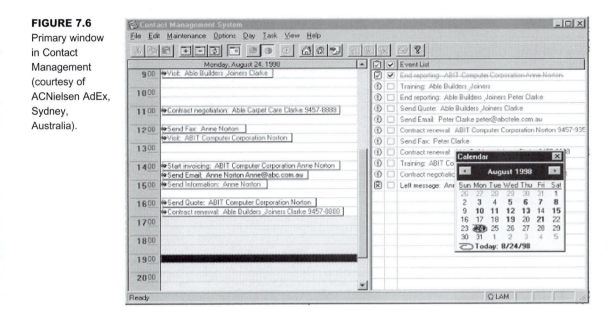

7.4.1.1 Row browser

A frequent use of the primary window in IS applications is to provide a 'row browse' display of database records, such as employee records. Such a window is sometimes called a *row browser*. The user can browse up and down through the records using the vertical scroll bar or keys on the keyboard (Page Up, Page Down, Home, End, and up and down arrows).

Figure 7.7 is an example of a row browser. The document – labeled `Ad Link` – inside the primary window is a *child window* (to be explained later). The child window has its own set of *window buttons* (minimize, restore, close) placed in the right corner of the menu bar. The columns of the browser's grid are *resizable* and their positions can be *rearranged*. The circular dents next to column names indicate that the column is *sortable* – clicking at the column will sort the records in an ascending or descending order of that column's values.

At any particular time, only one row (record) is active in the browser. Double-clicking at that record would normally display an 'edit window' with details for that record. The *edit window* allows modifying the content of the record.

Panes can be used to split the window vertically or horizontally, or even both ways. Figure 7.8 demonstrates a horizontal split. As the window title informs, the three panes are used to display the products by advertiser and by agency. The middle pane shows the advertisers belonging to the advertising agency currently selected (highlighted) in the top pane. The bottom pane then shows the products advertised by a selected advertiser.

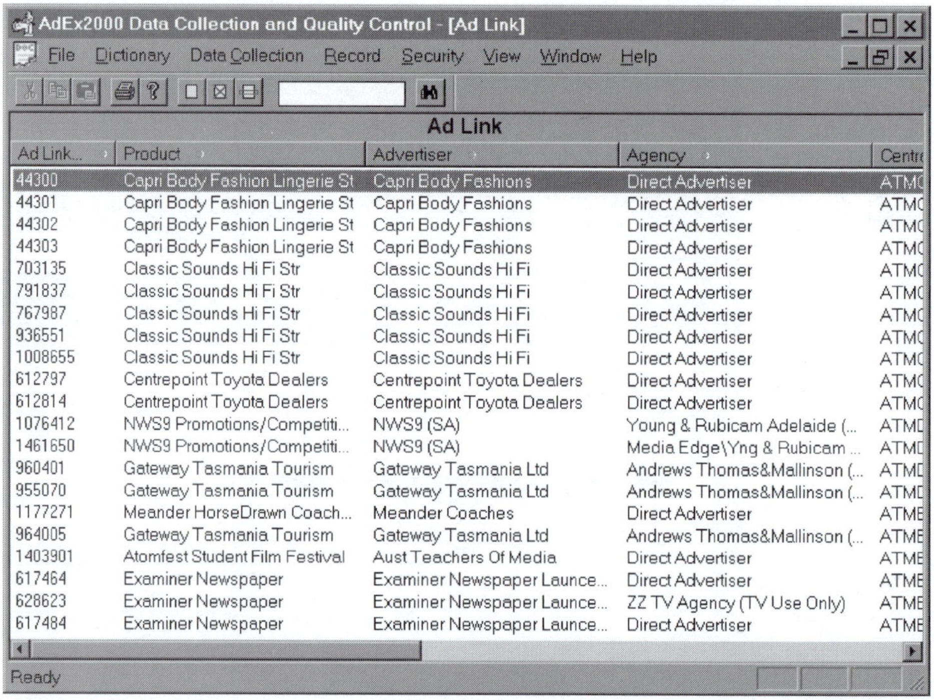

FIGURE 7.7
Row browse
window (courtesy
of ACNielsen
AdEx, Sydney,
Australia).

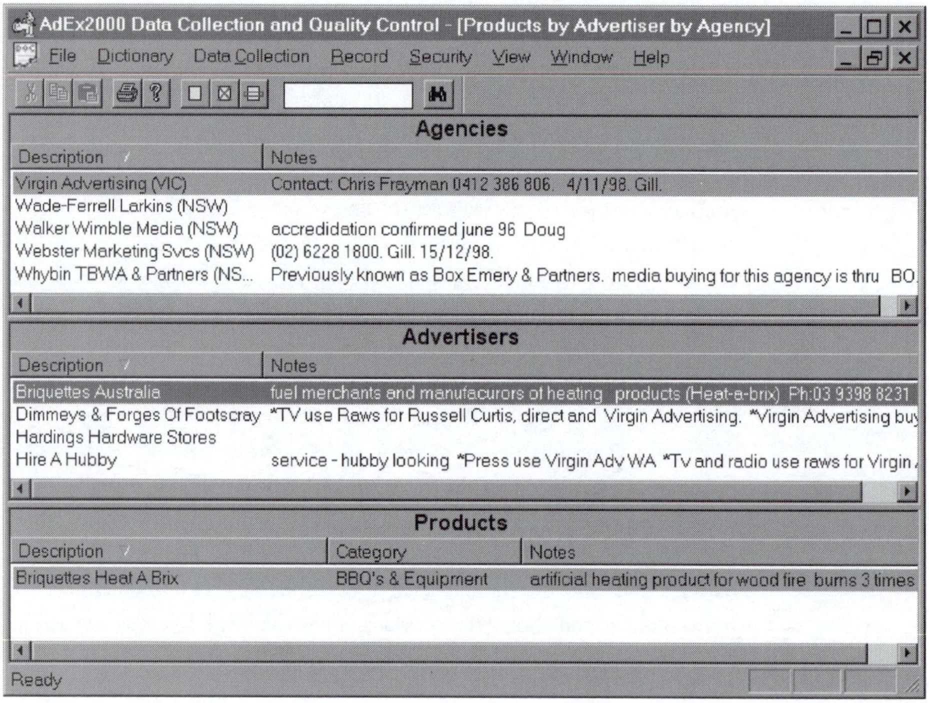

FIGURE 7.8
Multi-pane row
browse window
(courtesy of
ACNielsen AdEx,
Sydney,
Australia).

FIGURE 7.9
Window with tree
browse and row
browse panes
(courtesy of
ACNielsen AdEx,
Sydney,
Australia).

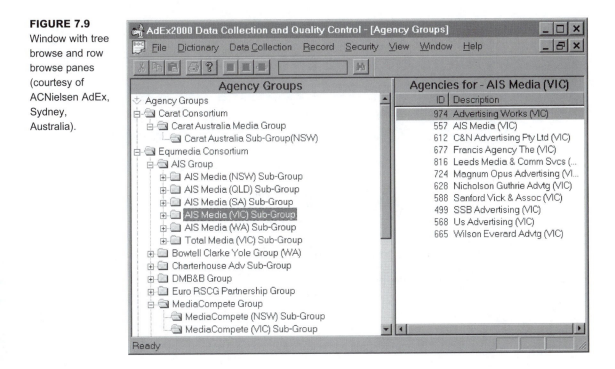

7.4.1.2 Tree browser

The other popular way of using the primary window is as a tree browser. A *tree browser* displays related records as an indented outline. The outline contains controls that allow the tree to be expanded or collapsed. A well-known example of a tree browser is the display of computer folders in Windows Explorer.

Unlike a row browser, a tree browser would allow in-place modifications, i.e. it would allow modifying the content of the window without activating an edit window. Modifications in a tree browser are done through 'drag and drop' operations.

Figure 7.9 demonstrates a tree browser in the left pane of the window. The right pane is a row browser. Selecting an agency group record in the tree browser displays the agencies of that agency group in the row browser.

7.4.1.3 Web page

A *web page* can also be treated as a special kind of primary window if it is used as an entry point of a web application. Unlike in conventional IS applications, the menu bar and toolbar of a web page are not used for application tasks. They are used for generic web surfing activities. The user events in web applications are normally programmed through action buttons and active hyperlinks.

FIGURE 7.10
Web page
window (courtesy
of Macquarie
University,
Sydney,
Australia).

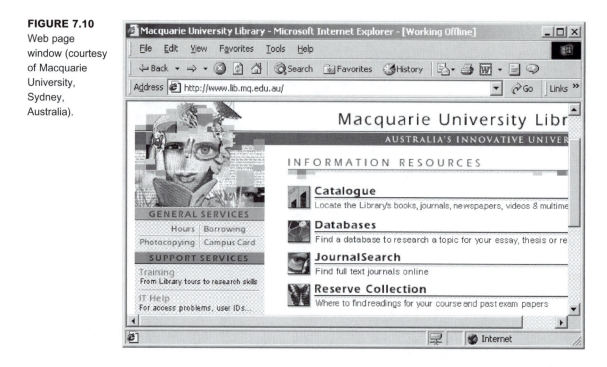

Figure 7.10 shows a web page that is an entry point to the Macquarie University Library web site. The menu bar and toolbar do not apply to the web page. Hyperlinks are used to search in the library database and to borrow books or other library items.

7.4.2 Secondary window

Disregarding some primitive IS applications, a *secondary window* supplements its primary window. It extends the functionality of the primary window, in particular for operations that modify the database (i.e. the insert, delete and update operations).

A secondary window is typically *modal* with respect to the primary window. The user must respond and close the secondary window before interacting with any other window of the application. *Modeless* secondary windows are possible but not recommended.

The *logon window* is a simple example of the secondary window. The logon screen example in Figure 7.11 demonstrates main visual differences between the primary and secondary window. A secondary window does not have any 'bars' – a menu bar, toolbar, scroll bars, or status bar. User events are achieved with *command buttons* (*action buttons*), such as OK, Cancel, Help.

Secondary windows come in various forms and shapes. A secondary window can be:

- a dialog box;
- a tab folder;
- a drop-down list;
- a message box.

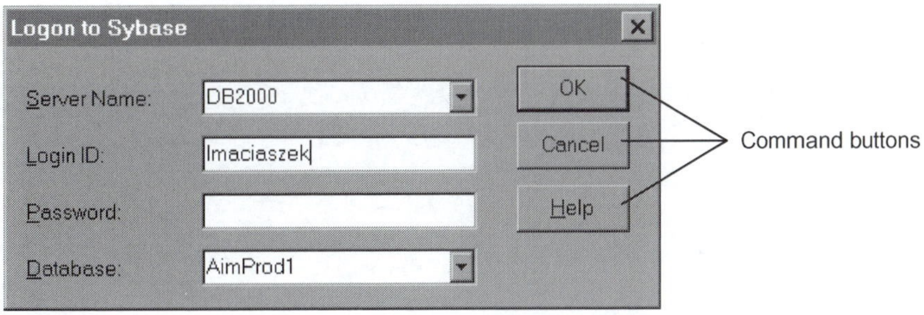

FIGURE 7.11
Simple
secondary
window – logon
window (courtesy
of ACNielsen
AdEx, Sydney,
Australia).

7.4.2.1 *Dialog box*

A *dialog box* is almost synonymous with the concept of the secondary window. It captures the most frequently needed properties of the secondary window. It supports the dialog between the user and the application. The dialog implies that the user enters some information to be considered by the application.

Figure 7.12 contains an example of the dialog box. It is an update window. It displays an advertising product corresponding to the currently selected product in the primary window's row product browser. The user can modify any *editable field* value in the white field frames.

Example 7.3 (Contact Management)

Refer to the Problem statement for Contact Management (Section 2.3.3) and to the successive examples for Contact Management in Chapter 4. Refer also to Examples 7.1 and 7.2 in this chapter.

The primary window for Contact Management (Figure 7.3) does not permit certain manipulations on events. For example, entering a new event or updating an existing event must be done through a secondary window – a dialog box.

By double-clicking on an event in the primary window, a dialog box should appear showing full details for that event. The dialog box displays not just the event information but also the data about its encompassing task as well as the organiza-tion and contact to which the event relates.

The event details that can be displayed and possibly modified include the event type (called action), a longer description (called notes), the date, time and user (employee) for an event's creation, and the scheduled, due, and completion time for the event.

Our task in this example is to design a dialog box for the event manipulation that conforms to the above requirements.

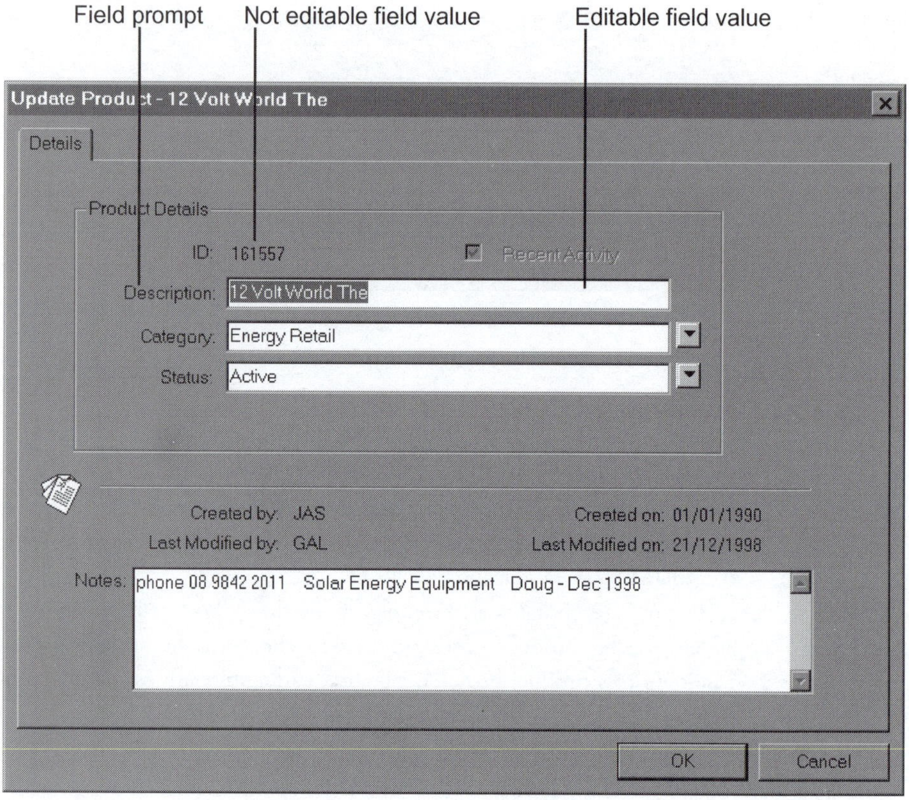

FIGURE 7.12
Dialog box
(courtesy of
ACNielsen AdEx,
Sydney,
Australia).

Field prompt   Not editable field value   Editable field value

Figure 7.13 is the proposed solution to the example. Note that Organization and Contact fields are not editable because the 'target' of the event cannot be changed. Similarly, the field values next to the prompt Created are not editable.

The field values adjacent to the prompt Completed are not editable in the sense that the user cannot type in them. However, pressing the Complete button will automatically insert the date, time, and the user values in these fields. After completing the event, the user still has the possibility of 'uncompleting' it because the Complete button is then renamed Uncomplete.

The user has a possibility of saving changes to the database and returning to the primary window by clicking the OK button. Alternatively, the user can Cancel the changes and stay in the dialog box. Finally, the user can press the New Event button that will save the changes (after the user's confirmation), clear all the fields in the dialog box, and allow the user to create a brand new event (without returning to the primary window).

7.4.2.2 Tab folder

A *tab folder* is useful when the amount of information to be displayed in a secondary window exceeds the window's 'real estate' and the subject matter can be broken logically apart into information groups. At any point in time, information from one tab is visible on the top of the

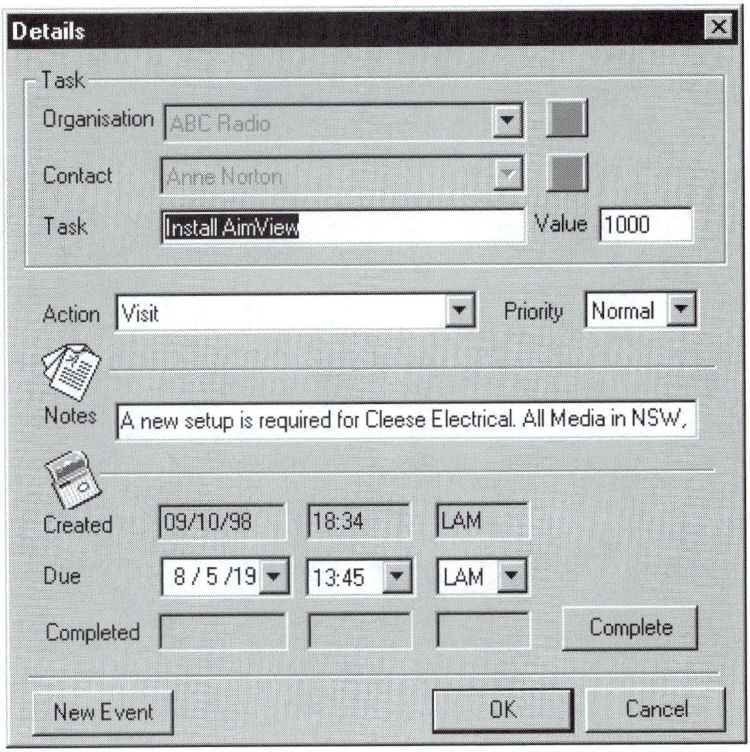

FIGURE 7.13
Dialog box
(Contact
Management)
(courtesy of
ACNielsen AdEx,
Sydney,
Australia).

stack of tab sheets. (Microsoft Windows name for the tab folder is a *tabbed property sheet* and each tab is called a *property page*.)

Figure 7.14 demonstrates a tab folder for inserting information about a new advertising organization. The four tabs divide the large volume of information to be entered by the user into four groups. The command buttons at the bottom of the screen apply to the whole window, not just to the currently visible tab page.

Example 7.4 (Contact Management)

Refer to the Problem statement for Contact Management (Section 2.3.3) and to the successive examples for Contact Management in Chapter 4. Refer also to Examples 7.1, 7.2, and 7.3 in this chapter.

Consider the tab folder for `Maintain Organizations` in Figure 7.2 (Example 7.1). One of the tabs is called `Contacts`. The purpose of it is to allow access and modification of `Contact` data (`Contact` class) from this tab folder. Otherwise, the user would always have to return to the primary window and activate a separate secondary window for `Contacts`.

The purpose of this example is to design the content of the `Contacts` tab.

FIGURE 7.14
Tab folder
(courtesy of
ACNielsen AdEx,
Sydney,
Australia).

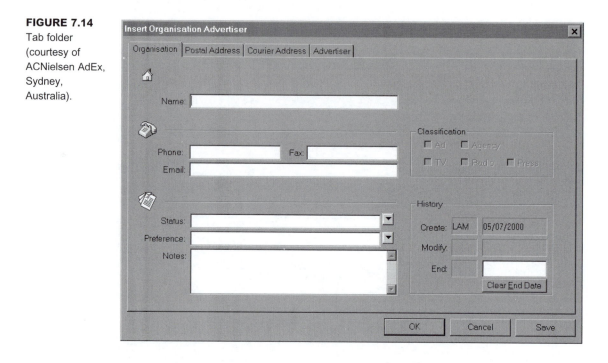

As shown in Figure 7.15, the `Contacts` tab displays only the names of the contacts in an organization. However, the tab has its own set of command buttons to `Add`, `Edit` or `Delete` the currently highlighted contact. An action to `Add` or `Edit` a contact will result in a `Maintain Contacts` secondary window opening up on the top of the `Maintain Organizations` window. The `Maintain Contacts` window will be modal with regard to the `Maintain Organizations` window.

7.4.2.3 Drop-down list

In some cases, a *drop-down list* (or a set of drop-down lists) is a convenient substitute for a tab page. A drop-down list provides a picklist of choices from which the user can select one that applies. For insert operations, the user can type in a new value to be added to the drop-down list next time it is opened.

As shown in Figure 7.16, a drop-down list does not need to be restricted to a simple list of values. It can be a tree browser of values.

7.4.2.4 Message box

A *message box* is a secondary window that displays a message to the user. The message can signify a warning, an explanation, an exceptional condition, etc. Command buttons in the message box offer one or more reply choices to the user.

FIGURE 7.15
Tab folder
(Contact
Management)
(courtesy of
ACNielsen AdEx,
Sydney,
Australia).

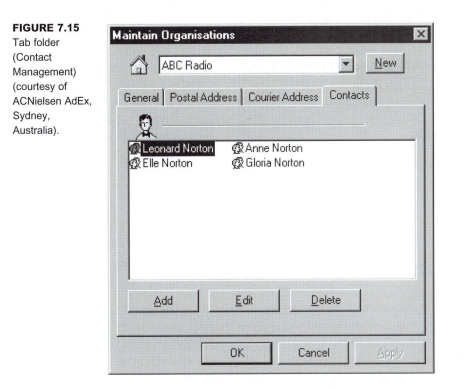

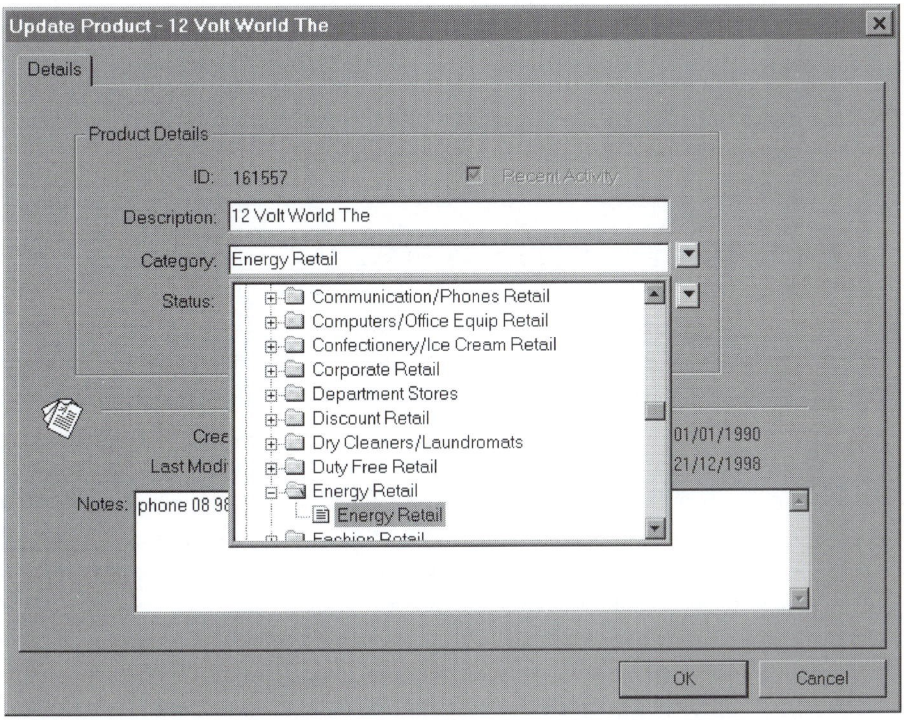

FIGURE 7.16
Drop-down list
(courtesy of
ACNielsen AdEx,
Sydney,
Australia).

FIGURE 7.17
Message box
(courtesy of
ACNielsen AdEx,
Sydney,
Australia).

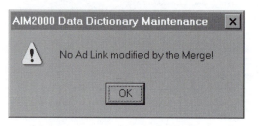

AIM2000 Data Dictionary Maintenance

No Ad Link modified by the Merge!

OK

Figure 7.17 shows a message. The message requires acknowledgment (OK button) from the user.

7.5 Dependencies between windows

To the user, the application appears as a set of collaborating windows. It is the task of the GUI designer to organize the dependencies between windows in a coherent, easy to understand structure. The user should never feel lost amongst opened windows.

Ideally, the link from the primary window to the top secondary window currently opened should be a path, not even a hierarchy. This can be achieved by making a secondary window *modal* with respect to the previous window. The MDI (multiple document interface) discussed in Section 7.5.3 would permit the handling of any complex situations without the need for modeless windows.

While the GUI design should facilitate the user's exploration of the interface, a good design of the *menu bar* structure remains the principal technique to explain the application's capabilities. The menu commands available to the user in pull-down and slide-off menus indirectly explain the dependencies between windows.

7.5.1 Document versus view

The GUI design in the Microsoft Windows environment depends directly on the library of classes provided by Microsoft that implement Windows objects and controls – the Windows API (application programming interface). The library is called MFC (Microsoft Foundation Classes).

Programming for Windows involves instantiating and using MFC objects as well as creating application-specific classes inheriting the generic functionality from the MFC classes. Programming for Windows involves also an acceptance of a specific structure for dependencies and interactions between windows. The structure is known as the document/view approach (Horton, 1997).

The *document* is an MFC mechanism for a collection of data in the application that the user can interact with. The document can contain any type of data, not just the text. In MFC, a document object derives from the class CDocument.

FIGURE 7.18
Document and
its view.

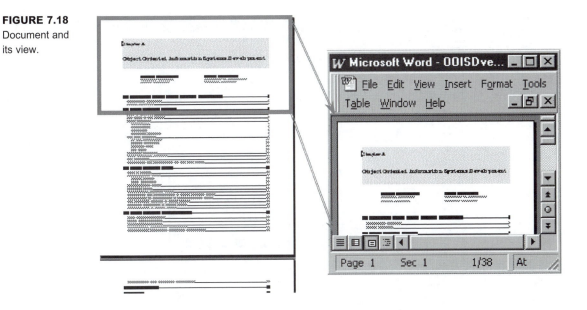

Normally, only a portion of data stored in a CDocument object can be displayed on the screen. This portion is called a *view*. It is derived from the class CView. There can be multiple views of the same document. Technically, a CView object and the window (frame) in which it is displayed are distinct.

Figure 7.18 visualizes the difference between the document and the view. In this case, the document is a word-processing document but in general it could be any file of information extracted from the database.

7.5.2 Single document interface

In some simple applications, the GUI design can consist of a single primary window with only one document opened in it at a time. The MFC library supports this under the title acronym SDI (single document interface).

The GUI design of Contact Management uses the SDI application. At any point in time, the user is presented with events for one day (Figure 7.19).

7.5.3 Multiple document interface

More complex applications would invariably require opening several documents at one time. The documents can be of the same type, but they are frequently of different types. MFC library supports such applications under the title acronym MDI (multiple document interface).

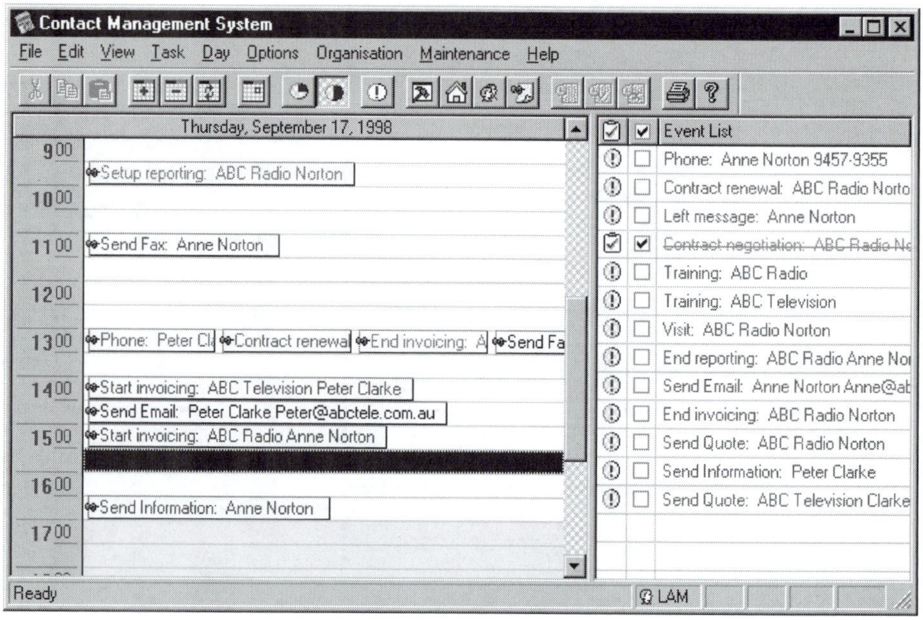

FIGURE 7.19
SDI application
(courtesy of
ACNielsen AdEx,
Sydney,
Australia).

FIGURE 7.19
SDI application (courtesy of ACNielsen AdEx, Sydney, Australia).

An MDI application still uses *only one primary window*. This is called a *parent window*. However, an MDI application allows opening of several documents within the parent window's frame. Each document is referred to as a *child window*. Logically, each child window performs as if it were the primary window that can only appear within the parent window (and not on the desktop).

The fact that the MDI framework has only a single primary window at its core is manifested by *one menu bar* that all child windows share. Similarly, child windows normally share toolbar and status bars. It is possible, however, to modify the available menu and toolbar actions to reflect the functionality of the currently active child window.

Figure 7.20 demonstrates an MDI application. Four documents (row browsers) are opened within the primary window's frame. A tree browser on the left is the fifth document.

7.6 Window navigation

The graphical depiction of GUI windows – through prototyping or other GUI layout tools – does not inform how the windows can be actually *navigated* by the user. We still need to design the *window navigation system*. A window navigation diagram should visualize application windows and control objects that allow the user to traverse from one window to another.

Unfortunately, UML does not have a graphical modeling technique to model window navigation. We need to develop our own model or to take advantage of UML stereotypes and customize one of the UML diagrams to represent window navigation.

FIGURE 7.20
MDI application
(courtesy of
ACNielsen AdEx,
Sydney,
Australia).

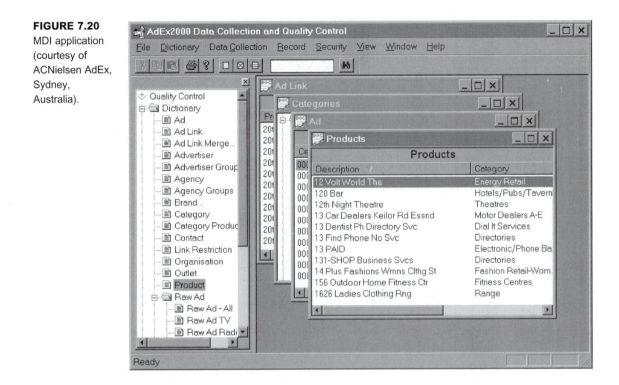

FIGURE 7.20
MDI application
(courtesy of
ACNielsen AdEx,
Sydney,
Australia).

7.6.1 Stereotyping the activity diagram for window navigation

It turns out that the UML activity diagram is a good candidate to stereotype for window navigation. The activity diagram shows the transitions between *activities* (Section 2.2.3.2). However, the activity diagram – being a kind of state machine – can also portray object *states*. This duality of activity diagrams can be used graphically to render the similar duality required in GUI objects. A GUI window is like a *state* awaiting events (*activities*).

States and activities in an activity diagram can be stereotyped. The *state stereotypes* can identify different kinds of windows and other GUI objects that 'persist' between events – i.e. which have duration. Figure 7.21 demonstrates the state stereotyped as a primary window. The state represents a *browser* (*grid*) *of products* displayed in the application's primary window. This is also the *initial state* in the model.

FIGURE 7.21
State
stereotyped as a
GUI object.

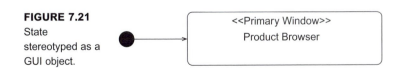

<<Primary Window>>
Product Browser

FIGURE 7.22
Activities
stereotyped as
GUI control
objects.

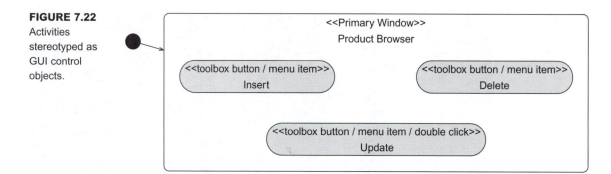

The *activity stereotypes* can identify different kinds of GUI controls that can be used to trigger events on the states (now stereotyped as GUI window objects). As opposed to states, the activities are of very short duration – we can say that they do not have duration on this relative time scale.

The activities (ovals) can be rendered inside a state (rounded rectangle) to which they apply. Figure 7.22 shows three activities in the state `Product Browser`. The `Product Browser` window can be used to initiate an event of inserting, deleting or updating a product. All three events can be triggered from a toolbox action button or a menu item. Double-clicking on the product row in the browser also supports the update event.

The complete list of state and activity stereotypes to support the design of a window navigation system would depend on the chosen GUI interface. The developers may also come up with iconic stereotypes. Below is an incomplete list of stereotypes for Microsoft Windows GUI:

■ *States (windows)*
  ■ Primary window
    ■ Pane in primary window
    ■ Row browser
    ■ Tree browser
    ■ Web page
  ■ Secondary window
    ■ Dialog box
    ■ Message box
    ■ Tab folder
  ■ Window data
    ■ Text box
    ■ Combo box
    ■ Spin box
    ■ Column
    ■ Row
    ■ Group of fields

- *Activities (window controls)*
    - Drop-down menu item
    - Pop-up menu item
    - Toolbar button
    - Command button
    - Double click
    - Picklist selection
    - Keyboard key
    - Keyboard function key
    - Keyboard accelerator key
    - Scrolling button
    - Window close button

7.6.2 Window navigation diagram

Once the state and activity stereotypes are determined, we can use *transition* lines to connect the activities and states. The result is a window navigation diagram in which activities trigger transitions on states.

Figure 7.23 extends the previous example and shows the states resulting from triggering the three activities available in the `Product Browser` window. The state triggered by the `Update` event is expanded. The window `Update Product` (a <<dialog box>>) contains four activities (<<command buttons>>). Pressing the `OK` or `Cancel` button causes the transition back to the window `Product Browser`. Pressing the `Save` or `Clear` button does not change the active window (if we wanted to capture the change of state within the active window, we would need to extend our model with additional stereotypes).

The model in Figure 7.23 is restricted to GUI objects. In Chapter 9, we show how the activity diagrams can be further stereotyped to visualize the entire application logic, including access to databases.

Example 7.5 (Contact Management)

Refer to the Problem statement for Contact Management (Section 2.3.3) and to examples for Contact Management in Chapter 4. Refer also to Examples 7.1, 7.2, and 7.3 in this chapter.

Consider the primary window in Figure 7.6 (Example 7.2) and the dialog box in Figure 7.13 (Example 7.3). Develop a window navigation diagram for windows in these two figures. The diagram should identify and model the main user events on the primary window and on the dialog box. It should also address the use of the Calendar – a dockable combo box.

FIGURE 7.23
Window
navigation
diagram.

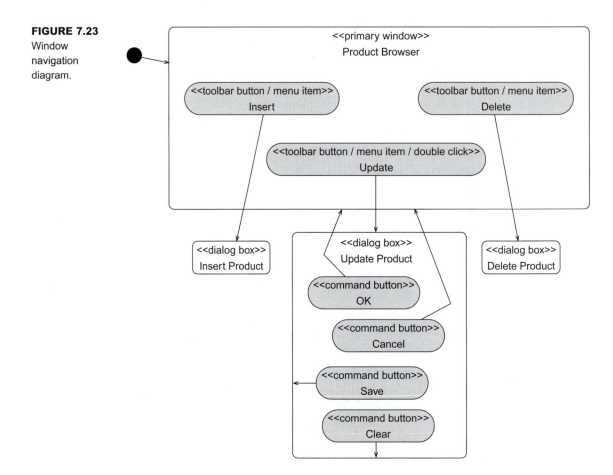

A window navigation diagram for the example should consider three windows: Contact Management (<<primary window>>), Task/Event Details (<<dialog box>>) and Calendar (<<combo box>>). The left and the right pane of the primary window may also be considered as possible states (sub-windows) of the primary window state. However, we overlook the panes in the solution.

As can be seen on the toolbar in Figure 7.6, there are a large number of activities (events) that can be triggered on the primary window. However, our task is to identify only the main user events, including those that activate the secondary windows Task/Event Details and Calendar.

Figure 7.24 shows the window navigation diagram for the example. The event Calendar (<<toolbar button>>) displays the Calendar (<<combo box>>). The combo box is screen-dockable. Clicking at the window close box can dismiss it. Selecting a month (<<scroll>>) or selecting a date (<<select>>) does not remove the combo box.

The Task/Event Details (<<dialog box>>) is reachable via the event Update Event (<<toolbar button/menu item/double click>>). The command buttons OK and Cancel

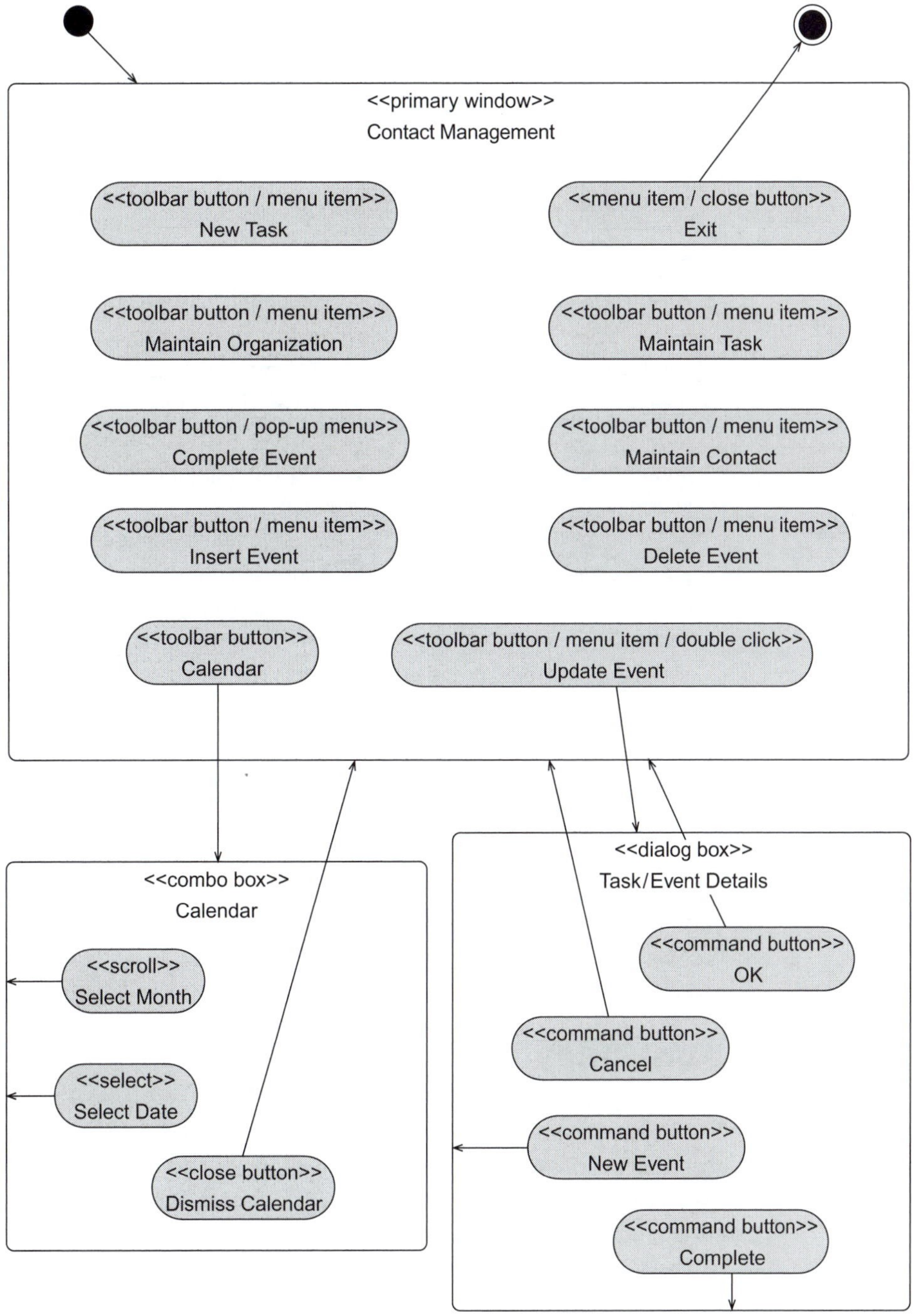

FIGURE 7.24
Window
navigation
diagram for
Contact
Management.

dismiss the dialog box and return the control to the primary window. Activating the button Complete fills in the 'complete' fields in the window but the control stays with the dialog box. This is because the user might want to create a new event. Pressing the button New Event clears the fields on the screen and allows the user to type details of a new event.

Example 7.6 (Telemarketing)

Refer to the Problem statement for Telemarketing (Section 2.3.4) and to the successive examples for Contact Management in Chapter 4. Consider the additional details below and design a window navigation diagram.

The main window interface for Telemarketing is an empty window with an application title and two command buttons. The buttons allow the telemarketer to get Next Call to a supporter or to Quit the application. Pressing the Next Call button displays a welcome message to the supporter and fills in the window with information about the currently dialed call.

While talking to a supporter, the telemarketer interacts with the system by pressing various command buttons. There is a range of toolbar buttons to record the call outcome (such as order for tickets, call re-scheduling, or unsuccessful out-come). There is also a range of command buttons to view more detailed information about the campaign or the supporter.

Figure 7.25 presents the window navigation diagram for the example. Although the Entry Window and Call Window is the same <<primary window>>, we explicitly represent the two states of the window. The state Entry Window is active after the initial launch of the program and when the call outcome is Unsuccessful. It is likely that events in secondary windows can return the control to the Entry Window but this is not captured in the model. Pressing Quit in either state terminates the application.

Summary

The development of the GUI spans the software production lifecycle – it starts in the analysis phase and extends to the implementation. In this chapter, we have addressed the GUI design, specifically for the Microsoft Windows environment. We have also introduced a graphical notation to depict the window navigation.

The GUI design is a *multidisciplinary activity* requiring the combined expertise of a few professions. The design must adhere to the *guidelines* published by the manufacturer of a windows interface adopted in the project. The guidelines specify such issues as the user in control principle, consistency, personalization, customization, forgiveness, feedback, aesthetics, and usability.

FIGURE 7.25
Window
navigation
diagram
(Telemarketing).

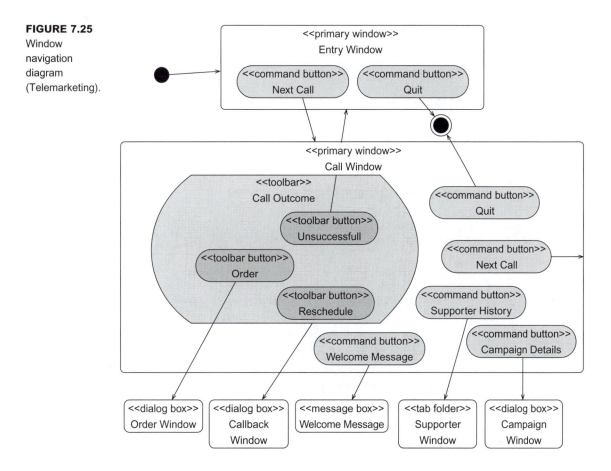

The Microsoft Windows interface distinguishes between the primary window and secondary window. The *primary window* can be a row browser, tree browser or web page. The *secondary window* can be a dialog box, tab folder, drop-down list or message box. A secondary window can be *modal* or *modeless* with regard to its primary window. The dependencies between windows are further formulated by the use of the *SDI interface* or the *MDI interface*.

The visual design of individual windows is only one aspect of the GUI development. The second relates to *window navigation* that captures the possible navigation paths between application windows. In this chapter, we introduced window navigation diagrams to address this issue. The windows navigation diagrams extend the UML activity diagrams. In effect, they offer a new UML *profile* for window navigation modeling.

Review questions

R1   List and briefly define the GUI design guidelines.

R2   How is a primary window different from a secondary window?

R3   What is a pane? How is it useful in GUI design?

R4   What is a tab folder? How is it different from a dialog box?

R5   What is the document/view approach?

R6   Does the MDI interface allow multiple primary windows? Explain.

R7   How are windows and window controls represented in window navigation diagrams? Is that representation consistent with the intent of the UML activity diagrams? Explain.

Exercise questions

Additional requirements (Telemarketing)

Consider the following additional requirements for Telemarketing:

1. The `Telemarketing Control` window is the primary control interface for the Telemarketing application. The window displays to the telemarketer a list of the calls in the current queue. When the telemarketer requests a call from the queue, the system establishes the connection and the telemarketer is able to process a connected call. The `Call Summary` information displays on the screen – it shows the start time, the finish time and the duration of the current call.

2. Once connected, the `Telemarketing Control` window displays information about the current call – who has been called, about what campaign, what kind of call is being made. If there is more than one call scheduled for the current phone number, then the telemarketer is given the option to cycle through these calls.

3. At any stage during the conversation, the telemarketer can view the supporter's history (the `Supporter History` window) with regard to the previous campaigns. Similarly, the details about the campaign to which the current call is pertaining can be viewed (the `Campaign` window).

4. The GUI interface provides for a quick recording of the call outcomes. The possible outcomes are: placement (i.e. tickets have been ordered), callback, unsuccessful, no answer, engaged, machine (i.e. answering machine), fax, wrong (i.e. wrong number), and disconnected.

5. The `Campaign` window displays campaign details, ticket details, and prize details for the campaign. The campaign details include the identifying number, the title, the start, the close and the prize drawing dates. The ticket details include the number of tickets in the campaign, how many have been sold and how many are still available. The prize details include the prize description, the prize value, and the place of the prize (the first, second or third).

6. The `Supporter History` window shows the past call history and the past campaign history for the supporter. The call history lists the recent calls, types of these calls, the outcomes, and the identification of the campaigns and of the telemarketers. The campaign history informs about the ticket placements and prize winnings by the supporter.

7. On selecting the `Placement` action, the `Placement` window is activated. The `Placement` window allows the user to allocate tickets to the supporter and to record the payment.

8. On selecting the `No Answer` or `Engaged` action, the 'no answer' or 'engaged' outcome is recorded in the system for each of the current calls. The calls are then re-scheduled by the system for another time tomorrow, provided each call is below the limit for attempts determined by the type of call.

9. Upon selecting the `Machine` action, the 'machine' outcome is recorded in the system. The duration of the call is set for the first of the current calls only. The calls are then re-scheduled by the system for another time tomorrow, provided each call is below the limit for attempts determined by the type of call.

10. On selecting the `Fax` or `Wrong` action, the 'fax' or 'wrong' outcome is recorded in the system. The duration of the call is set for the first of the current calls only. The supporter data is then updated to 'bad phone' for each supporter with the current phone number.

11. Upon selecting the `Disconnected` action, the 'disconnected' outcome is recorded in the system. The supporter data is then updated to 'bad phone' for each supporter with the current phone number.

12. Upon selecting the `Callback` action, the 'callback' outcome is recorded in the system. The duration of the call is set for the first of the current calls only. The `Call Scheduling` window is invoked to obtain the date and time for the callback to be arranged. The calls are then re-scheduled by the system (with the new priority) for the date and time obtained by the `Call Scheduling` window. The types of new calls are set to 'callback'.

13. Upon exiting the `Placement` window, if all of the remaining tickets in the campaign have just been allocated, then all further calls to supporters for that campaign are pointless. Any such calls must be removed from the call queue.

E1 *Telemarketing* – refer to the additional requirements above and to the solutions to the Telemarketing case study as defined in the book activity diagram for Telemarketing. Consider the class diagram in Example 4.7 (Section 4.2.1.2.3).

Modify and extend the class diagram in Figure 4.4 to support the additional requirements specified above.

E2 *Telemarketing* – refer to the additional requirements above and to the solutions to the Telemarketing case study as defined in the book activity diagram for Telemarketing.

Design and sketch the primary window for Telemarketing, i.e. the `Telemarketing Control` window. Explain how this window satisfies the relevant application requirements.

E3 *Telemarketing* – refer to the additional requirements above and to the solutions to the Telemarketing case study as defined in the book activity diagram for Telemarketing.

Design and sketch the `Supporter History` window. Explain how this window satisfies the relevant application requirements.

E4 *Telemarketing* – refer to the additional requirements above and to the solutions to the Telemarketing case study as defined in the book activity diagram for Telemarketing.

Draw the window navigation diagram for the Telemarketing application. If the complexity of the solution warrants it, split the diagram into a number of smaller diagrams. Do not be unduly influenced by the window navigation diagram in Example 7.6 (Section 7.6.2). Explain how your solution satisfies the application requirements.

E5 *OnLine Shopping* – refer to the solutions to the OnLine Shopping tutorial as defined in the book activity diagram for OnLine Shopping.

Design and sketch the web page that displays the current order status to the customer. Explain any intricacies.

E6 *OnLine Shopping* – refer to the solutions to the OnLine Shopping tutorial as defined in the book activity diagram for OnLine Shopping.

Draw the window navigation diagram for the OnLine Shopping application. If the complexity of the solution warrants it, split the diagram into a number of smaller diagrams. Explain how your solution satisfies the application requirements.

Database Design

Information systems are almost by definition multi-user systems. This characteristic alone demands a database that many users and application programs can concurrently access. The application programs depend on the database but not really vice versa. The conclusion is obvious – a good database design, that can accommodate and support *all* application programs, is the necessary condition for an information system to deliver the intended functionality.

In UML, the class diagrams define the data structures required by an application. The data structures that have persistent presence in the database are modeled as the entity classes and as the relationships between entity classes. The entity classes need to be mapped to the data structures recognized by the database. These data structures vary depending on the underlying database model, which can be object-oriented, object-relational or relational.

In this chapter, we discuss the mapping of objects to databases. We explain the conversions from the entity classes, associations, aggregations, and generalizations to the data structures available in the three database models. The scope of the textbook has not allowed us to explain the 'schema integration', i.e. the integration of overlapping database structures resulting from the demands of many application programs competing for the same database resources.

8.1 Persistent database layer

Througout the book we have been carefully distinguishing between the development of a client application and the design of a server database. We emphasized that the class models and the BCED class packages (Section 6.1.3.2) reflect the application classes, not the storage database structures.

The *entity classes* represent persistent database objects in the application but *they are not* persistent classes in the database. The *database classes* encapsulate communication between the application and database, but neither are they persistent classes. We still need to design the *persistent database layer*.

The persistent database layer can be a relational (e.g. Sybase, DB2, Oracle8), object-relational (e.g. UniSQL, Oracle8) or object database (e.g. ObjectStore, Versant). It is unlikely that the storage model for a new system can be any of the older models such as hierarchical (e.g. IMS), network (e.g. IDMS), inverted or similar model (e.g. Total, Adabas). In some cases, but not really in modern IS applications, the persistency can be implemented in simple flat files.

8.1.1 Data models

The database community has developed its own view on the world of modeling. Databases *store data*. Historically, the database community has concentrated on *data models* (i.e. state models in UML parlance). The current capability of databases to *store and execute programs* has extended this perspective to include *behavior models* (centered on triggers and stored procedures) but data modeling remains the 'bread and butter' of database development.

A *data model* (called also a *database schema*) is an abstraction that presents the database structures in more understandable terms than as raw bits and bytes. A popular classification of data model layers recognizes three abstractions:

1. External (conceptual) data model.
2. Logical data model.
3. Physical data model.

The *external schema* represents a high-level *conceptual data model* required by a single application. Because a database normally supports many applications, multiple external schemas are constructed. They are then integrated into one conceptual data model. The most popular conceptual data modeling technique is ER (entity relationship) diagrams (e.g. Maciaszek, 1990).

The *logical schema* (sometimes called also the *global conceptual schema*) provides a model that reflects the storage structures of the DBMS (database management system). It is a global integrated model to support any current and expected applications that need access to the information stored in the database.

The *physical schema* is specific to a particular DBMS. It defines how data is actually stored on persistent storage devices, typically disks. The physical schema defines such issues as the use of indexes and clustering of data for efficient processing.

The *lower-engineering CASE tools* (i.e. the CASE tools targeting system design and implementation) provide a single data modeling technique for logical and physical schema. They tend to call such a combined model a physical data model.

Figure 8.1 demonstrates how UML models for an application relate to persistent database models. Classes of the entity package represent the 'business objects' of an application. A UML class diagram (for entity classes) can replace an ER diagram as a tool of choice for the conceptual database modeling.

The database package does not 'drive' the database modeling; it is rather driven by it. The database package isolates the application model from the database model. The database package is designed in parallel or after the persistent database layer has been defined. The database package decouples the entity classes from the database schema. It establishes the mapping between objects and database.

FIGURE 8.1
UML and
persistence
models.

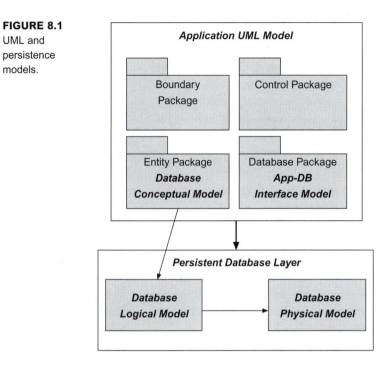

8.1.2 Mapping objects to the database

The mapping between the application and the database – for which the database package is responsible – may be a convoluted issue (Section 6.1.3). There are two fundamental reasons for the mapping difficulty. Firstly, the storage structures of the database may have little to do with the object-oriented paradigm. Secondly, the database is almost never designed for a single application.

The first reason amounts to the conversion of classes in the entity package (Sections 5.2.4 and 6.1.3.2) to *non object-oriented structures*, typically to relational tables. Even if the target database is an object database, the peculiarities of the database will necessitate a careful conversion.

The second reason demands an optimal database *design for all applications*, not just the one under consideration. The applications should be prioritized for business significance so that those applications that are most important to the organization have the database structures tuned to them. Equally important, the database designer should always look into the future, anticipate future demands for data by forthcoming applications and design the database to accommodate these demands.

The odds are that the persistent database layer is going to be a *relational database*. The relational database technology dominates the marketplace. For large enterprise databases, the change to the *object database* technology will be evolutionary and will go through an intermediate (if not final) stage of the *object-relational* technology.

We begin by presenting an ideal, albeit unlikely, scenario where the persistent storage is provided by a pure *object database*. We then discuss the mapping from objects to an *object-relational database*. Finally, we consider the *relational database* model – the most restrictive and therefore the most difficult model to map.

8.2 Object database model

The object database (ODB) model provides for the least troublesome mapping between the application program and the database. In fact, an overwhelming objective of an object database management system (ODBMS) is the transparent integration of the database with the application programming language.

The Object Data Management Group (ODMG) has standardized the ODB model. The ODMG member organizations represent all major vendors of ODBMS software. More recently, ODMG changed its charter to concentrate on the *mapping of objects to relational and other databases*. This makes the standard an *Object Storage API* that can work with any persistent data sources. In effect, the standard can be used as a database package (Figure 8.1) for mapping between an application and the database. The latest standard (January 2000) is called the Object Data Standard: ODMG 3.0 (ODMG, 2000).

The standard defines that an ODBMS does not provide a separate database language (such as SQL) for data manipulation *within* a programming language environment. It instead makes database objects appear in the application programming language as normal programming language objects. In other words, the programming language is extended with database objects that implement data persistency, transaction management, navigational queries (i.e. queries that 'navigate' along relationships), etc.

A separate query language, to access the database *outside* of the programming language environment, is also included. Such a language is typically called the Object SQL (OSQL). The OSQL extends the querying capabilities of the relational SQL with navigational queries and the ability to process more complex data types, such as templates (Section 6.2.2.5).

8.2.1 ODB modeling primitives

The basic modeling primitives of an object database model are the object and the literal (ODMG, 2000; Eaglestone and Ridley, 1998). Each *object* has an OID (Section 2.1.1.3). A *literal* has no OID – its value is like its identifier.

An ODB makes a distinction between a *class* (*implementation*) and a *type* (*specification*). A type can have multiple classes. For example, the type Employee can be implemented in a Smalltalk class and/or in a Java class. The semantics of the type enables separating the specification from its various implementations. The specification of the abstract behavior of a type is called an *interface*. An interface cannot be directly instantiated.

An ODB class has *properties* and *operations*. A property can be an *attribute* or a *relationship* (i.e. an attribute that links the object to one or more other objects).

8.2.1.1 *Literal and object types*

One of the main benefits of an ODB is the built-in support for literal and object types. This makes an ODB a natural implementation platform for an object-oriented IS development. If IS developers are not turning to ODB in great numbers, that's only because of certain other ODB weaknesses (like the deficient multi-user support) as well as the commercial and political power play by the more influential database vendors.

A *literal type* can be (ODMG, 2000):

- atomic (simple);
- structured;
- collection (template);
- null.

An *atomic literal* can be:

- numeric
    - short (signed short integer);
    - long (signed long integer);
    - unsigned short;
    - unsigned long;
    - float (single precision floating point (decimal) number);
    - double (double precision floating point number);
- alphanumeric and special characters
    - char (single character);
    - string (string of characters);
    - boolean (i.e. logical values 'true' or 'false');
    - octet (bit string to represent 'raw' data);
    - enum (enumerated list of allowed values).

A *structured literal* is a predefined data structure that consists of more than one atomic literal. A structured literal can be:

- date (e.g. 9 July 2000);
- time (e.g. 11:14);
- timestamp (e.g. 9 July 2000 11:14:56);
- interval (e.g. 11:14, 11:19).

A *collection literal* is a parameterized type (Section 6.2.2.5) where formal parameters are usually literal types, but they can be object types. Either way, a collection literal does not have an object identifier. A collection literal can be:

- set<t> (i.e. a set where all the elements are of the same literal type or object type t; e.g. set<dept_name>, where dept_name is a string);
- bag<t> (i.e. a multi-set (set that allows duplicate elements));

- list<t> (i.e. an ordered (sorted) set);
- array<t> (i.e. a dynamically sized, ordered collection of elements where each element can be located by its position);
- dictionary<t,v> (i.e. an unordered sequence (index) of key-value pairs with no duplicate keys).

A *null literal* can be specified for every other literal type (e.g. string or list<>). The null literal signifies a null value. As in relational databases, the null value represents one of two possibilities: 'value at present unknown' (e.g. I don't know your birth date) or 'value not applicable' (e.g. you cannot have a maiden name if you are a man). The null value is not zero or space (empty) character; it is a special stream of bits that denotes the null value.

An *object type* can be (ODMG, 2000):

- atomic object;
- structured object;
- collection (the same set of possibilities as for the collection literal but a collection object has an object identifier; e.g. set<Dept>, where Dept is a class and instances of set<Dept> are objects).

Figure 8.2 is an example for type declarations. The class Employee has five properties. One of these properties (emp_name) is a structured object. The value of emp_name is an OID of an instance of PersonName. The class PersonName is not shown but it presumably consists of attributes such as family_name, first_name, middle_initial.

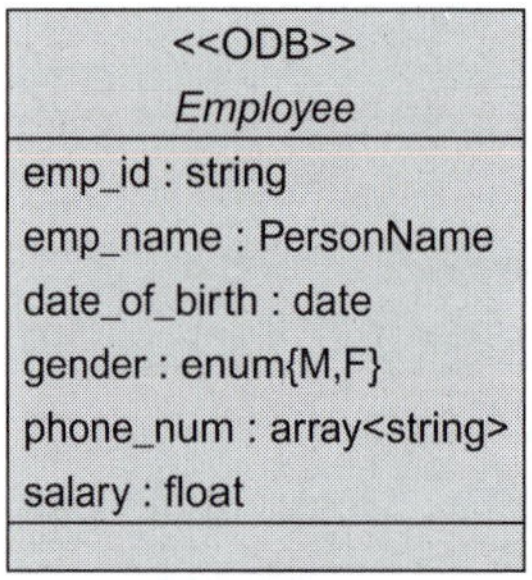

FIGURE 8.2
Type declarations
in ODB.

<<ODB>>
Employee
emp_id : string
emp_name : PersonName
date_of_birth : date
gender : enum{M,F}
phone_num : array<string>
salary : float

8.2.1.2 *Relationships and inverses*

The ODB model builds on the modeling primitives discussed in the previous section. Of the three types of relationships (i.e. association, aggregation, generalization), the ODB model directly supports association and generalization. The *aggregation* is only supported by constraining an association.

Associations are implemented with collection object types, in particular Set<> and List<>. In practice, the associations are responsible for the switch from a relational-style value-based database access back to navigational database access. (We say 'the switch back' because the older-style network databases have been using navigation as their modus operandi.)

Figure 8.3 shows how a many-to-many association between the classes Student and CourseOffering is represented in an ODB. The graphical model makes a distinction

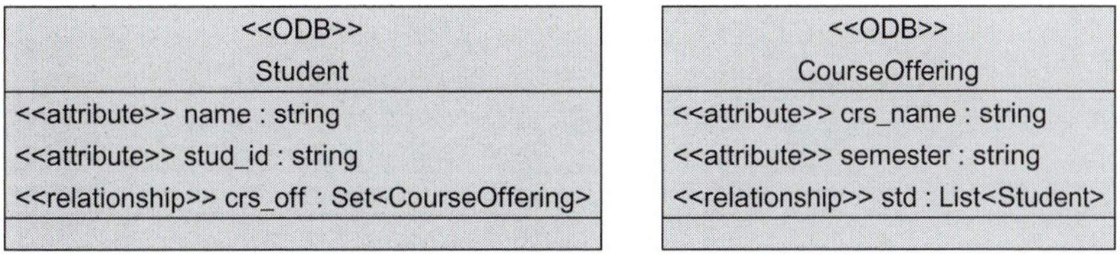

FIGURE 8.3
Association in
ODB.

<<ODB>> Student
<<attribute>> name : string
<<attribute>> stud_id : string
<<relationship>> crs_off : Set<CourseOffering>

<<ODB>> CourseOffering
<<attribute>> crs_name : string
<<attribute>> semester : string
<<relationship>> std : List<Student>

```
class Student
{
    attribute    string              name;
    attribute    string              stud_id;
    relationship Set<CourseOffering> crs_off
                 inverse CourseOffering::std;
};

class CourseOffering
{
    attribute    string              crs_name;
    attribute    string              semester;
    relationship List<Student>       std
                 inverse Student::crs_off;
};
```

between attributes and relationships. No association line is drawn between the classes because the relationship properties (`crs_off` and `std`) implement that association already.

The `inverse` keyword, explicit in the schema definition, enforces *referential integrity* on the association and eliminates the possibility of *dangling pointers*. For example, to add a `Student` to a `CourseOffering` the programmer can either add the `CourseOffering` object (OID to be precise) to `Set<CourseOffering>` or add the `Student` object to `List<Student>`. Once the programmer changes one end of the association, the opposite end (the inverse) is automatically modified by the ODBMS.

Although not shown in the above class definitions, the ODB model allows for the specification of *keys* – unique identifying values for objects of the class. Unlike in relational databases, the key is not the only, or even principal, means of object identification (the OID values serve this purpose). However, at times, searching in the ODB by a key value may be an option.

The key can be *simple* or *compound* (when it consists of more than one attribute). Because a class can have many keys, sequential numbers (or other visual technique) may be used to distinguish between them.

8.2.1.3 *ISA and EXTENDS inheritance*

The ODMG object model defines two kinds of generalization relationships: ISA and EXTENDS relationships. The *ISA relationship* corresponds (loosely speaking) to our earlier definition of *interface inheritance* (Section 5.3.3). The *EXTENDS relationship* corresponds to *implementation inheritance* (Section 5.3.4).

FIGURE 8.4
Inheritance in
ODB.

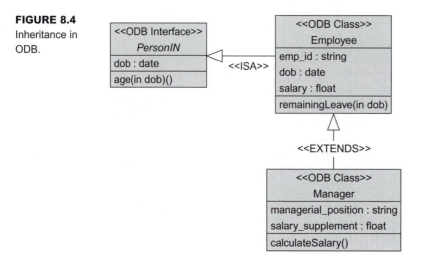

Employee inherits only the behavior from PersonIN. The properties of PersonIN are not inherited – a copy of dob must be explicitly included in Employee. Manager inherits both the state (declarations of properties) and the behavior (code of operations) from Employee.

The ODMG standard permits *multiple ISA inheritance* of interfaces (i.e. multiple inheritance of behavior). Both interfaces and classes can inherit from interfaces but interfaces cannot inherit from classes. Also, the ISA inheritance is not allowed between classes. Finally, the standard permits only *single EXTENDS inheritance* of state and behavior.

8.2.1.4 *Built-in operations*

An ODBMS comes equipped with *built-in operations* in support of literal and object types. The most interesting operations are those that support structured types and collections. The system designer must be familiar with ODBMS interfaces to take advantage of them in the design models.

In what follows we list the signatures of all but a few supported (or expected to be supported) interfaces for *structured types* and *collections* (ODMG, 2000). We hope that the signatures explain the intended purpose of the operations.

- *Date*
    - ushort day_of_year()
    - Month month_of_year()
    - Weekday day_of_week()
    - boolean is_leap_year()
    - boolean is_greater(in Date a_date)
    - boolean is_between(in Date a_date, in Date b_date)
    - Date add_days(in long days)
    - long subtract_date(in Date a_date)

- *Time*
    - ushort millisecond()
    - boolean is_equal(in Time a_time)
    - boolean is_between(in Time a_time, in Time b_time)
    - Time subtract_interval(in Interval an_interval)
    - Interval subtract_time(in Time a_time)
- *Timestamp*
    - ushort millisecond()
    - ushort month()
    - boolean is_between(in Timestamp a_stamp, in Timestamp b_stamp)
    - Timestamp plus(in Interval an_interval)
    - Timestamp minus(in Interval an_Interval)
- *Interval*
    - ushort second()
    - Interval plus(in Interval an_interval)
    - boolean is_less_or_equal(in Interval an_interval)
    - boolean is_zero()

Collection objects share a number of operations. Hence, a superclass called `Collection` is normally defined by an ODBMS. The specific collection classes inherit the common behavior from the superclass `Collection` (as always, the inherited operations can be refined or overridden, if necessary). Common operations include:

- unsigned long cardinality()
- boolean is_ordered()
- boolean contains_element(in any element)
- void insert_element(in any element)
- void remove_element(in any element) raises(ElementNotFound)
- *Set*
    - Set create_union(in Set other_set)
    - boolean is_subset_of(in Set other_set)
    - boolean is_proper_superset(in Set other_set)
- *Bag*
    - unsigned long occurrences_of(in any_element)
    - Bag create_intersection(in Bag other_bag)
- *List*
    - any retrieve_element_at(in unsigned long index) raises(InvalidIndex)
    - void insert_element_after(in any element, in unsigned long index) raises(InvalidIndex)

- void insert_element_first(in any element)
- void remove_last_element() raises(ElementNotFound)
- List concat(in List other_list)
- void append(in List other_list)

- *Array*

  - void remove_element_at(in unsigned long index) raises(InvalidIndex)
  - any retrieve_element_at(in unsigned long index) raises(InvalidIndex)
  - void resize(in unsigned long new_size)

- *Dictionary*

  - any lookup(in any key) raises(KeyNotFound)
  - boolean contains_key(in any key)

8.2.2 Mapping to ODB

The mapping from UML models to an ODB is relatively seamless. The very task of an ODB is to deliver an object-oriented implementation for an object-oriented model. In fact, we model the ODB designs with the UML class diagrams stereotyped to express the ODB features and constraints.

The mapping process must be done for those parts of state and behavior models that relate to persistent objects. In essence, the mapping is restricted to the state and behavior aspects of classes in the entity package.

The state mapping dominates the task. The behavior mapping is normally done as part of the architectural design (Section 6.1), collaboration design (Section 6.2), and client/server program design (Chapter 9). In particular, it is the responsibility of the architectural design to take the initial decision where the various processes should run – on the client or on the server. This decision affects the detailed collaboration design and the client/server program design.

8.2.2.1 *Mapping entity classes*

A careful reader would have noticed an awkward assumption in UML modeling that the attributes in classes are defined on *atomic data types* and on a few *built-in structured data types* (Date, Currency). The association roles imply that the *collections* (templates) will be used in the design but the decision on collections is normally delayed until the support for them in the chosen database and programming environment is known.

But what about simple questions like: 'What if an employee has many phone numbers? How should I model this during analysis? Do I really need to have a separate class of phone numbers?' A similarly troublesome question seems to be: 'Can I model an employee name as a single attribute but with the internal structure recognizing that the name consists of the family name, first name and middle initial? Do I really need to have a separate class of employee names?'

Theoretically, UML does not restrain us from extending the type system by defining new classes (in analysis) and by using templates (in design). In practice, to avoid the proliferation of minor classes, we do not want to do this until we know the support that we can get from an implementation platform for the extendible type system and for the built-in structured and collection types. As a result, questions like those above are frequently swept aside until the detailed design.

Let us explain these and similar issues by taking some of our analysis models and mapping them to an ODB class schema. In this section, we look at classes other than the entity classes. In subsequent sections, we also consider the relationships between entity classes.

Example 8.1 (Contact Management)

Refer to the class specifications for Contact Management in Example 4.6, Figure 4.3 (Section 4.2.1.2.3). Consider the classes `Contact` and `Employee`. Note that the questions formulated above apply to these two classes.

`Contact` has the attributes `family_name` and `first_name` but does not have the concept of a contact name. Similarly, `Employee` contains `family_name`, `first_name`, and `middle_name` but we could not ask the database about an employee name because such a concept does not exist.

`Contact` has also the attributes `phone`, `fax` and `email`. The current model does not allow for a contact to have more than one `phone`, `fax` or `email` – quite an unrealistic assumption in practice.

Our task in this example is to map the entity classes `Contact` and `Employee` to an ODB design. The mapping should address the identified problems.

Figure 8.5 demonstrates the mapping. We introduced two ODB abstract classes to represent the types `PersonShortName` and `PersonLongName`. The first class defines the type for `contact_name` within the class `Contact`. The second class inherits the two attributes of `PersonShortName` via the EXTENDS relationship and together with its own attribute provides the data type for `employee_name` within the class `Employee`.

The possibility of a `Contact` having many phones, faxes and emails is designed with the set type – one of the collection types supported by ODB systems.

8.2.2.2 Mapping associations

In UML models, the associations between classes permit the navigation between the objects of these classes. This is exactly what the object databases are good at – the navigation between objects linked by persistent object identifiers.

The mapping of associations to ODB is therefore a pretty straightforward activity, as already demonstrated for the association between `Student` and `CourseOffering` in

FIGURE 8.5

Mapping entity classes to ODB design (Contact Management).

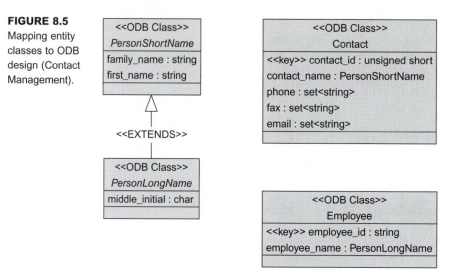

Section 8.2.1.2 (Figure 8.3). The relationship property in an ODB class is typed with the name of the class (or a collection of the class) to which it is associated.

This said, we might want to optimize the design during the mapping. In particular, we might decide to model some UML attributes (or UML classes) as ODB interfaces with the intention to use these interfaces as types for properties in ODB classes (as demonstrated in Figure 8.5).

Example 8.2 (Contact Management)

Refer to the association specifications for Contact Management in Example 4.8, Figure 4.5 (Section 4.2.2.3). Refer also to the previous example of mapping entity classes (Figure 8.5).

Our task is to map the model in Figure 4.5 to an ODB design. During the mapping we would like to consider which UML attributes or classes are good candidates for ODB interfaces. We can then use (reuse) these interfaces in relevant ODB classes.

Figure 8.6 is one possible solution to the example. Apart from the previously introduced *ODB classes* (PersonShortName and PersonLongName), we created an EXTENDS *inheritance hierarchy* for the ODB class Address. We then nested the *object attributes* postal_address and courier_address inside the ODB classes Organization and Contact. No association links are drawn because the relationships are represented as class properties.

FIGURE 8.6
Mapping
associations to
ODB design
(Contact
Management).

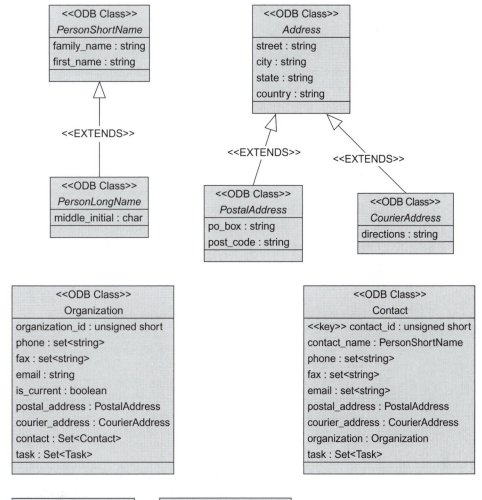

8.2.2.3 Mapping aggregations

As explained before (Sections 2.1.4, 4.2.3 and 5.4), UML recognizes only two semantics of aggregation – the *aggregation* with the reference semantics and the *composition* with the value semantics. Limited as it is, the UML notion of aggregation is likely not to be directly supported by an ODB implementation (or any other database for that matter).

Aggregations in databases are modeled as associations or as nested attributes. If a special aggregation semantics is to be enforced then this is achieved through procedural means (in programs) rather than declaratively (in data structures).

The mapping principle for aggregations is simple. A *UML aggregation* maps to an ODB model as if it were an association. A *UML composition* results in a composite ODB class that contains a nested attribute representing the component class. Since the component class has an internal structure (i.e. it is not atomic), an ODB interface has to be first defined as a structured object type. The nested attribute can then take values of that object type. Some variations to the above mapping strategies are possible for the sake of processing efficiency, reusability, scalability, maintainability, etc.

Example 8.3 (University Enrolment)

Refer to the aggregation specifications for University Enrolment in Example 4.9, Figure 4.6 (Section 4.2.3.3).

Our task is to map the model in Figure 4.6 to an ODB design. To handle nested attributes and to simplify the model, some ODB interfaces may need to be defined and used as types for the class attributes.

Figure 8.7 is the proposed model. Two abstract ODB classes are defined: `YearSemester` and `AcademicRecord`. The former is of only cosmetic significance – the model could do without it. The latter is necessary to define the UML composition as a nested attribute `academic_record` in the class `Student`.

The UML aggregation between `Course` and `CourseOffering` is modeled as a normal association. The semantics of aggregation would need to be enforced procedurally. The relationship properties define the aggregation and association relationship present in Figure 4.6.

8.2.2.4 Mapping generalizations

Mapping UML generalization relationships is likely to rely predominantly on the ODB *EXTENDS* relationship. UML has neither a notion of *interface* (in the ODMG sense), nor a separate category of generalization relationship that would correspond to the ODB *ISA* relationship. Inheritance of behavior is supported in UML through property visibility (attributes with private visibility are not inherited).

FIGURE 8.7
Mapping
aggregations to
ODB design
(University
Enrolment).

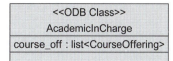

```
        <<ODB Class>>
          YearSemester
    ──────────────────────────
    year : date
    semester : unsigned short
```

```
            <<ODB Class>>
              Course
    ──────────────────────────────────
    course_code : string
    course_name : string
    credit_points : unsigned short
    course_offering : list<CourseOffering>
```

<<EXTENDS>>

```
      <<ODB Class>>
       AcademicRecord
    ────────────────────
    course_code : string
    grade : string
```

```
            <<ODB Class>>
             CourseOffering
    ──────────────────────────────────────
    year_sem : YearSemester
    enrolment_quota : unsigned short
    course : Course
    student : list<Student>
    academic_in_charge : AcademicInCharge
```

```
          <<ODB Class>>
            Student
    ──────────────────────────────────────
    student_id : string
    student_name : string
    current_fees : float
    course_off : list<CourseOffering>
    academic_record : set<AcademicRecord>
```

```
          <<ODB Class>>
          AcademicInCharge
    ────────────────────────────────
    course_off : list<CourseOffering>
```

Example 8.4 (Video Store)

Refer to the generalization specifications for Video Store in Example 4.10, Figure 4.7 (Section 4.2.4.3).

Our task is to map the model in Figure 4.7 to an ODB design. Although the subclasses in the UML model do not contain their own attributes (as yet), we assume that they differ in state and behavior and that the properties will be added to these classes in due course.

The transformation from the UML to the ODB generalization model is shown in Figure 8.8. The UML class RentalConditions is transformed to an abstract ODB class. The ODB class VideoMedium contains the atrribute rental_cond of the type RentalConditions. That attribute, together with other properties of VideoMedium, is inherited down to the concrete classes at the bottom of the inheritance tree (i.e. BetaTape, VHSTape and DVDDisk).

FIGURE 8.8
Mapping
generalizations
to ODB design
(Video Store).

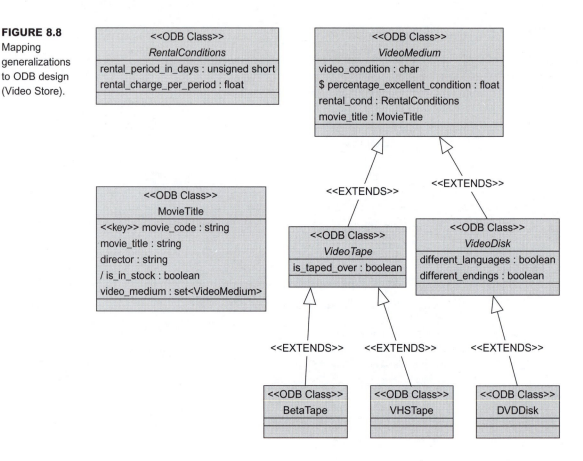

8.3 Object-relational database model

The 'next great wave' in database technology is the object-relational model (Stonebraker and Moore, 1996). As the name informs, an object-relational database (ORDB) combines the old-style relational model and the new-style object model. A single object-relational database management system (ORDBMS) is capable of processing the relational data structures (*relational tables*) and the object data structures (*object tables*).

The standard for the ORDB model was ratified in 1999 after more than six years in the making (under the nickname SQL3). The standard is the work of the American National Standards Institute (ANSI) and the International Organization for Standardization (ISO). The ORDB standard is called SQL:1999 (Eisenberg and Melton, 1999). The standard leaves many ORDB issues unresolved and it is expected that it will be revised roughly every three years.

The ORDB model is upward compatible with the last relational database standard – namely SQL92. The model extends the conventional relational table facility with a new mechanism to store objects in SQL tables. The model extends also the limited relational support for user-defined types with arbitrary complex *structured types* (to encapsulate attributes and operations in a single object type – class).

While the standard has been and still is evolving, major relational database vendors (Oracle, IBM, Informix) have been on a mission to deliver ORDBMS products with at least partial support for the ORDB model. One of the major problems for ORDBMS vendors is how to integrate the pre-existing relational features with the new object features to allow for a smooth migration of relational systems to ORDB solutions. This problem is not really addressed by the SQL:1999 standard.

In what follows, we try to conform to SQL:1999 specifications (Eisenberg and Melton, 1999) but we make occasional detours to real ORDBMS products (in particular Oracle8) to highlight the differences between the theory and practice.

8.3.1 ORDB modeling primitives

The ORDB modeling primitives consist of the new object primitives and the old relational primitives. The principal new object primitive is a user-defined *structured type* that corresponds to the ODB notion of *interface* and the UML notion of *class*.

A structured type is defined by specifying its *attributes* and *operations*. A structured type can also be defined as a *subtype* of another structured type. In effect, the ORDB model supports *multiple interface inheritance* (Section 5.3.3).

The storage mechanism is a *table*. Table *columns* may take values of user-defined structured types. Such tables are called in some ORDBMS implementations (e.g. Oracle8) the *object tables* – to distinguish them from the conventional *relational tables*.

The ODB-style structured and collection types are supported as well. A special kind of the structured type – called the *row type* – permits specifying nested data structures within object tables. A row type can also be used to define a *reference type*. References provide navigational capability on objects.

8.3.1.1 Distinct and structured types

Columns in an ORDB table can take values of *built-in types* or *user-defined types*. The *built-in type* facility of an ORDB is similar to that expected from an ODB (Section 8.2.1.1). The same applies to the built-in operations.

A *user-defined type* is represented as either:

■ *distinct type* – expressed as a single pre-defined data type, called a *source type* (the *distinct type* corresponds to the ODMG *atomic object type*); or

■ *structured type* – expressed as a list of attribute and operation definitions (the *structured type* corresponds to the ODMG *structured object type*).

A *structured type* permits database users to define their own named types. A structured type definition consists of declarations of:

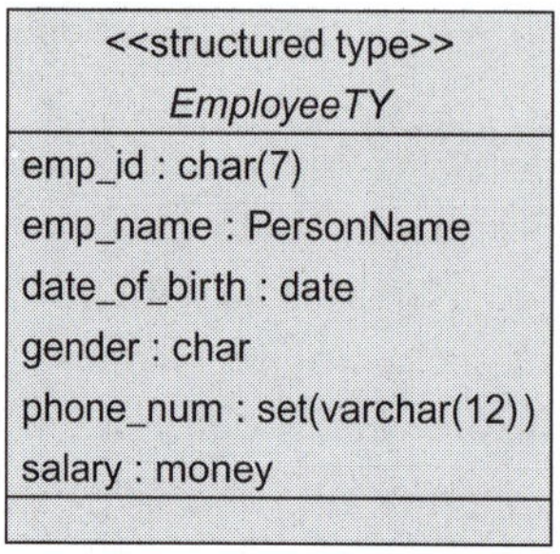

FIGURE 8.9

Type
declarations in
ORDB.

<<structured type>> *EmployeeTY*
emp_id : char(7)
emp_name : PersonName
date_of_birth : date
gender : char
phone_num : set(varchar(12))
salary : money

- *attributes* that represent the state of the structured type objects;
- *operations* that define the behavior of the structured type objects;
- operations that define the *equality/inequality*, *ordering*, and *conversion* of the structured type objects (necessary if we want to compare whether two structured type objects are equal, or to sort them in some way, or to convert from one structured type to another).

A structured type *attribute* can be typed with a *source type*, *distinct type*, *collection type* or another structured type. SQL:1999 defines several collection types (ORDB products can define more collection types):

- set;
- list;
- multiset (the same as the ODB bag);
- array.

Figure 8.9 shows a structured type definition for Employee corresponding to the ODB definition in Figure 8.2. The differences are minor and relate to built-in source types (a somewhat arbitrary issue if no particular ORDBMS is considered). The attribute gender is typed as char because a typical ORDBMS is unlikely to support the enum type. An ORDB achieves the same result by specifying a *check constraint* on gender (Section 8.4).

8.3.1.2 Object tables

The *table* (*object table*) is a set of rows having one or more columns. The *row* is an object (instance) of a *row type* (Section 8.3.1.3 below). Every row in an object table is an object uniquely identified by an OID. Accordingly, the row is the smallest unit of data that can be inserted or deleted from a table.

The suffix TY used in the structured type name is a recommended practice that permits a quick differentiation between an *object type* and an *object table*. In order to store instances of the type EmployeeTY persistently in an ORDB, a *table* of EmployeeTY has to be created. It is convenient to name such a table with the name of the type but without the suffix TY. The SQL:1999 declaration could be:

```
create table Employee of EmployeeTY;
```

The *encapsulation* of attributes of a structured type by operations (e.g. Sections 2.1.2.1.2 and 5.1.4) has not been defined in SQL:1999 (Eisenberg and Melton, 1999). However, SQL:1999 assumes that an ORDB would generate for each attribute an *observer* (get) and *mutator* (set) *operation*. They allow, respectively, reading and modifying each attribute.

8.3.1.3 Row types

A *row type* allows a table to have a relatively complex internal structure without necessarily even using structured types or collections. A row type is a sequence of *fields* (<field name><data type> pairs). In effect, a row type allows a table within another table. A column in a table can contain row values.

The following example explains how row types can be used to define a table with a complex internal structure. The example is inspired by some classes in Contact Management (see Figure 8.6).

```
create table Contact
    (contact_id   integer,
     contact_name row
        (family_name varchar(30),
         first_name  varchar(20)),
     postal_address row
        (po_box     varchar(10),
         post_code varchar(10),
         address    row
            (street   varchar(30),
             city     varchar(20),
             state    varchar(20),
             country varchar(25)))));
```

From a database programming point of view, row types allow storage of complete rows in variables, passing them as operation input arguments, and returning them as operation output arguments or return values.

8.3.1.4 Reference types

A structured type can be used to define a *reference type*. The keyword ref is used to define references. For example emp ref(EmployeeTY) is a reference in an object table to a structured type. In SQL:1999, the reference types are *scoped* – the table that they reference is known at compilation time (i.e. dynamic classification is not supported (see Section 2.1.5.2.3)).

As expected, the value of a reference type is an OID and is unique within the database. It references a row in a *referenceable table*. A referenceable table must be a *typed table*, i.e. a table with an associated *structured type*. Reference types can be used in an ORDB to implement *one-to-one associations*.

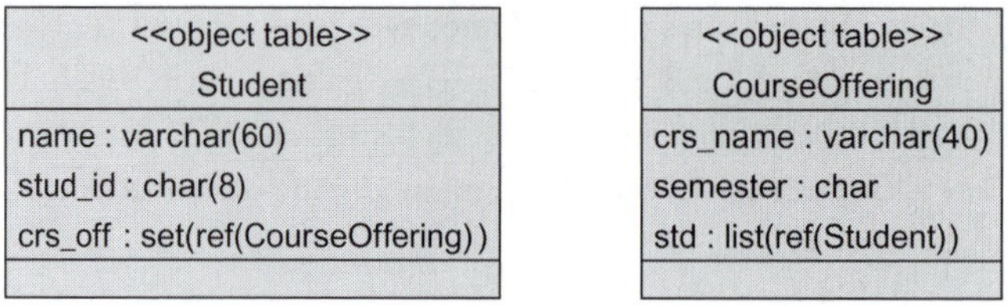

FIGURE 8.10
Association in
ORDB.

<<object table>>
Student
name : varchar(60)
stud_id : char(8)
crs_off : set(ref(CourseOffering))

<<object table>>
CourseOffering
crs_name : varchar(40)
semester : char
std : list(ref(Student))

To implement *many-to-many associations*, *collections* (Section 8.3.1.1) *of references* could be used, if available. Figure 8.10 uses the example presented in Figure 8.3 to show how the many-to-many association between `Student` and `CourseOffering` can be represented in an ORDB.

8.3.1.5 Columns, fields and attributes

SQL:1999 makes a careful distinction between the notions of column, field and attribute (SQL, 2000). This is an important terminological clarification. The distinction is as follows:

■ *column* is a structural component of a *table*;

■ *field* is a structural component of a *row type*;

■ *attribute* is a structural component of a *structured type*.

A column can be *nullable* – it can then take NULL values. A column can also be an *identity* column (taking OID values). A data type for a column, field, or attribute can be a *reference type*.

8.3.1.6 OF and UNDER inheritance

SQL:1999 allows the specialization of existing types. Currently, only the *single inheritance* is allowed. Table hierarchies can be created to correspond to the type hierarchies. That is, a supertable must be declared as 'of' a sypertype, and a subtable as 'of' a subtype. However, a type can be 'skipped' in the table hierarchy, as shown in Figure 8.11.

The SQL:1999 code below the diagram in Figure 8.11 relates to the most specialized type (`ManagerTY`) and to the table (`Manager`). The `under` keyword is used in SQL:1999 to determine the hierarchy of types and the hierarchy of tables. The `of` keyword determines the structured type of a table. We also used `OF` as the name of generalization relationships between the tables and their types in the diagram.

We have declared the type `ManagerTY` to be `instantiable` – i.e. we can create objects of that type. We have also declared it to be the `final` specialization type – no more subtypes are allowed.

Note that SQL:1999 does not have any explicit notion of *interface*. The *encapsulation* (private, protected, public) is not defined. The SQL:1999 inheritance is a *single implementation inheritance*.

FIGURE 8.11
Inheritance in
ORDB.

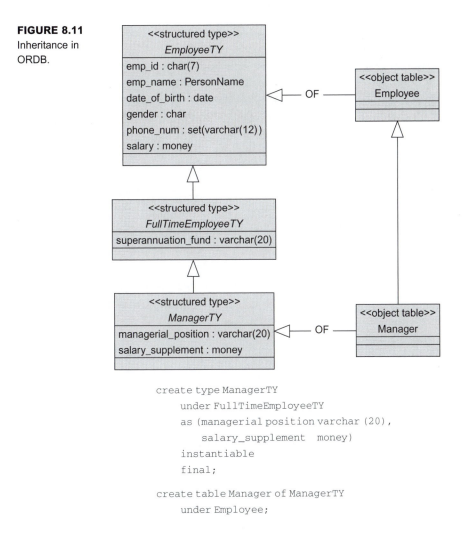

```
create type ManagerTY
    under FullTimeEmployeeTY
    as (managerial position varchar (20),
        salary_supplement  money)
    instantiable
    final;

create table Manager of ManagerTY
    under Employee;
```

8.3.2 Mapping to an ORDB

As in the case of the ODB model, the mapping from UML classes contained in the entity package to an ORDB design can be done in UML itself. The UML stereotypes and other extensibility mechanisms should be sufficient to express the ORDB concepts.

Note, however, that in practice, the mapping is not done to an 'abstract' SQL:1999 standard but to a real ORDB product. The real product may not support some SQL:1999 features and may have other features not mentioned in SQL:1999.

Hence, for example, the current version of Oracle8 (Oracle8i Release 8.1.5.0.0) supports neither the inheritance nor the row type. It does have the array collection but no other collections. It has the notion of a nested table that also allows a nested table of references. It has the notion of an object view to 'transform' relational tables into objects, etc.

FIGURE 8.12

Mapping entity classes to ORDB design (Contact Management).

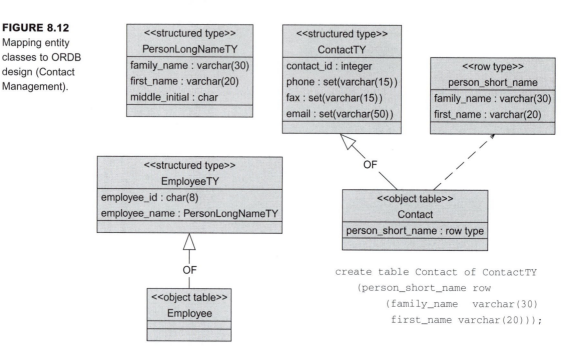

```
create table Contact of ContactTY
         (person_short_name row
               (family_name   varchar(30)
                first_name varchar(20)));
```

8.3.2.1 *Mapping entity classes*

Example 8.5 (Contact Management)

Refer to the class specifications for Contact Management in Example 4.6, Figure 4.3 (Section 4.2.1.2.3). Refer also to Example 8.1 (Section 8.2.2.1).

Our task in this example is to develop an ORDB design model semantically corresponding to the ODB design in Figure 8.5.

A solution to this example requires taking a decision on how to show ODB interfaces (Figure 8.5) in the ORDB design model. The interfaces are not supported in SQL:1999, but we still need to model somehow PersonShortName and PersonLongName.

Figure 8.12 demonstrates two possible solutions. In the case of PersonLongName, a structured type for it has been created. It is then used as the type for an attribute in EmployeeTY. In the case of PersonShortName, we created a class (person_short_name) to 'simulate' the row type (the row type is not an object-oriented concept!). The table Contact is of the type ContactTY but it has an additional column person_short_name of the row type. A dependency relationship to the class person_short_name is used to show the structure of the row type.

8.3.2.2 Mapping associations

Example 8.6 (Contact Management)

Refer to the association specifications for Contact Management in Example 4.8, Figure 4.5 (Section 4.2.2.3). Refer also to the previous mapping examples for Contact Management in Sections 8.2.2.2 and 8.3.2.1.

Our task in this example is to develop an ORDB design model semantically corresponding to the ODB design in Figure 8.6 (Section 8.2.2.2). To simplify the solution while concentrating on association specifications, we assume that all ODB interfaces in Figure 8.6 are converted to row types in our ORDB design (there is no need to show the definitions of the row types in the solution).

Figure 8.13 presents our solution to the example. Object tables contain columns typed as row types and columns typed as reference types. Structured types contain attributes typed as atomic source types or as collections of source types.

8.3.2.3 Mapping aggregations

Example 8.7 (University Enrolment)

Refer to the aggregation specifications for University Enrolment in Example 4.9, Figure 4.6 (Section 4.2.3.3).

Our task in this example is to map the UML model in Figure 4.6 to an ORDB design. Although we have developed an ODB design for this problem in Example 8.3, we do not want to be influenced by it when solving this example. We assume that collections of structured types (not just collections of primitive source types) are supported as attribute types in the structured types.

When solving this example we need to decide how to model in ORDB the UML aggregation and the UML composition. The assumption specified in the example definition gives us a strong hint. The composition between `Student` and `AcademicRecord` can be modeled in `Student` with an attribute typed as a collection of `AcademicRecord`. This is shown in Figure 8.14. The collection is `set(AcademicRecordTY)`.

The UML aggregation between `Course` and `CourseOffering` is modeled as a normal association – with references. For every object table we have to specify the corresponding structured type. This is necessitated, among other things, by the SQL:1999 requirement that a value of a `ref` type must identify a row in a typed table (i.e. a table of a specified structured type).

FIGURE 8.13
Mapping
associations to
ORDB design
(Contact
Management).

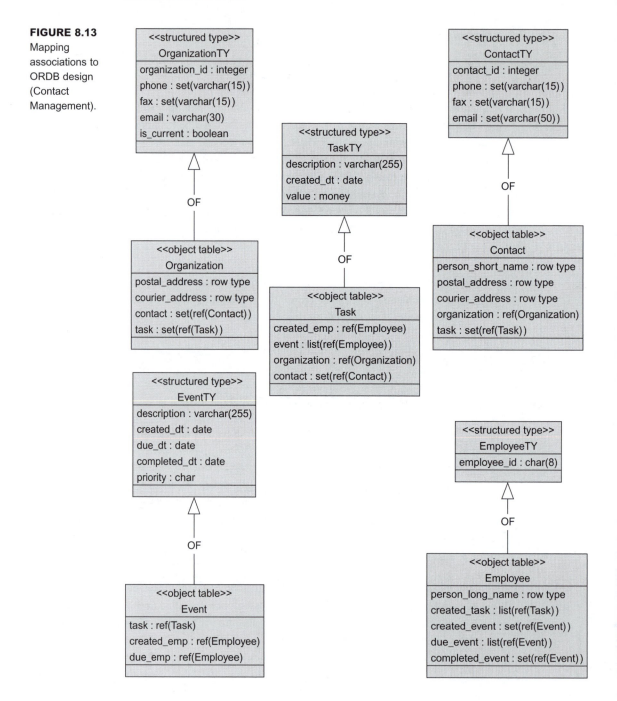

FIGURE 8.14
Mapping
aggregations to
ORDB design
(University
Enrolment).

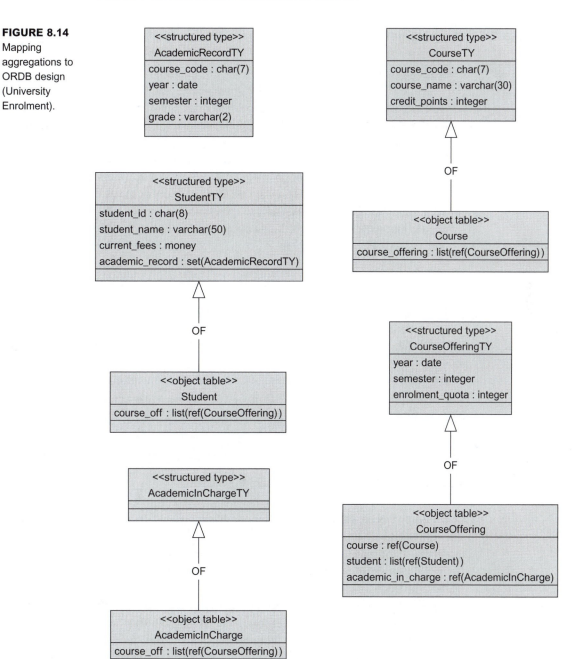

8.3.2.4 *Mapping generalizations*

📁 **Example 8.8 (Video Store)**

Refer to the generalization specifications for Video Store in Example 4.10, Figure 4.7 (Section 4.2.4.3). Refer also to the previous example of mapping generalizations to the ODB design in Section 8.2.2.4.

Our task in this example is to develop an ORDB design model semantically corresponding to the ODB design in Figure 8.8 (Section 8.2.2.4).

Because we are not sure how the ORDB model would support the derived and static attributes, we assume that they will be computed procedurally and there is no need to model them in the ORDB data structures. The two attributes of concern here are: `is_in_stock` and `number_currently_available`.

The main difficulty when solving this example is only indirectly linked to the generalization mapping. The main challenge relates to the SQL:1999 restriction that a value of a `ref` type is 'scoped'. Only one table can be in the scope of a `ref` type and the scope must be known statically – at compilation time.

Previously, we linked `MovieTitle` to `VideoMedium`, implying that any object of `VideoMedium` (i.e. a `BetaTape`, `VHSTape` or `DVDDisk`) will be linked to `MovieTitle`. Now we are forced to create three associations in `MovieTitle` to handle the problem. The complete solution is shown in Figure 8.15.

8.4 Relational database model

Over the last twenty years, the relational model has conquered the database software market. The relational database (RDB) model has replaced the hierarchical and network database models. In the second half of the 1990s, vendors of relational database management systems (RDBMS) have been put on notice by the ODB model, the ODMG standards and various ODBMS products.

As a consequence, ORDBMS products emerged which are destined to play a dominant role in the future. The traditional RDBMS vendors, such as Oracle, IBM or Informix, offer the most influential of these products today. In the meantime, pure ODBMS products have not increased their market share – they have shifted to become object storage APIs to support interoperability between client applications and any server data sources, in particular relational databases.

Although the future no longer belongs to the RDB model, business inertia is such that a decade or more will pass before large systems migrate to the ORDB or ODB technology. There will be also many new applications developed in the RDB technology, simply because businesses will not need the sophisticated and difficult-to-master object solutions.

FIGURE 8.15
Mapping
generalizations
to ORDB design
(Video Store).

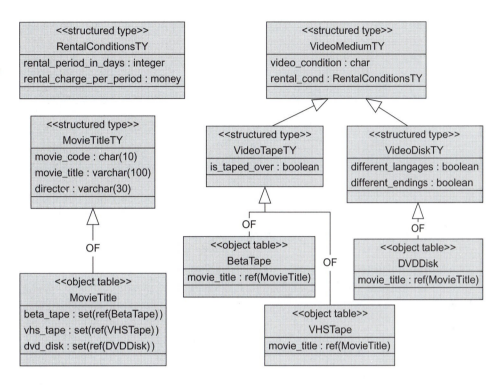

The current (and the last) standard for the RDB model is known as SQL92. It was ratified in 1992 by ANSI and ISO. All major RDBMS products on the market (Oracle, DB2, Sybase, Informix, SQL Server, etc.) conform to the standard, albeit in their unique ways. In fact, some RDB concepts (e.g. *trigger*) have been widely implemented in RDBMS products but recognized only in the SQL:1999 standard.

8.4.1 RDB modeling primitives

The RDB modeling primitives are primitive indeed. The simplicity of the RDB model, which derives from the mathematical *set* concept, is both its strength and its weakness. The mathematical foundations make the model *declarative* in nature (as opposed to *procedural*). The user declares *what* is needed from the database rather than instructing the system *how* to find the information (an RDBMS knows how to find data in its own database).

But what is simple at first becomes quite complex when the problem to solve gets complicated. There are no simple solutions for complex problems. To solve a complex problem we need sophisticated machinery. To start with, we need sophisticated data modeling primitives.

Perhaps the best way to characterize the RDB model is to state what it does not support. From the major modeling primitives available in the ODB and/or ORDB models, the RDB does not support:

FIGURE 8.16
Dependencies
between RDB
modeling
primitives.

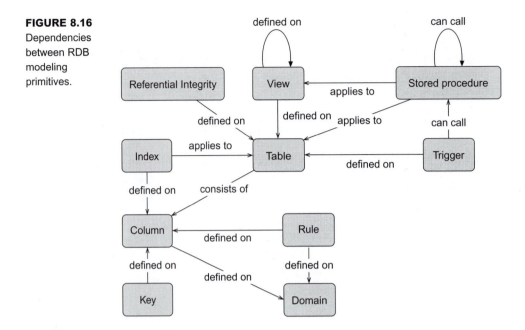

- object types and associated concepts (such as inheritance or methods);
- structured types;
- collections;
- references.

The main modeling primitive in the RDB model is a *relational table* that consists of columns. Table *columns* can only take *atomic values* – structured values or collections of values are not permitted.

The RDB model is adamant about any user-visible *navigational links* between tables – they are explicitly *precluded*. The relationships between tables are maintained by comparing values in columns. There are no persistent links. The ORDB utility to maintain pre-defined relationships between tables is called the *referential integrity*.

Figure 8.16 shows RDB modeling primitives and dependencies between them. All concepts are named with singular nouns but some dependencies apply to more than one instance of the concept. For example, a referential integrity is defined on one or more tables. Most of the concepts shown in Figure 8.16 are discussed next in this chapter. Others are addressed more fully in Chapter 9.

8.4.1.1 Columns, domains and rules

Relational databases define data in tables of columns and rows. A data value stored on the intersection of any column and row must be a simple (indivisible) and a single (not repeating) value. We say that the *columns* have *atomic domains* (data types).

A *domain* defines the legal set of values that a column can take. The domain can be anonymous (e.g. gender char(1)) or it can be named (e.g. gender Gender). In the latter case, the domain Gender has been defined earlier and used in the definition of the column. A possible syntax for the domain definition could be:

```
create domain Gender char(1);
```

A *named domain* can be used in definition of many columns in different tables. This enforces consistency between these definitions. Changes to the domain definition are automatically reflected in column definitions. Although an attractive option at first glance, its use is impeded once the database has been *populated*, i.e. loaded with data.

Columns and domains can have *business rules* which constrain them. The business rule can define:

- *default value* (e.g. if no value is provided for city, assume 'Sydney');
- *range of values* (e.g. the allowed age is in the range 18 to 80);
- *list of values* (e.g. the allowed color is 'green', 'yellow' or 'red');
- *case of value* (e.g. the value must be in uppercase or lowercase);
- *format of value* (e.g. the value must start with letter 'K').

Only very simple business rules concerning single columns or domains can be defined with the *rule* facility. More complex rules spanning tables can be defined as *referential integrity* constraints. The ultimate mechanism for defining business rules is a *trigger*.

8.4.1.2   *Relational tables*

A *relational table* is defined by its fixed set of columns. Columns have built-in or user-defined types (i.e. domains). Tables can have any number or *rows* (records). As the table is a mathematical *set*, there are no duplicate rows in a table.

A column value in a particular row may be allowed to be NULL. The NULL value means one of two things: 'the value at present unknown' or 'the value does not apply' (Section 8.2.1.1).

A consequence of the RDB model's requirement of 'no duplicate rows' is that every table has a *primary key*. A *key* is a *minimal* set of columns (possibly one) such that the values in these columns *uniquely* identify a single row in the table. A table can have many such keys. One of these keys is arbitrarily chosen as the most important for the user – this is the *primary key*. Other keys are called the *candidate* or *alternate keys*.

In practice, an RDBMS table does not have to have a key. This means that a table (without a unique key) may have duplicate rows – a pretty useless feature in a relational database as two rows with the same values for all their columns are not distinguishable. This is different to ODB and ORDB systems where the OID provides such a distinction (two objects may be equal but not identical, like two copies of this book, for example).

Although UML can be stereotyped for modeling relational databases, it is more convenient to use a specifically targeted diagramming technique for the logical modeling of relational databases. Figure 8.17 demonstrates one such notation. The target database is DB2.

FIGURE 8.17

Table definition
in RDB.

Employee			
emp_id	CHAR(7)	<pk>	not null
family_name	VARCHAR(30)	<ak>	not null
first_name	VARCHAR(20)		not null
date_of_birth	DATE	<ak>	not null
gender	Gender		not null
phone_num1	VARCHAR(12)		null
phone_num2	VARCHAR(12)		null
salary	DEC(8,2)		null

The table Employee consists of eight columns. The last three columns accept NULL values. The column emp_id is the primary key. The columns {family_name, date_of_birth} define the candidate (alternate) key. The column gender is defined on the domain Gender.

Because of the RDB restriction that a column can take only atomic single values, we have encountered difficulty with modeling the employee name and phone numbers. In the former case, we used two columns: family_name and first_name. The columns are not grouped or otherwise related in the model. In the latter case, we opted for a solution with two columns (phone_num1, phone_num2) allowing a maximum of two phone numbers per employee.

Once the table has been defined in a CASE tool, the code to create the table can be automatically generated, as shown below. The generated code includes the definition of the domain Gender and the definition of the business rule defined on that domain.

```
-- ================================================================
-- Domain: Gender
-- ================================================================
create distinct type Gender as CHAR(1) %WITHCOMPAR%;

-- ================================================================
-- Table: Employee
-- ================================================================
create table Employee (
    emp_id              CHAR(7)                         not null,
    family_name         VARCHAR(30)                     not null,
    first_name          VARCHAR(20)                     not null,
    date_of_birth       DATE                            not null,
    gender              Gender                          not null
        constraint C_gender check (gender in ('F','M','f','m')),
    phone_num1          VARCHAR(12),
    phone_num2          VARCHAR(12),
    salary              DEC(8,2),
primary key (emp_id),
unique (date_of_birth, family_name)
);
```

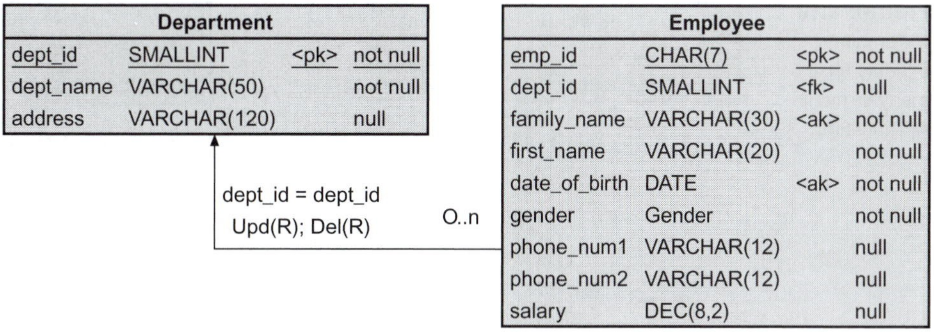

FIGURE 8.18
Referential
integrity.

Department			
dept_id	SMALLINT	\<pk\>	not null
dept_name	VARCHAR(50)		not null
address	VARCHAR(120)		null

Employee			
emp_id	CHAR(7)	\<pk\>	not null
dept_id	SMALLINT	\<fk\>	null
family_name	VARCHAR(30)	\<ak\>	not null
first_name	VARCHAR(20)		not null
date_of_birth	DATE	\<ak\>	not null
gender	Gender		not null
phone_num1	VARCHAR(12)		null
phone_num2	VARCHAR(12)		null
salary	DEC(8,2)		null

dept_id = dept_id
Upd(R); Del(R)   O..n

8.4.1.3 *Referential integrity*

The RDB model maintains relationships between tables by means of *referential integrity* constraints. The relationships are not fixed row-to-row connections. Instead, an RDB 'discovers' row-to-row connections each time the user requests the system to find a relationship. This 'discovering' is done by comparing the *primary key* values in one table with the *foreign key* values in the same or another table.

A *foreign key* is defined as a set of columns in one table whose values are either NULL or are required to match the values of the primary key in the same or another table. That primary-to-foreign key correspondence is called the *referential integrity*. The primary and foreign keys in a referential integrity must be defined on the same domain, but they do not have to have the same names.

Figure 8.18 shows a graphical representation for referential integrity. As the result of drawing a relationship between the tables Employee and Department, the foreign key dept_id has been added to the table Employee. For each Employee row, the foreign key value must be either NULL or must match one of the dept_id values in Department (otherwise an employee would work for a department which does not exist).

The additional description on the relationship line defines *declaratively* the behavior associated with the referential integrity. There are four possible *declarative referential integrity constraints* associated with *delete* and *update* operations. The question is what to do with Employee rows if a Department row is deleted or updated (i.e. when dept_id gets updated). There are four possible answers to this question:

1. Upd(R); Del(R) – *restrict* the update or delete operation (i.e. do not allow the operation to go ahead if there are still Employee rows linked to that Department).
2. Upd(C); Del(C) – *cascade* the operation (i.e. delete all linked Employee rows).
3. Upd(N); Del(N) – *set null* (i.e. update or delete the Department row and set dept_id of the linked Employee rows to NULL).
4. Upd(D); Del(D) – *set default* (i.e. update or delete the Department row and set dept_id of the linked Employee rows to the default value).

The modeling of referential integrity gets complicated when the relationship between tables is many-to-many, as between Student and CourseOffering (Figure 8.3 in Section

FIGURE 8.19

Referential integrity for many-to-many relationship.

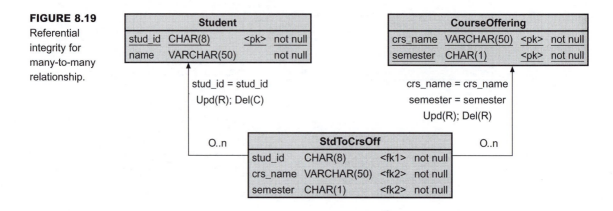

8.2.1.2). To be able to manage the problem under the RDB restriction that a column cannot take multiple values, we need to introduce an *intersection table*, such as StdToCrsOff in Figure 8.19. The only purpose of the table is to model the many-to-many relationship and specify the declarative referential integrity constraints.

8.4.1.4 *Triggers*

The *rules* and *declarative referential integrity* constraints allow defining simple business rules on the database. They are not sufficient to define more complex rules or to define any exceptions to the rules. An RDB solution to this problem (standardized in SQL:1999) is a trigger.

A *trigger* is a small program, written in an extended SQL, that is executed automatically (triggered) as a result of a modification operation on a table on which the trigger has been defined. A modification operation can be any of the SQL modification statements: insert, update or delete.

A trigger can be used to implement *business rules* that go beyond the capability of the SQL rule statement (Section 8.4.1.1). For example, the business rule that forbids changes to the Employee table during the weekends can be programmed into a trigger. Any attempt to issue an SQL insert, update or delete on the table during a weekend will result in the trigger firing and the database refusing to execute the operation.

A trigger can also be used to enforce more complex referential integrity constraints. For example, our business rule may state that on deleting a Department row, the Employee who is the manager of that department should also be deleted but all other employees should have dept_id values set to NULL. Such a business rule cannot be enforced declaratively. We need a procedural trigger to enforce it.

Once triggers are used to enforce referential integrity in the database, the declarative referential integrity constraints are normally abandoned. Mixing procedural and declarative constraints is a bad idea because of occasionally intricate interdependencies between them. Consequently, the dominant practice today is to program the referential integrity in triggers alone. The issue is not as daunting as it may look because a good CASE tool can generate much of the code automatically.

For example, the trigger code, generated by a CASE tool for the Sybase RDBMS, is shown below. The trigger implements the `Del(r)` declarative constraint – i.e. it does not allow the `Department` row to be deleted if there are still `Employee` rows associated with it.

```
create trigger keepdpt
        on Department
        for delete
        as
        if @@rowcount = 0
                return /* avoid firing trigger if no rows affected */
        if exists
                (select * from Employee, deleted
                where Employee.dept_id =
                    deleted.dept_id)
        begin
                print 'Test for RESTRICT DELETE failed. No deletion'
                rollback transaction
                return
        end
        return
go
```

The `if` statement checks if the SQL `delete` operation (which fired the trigger) is going to delete any rows at all. If not, the trigger does not proceed – no harm can be done. If `Department` rows can be deleted then Sybase stores these (about to be deleted) rows in an internal table called `deleted`. The trigger then does an *equality join* operation on `dept_id` on the tables `Employee` and `deleted` to find out if there are any employees working for the department(s) to be deleted. If so, the trigger refuses the `delete` action, displays a message and rolls back the transaction. Otherwise, the `Department` rows are allowed to be deleted.

8.4.1.5   *Relational views*

A *relational view* is a stored and named SQL query. Because a result of any SQL query is a transient table, a view can be used in place of a table in other SQL operations. A view can be derived from one or more tables and/or one or more other views (Figure 8.16).

Figure 8.20 show a graphical representation for the view `EmpNoSalary` – the view displays all information from the table `Employee` except the `salary` column. The `create view` statement below the figure demonstrates that a view is really a named query that executes each time a SQL query or update operation is issued on the view.

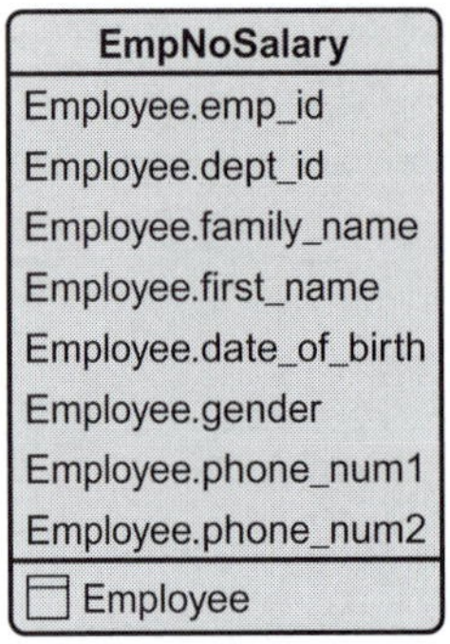

FIGURE 8.20
Relational view.

EmpNoSalary
Employee.emp_id
Employee.dept_id
Employee.family_name
Employee.first_name
Employee.date_of_birth
Employee.gender
Employee.phone_num1
Employee.phone_num2
☐ Employee

```
=================================================================
-- View: EmpNoSalary                                          --
=================================================================
create view EmpNoSalary () as
    select Employee.emp_id, Employee.dept_id,
           Employee.family_name, Employee.first_name,
           Employee.date_of_birth, Employee.gender,
           Employee.phone_num1, Employee.phone_num2
    from Employee;
```

Theoretically, a view is a very powerful mechanism with many uses. It can be used in support of *database security* by restricting the users from seeing the table data. It can present data to the users in *different perspectives*. It can *isolate the application from changes* to table definitions, if the changed definition is not part of the view. It allows easier expression of *complex queries* – the query can be built in a 'divide and conquer' fashion by using multiple levels of views.

In practice, the use of the view concept in the RDB model is severely restricted by its inability to allow view updates. A *view update* is the possibility of sending a modification operation (a SQL insert, update, or delete) to the view and changing the underlying base table(s) as a result. The SQL92 support for view updating is very limited – practically non-existent.

8.4.1.6 *Normal forms*

Arguably, one of the most important but at the same time least understood concepts in the RDB design is *normalization*. A relational table must be in a *normal form* (NF). There are six normal forms:

- 1st NF
- 2nd NF
- 3rd NF
- BCNF (Boyce–Codd NF)
- 4th NF
- 5th NF

A table that is in a higher NF is also in all lower NFs. A table must be at least in the 1st NF. A table with no structured or multi-valued columns is in the 1st NF (and that's the fundamental requirement of the RDB model).

A table in a low NF can exhibit so-called update anomalies. An *update anomaly* is an undesirable side effect as a result of a modification operation (`insert`, `update`, `delete`) on a table. For example, if the same information is repeated many times in the same column in the table then an update of that information must be performed in all places or the database will be left in an incorrect state. It can be shown that update anomalies are incrementally eliminated with the table reaching higher NFs.

So, how do we normalize a table to a higher NF? We can bring a table to a higher NF by splitting it vertically along columns into two or more smaller tables. These smaller tables are likely to be in higher NFs and they replace the original table in the RDB design model. The original table can, however, always be reconstructed by joining the smaller tables in a SQL `join` operation.

The scope of this book does not allow us to treat the normalization theory in any detail. The reader is referred to such textbooks as Date, 2000; Maciaszek, 1990; Silberschatz *et al.*, 1997; Ramakrishnan and Gehrke, 2000. The main point that we would like to make is that a good RDB design naturally arrives at a good normalization level.

What do we mean by a good design in the normalization context? A *good design* means that we understand how the RDB is going to be used by a mix of update and retrieval operations. If the database is very dynamic, i.e. it is subjected to frequent update operations, then we will naturally create smaller tables to better localize and facilitate these updates. The tables will be in higher NFs and the update anomalies will be reduced or eliminated.

On the other hand, if the database is relatively static, i.e. we frequently search for information but we update the database content sporadically, then a *denormalized design* will pay off. This is because a search in a single large table is going to be much more efficient than the same search on multiple tables that need to be joined together before the search starts.

8.4.2 Mapping to the RDB

Mapping from a UML class model to the RDB schema design has to consider the limitations of the RDB model. The issue is that of trading some *declarative semantics* of class diagrams for the *procedural solutions* in logical schema designs. In other words, it might not be possible to express some built-in declarative semantics of classes in the relational schema. Such semantics will have to be resolved procedurally in database programs, i.e. in stored procedures (Section 9.1.2.1).

The mapping to the RDB models has been extensively studied in the context of the ER and extended ER modeling (e.g. Maciaszek, 1990; Elmasri and Navathe, 2000). The principles are the same and all major issues have been identified in those studies. Just as in the case of the ORDB and ODB models, the mapping must not simply conform to some standard (SQL92 in the RDB case), but must relate to the target implementation RDBMS.

8.4.2.1 Mapping entity classes

The mapping of entity classes to relational tables must obey the 1st NF of tables. The columns must be atomic. However, and awkwardly enough, as we pointed out in Section 8.2.2.1, the class attributes (as opposed to the class relationships) in UML analysis models are already atomic. This simplifies the mapping.

> ## Example 8.9 (Contact Management)
>
> Refer to the class specifications for Contact Management in Example 4.6, Figure 4.3 (Section 4.2.1.2.3). Consider also the discussion regarding the non-atomic attributes in Example 8.1.
>
> Map the classes `Contact` and `Employee` to a RDB design such that a number of alternative mapping strategies is demonstrated.

Our solution to this example is shown in Figure 8.21. The solution assumes the Oracle RDBMS. We modeled `contact_name` as an atomic data type in the table `Contact`. Each `Contact` is allowed only one `fax` and one `email`. However, we do allow any number of `phones`. The table `ContactPhone` serves this purpose.

In the table `Employee`, we maintain three separate attributes for `family_name`, `first_name` and `middle_initial`. However, the database does not have any knowledge of `employee_name` as a combined concept for these three attributes.

8.4.2.2 Mapping associations

The mapping of associations to RDB involves the use of *referential integrity* constraints between tables. Any association that is one-to-one or one-to-many can be directly expressed by inserting a *foreign key* in one table to match the primary key of the other table.

In the case of *one-to-one association*, the foreign key can be added to either table (to be decided on the basis of the association usage patterns). Also, in the case of one-to-one association, it

FIGURE 8.21
Mapping entity classes to RDB design (Contact Management).

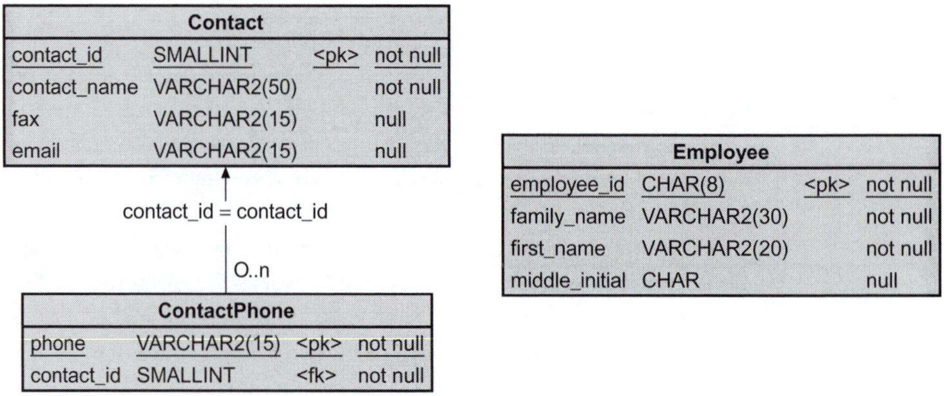

may be desirable to combine the two entity classes in one table (depending on the desired normalization level).

For *recursive* one-to-one and one-to-many associations, the foreign key and primary key are in the same table. Each *many-to-many association* (whether recursive or not) requires an intersection table as demonstrated in Figure 8.19.

Example 8.10 (Contact Management)

Refer to the association specifications for Contact Management in Example 4.8, Figure 4.5 (Section 4.2.2.3).
    Map the diagram in Figure 4.5 to a RDB model.

This example proves to be quite straightforward due to the lack of many-to-many associations in the UML association specifications. The RDB diagram (for the DB2 RDBMS) is shown in Figure 8.22. Consistently with the RDB principles, we created a number of new columns as primary keys. We decided to retain the model in Figure 8.21 as a partial solution to this example. To conserve space, we suppressed the display of the columns' nullabilities and key indicators.

The referential integrity constraints between `PostalAddress` and `CourierAddress` on one hand and `Organization` and `Contact` on the other hand are modeled with foreign keys in the address tables. This is slightly arbitrary and the constraints could have been modeled in the opposite direction (i.e. with foreign keys in `Organization` and `Contact`).

8.4.2.3 *Mapping aggregations*

An RDB does not understand the difference between association and aggregation except when implemented procedurally in triggers or stored procedures. The main principles for the association mapping (Section 8.4.2.2) apply to the mapping of aggregations. Only when an association can be converted to a number of resultant relational solutions would the semantics of aggregation (as a special form of association) influence the decision.

In the case of the strong form of aggregation (i.e. *composition*), an attempt should be made to combine the subset and superset entity classes in a single table. This is possible for one-to-one aggregations. For *one-to-many aggregations*, the subset class (in the strong and weak forms of aggregation) must be modeled as a separate table (with a foreign key linking it to its owning table).

Example 8.11 (University Enrolment)

Refer to the aggregation specifications for University Enrolment in Example 4.9, Figure 4.6 (Section 4.2.3.3).
    Map the diagram in Figure 4.6 to an RDB model.

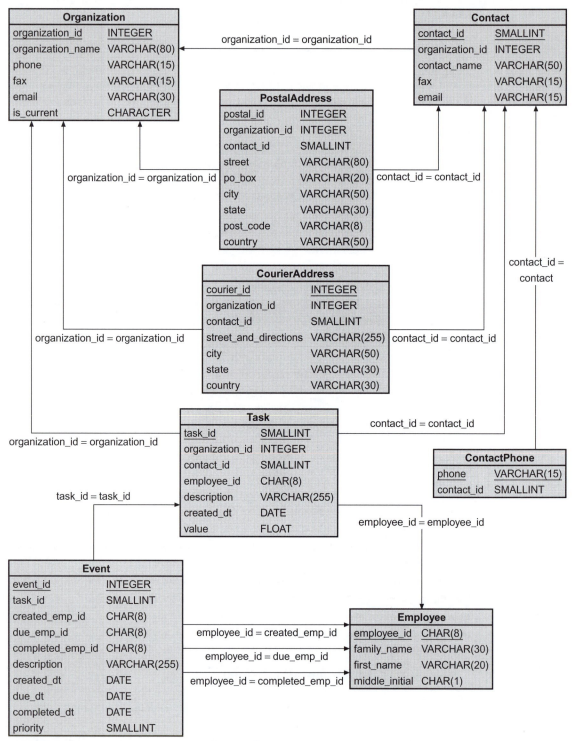

FIGURE 8.22 Mapping associations to RDB design (Contact Management).

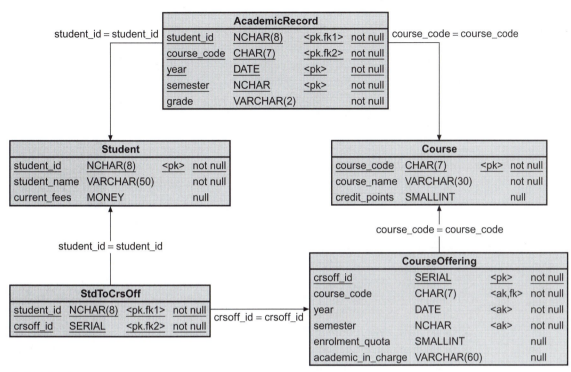

FIGURE 8.23 Mapping aggregations to RDB design (University Enrolment).

This example includes two aggregation relationships – a composition from Student to AcademicRecord and a weak aggregation from Course to CourseOffering. Both are one-to-many aggregations and require separate 'subset' tables.

In the UML model in Figure 4.6, we assumed (naturally enough) an indirect navigational link from AcademicRecord to Course. In an RDB design, we may want to establish a direct referential integrity between the tables AcademicRecord and Course. After all, AcademicRecord has the attribute course_code as part of its primary key. The same attribute can be made into a foreign key to the table Course. This is shown in Figure 8.23 (for the Informix RDBMS).

The *many-to-many association* between the classes Student and CourseOffering leads to another interesting observation, albeit not related to the aggregation mapping. The association results in an intersection table StdToCrsOff with the primary key to be concatenated from the primary keys of the two main tables.

The primary key for CourseOffering could be {course_code, year, semester}. However, such a key would result in a cumbersome primary key for StdToCrsOff. We opted, therefore, for a system-generated primary key in CourseOffering. It is called crsoff and its type is SERIAL (in Informix, the type to generate unique identifiers is called SERIAL; the same type may be called something else in other RDBMSs – for example, it is called IDENTITY in Sybase, UNIQUEIDENTIFIER in Microsoft SQL Server, and SEQUENCE in Oracle).

FIGURE 8.24
Generalization
hierarchy to
exemplify
mapping to RDB.

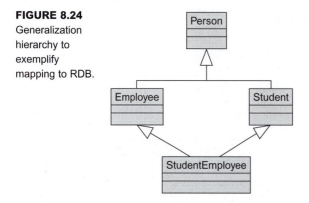

8.4.2.4 *Mapping generalizations*

The mapping of generalization relationships to RDB can be done in a variety of ways but the principles are less convoluted than might be expected. It must be remembered, however, that expressing a generalization in an RDB data structure ignores issues that make the generalization tick – inheritance, polymorphism, code reuse, etc.

To illustrate the generalization mapping strategies consider the example in Figure 8.24. There are four strategies for converting a generalization hierarchy to an RDB design model (although some further variations of these strategies are possible):

1. Map each class to a table.

2. Map the entire class hierarchy to a single 'superclass' table.

3. Map each concrete class to a table.

4. Map each disjoint concrete class to a table.

The first mapping strategy is illustrated in Figure 8.25. Each table has its own primary key. The presented solution does not tell us if a 'subclass' table 'inherits' some of its columns from the 'superclass' table. For example, is person_name stored in Person and 'inherited' by Employee, Student and StudentEmployee? 'Inheriting' means really a join operation and the performance penalty of the join may force us to have person_name duplicated in all tables of the hierarchy.

The second mapping strategy is illustrated in Figure 8.26 (in Microsoft SQL Server RDBMS). The table Person would contain the combined set of attributes in all classes of the generalization hierarchy. It contains also two columns (is_employee and is_student) to record whether a person is an employee, a student, or both.

To illustrate the third mapping strategy, we assume that the class Person is abstract. Any attributes of the class Person are 'inherited' by the tables corresponding to the concrete classes. The result will be similar to that shown in Figure 8.27.

FIGURE 8.25
Mapping each
class to a table.

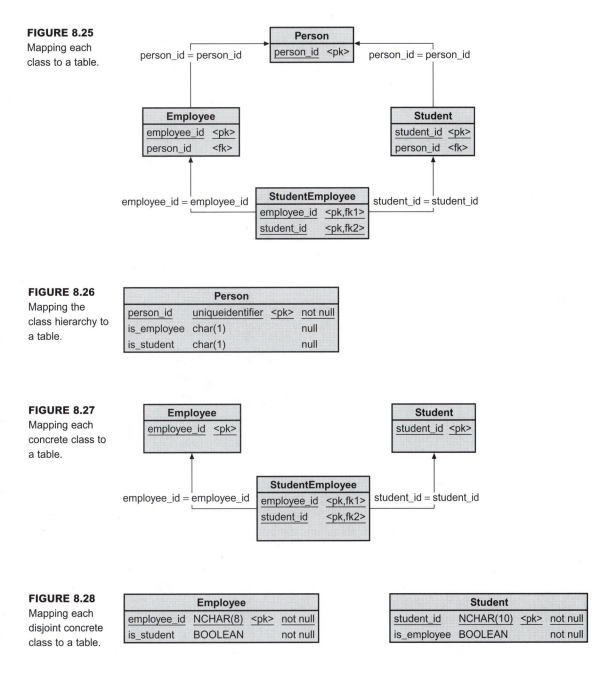

FIGURE 8.26
Mapping the
class hierarchy to
a table.

FIGURE 8.27
Mapping each
concrete class to
a table.

FIGURE 8.28
Mapping each
disjoint concrete
class to a table.

Still assuming that the class Person is abstract, the last strategy is illustrated in Figure 8.28 (in Informix RDBMS). As opposed to the model in Figure 8.25, we assume that the fact that an employee is also a student, and vice versa, is always known. Hence, not null for the two BOOLEAN columns.

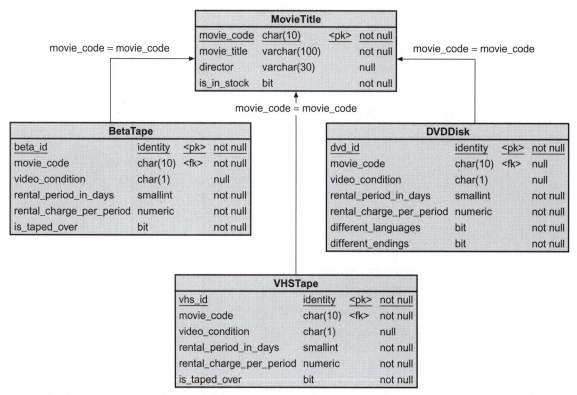

FIGURE 8.29 Mapping generalizations to RDB design (Video Store).

 Example 8.12 (Video Store)

Refer to the generalization specifications for Video Store in Example 4.10, Figure 4.7 (Section 4.2.4.3). Refer also to the few modeling extensions introduced in Example 8.4 (Section 8.2.2.4).

Our task is to map the diagram in Figure 4.7 to an RDB model while considering the extensions in Figure 8.8 (Example 8.4). We will use the third strategy of mapping each concrete class to a table.

We need to consider how to handle the derived attribute `is_in_stock` and the static attribute `number_currently_available`. As in the previous models for Video Store, we will ignore the possibility of having more than one rental condition for the same video medium (i.e. beta tape, VHS tape or DVD disk).

The RDB design (for Sybase RDBMS) in Figure 8.29 contains a table for each of the three concrete classes (`BetaTape`, `VHSTape`, and `DVDDisk`). The tables duplicate information about `video_condition`, `rental_period_in_days`, and `rental_charge_per_period`. Only one `rental_period_in_days` and one `rental_charge_per_period` can be recorded per tape or disk.

The columns `is_taped_over`, `different_languages`, `different_endings` and `is_in_stock` are typed as `bit`. By definition, the `bit` type does not allow null values (`bit` is either zero or one).

The column `is_in_stock` is set to true (one) if there is at least one tape or disk with a particular movie in stock. This is not terribly useful information if a customer is only interested in one of the three video mediums. A better solution would be to have three `bit` columns or to assume that this information is never stored, i.e. it is derived (calculated) whenever a customer requests a tape or disk.

The static attribute `number_currently_available` is not stored in any table in our design. The only table where it could be sensibly stored is `MovieTitle`. If stored, the same considerations as for the attribute `is_in_stock` would apply.

Summary

This chapter has reflected on the paramount importance of databases in software development. A bad database design cannot be set right by other means, including a good application design. All three major database models have been discussed – the object, object-relational, and relational model.

There are three levels of database models – external, logical and physical. In this chapter, we have concentrated on the *logical model*. The *mapping of objects to databases* is understood as the mapping of a UML class model to a database logical model.

The mapping to the *ODB logical model* is the easiest. The ODB model supports *object types* as well as *structured and collection literals*. The relationships are modeled with *inverses*. The *ISA* and *EXTENDS* inheritance can be used to map UML generalizations. UML aggregations can be mapped using *collections*.

The *ORDB logical model* is more complex than the ODB model. The ORDB model makes a strong distinction between the *structured type* and the *table* as the only storage mechanism. A *row type* allows the specification of nested data structures – a possibility that is not readily available in UML. *References* and *collections of references* are also supported. The *OF* and *UNDER* inheritance can be used for mapping from UML generalizations.

The mapping to the *RDB logical model* is the most cumbersome. The RDB model does not support object types, inheritance, structured types, collections or references. Data is stored in *tables* related by *referential integrity* constraints. *Triggers* can be used to program the semantics captured in business rules implied in UML class models. *Normalization* can further influence the mapping.

Review questions

R1   Explain the three levels of database models: the external, the logical, and the physical model.

R2   How have the ODB standards evolved? What is the practical significance of this evolution?

R3   What is the difference between the ODB type and the ODB class?

R4   What is the ODB collection literal? How is it useful for the mapping from UML class models?

R5   What is the ODB collection object type? How is it useful for the mapping from UML class models?

R6   Explain the semantics and applicability of the inverse keyword in an ODB schema.

R7   What is the difference between the ISA and EXTENDS inheritance in an ODB schema?

R8   What is the main use of the ORDB row type? Can it be used to define reference types? Explain.

R9   What is the difference between a row of references and a collection of references in an ORDB?

R10   Do ORDB systems support dynamic classification? Explain.

R11   Explain the difference between the ORDB column, field, and attribute.

R12   What is the difference between the OF and UNDER inheritance in an ORDB schema?

R13   What is RDB referential integrity? How is it useful for the mapping from a UML class model?

R14   Explain the four RDB declarative referential integrity constraints.

R15   What is the RDB trigger? How is it related to referential integrity?

R16   What is a good normalization level in an RDB? Explain.

Exercise questions

E1   *Telemarketing* – refer to the Telemarketing case study as defined in the book activity diagram for Telemarketing and to the solution to Exercise E1 in Chapter 7.

Map the class diagram to an ODB schema. Explain the mapping.

E2   *Telemarketing* – refer to the Telemarketing case study as defined in the book activity diagram for Telemarketing and to the solution to Exercise E1 in Chapter 7.

Map the class diagram to an ORDB schema. Explain the mapping.

E3   *Telemarketing* – refer to the Telemarketing case study as defined in the book activity diagram for Telemarketing and to the solution to Exercise E1 in Chapter 7.

Map the class diagram to an RDB schema. Explain the mapping.

Chapter

9

Program and Transaction Design

We make a distinction between a system design and program design. The program design is that aspect of the system design that models the execution logic of the program and defines the framework for the client/server object collaboration. The IS programs perform business transactions. A transaction is a unit of database consistency that a DBMS can enforce provided that the scope of the transaction is defined within the program.

The program and transaction design puts together the system design artifacts and culminates the system design process. It delivers the application logic to the GUI and database design. The outcome is a design document that provides sufficient programming instructions for a programmer to start 'cutting the code.' In fact, some initial code can be automatically generated (forward-engineered) from the design. The programmer's extensions of that initial code can be reverse-engineered back to the design, concluding a 'round-trip' engineering cycle.

9.1 Designing the program

The *program design* is an intrinsic part of the overall system design (Chapters 6, 7, and 8). The *architectural design* of class packages and components establishes the generic execution framework. The *detailed design* of the GUI and database specifies the front-end and the back-end of that framework. The program design fills in the gaps in this generic framework and turns it into a design document that can be handed over to a programmer for implementation.

The program design concentrates on one application program at a time. In this sense, the program design is a direct extension of the *user interface design* discussed in Chapter 7. The program design uses a portion (subschema) of the *database design* (Chapter 8) and it defines database procedural aspects – stored procedures and program-specific triggers.

The program's execution logic splits up between the client and the server processes. The *client process* embodies most of the dynamic object collaboration (Section 6.2) in the program. A proper balance between object cohesion and coupling (Section 9.1.1) can harness the complexity of that collaboration. The *server process* takes care, among other things, of executing business transactions initiated by the *client process*.

9.1.1 Class cohesion and coupling

In passing, in particular in Chapters 5 and 6, we have identified the main principles of good program design, albeit more in the context of good system design. *Class layering* is the cornerstone for writing understandable, maintainable, and scalable programs. The proper use of *inheritance* and *delegation* is necessary to avoid delivering object-oriented programs that become legacy systems the day after release to the stakeholders.

A good program design ensures a well-balanced *cohesion* and *coupling* of classes. The terms cohesion and coupling were coined by the structured design methods. However, the terms have a similar connotation and importance in the object-oriented design (Page-Jones, 2000; Schach, 1996).

Class cohesion is the degree of inner self-determination of the class. It measures the strength of the class independence. A highly cohesive class performs one action or achieves a single goal. The stronger the cohesion the better.

Class coupling is the degree of connections between classes. It measures the class interdependence. The weaker the coupling the better (however, the classes have to be 'coupled' to cooperate!).

Cohesion and coupling are at odds with each other. Better cohesion induces worse coupling and vice versa. The task of the designer is to achieve the best balance between the two. Riel (1996) proposed a number of heuristics to address this issue:

- Two classes should either be not dependent on one another or one class should be only dependent on the public interface of another class.
- Attributes and the related methods should be kept in one class (this heuristic is frequently violated by classes who have many *accessor* (`get`, `set`) methods defined in their public interface).
- A class should capture one and only one abstraction. Unrelated information, when a subset of methods operates on a proper subset of attributes, should be moved to another class.
- The system intelligence should be distributed as uniformly as possible (so that classes share the work uniformly).

9.1.1.1 *Kinds of class coupling*

In order for two classes to communicate, they need to be 'coupled'. The *coupling* between the class X and the class Y exists if the class X can *directly* refer to the class Y. Page-Jones (2000) lists eight kinds of class coupling (that he calls direct class-reference set):

1. X inherits from Y.
2. X has an attribute of class Y.
3. X has a template attribute with a parameter of class Y.
4. X has a method with an input argument of class Y.

5. X has a method with an output argument of class Y.

6. X knows of a global variable of class Y.

7. X knows of a method containing a local variable of class Y.

8. X is a friend of Y.

9.1.1.2 The Law of Demeter

Class coupling is necessary for object communication but – as we reasoned in Section 5.2 – it should be confined, as much as possible, to *within* the class layers (i.e. to the *intra-layer coupling*). The *inter-layer coupling* should be minimized and carefully channeled. An additional guidance for restricting the arbitrary communication between classes is offered in the Law of Demeter (Lieberherr and Holland, 1989).

The Law of Demeter specifies what targets are allowed for the messages within the class methods. It states that a target of a message can only be one of the following objects (Page-Jones, 2000):

1. The method's object itself (i.e. this in C++ and Java, self and super in Smalltalk).

2. An object that is an argument in the method's signature.

3. An object referred to by the object's attribute (including an object referred to within a collection of attributes).

4. An object created by the method.

5. An object referred to by a global variable.

To restrict the coupling induced by inheritance, the third rule can be limited to the attributes defined in the class itself. An attribute inherited by the class cannot then be used to identify a target object for the message. This constraint is known as the *Strong Law of Demeter* (Page-Jones, 2000).

9.1.1.3 Accessor methods and mindless classes

As mentioned in Section 9.1.1, attributes and the related methods should be kept in one class (Riel, 1996). A class should decide its own destiny. A class can restrict other classes from accessing its own state by limiting the accessor methods in its interface. *Accessor methods* define the *observer* (get) or *mutator* (set) operations (Section 8.3.1.2).

Accessor methods 'open up' a class to the internal manipulation by other classes. While the coupling implies a certain amount of exploitation, an excessive availability of accessor methods may lead to a non-uniform distribution of intelligence among classes. A class with many accessor methods risks becoming *mindless* – other classes decide what is good for it.

This said, there are situations when a class has to open up to other classes. This happens whenever there is a need to implement a *policy between two or more classes* (Riel, 1996). Examples are abounding.

Suppose that we have two classes INTEGER and REAL and we need to implement a 'policy' for the conversion between integer and real numbers. In which of the two classes is the policy to be implemented? Do we need a CONVERTER class to implement the policy? Either way, at least one of these two classes must allow accessor methods and it will then become 'mindless' with regard to that policy.

A famous quote from Page-Jones is in place: 'On an object-oriented farm there is an object-oriented milk. Should the object-oriented cow send the object-oriented milk the uncow_yourself message, or should the object-oriented milk send the object-oriented cow the unmilk_yourself message?' (Page-Jones at OOPSLA'87.)

Example 9.1 (University Enrolment)

In Chapter 6, we have designed collaborations for a part of University Enrolment (Examples 6.3 and 6.4 in Sections 6.2.4.1 and 6.2.4.2). The collaboration models provided a relatively uniform distribution of intelligence but no alternative solutions were discussed.

For this example, assume that we need to add a student to a course offering. To do so, we need to do two checks. Firstly, we have to find out prerequisite courses for the course offering. Secondly, we have to check the student's academic record to establish whether the student satisfies the prerequisites. With this knowledge, we can decide whether the student can be added to the course offering.

Consider that a message enrol() is to be sent by a boundary object :EnrolmentWindow. Consider that three classes – CourseOffering, Course, and Student – collaborate to accomplish the task. Our job is to design a range of possible collaboration diagrams to solve the problem. Discuss the pros and cons of different solutions.

Figure 9.1 illustrates the first solution. The boundary object :EnrolmentWindow initiates the transaction by sending the enroll() message to aCourse. aCourse asks aStudent for the academic record and checks it against its prerequisites. aCourse decides if aStudent can be enrolled and requests that aCourseOffering adds aStudent to its list of students.

FIGURE 9.1
aCourse as policy maker (University Enrolment).

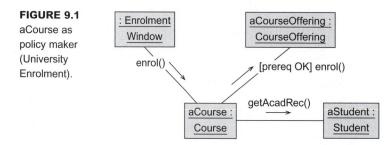

FIGURE 9.2
aStudent as
policy maker
(University
Enrolment).

FIGURE 9.3
aCourseOffering
as policy maker
(University
Enrolment).

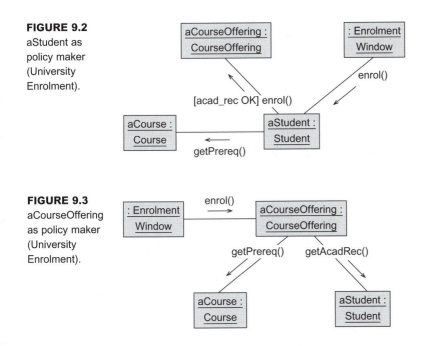

The scenario in Figure 9.1 gives too much power to the object aCourse. aCourse is the policy maker. aStudent is mindless. The solution is unbalanced but there is no clear way out.

We could switch the emphasis from aCourse to aStudent to obtain the solution presented in Figure 9.2. Now :EnrolmentWindow asks aStudent to do the main job. aStudent invokes an observer method getPrereq() in aCourse. aStudent decides if the enrolment is possible and instructs aCourseOffering to enroll the student.

Figure 9.3 illustrates a more balanced solution in which aCourseOffering is the policy maker. The solution is impartial with regard to aCourse and aStudent but it makes these two objects quite idle and mindless. aCourseOffering acts like the 'main program' (a '*God*' *class* in Riel's parlance (Riel, 1996)).

The solution in Figure 9.3 can be improved by introducing a *control object* to handle the policy information (see the BCE approach – Section 5.2.4). The *control object* :EnrolmentPolicy in Figure 9.4 decouples the three entity classes from the enrolment policy. This is beneficial because any changes to the enrolment policy are encapsulated in a single control class. However, there is a risk that the class EnrolmentPolicy can grow into a 'God' class.

9.1.1.4 *Dynamic classification and mixed-instance cohesion*

In Section 2.1.5.2.3 we raised the issue of the *dynamic classification* and observed that the popular object-oriented programming environments do not support it. The price for this lack of support is frequently reflected in designing classes with a *mixed-instance cohesion*.

FIGURE 9.4
:EnrolmentPolicy
as policy maker
(University
Enrolment).

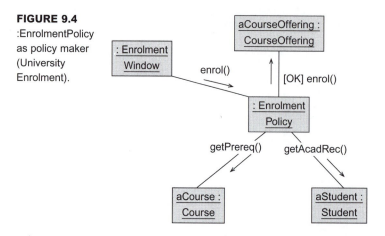

Page-Jones (2000) defines that 'a class with *mixed-instance cohesion* has some features that are undefined for some objects of the class.' Some methods of the class apply only to a subset of objects in that class and some attributes make sense only for a subset of objects.

For example, the class `Employee` may define objects that are 'ordinary' employees and managers. A manager is paid an allowance. Sending a message `payAllowance` to an `Employee` object does not make sense if that `Employee` object is not a manager.

To eliminate the mixed-instance cohesion, we need to extend the generalization hierarchy to identify `Employee` subclasses such as `OrdinaryEmployee` and `Manager`. However, an `Employee` object may be an `OrdinaryEmployee` one day and a `Manager` another day, or vice versa. To eliminate the mixed-instance cohesion we need to allow objects to dynamically change classes at run time – the proverbial catch-22 if the dynamic classification is not supported.

Example 9.2 (University Enrolment)

Consider the following variations to Example 9.1:

■ Evening course offerings are only available to part-time students.

■ Full-time students may only enroll in daytime course offerings.

■ There is a small extra fee if a part-time student wants to enroll in an evening course offering.

■ A part-time student is automatically considered full-time when enrolled in more than six credit points (i.e. normally more than two course offerings) in a given semester (and vice versa).

Our task is to propose a highly cohesive *structural collaboration* model with no mixed-instance cohesion. The model should then be critically appraised and an alternative solution that avoids the problem of dynamic classification should be suggested and discussed.

FIGURE 9.5

Structural
collaboration
eliminating
mixed-instance
cohesion
(University
Enrolment).

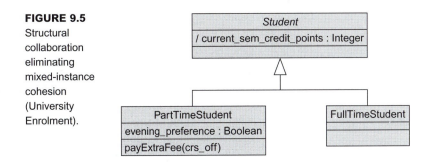

FIGURE 9.5

Structural
collaboration
eliminating
mixed-instance
cohesion
(University
Enrolment).

To eliminate the mixed-instance cohesion, we need to specialize `Student` into two subclasses `PartTimeStudent` and `FullTimeStudent` (Figure 9.5). If every student must be either part-time or full-time, then the class `Student` is *abstract*. The message `payExtraFee(crs_off)` will never be sent to an object of class `FullTimeStudent`, because `FullTimeStudent` does not have a method for it.

Granted, we still have a problem. A part-time student may have a preference for daytime course offerings (i.e. `evening_preference = 'False'`) and no extra fees are then paid. In other words, we still have a *mixed-instance cohesion* in `PartTimeStudent`. Sending a message `payExtraFee(crs_off)` to a `PartTimeStudent` will not make sense if the student takes a daytime course offering.

Figure 9.6 extends the design to eliminate this second aspect of mixed-instance cohesion. The class `DayPrefPartTimeStudent` does not have the method `payExtraFee(crs_off)`. But what if a `DayPrefPartTimeStudent` is forced to take an evening course offering because there are no more places available in daytime course offerings? Perhaps, some other fee would then apply. Should we specialize further to derive a class `UnluckyDayPrefPartTimeStudent`?

FIGURE 9.6

Structural
collaboration
eliminating
another aspect of
mixed-instance
cohesion
(University
Enrolment).

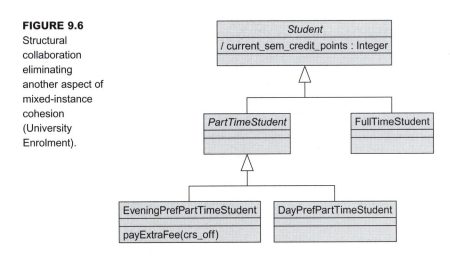

Short of getting into ridiculous situations, we may opt for abandoning the idea of pushing the elimination of the mixed-instance cohesion any further. And we have not even mentioned the dynamic classification yet.... In reality, the current value of the attribute `current_sem_credit_points` determines if a student is part-time or full-time.

Similarly, a student can change his/her preference for the evening or daytime course offerings at any time. In the absence of the programming environment's support for *dynamic classification*, it would be a programmer's responsibility to allow an object to change the class at run time. That's tough – very tough in the case of persistent objects with OID values containing class identifiers.

The alternative is to restrict the depth of the inheritance hierarchy, eliminate the need for dynamic classification, and reintroduce a certain amount of mixed-instance cohesion. For example, we can hang on to the structural collaboration in Figure 9.5 and resolve the problem of the evening preference by allowing an object to respond differently to the message `payExtraFee(crs_off)` depending on the value of the attribute `evening_preference`. This can be programmed with an `if` statement as shown in the pseudocode below:

```
method payExtraFee(crs_off) for the class PartTimeStudent
      if evening_preference = 'False'
          return
      else
          do it
end method
```

Although the use of `if` statements in an object-oriented code signifies an abandoning of inheritance and polymorphism, it may be unavoidable for purely pragmatic reasons. Rather than struggling with the *dynamic classification*, the programmer introduces the *dynamic semantics* to a class. An object responds differently to the same message depending on its current local state. A statechart diagram would be used to design the dynamic semantics for the class. Admittedly, the *cohesion* of the class suffers in the process.

9.1.2 Designing client/server collaboration

The IS programs interact with the databases for data. A client program must use a database language – typically SQL – to access and modify the database. To understand how a client program communicates with a database server, we need to recognize that SQL comes in different dialects and can be used at different levels of programming abstraction.

Figure 9.7 distinguishes five levels of SQL interface. At *Level 1*, SQL is used as a data definition language (DDL). DDL is a specification language for defining the database structures (database schema). A database designer and a database administrator (DBA) are the main users of Level 1 SQL.

At *Level 2*, SQL is used as a data manipulation language (DML) or the query language. The term *query language* is, however, a misnomer because SQL at Level 2 serves not only the purpose of retrieving data but also of modifying it (with insert, update and delete operations).

FIGURE 9.7
SQL interfaces.

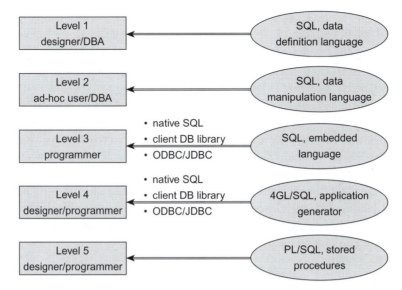

A wide range of users use Level 2 SQL – from 'naive' ad-hoc users to experienced DBAs. SQL at this level is *interactive*, which means that a user can formulate a query outside any programming environment and immediately run it on a database. Level 2 SQL is an entry point to learning more elaborated SQL at the next levels.

Application programmers use SQL at levels above Level 2. At these higher levels, SQL permits *record-at-a-time processing* in addition to the *set-at-a-time processing* facility available (as the only option) at Level 2. The set-at-a-time processing takes one or more tables (sets of records) as the input to a query and returns a table as the output. Although a powerful facility, it is difficult and dangerous to use with complicated queries.

To be certain that a query returns correct results, the programmer must have a possibility of browsing one-by-one through the records returned by a query and deciding what to do with these records on a one-at-a-time basis. Such record-at-a-time processing capability is called a *cursor* and is available in SQL at levels above Level 2.

Level 3 SQL is *embedded* in a conventional programming language, such as C or COBOL. Because a programming language compiler does not understand SQL, a precompiler (pre-processor) is needed to translate SQL statements to function calls in the DB library provided by a DBMS vendor. A programmer may elect to program using the DB library functions directly in which case the precompiler is not needed.

A popular way of interfacing a client program with databases is via *Open Database Connectivity* (ODBC) or *Java Database Connectivity* (JDBC) standards. To program this way, an ODBC or JDBC software driver for a particular DBMS is required. ODBC and JDBC provide a standard database language, above SQL, which is translated by the driver to the native DBMS SQL.

ODBC/JDBC have an advantage of decoupling the program from the native DBMS SQL. If the program needs to be migrated in the future to a different target DBMS, then a straightforward replacing of the driver should do the trick. More importantly, working with ODBC/JDBC allows a single application to issue queries to more than one DBMS.

The disadvantage of ODBC/JDBC is that it is the 'lowest common denominator' for SQL. A client application cannot take advantage of any special SQL features or extensions supported by a particular DBMS vendor.

Level 4 SQL uses the same strategies for embedding SQL in client programs as Level 3 SQL. Level 4 SQL provides, however, a more powerful programming environment of an application generator or a fourth generation language (4GL). A 4GL comes equipped with 'screen painting' and GUI building capabilities. Since IS applications require sophisticated GUI, a 4GL/SQL is a frequent choice for building such applications.

Level 5 SQL complements Levels 3 and 4 by providing the possibility of moving some SQL statements from the client program to an active (programmable) server database. SQL is used as a programming language (PL/SQL). The server programs can be called from within the client programs, as discussed next.

9.1.2.1 *Stored procedures*

The Sybase RDBMS first introduced *stored procedures* and they are now part of every major commercial DBMS. Stored procedures turn a database into an active programmable system.

A *stored procedure* is written in an extended SQL that allows for such programming constructs as variables, loops, branches, and assignment statements. A stored procedure is given a name, can take input and output parameters, it is compiled and stored in the database. A client program can call a stored procedure very much as it calls subroutines.

Figure 9.8 illustrates the advantages of a client program calling a stored procedure rather than sending a complete query to the server. A query constructed in a client program is sent to the database server over the network. The query may contain syntax and other errors, but the client is not able to eliminate them – the database system is the only place where such verification can be done. Once verified, the DBMS checks if the caller is authorized to run the query. If so, the query is optimized to determine the best access plan to data. Only then can it be compiled, executed and the results returned to the client.

On the other hand, if a query (or the whole set of queries) is written as a stored procedure, then it is optimized and compiled into the server database. A client program does not need to send a (possibly large) query over the network – it instead sends a short call with the procedure name and a list of actual parameters. If lucky, the procedure may reside in the DBMS memory cache. If not, it will be brought to memory from the database.

The user's authorization is scrutinized as in the case of a SQL query. Any actual parameters replace formal parameters and the stored procedure executes. The results are returned to the caller.

As seen in the above scenario, stored procedures provide much more efficient ways of accessing the database from a client program. The performance advantages are due to the savings in *network traffic* and no need for *parsing and compilation* each time a client request is received. Even more importantly, a stored procedure is *maintained in a single place* and can be called from many client programs.

FIGURE 9.8
Comparison of client SQL and stored procedure invocation.

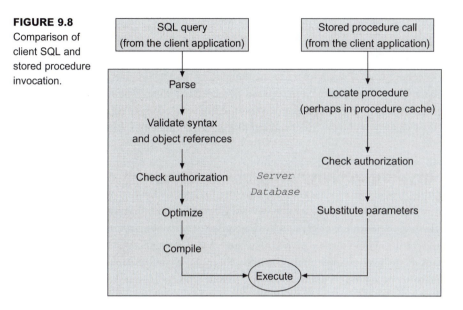

9.1.2.2 *Triggers*

Triggers (Section 8.4.1.4) are a special kind of stored procedure that cannot be called – they trigger themselves on `insert`, `update` or `delete` events on a table. This implies that each table can have up to three triggers. Indeed, in some systems this is the case (e.g. Sybase). In other systems (e.g. Oracle), additional variants of events are identified leading to the possibility of having more than three triggers on each table. (Availability of more kinds of triggers does not provide more expressive power in trigger programs, though.)

Triggers can be programmed to enforce *any business rules* that apply to the database and cannot be violated by any client program or an interactive SQL DML statement. This means that triggers can be used beyond the procedural enforcement of referential integrity constraints (as discussed in Section 8.4.1.4). For example, a trigger may be written to disallow access to the database during some time periods or on some days.

A user of a client program may not even be aware that the triggers 'watch' what is being modified in the database. If the modifications do not violate business rules, the triggers are not visible to the programs. A trigger makes itself known to the user when a DML command cannot be allowed. The trigger will notify the user of the problem by displaying an informational message on the program's screen and refusing to perform the DML operation.

9.2 Program navigation

In the presence of active databases, the number of programming objects increases and the object collaboration gets more complex. The window navigation diagrams (Section 7.6.2) are not sufficient any more as design documents from which a programmer can undertake implementation. They need to be extended into (subsumed by) more complete program navigation diagrams.

The concept of *program navigation* is not standardized or discussed in UML. It is nevertheless a fundamental modeling abstraction required to eliminate a gap between the design and implementation of the system. The alternative is bad software engineering – the *architecture and logic* of the program is undocumented and left to the programmer's decisions.

9.2.1 Stereotyping activity diagram for program navigation

To convert window navigation diagrams into program navigation diagrams, we need to add server-side stereotypes to the UML activity diagrams. Both the *states* (rounded rectangles) and the *activities* (ovals) should be stereotyped. The stereotypes must account for the peculiarities of a DBMS model or even a particular DBMS. (This is, of course, the main reason, or rather excuse, why the navigation diagrams are not offered in UML.)

The following list of stereotypes may be used for designing program navigation with an RDBMS. Depending on the level of abstraction at which a program navigation diagram is to be constructed, the list can shrink or extend with additional objects:

- *States (data objects)*:
  - Database
  - Relational table
    - Column
    - Record
  - Relational View
    - Column
    - Record
  - Index
  - Cluster
- *Activities (program objects)*:
  - Stored procedure
  - Trigger
    - On Insert
    - On Update
    - On Delete
    - Other kinds of trigger…
  - Client SQL query
    - Native query
    - DB library query
    - ODBC/JDBC query

9.2.2 Program navigation diagram

To illustrate program navigation diagrams, we will simply extend examples of window navigation diagrams presented in Section 7.6.2. Figure 9.9 is the program navigation diagram that extends (and slightly rearranges) the window navigation diagram in Figure 7.23.

FIGURE 9.9
Program navigation diagram.

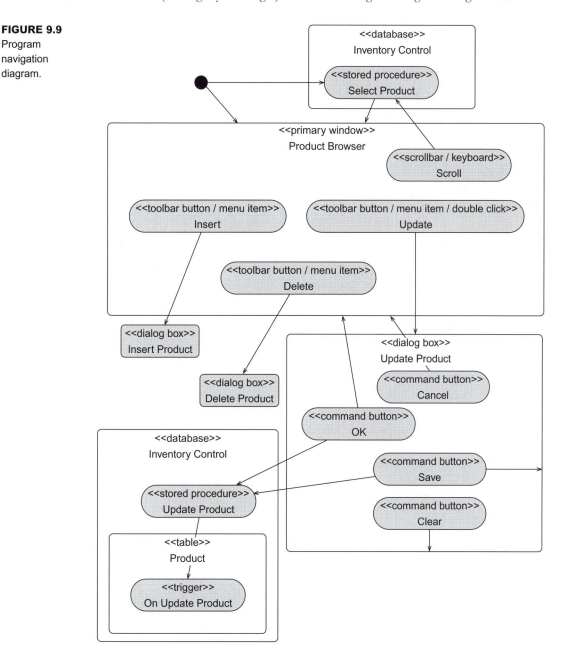

Figure 9.9 introduces two *server states*: Inventory Control (<<database>>) and Product (<<table>>). Three *server activities* are added: Select Product (<<stored procedure>>), Update Product (<<stored procedure>>) and On Update Product (<<trigger>>). We also added a client activity Scroll (<<scrollbar/keyboard>>).

With added information, the program navigation diagram in Figure 9.9 informs the programmer that to display products in Product Browser a stored procedure (Select Product) must be called. The same stored procedure is involved when the user scrolls up and down in the browser window and the information content of the window must be refreshed from the database.

In the lower part of the diagram, we can see that pressing the OK or Save button in Update Product (<<dialog box>>) invokes Update Product (<<stored procedure>>). A trigger controls the modification outcome (On Update Product).

Example 9.3 (Contact Management)

Consider the following extensions to Example 7.5 (Section 7.6.2):

■ Stored procedures are used to modify (insert, delete, update, complete) an event.

■ There are triggers to monitor inserts and updates on the Event table.

Our task is to design a program navigation diagram for this part of the Contact Management application that handles event modifications.

Our solution to the example (Figure 9.10) includes only those client states and activities from Figure 7.24 that are relevant to event modifications. Note that the stored procedure Complete Event can be invoked from either the primary window or dialog box. Because Complete Event updates the table Event, the trigger On Update Event fires. The same trigger can be activated by the stored procedure Save Event.

The dialog box Task/Event Details serves the double purpose of inserting a new event and updating an existing event. The command button OK calls the stored procedure Save Event. The parameter list in the call informs the procedure if OK means insert or update. Correspondingly, the procedure execution fires one of the two triggers: On Insert Event or On Update Event.

9.3 Designing the transaction

A *transaction* is a logical unit of work that comprises one or more SQL statements executed by a user. A transaction is a unit of *database consistency* – the state of the database is consistent after the transaction completes. To ensure that consistency, a transaction manager of a DBMS serves two purposes: *database recovery and concurrency control*.

FIGURE 9.10
Program
navigation
diagram (Contact
Management).

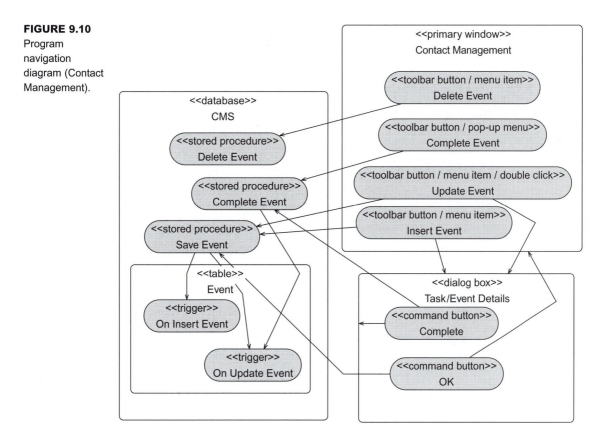

According to SQL standards, a transaction begins with the first executable SQL statement (in some systems, an explicit `begin transaction` statement may be required). A transaction ends with a `commit` or `rollback` statement. The `commit` statement writes the changes persistently to the database. The `rollback` statement erases any changes made by the transaction.

The transaction is *atomic* – the results of all SQL statements in the transaction are either committed or rolled back. The user determines the duration (size) of a transaction. Depending on the business needs, application domain and user–computer interaction style, a transaction can be as short as one SQL statement or it can involve a series of SQL statements.

9.3.1 Short transaction

Most conventional IS applications require *short transactions*. A short transaction contains one or more SQL statements that must be completed as quickly as possible, so that other transactions are not held up.

Consider an airline reservation system in which many travel agents make flight bookings for travelers around the world. It is essential that each booking transaction is performed quickly by the DBMS, so that the availability of flight seats is updated, and the database gets ready to process the next transaction waiting in the queue.

9.3.1.1 *Pessimistic concurrency control*

The conventional DBMSs, with the notable exception of ODBMSs, have been architected with short transactions in mind. These systems work according to a *pessimistic concurrency control*. *Locks* are acquired on every persistent object that a transaction processes. There are four kinds of locks on an object:

1. *Exclusive (write) lock* – other transactions must wait until the transaction holding such a lock completes and releases the lock.

2. *Update (write intent) lock* – other transactions can read the object but the transaction holding the lock is guaranteed to be able to upgrade it to the exclusive mode, as soon as it has such a need.

3. *Read (shared) lock* – other transactions can read and possibly obtain an update lock on the object.

4. *No lock* – other transactions can update an object at any time; suitable only for applications that allow '*dirty reads*' – i.e. a transaction reads data that can be modified or even deleted (by another transaction) before the transaction completes.

9.3.1.2 *Levels of isolation*

Associated with these four kinds of lock are the four *levels of isolation* between concurrently executing transactions. It is the responsibility of the system designer to decide which level of isolation is appropriate for the mix of transactions on the database. The four levels are (Khoshafian *et al.*, 1992):

1. *Dirty read possible* – transaction t1 modified an object but it has not committed yet; transaction t2 reads the object; if t1 rolls back the transaction then t2 obtained an object that in a sense never existed in the database.

2. *Nonrepeatable read possible* – t1 has read an object; t2 updates the object; t1 reads the same object again but this time it will obtain a different value for the same object.

3. *Phantom possible* – t1 has read a set of objects; t2 inserts a new object to the set; t1 repeats the read operation and will see a 'phantom' object.

4. *Repeatable read* – t1 and t2 can still execute concurrently but the interleaved execution of these two transactions will produce the same results as if the transactions executed one at a time (this is called *serializable execution*).

Typical GUI-based interactive IS applications require short transactions. The level of isolation, however, may differ between different transactions in the same application. The SQL statement set transaction can be used for that purpose. The trade-off is obvious – increasing the level of isolation reduces the overall concurrency of the system.

One crucial design decision is, however, independent from the above considerations. The beginning of the transaction must always be delayed to the last second. It is unacceptable to start a transaction from a client window and then make the transaction wait until it obtains some additional information from the user before it can actually complete the job.

The user may be very slow in providing that information or may even elect to shut the computer down while the transaction is running. The *transaction timeout* will eventually roll back the transaction, but the harm to the overall system throughput has been done.

9.3.1.3 *Automatic recovery*

Murphy's Law states that if something can go wrong, it will. Programs may contain errors, running processes can hang or be aborted, the power supply can fail, a disk head can crash, etc. Fortunately, a DBMS provides an *automatic recovery* for most situations. Only in the case of the physical loss of disk data is a DBA's intervention necessary to instruct the DBMS to recover from the last database *backup*.

Depending on the state of the transaction at failure point, a DBMS will automatically perform a *rollback* or *roll forward* of the transaction as soon as the cause of the problem is eliminated. The recovery is automatic but a DBA can control the amount of recovery time by setting the frequency of *checkpoints*. A checkpoint forces the DBMS to temporarily stop all transactions and write all the transactional changes (made since the previous checkpoint) to the database.

Figure 9.11 illustrates the issues involved in automatic recovery from failure (Kirkwood, 1992). The transaction t1 committed after the checkpoint but before the system failure. As the DBMS does not know if all changes after the checkpoint have been physically written to the database, it will *roll forward* (*redo*) the transaction t1 after it recovers from the failure.

The transaction t2 had a rollback applied to it between the checkpoint and the failure. As in the case of the transaction t1, the DBMS does not know if the rollback changes reached the disk – the DBMS will perform the *rollback* again.

FIGURE 9.11
Automatic recovery.

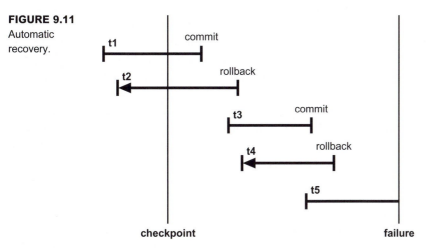

The other transactions started after the checkpoint. The transaction t3 will be *rolled forward* to guarantee that its changes are affected in the database. Similarly, the transaction t4 will be repeated, i.e. *rolled back*.

The transaction t5 would not require any remedial action by the DBMS because it was executing at the time of failure. Any changes done by t5 before the failure have not been written to the database. All intermediate changes have only been written to the log file. The user is aware that the transaction was executing at the time of failure and may re-send the transaction when the DBMS is up and running again.

9.3.1.4 *Programmable recovery*

While unexpected system failures are automatically recovered from by a DBMS, the designers and programmers should control any anticipated transaction problems. A DBMS provides a range of rollback options to apply in the program so that it can gracefully recover from a problem, possibly without the user realizing that things went wrong at some point.

To start with, the GUI guidelines such as the user in control or forgiveness (Section 7.3) demand that a program allow the user to make mistakes and recover from them. A programmer-controlled rollback applied in the right places in the program can restore the database to the previous state (i.e. *undo* the mistake), provided that the transaction has not committed.

If the transaction has committed then the programmer may still have an option of writing a *compensating transaction*. The user can then request the execution of the compensating transaction to undo the changes to the database. Compensating transactions are designed specifically to allow programmable recovery and should be modeled in use cases.

9.3.1.4.1 Savepoint

A *savepoint* is a statement in a program that divides a longer transaction into smaller parts. *Named savepoints* are inserted in strategic places in the program. The programmer has then an option of rolling back the work to a named savepoint rather than to the beginning of the transaction.

For example, a programmer may insert a savepoint just before an update operation. If the update fails, then the program rolls back to the savepoint and attempts to execute the update again. Alternatively, the program may take any other action to avoid aborting the transaction altogether.

In larger programs, savepoints may be inserted before each subroutine. If a subroutine fails, it may be possible to roll back to the beginning of that subroutine and re-execute it with revised parameters. If necessary, a specially designed and programmed recovery subroutine can do the mopping up so that the transaction can resume the execution.

9.3.1.4.2 Trigger rollback

A *trigger rollback* is a special kind of savepoint. As explained in Section 9.1.2.2, a trigger can be used to program a business rule of any complexity. At times it may be undesirable to roll back the whole transaction when a trigger refuses to modify a table (due to the transaction attempt to breach the business rule). The transaction may want to take a remedial action.

For the above reason, a DBMS may provide a trigger programming possibility to roll back either the whole transaction or just the trigger. In the latter case, the program (possibly a stored procedure) can analyze the problem and decide on further action. Even if the whole transaction has to be eventually rolled back, the program may have a possibility of better interpreting the cause of the error and display a more intelligible message to the user.

9.3.1.5 *Designing stored procedures and triggers*

A program navigation diagram (Section 9.2.2) can be further extended to include *transaction states*. This may, however, be cumbersome from a graphical layout point of view. An alternative solution might be to design multiple program navigation diagrams each presenting a different navigation perspective. One such perspective may concentrate on capturing navigation in transactions.

In any case, program navigation diagrams identify stored procedures and triggers. The purpose, definition and detailed design for each stored procedure and trigger need to be provided. In particular, some pseudocode notation ought to be employed to define the algorithms.

As an example, we present below an algorithm for the stored procedure `DeleteEvent` in the Contact Management application (see Figure 9.10, Section 9.2.2). The procedure checks whether the user (employee) attempting the delete is the same employee who created the event. If not, the delete operation is rejected. The procedure also checks if the event is the only one remaining for the task. If so, the task is deleted as well.

```
BEGIN
INPUT PARAMETERS (@event_id, @user_id)
Select Event (where event_id = @event_id)
IF @user_id = Event.created_emp_id
   THEN
      delete Event (where event_id = @event_id)
      IF no more events for
         Task.task_id = Event.task_id AND
         Event.event_id = @event_id
      THEN
         delete that Task
      ENDIF
   ELSE
      raise error ('Only the creator of the event can
                   delete that event')
ENDIF
END
```

The stored procedure `DeleteEvent` contains `delete` statements to delete records from the tables `Event` and `Task`. These `delete` statements would fire delete triggers on these tables, if present. If the algorithms for these triggers go beyond the normal referential integrity checking, the designer should provide pseudocode specifications for them as well (including the decision on rollback strategy – a trigger rollback or a transaction rollback).

9.3.2 Long transaction

Some new classes of IS applications encourage cooperation among users. These applications are known as *workgroup computing* applications or *computer-supported cooperative work* (CSCW) applications. Examples include many office applications, collaborative authoring, computer-aided design, CASE tools, etc.

In many ways, workgroup computing applications have database requirements that are orthogonal to the traditional database model with short transactions that isolate users from each other. Workgroup computing applications require long transactions, version management, collaborative concurrency control, etc.

The ODB model provides a framework for workgroup computing and many ODBMS products target this application domain. Users in a workgroup computing application share information and are made aware of the work they do on shared data. They work in their own *workspaces* using personal databases of data *checked-out* (copied) from the common workgroup database. They work in a *long transaction* that can span computer sessions (users can take breaks then continue working in the same long transaction after returning).

The dominant aspect of a long transaction is that it is not allowed to be automatically rolled back without trace by the system because of failures. To appreciate this requirement, imagine my despair if this textbook were now 'rolled back' due to a computer failure! A rollback of a long transaction is controlled by the users by means of *savepoints* that persistently store objects in the users' private databases.

The notion of *short transaction* is not eradicated from a workgroup computing application. Short transactions are necessary to guarantee atomicity and isolation *during* the check-out and check-in operations between the group database and private databases. *Short locks* are released afterwards and *long persistent locks* are imposed by the group database on all checked-out objects.

Related objectives of the long transaction model include (Hawryszkiewycz *et al.*, 1994; Maciaszek, 1998):

■ Allowing the exchange of information (even if temporarily inconsistent) between cooperating users.

■ Detecting data inconsistencies and mediating their resolutions.

■ Taking advantage of object versionability to provide a controlled sharing without loss of work in case of system failures.

9.4 Round-trip engineering

The iterative and incremental process (Section 1.1.3.1) of modern software production requires strong support from the *round-trip engineering* between the design and implementation. Round-trip engineering is defined as the coming together of the forward code generation and the reverse engineering from the code to design models. Round-trip engineering gives '. . . the ability to work in either a graphical or textual view, while tools keep the two views consistent.' (Booch *et al.*, 1999, p. 16.)

In client/server applications, round-trip engineering is applied separately to *client* application programs and to *server* database programs. It is possible, and indeed likely, that a different CASE tool is used on the same project for the client design and for the server design. Also, the CASE tools used for round-trip engineering have to be tightly integrated with particular client and/or server programming environments.

9.4.1 Round-trip engineering with client programs

The principles of *round-trip engineering with client applications* are relatively straightforward – the villain is in the detail. Figure 9.12 is an activity diagram for a typical cycle of round-trip engineering with an object programming language (Paradigm, 1997; Rational, 1998). UML models are stored in a CASE repository (as explained in passing, the CASE repository is itself a database system, frequently an object database).

The UML Design Model (a UML state) has to be specifically developed to target the programming language. The Code Generation (a UML activity) uses the UML Design Model to generate the Source Code (header and implementation files). Any user-supplied definitions and auxiliary declarations from the previous round-trip engineering iterations are preserved.

The Source Code undergoes later normal programming changes and extensions. The Modified Code is reverse-engineered to the UML Implemented Model by the activity called in Figure 9.12 the UML Generation. Some form of a visual Model Differencing

FIGURE 9.12
Round-trip engineering with the client program.

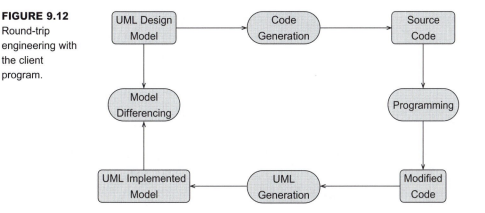

tool is then used to reveal design changes by comparing the current `UML Implemented Model` and the last `UML Design Model`. All accepted changes are propagated to the `UML Design Model` and the next round-trip engineering iteration can begin.

As observed above, the villain is in the detail. In practice, there will be many 'missing links' between the CASE tool's understanding of the programming language and the realities of a particular compiler for that language. The CASE tool may report analysis errors in the code that compiles cleanly because it may not recognize variations supported by the specific compiler.

The CASE tool may not resolve some references to declarations in the compiler-specific or library-specific source files. For example, references will not be resolved if the source file refers to symbols defined in another file without explicitly including that file. Although workarounds for many such problems may exist, they invariably lead to imperfect solutions that will require manual adjustments.

This said, imperfections are not an excuse for not conducting round-trip engineering with a client program. Imperfections can be corrected by manual means and once corrected the UML models deliver a matching documentation for the current program. The alternative is the complete loss of control over the application implementation.

9.4.2 Round-trip engineering with databases

Round-trip engineering with databases (Maciaszek, 2000) involves a *physical data model* (PDM) at the design end and a *database* (DB) at the implementation end. The PDM model is used in lieu of UML because UML does not support physical database design (Section 8.4). The PDM model must target a particular DBMS.

Figure 9.13 is an activity diagram for the round-trip engineering with a relational database. After the PDM model for a database is constructed (the state `Initial PDM`), it can be

FIGURE 9.13
Round-trip
engineering with
a database.

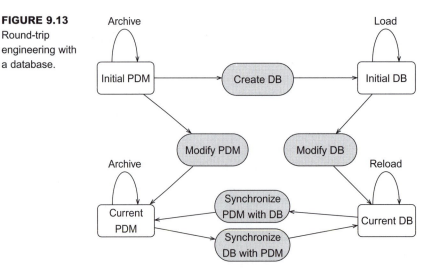

archived (the activity `Archive`). Comparing the archived and the current PDM allows the latest changes to the model to be captured.

The forward engineering of `Initial PDM` to `Initial DB` is done by the activity `Create DB`. The activity generates a DB schema, including triggers. `Initial DB` is populated with data by the recursive activity `Load`. The activity `Modify DB` introduces changes to the schema and causes the database transition to the state `Current DB`.

At this stage, two possibilities exist: the changes to `Current PDM` can be synchronized with `Current DB` (the activity `Synchronize PDM with DB`) or vice versa – the changes to `Current DB` can be synchronized with `Current PDM` (the activity `Synchronize DB with PDM`). As a result of these activities, `Current PDM` may need to be archived and `Current DB` may need to be reloaded.

Figure 9.14 shows the screen from a reverse engineering session (the activity `Synchronize PDM with DB`) from `Current DB` (Sybase DB) to `Current PDM` (PowerDesigner PDM).

The round-trip engineering process with the database should take into consideration that (Maciaszek, 2000):

■ The PDM model can be archived and versioned by the CASE tool, but a typical RDBMS or ORDBMS does not have a built-in capability to maintain DB versions (other than by creating a new DB).

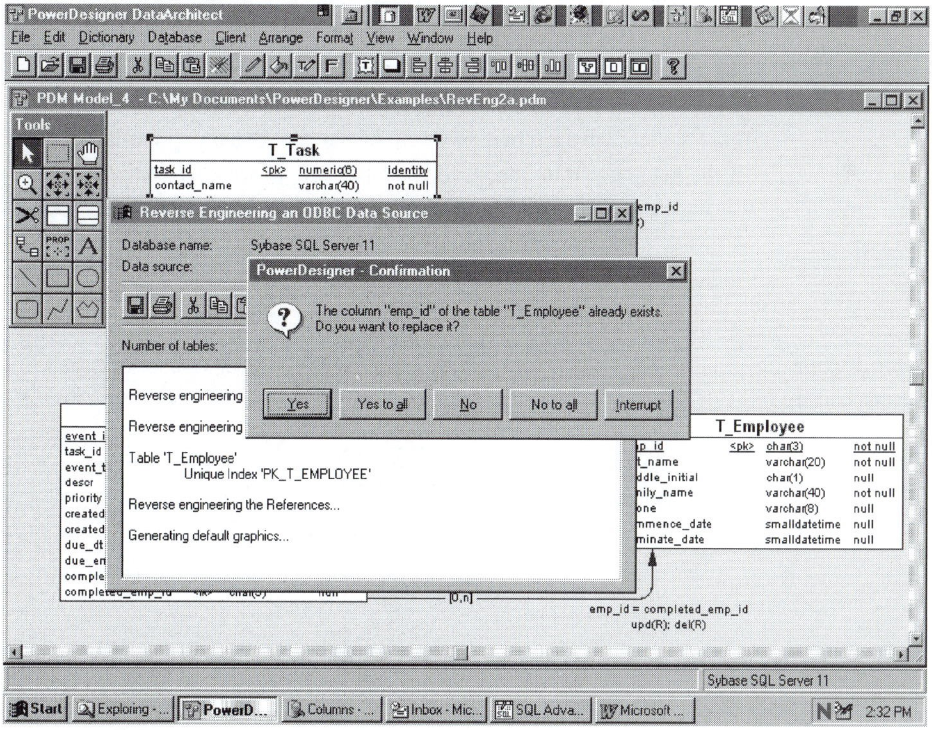

FIGURE 9.14
Reverse engineering session from Sybase DB to PowerDesigner PDM.

■ After the initial generation of the DB schema, the DB is loaded with data and the server programming begins. The programmers should have the possibility of modifying (or requesting the modification of) the DB schema as long as the modifications are eventually synchronized with the current PDM. The activity `Synchronize PDM with DB` should be done in bulk at specific synchronization times and PDM should be then archived.

■ Any later changes to the archived PDM, that need to be synchronized with DB, should be forward engineered to a new DB instance (in the absence of DB versions).

9.4.3 Reengineering from relational to object-relational databases

As discussed in Chapter 8, the next generation of database technology will adopt the ORDB model. There will be, therefore, a growing need for the migration of the existing (legacy) relational databases to object-relational platforms. *Reengineering* is the process that examines and alters a legacy system to recover its design and re-implement it in a new form.

Reengineering and round-trip engineering share the technologies of the forward and reverse engineering. The difference is that round-trip engineering is concerned with the evolutionary development of *new systems*. Reengineering precedes round-trip engineering and it is concerned with obtaining the initial PDM from the studies of *legacy code*.

Today, most reengineering projects aim at addressing the old-style COBOL-based systems to retarget them to the relational database technology. In the future, relational databases will become legacy systems to be reengineered to ORDB or ODB solutions. However, the pure ODB market is not expected to grow as fast as the ORDB market – partly because of the natural inertia in switching to brand new technologies and partly because ODBMSs address a niche market of multimedia and collaborative processing systems.

Figure 9.15 is an activity diagram depicting the sequence of activities in reengineering from an RDB to an ORDB system. The successive round-trip engineering with an ORDB is also indicated.

FIGURE 9.15
Reengineering from RDB to ORDB.

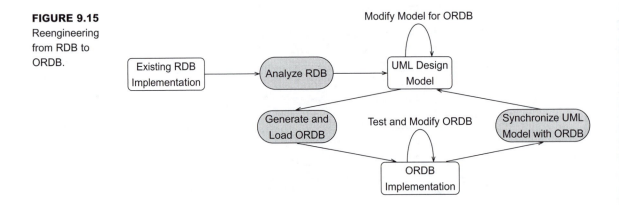

An `Existing RDB Implementation` is analyzed (the activity `Analyze RDB`) to determine database structures, business rules and the logic of application programs. This analysis leads to the construction of a `UML Design Model` that reflects the status operandi of the existing (legacy) RDB implementation. The UML model is then modified for an `ORDB Implementation`.

The ORDB schema, triggers, and methods (procedures) can now be generated and the ORDB can be loaded with data. Application programs are written for the ORDB and tested. This invariably leads to changes in the ORDB that need to be reflected in the UML design model. Once this is done, we say that the changes have been reengineered and the first iteration of the round-trip engineering cycle has been completed.

The process of reengineering and round-trip engineering with object-relational databases encounters two major challenges. The first one has to do with the round-trip engineering aspect and the second relates to the UML modeling power.

The process of round-trip engineering between UML design models and ORDB implementations is similar to round-trip engineering with a relational database, as discussed in the previous section. The process is similar but the underlying technical issues are considerably more difficult. This is because the ORDB model is much more complex and semantically much richer than the RDB model (Chapter 8). To start with, the CASE tools have to target the new SQL1999 standard and understand various variations of SQL1999 in commercial ORDBMSs.

As in the case of the RDB model, it is unlikely that UML will provide a PDM capability for ORDB systems. UML is predominantly the language for system analysis. The UML *profiles* to model ORDB systems are available (e.g. Maciaszek and Wong, 2000) but they do not provide lower-engineering features capable of understanding all nuances of an ORDBMS, including the nuances in different releases of the same ORDBMS.

For example, Oracle8 uses object views to facilitate migration from a relational to an object-relational database. Like other kinds of ORDB objects, an object view can be represented by a stereotyped class, and possibly given its own graphical icon. Ultimately, however, a stereotyped class has to be given its own precise semantics so that the CASE tool can understand any constraints and possibilities with regard to that stereotyped class (such as what kinds of relationship and other links are allowed between that stereotyped class and any other class in the model). A lower-engineering CASE tool from Oracle Corporation (in this case) has a much better chance to address such issues properly than a generic UML with stereotypes.

Summary

In this chapter, we have explained some more intricate concepts of program and transaction design and we have described design undertakings on the transition line between the design and implementation. We proposed program navigation diagrams. We also explained round-trip engineering with the client programs and with server databases.

A well-designed program maximizes the *class cohesion* while minimizing the *class coupling*. The coupling and cohesion principles can be achieved if the design obeys the *Law of Demeter*, which specifies the allowed object targets for the messages within the class methods. The excessive use of *accessor methods* can lead to *mindless classes*. The *mixed-instance cohesion*, albeit undesirable, may need to be sporadically allowed because the programming environments do not support the *dynamic classification*.

When designing the C/S collaboration, a consideration needs to be given to the five levels of *SQL interfaces*. *Level 5 SQL* is of particular interest because it allows the user to directly program the database. *Stored procedures* and *triggers* heavily influence the server aspect of the program design. The *program navigation diagrams* extend the window navigation diagrams to include the database considerations.

A *transaction* is a logical unit of database work that starts in a consistent database state and ensures the next consistent state when finished. Transactions ensure *database concurrency* and *database recovery*. Conventional database applications require *short transactions*. Some new database applications work in *long transactions*.

Round-trip engineering is the process whereby the design models and the programs are in sync but they can evolve individually. Round-trip engineering combines *forward engineering* from the design models and *reverse engineering* from the programs. Round-trip engineering is normally applied separately to *client programs* and to *database programs*.

Review questions

R1   How is the design affected by the principles of class cohesion and coupling?

R2   Which objects are permitted to be the targets of a message according to the Law of Demeter?

R3   What is a 'mindless class'?

R4   Explain the correlations between the dynamic classification and the mixed-instance cohesion.

R5   Describe briefly the five levels of SQL interfaces.

R6   What are the advantages of a stored procedure call over a SQL query submitted from the client program to the database? Are there any circumstances that would make us use a SQL query instead of a stored procedure call?

R7   List the main server objects modeled in program navigation diagrams as states and as activities.

R8   Describe briefly the locks in pessimistic concurrency control.

R9   Describe briefly the levels of transaction isolation.

R10   Can the amount of database recovery time be controlled by the designer/DBA? Explain.

R11   What is a compensating transaction? How can it be used in program design?

R12   What is a savepoint? How can it be used in program design?

R13   What is the function of the model differencing in round-trip engineering with a client program?

R14   Conventional databases do not have a built-in capability to maintain DB versions. How does this affect round-trip engineering with them?

Exercise questions

E1 *Telemarketing* – refer to the Telemarketing case study as defined in the book activity diagram for Telemarketing and to the solution to Exercise E4 in Chapter 7.

Extend the window navigation diagram for the Telemarketing application into a program navigation diagram. If the complexity of the solution warrants it, split the diagram into a number of smaller diagrams. Explain how your solution satisfies the application requirements.

E2 *Contact Management* – refer to the solutions to the Contact Management case study as defined in the book activity diagram for Contact Management. In particular, consider the window navigation diagram in Example 7.5 (Section 7.6.2).

Identify the stored procedures, triggers and other database objects (unidentified in the solutions so far) required in the Contact Management system.

Extend the window navigation diagram for Contact Management (Figure 7.24) into a program navigation diagram. If the complexity of the solution warrants it, split the diagram into a number of smaller diagrams. Explain how your solution satisfies the application requirements.

Testing and Change Management

Testing and change management are not separate phases of the lifecycle – they span the lifecycle. Testing is not just the debugging of programs. Development artifacts of every lifecycle phase must be tested. Similarly, change management does not just apply to enhancements requested by the stakeholders or to defects found during testing. Change management is the fundamental aspect of the overall project management – the change requests must be documented and the impact of each change on development artifacts must be tracked and retested after the change is realized.

Traceability underlies the testing and change management. Traceability captures, links and tracks all important development artifacts, including requirements. The ultimate aim of traceability is to enable the generation of a complete system documentation that is guaranteed to be correct and consistent across various documents and models – from the requirements to the technical and user documentation.

The traceability items can be textual statements or graphical models. Traceability establishes explicit links between the traceability items. The links can be direct or indirect. The links allow an impact analysis to be undertaken if any item on the traceability path is changed.

Earlier in the book, we distinguished between the system services and system constraints. Traceability, testing and change management are frequently associated with system services that manifest themselves in the use case requirements. However, one must not forget that the enforcement of the system constraints must also be tested and managed.

10.1 Testing system services

Schach (1996) distinguishes between the informal and methodical testing of system services. Every developer performs an *informal test* while modeling or implementing a system service. By its nature, the informal testing is imperfect. A person who developed a service is the least likely person to find faults in that service.

The informal testing is only of marginal significance and it must be supplemented by a methodical testing. There are two main kinds of *methodical testing* (Schach, 1996):

1. Non-execution-based (formal reviews)
   - ■ Walkthroughs
   - ■ Inspections
2. Execution-based
   - ■ Testing to specs
   - ■ Testing to code

10.1.1 Walkthroughs

A *walkthrough* is a type of formal brainstorm review that can be conducted in any development phase. It is a friendly meeting of developers, carefully planned and with clear objectives, an agenda, duration, and membership. Many IS development teams conduct walkthroughs on a weekly basis.

A few days *prior to a walkthrough meeting*, the participants are handed the materials (models, documents, program code, etc.) that are to be reviewed at the meeting. The materials are collected and distributed to the participants by the walkthrough moderator. The participants study the materials and supply the moderator with their comments, still prior to the meeting.

The meeting is relatively short (two–three hours at most). *During the meeting* the moderator presents the comments and opens a discussion on each item. The purpose of the meeting is to pinpoint the problem, not to harass the developer! The developer behind the problem is not important and may even be anonymous (although normally this would not be the case). The whole idea is to confirm the existence of a problem. A solution to the problem must not be even attempted.

There is lots of evidence that walkthroughs work very well. They introduce rigor and professionalism to the development process, contribute to productivity and to meeting the deadlines, have very important informational outcomes, and improve software quality.

10.1.2 Inspections

Like the walkthrough, an *inspection* is a friendly meeting but done under close supervision by the project management. Its purpose is also to identify defects, validate that they are in fact defects, record them, and schedule when and by whom they have to be fixed.

Unlike the walkthroughs, inspections are conducted less frequently, may target only selected and critical issues, and are more formal and more rigorous. An inspection is organized in a number of stages. It starts with the *planning stage* that identifies the inspection membership and the inspection target area.

Prior to the inspection session, a short *informational meeting* may be set. During the informational meeting, the developer whose product is to be inspected introduces the subject. The inspection materials are handed over to the participants during or before the informational meeting.

The *informational meeting* usually takes place one week before the inspection meeting. This gives the inspection team time to study the materials and prepare for the meeting. During the meeting, the defects are identified, recorded and numbered. Immediately after the meeting, the moderator prepares the *defect log* – ideally recorded in a *change management tool* associated with the project.

The developer is normally requested to resolve the defects quickly and record the resolution in the change management tool. The moderator would verify the defect resolution and decide if *reinspection* is needed. Once satisfied with the resolution, the moderator – in consultation with the project manager – submits the development module to the *Software Quality Assurance* (SQA) group in the organization (if such a group exists).

The SQA group should consist of some of the best people that the organization has. The group must not be associated with the project except in the capacity of quality assurance. The group (not the original developers!) is made responsible for the final quality of the product.

10.1.3 Testing to specs

Testing to specs is an execution-based test type. It applies to executable software products, not to documents or models. It is also known under a variety of different names, such as *black-box testing*, functional testing, input/output driven testing, etc.

The principle of testing to specs is that the developer treats the test module as a black box that takes some input and produces some output. No attempt is made to understand the program logic or computational algorithms.

The testing to specs requires that the *test requirements* are derived from the *use case requirements*, and then identified and documented in a separate test plan and test case documents. These documents provide a test scenario to the tester. The scenarios can be recorded in a *capture-playback tool* and used repeatedly. This is particularly valuable for *regression testing* (Section 1.3.10).

The testing to specs is likely to discover defects normally difficult to catch by other means. In particular, the testing to specs discovers *missing functionality* – something that (hopefully) has been documented as a use case requirement (and therefore a test requirement) but it has never been programmed. It can also discover the missing functionality that has never been documented in the use cases but is manifestly missing in the system implementation.

10.1.4 Testing to code

Testing to code is the second form of execution-based testing. It is also known under the names of *white-box testing*, glass-box testing, logic-driven testing, and path-oriented testing.

Testing to code starts with the careful analysis of the program's algorithms. Test cases are derived to *exercise the code* – i.e. to guarantee that all possible execution paths in the program are verified. The test data are specially contrived to exercise the code.

Testing to code can be supported by the capture-playback tools and used then for regression testing. However, the nature of testing to code requires the extensive involvement of the programmer in utilizing the tools. Many of the playback scripts need to be written by the programmer rather than generated by the tool. Even if generated, they may need to be extensively modified by the programmer.

Like all other forms of execution-based testing, testing to code cannot be exhaustive because of the combinatorial explosion in the number of possible test cases with even a modest growth in the program's complexity. Even if it were possible to test every execution path, we could not guarantee that we have detected every defect. The old testing adage holds – testing can only eliminate some errors, it cannot prove the program correct!

10.2 Testing system constraints

The *testing of system constraints* is predominantly *execution-based*. Its purpose is to determine that the system constraints were implemented as listed in the requirements and test documents. The testing of system constraints includes such issues as:

- user interface testing;
- database testing;
- authorization testing;
- performance testing;
- stress testing;
- failover testing;
- configuration testing;
- installation testing.

The first two types of system constraint tests – the *user interface* and *database testing* – are very closely associated with the testing of system services. They are normally conducted in parallel with tests of system services. As such, they are included in test case documents (Section 10.3) produced for the testing of system services.

10.2.1 User interface testing

The GUI testing is intertwined with the overall software development process. It starts as early as in the requirements phase with activities such as storyboarding, inclusion of window drawings in use case documents and GUI prototyping. These early GUI tests concentrate on the fulfillment of functional requirements and on usability.

Later, when the system has been implemented, methodical *post-implementation GUI testing* is required. The tests are first conducted by the developers, then by the testers, and – prior to the software release – by the customers (*pilot tests*). The following is a sample list of questions in a test document designed for post-implementation GUI tests (Bourne, 1997):

- Does the window name correspond to its function?

- Is the window modal or modeless? Which should it be?

- Is a visual distinction made between the required and optional fields?

- Can the window be resized, moved, closed and restored? Should it be?

- Are any fields missing?

- Are there any spelling mistakes in titles, labels, prompt names, etc.?

- Are command buttons (`OK`, `Cancel`, `Save`, `Clear`, etc.) used consistently across all dialog boxes?

- Is it possible always to abort the current operation (including the delete operation)?

- Are all static fields protected from editing by users? If the application can change the static text, is this being done correctly?

- Are consistent font types and sizes applied to static text fields? Are they spelled correctly?

- Do the sizes of edit boxes correspond to ranges of values that they take?

- Are all edit boxes initialized with correct values when the window opens?

- Are the values entered into edit boxes validated by the client program?

- Are the values in drop-down lists populated correctly from the database?

- Are edit masks used in entry fields as specified?

- Are error messages legible and easy to act on?

10.2.2 Database testing

Like the GUI testing, the database testing is inherent in many other kinds of test. Much of the black-box testing (testing to specs) is based on the database input and output. However, separate methodical database testing is still necessary.

The *post-implementation database testing* includes extensive white-box (to code) testing. The most significant part of database testing is *transaction testing*. Some other aspects of the database can be extracted into separate tests, e.g. performance, concurrency, authorization.

As with GUI tests, the same database tests need to be conducted repeatedly for all different application functions. The issues to be addressed in the database tests should be extracted into a generic document. This generic document should then be attached to all function (system services) tests. The following is an exemplary set of issues that the database tests should address (Bourne, 1997):

- Verify that the transaction executes as expected with correct input. Is the system's feedback to the GUI correct? Is the database content correct after the transaction?

- Verify that the transaction executes as expected with incorrect input. Is the system's feedback to the GUI correct? Is the database content correct after the transaction?

- Abort the transaction before it finishes. Is the system's feedback to the GUI correct? Is the database content correct after the transaction?

- Run the same transaction concurrently in many processes. Deliberately make one transaction hold a lock on a data resource needed by other transactions. Are the users getting understandable explanations from the system? Is the database content correct after the transactions have terminated?

- Extract every client SQL statement from the client program and execute it interactively on the database. Are the results as expected and the same as when the SQL is executed from the program?

- Perform interactive white-box testing of every more complex SQL query (from a client program or from a stored procedure) involving outer joins, union, subqueries, null values, aggregate functions, etc.

10.2.3 Authorization testing

The *authorization testing* may be treated as an inherent extension of the first two types of system constraint tests. Both the client (user interface) and server (database) objects should be protected from an unauthorized use. The authorization testing should verify that the security mechanisms built into the client and the server will in fact protect the system from unauthorized penetration.

Although ultimately the database bears the consequences of security breaches, the protection starts at the client. The *user interface* of the program should be able to configure itself dynamically to correspond to the *authorization* level of the current user (*authenticated* by the user id and password). Menu items, command buttons or even entire windows should be made inaccessible to the users if they do not have proper authorization.

Not all security loopholes can be addressed at the client. The support for authorization is a significant component of any DBMS. *Server permissions* (*privileges*) fall into two categories. A user may be given selective permissions to:

- access individual *server objects* (tables, views, columns, stored procedures, etc.);
- execute SQL statements (select, update, insert, delete, etc.).

Permissions for a user may be assigned directly at a *user level* or at a *group level*. Groups allow the security administrator to assign permissions to a group of users in a single entry. A user may belong to none or to many groups.

To allow greater flexibility with managing authorization, most DBMSs introduce one more authorization level – the *role level*. The role allows the security administrator to grant permissions to all users who play a particular role in the organization. Roles can be nested – i.e. the permissions granted to different role names can overlap.

In larger IS applications, the *authorization design* is an elaborate activity. Frequently an *authorization database* is set up alongside the application database to store and manipulate the client and server permissions. The application program consults the database after the user's logon in order to identify the user's authorization level and configure itself to that user.

Any changes to database permissions are driven from the authorization database – i.e. nobody, even the security administrator, is allowed to directly change the application database permissions without first updating the authorization database. Figure 10.1 demonstrates a possible design of the authorization database.

10.2.4 Testing of other constraints

The testing of system constraints also includes:

- performance testing;
- stress testing;
- failover testing;
- configuration testing;
- installation testing.

Performance testing measures the performance constraints demanded by the customer. The constraints relate to the *transaction speed and throughput*. The tests are conducted for different system workloads, including any anticipated *peak loads*. The performance testing is an important part of *system tuning*.

Stress testing is designed to break the system when abnormal demands are placed on it – low resources, an unusual contention for resources, abnormal frequency, quantity or volume. The stress testing is frequently coupled with performance testing and may require similar hardware and software *instrumentation*.

Failover testing addresses the system's response to a variety of hardware, network or software malfunctions. This kind of testing is closely related to the *recovery* procedures supported by the DBMS.

Configuration testing verifies how the system operates on various software and hardware configurations. In most production environments, the system is expected to run successfully on various client workstations that connect to the database using a variety of network protocols. The client workstations may have different software installed (e.g. drivers) that can conflict with the expected setups.

Installation testing extends the configuration testing. It verifies that the system operates properly on every platform installed. This means that the tests of system services are rerun.

FIGURE 10.1
Design of an
authorization
database.

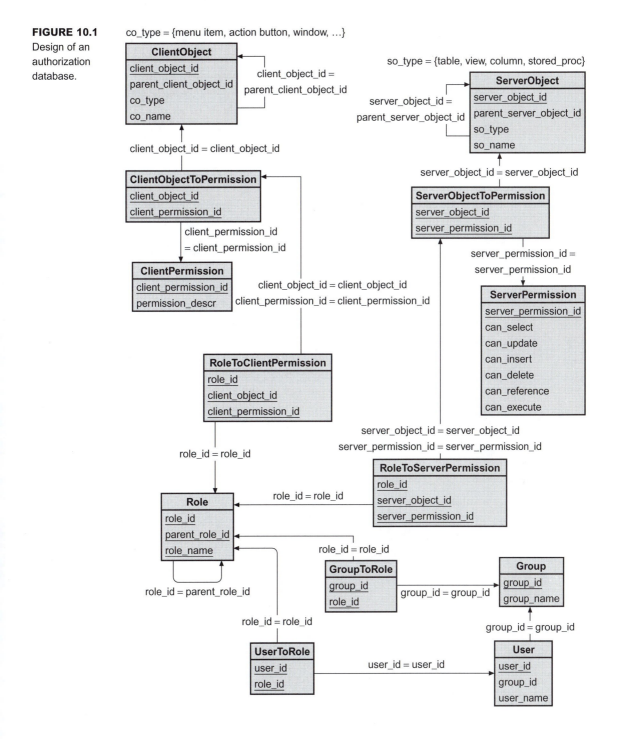

10.3 Test and change management documents

The *test and change management documentation* is an integral part of other system documents, including the use case documents (Figure 10.2). The system *features* identified in the business use case model (Section 3.5.2) can be used to write the initial test plan. The use case model is then used to write test case documents and determine *test requirements*. *Defects* found during testing are documented in the *defects document*. Any unimplemented *use case requirements* are listed in the enhancements document.

When a CASE tool is used, the developers have an option of either:

- producing narrative documents and then using them to create requirements (test requirements, use case requirements, etc.) in the CASE repository; or

- using the CASE tool to enter the requirements into the repository and then generating documentation.

Figure 10.3 shows an excerpt from a test case document used to enter *test requirements* into the repository. Similarly to the use case requirements, the test requirements are numbered and hierarchically organized. Many test requirements correspond directly to use case requirements. Hence, the main section in the document is called 'Conformance to Use Case Specs'.

Other sections of a test case document would identify requirements for GUI testing, database testing, and testing of generic reusable components. These kinds of test must be included as part of testing of functional units for two reasons. Firstly, to test the GUI, database or generic components (such as those that end up in the dynamic link library) we need the functional context within which the input and output data make sense. Secondly, the GUI, database and generic components may show defects only in the context of some, but not all, functional tests.

FIGURE 10.2
Documents relevant to testing and change management.

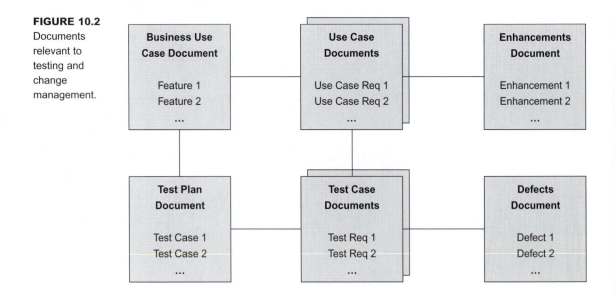

Business Use Case Document	Use Case Documents	Enhancements Document
Feature 1 Feature 2 ...	Use Case Req 1 Use Case Req 2 ...	Enhancement 1 Enhancement 2 ...

Test Plan Document	Test Case Documents	Defects Document
Test Case 1 Test Case 2 ...	Test Req 1 Test Req 2 ...	Defect 1 Defect 2 ...

FIGURE 10.3
Test case
document.

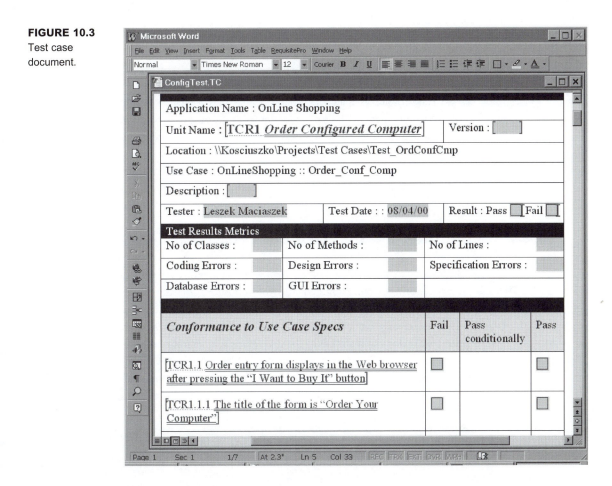

The test case documents are used to record the test outcomes. Hence, the three columns next to each test requirement in Figure 10.3. A test requirement can fail the test, pass it conditionally (in which case an explanation is required), or pass it unconditionally.

10.4 Managing change

The testing reveals *defects*. The defects need to be fixed. To be fixed, the defects must be submitted as *change requests* and allocated to developers. Some change requests may relate to *enhancements* rather than defects. Both defects and enhancements undergo status changes, may be prioritized, have owners, need to be traced to their origins in test and use case documents, etc.

Managing change is a big task in any multi-developer software project. Consider a scenario where two different defects are allocated to two different developers for fixing but it turns out that correcting these seemingly unrelated defects requires changes in the same code component. Unless the developers are made aware of the possible conflict, both developers can simultaneously work on the corrections and eventually the more recent fix will undo the earlier fix.

To properly manage change, a *change request management tool* (part of the CASE tool) is necessary. The tool allows managing change online and it ensures that all developers work with the latest documents. Changes to documents introduced by one project member are immediately available to fellow developers. Potential conflicts are resolved through *locking* or *version control* mechanisms. In the former case, a locked document is temporarily unavailable to other developers. In the latter case, multiple versions of the same document can be created and any conflicts between versions are resolved through negotiations at some later time.

10.4.1 Submitting change request

Typically, a *change request* is either a defect or an enhancement. A change request is entered into the project repository. Once entered into the repository, the developers can monitor the progress made on the change request, observe its *status* and act on it. *Actions* that can be performed on a change request depend on the current status of the request.

Figure 10.4 shows the main tab in the dialog box for entering defects (Rational, 2000). A defect will be numbered and described in detail. The priority, severity, project, and owner information can be entered from the drop-down lists of applicable choices (the attribute values in drop-down lists and elsewhere on the form can be customized to suit the project's

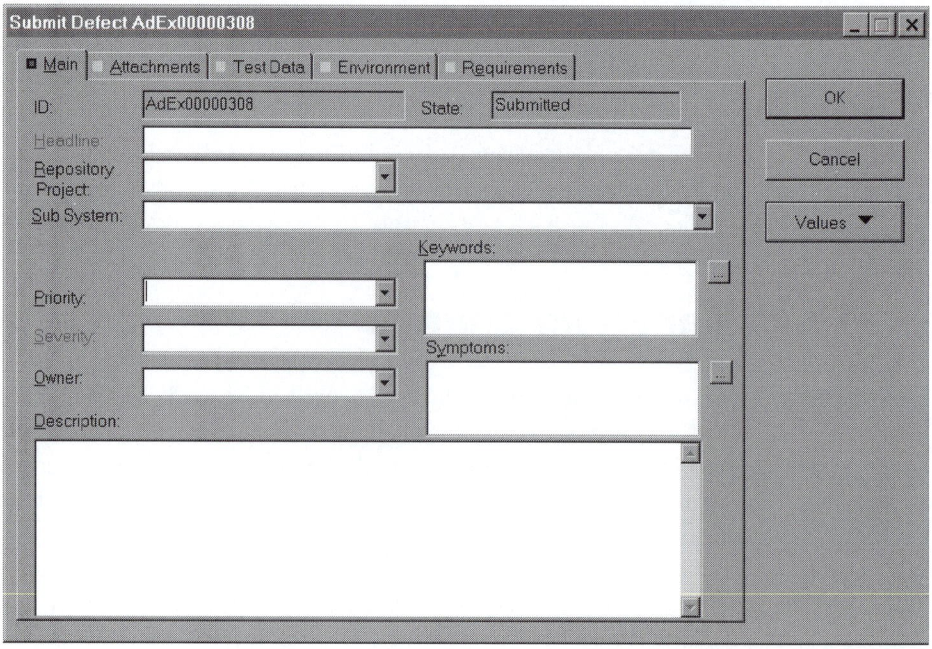

FIGURE 10.4
Window to
submit a defect.

needs). Other fields allow entering descriptive information, including the possibility of attaching a related documentation such as code fragments.

The action of *submitting* a change request can result in automatic *e-mail notifications* to team members. The change request is then in the *Submitted status*. The project management can customize the tool to allow predefined actions in each status. For example, when in the Submitted status, the possible actions can be: `Assign` (to a team member), `Modify` (some details of the request), `Postpone`, `Delete` (without fixing), `Close` (probably as a result of fixing it).

10.4.2 Keeping track of change requests

Each change request is assigned to a team member. The team member can `Open` the change request. When in the *Open state*, no other team member can modify the state of the request.

When the change request is resolved, the developer can execute the `Resolve` action on it. The details of the resolution can be entered and the e-mail notification can be sent to the project managers and testers. The testers may need to perform the `Verify` action on the resolved change request.

At any stage, the change request management tool can track the requests and produce easy-to-understand charts and reports (*project metrics*). Charts and reports can assess the number of unassigned defects, reveal workloads of each team member, show how many defects are still unresolved, etc.

Figure 10.5 shows the chart for active defects by priority. Six defects are to be resolved immediately, fifty-five should be given high attention, sixty-seven are in the normal queue, and sixty-eight have low priority.

10.5 Traceability

The traceability, testing and change management are not the aims in themselves and must not be overdone. The developers should concentrate on developing, not tracing, testing or managing change. There is a significant cost to the project associated with these issues. However, there is also a significant long-term cost to the project associated with *not* managing these issues.

Since the traceability underpins the testing and change management, the *cost-benefit analysis* should determine the scope and depth of project traceability. As a minimum, the traceability should be maintained between the use case requirements and defects. In a more elaborated model, the test requirements could be added between the use case requirements and defects on the traceability path. In an even more sophisticated model, the traceability agenda can include the system features, test cases, enhancements, test verification points, and other software development artifacts.

In the rest of this chapter, we will consider the traceability model consistent with the links between system documents shown in Figure 10.2. The business use case document lists *system*

FIGURE 10.5
Metric chart.

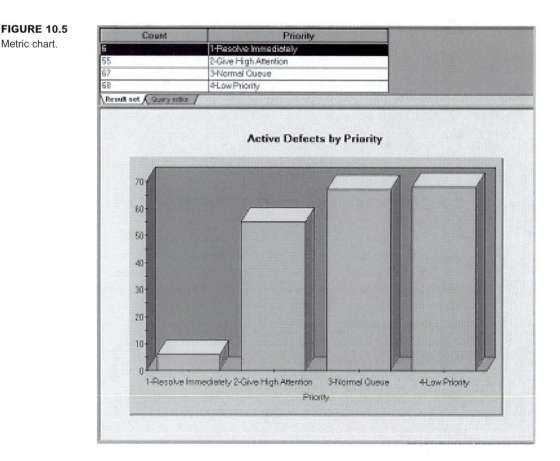

Count	Priority
6	1-Resolve Immediately
55	2-Give High Attention
67	3-Normal Queue
68	4-Low Priority

Result set   Query editor

Active Defects by Priority

features. The test plan document identifies *test cases*. *Features* are linked to *test cases* and to *use case requirements* in the use case documents. *Test requirements* in the test case documents can be traced back to *test cases* and *use case requirements*. *Test requirements* are linked to *defects* and *enhancements* are traced to *use case requirements*. The trace from *defects* to *enhancements* is not needed.

10.5.1 System features to use cases and use case requirements

A *system feature* is a generic piece of functionality to be implemented in the system. It is a business process shown as an important benefit of the system. Normally, a system feature corresponds to a *business use case* in a business use case model (Section 3.5.2). If a business use case model is not formally developed, then system features are identified in a *vision document* (or similarly named strategic project document).

Each system feature is realized by a set of *use case requirements* in one or more *use cases*. Tracing use cases back to the stakeholder needs (expressed in system features) helps to validate the correctness of the use case model. This strategy 'scopes' the requirements capture and facilitates the completion of the requirements phase. It can also assist in incremental development and delivery of the product.

A problem may arise with this strategy if the use case requirements within each use case are only indirectly linked to features. This can lead to situations where there is a trace between a feature and a use case yet most use case requirements have nothing to do with the feature. Deciding whether or not the trace between the feature and the use case is still valid may prove to be a daunting and unsustainable task.

To avoid the scalability and long-term problems associated with this strategy, the traceability matrix should trace the features not only to the use cases but also directly to the use case requirements. This is possible if each use case is itself treated as the highest-level use case requirement with a hierarchy of specific use case requirements under it.

This is shown in Figure 10.6. The columns contain use cases and use case requirements within use cases. The hierarchical display of use case requirements can be expanded or collapsed. The arrows signify the traces from features to use cases and use case requirements. Some arrows are crossed over. These are *suspect traces*. A trace becomes suspect when a *from* or *to* requirement changes. The developer needs to examine the suspect links before clearing them.

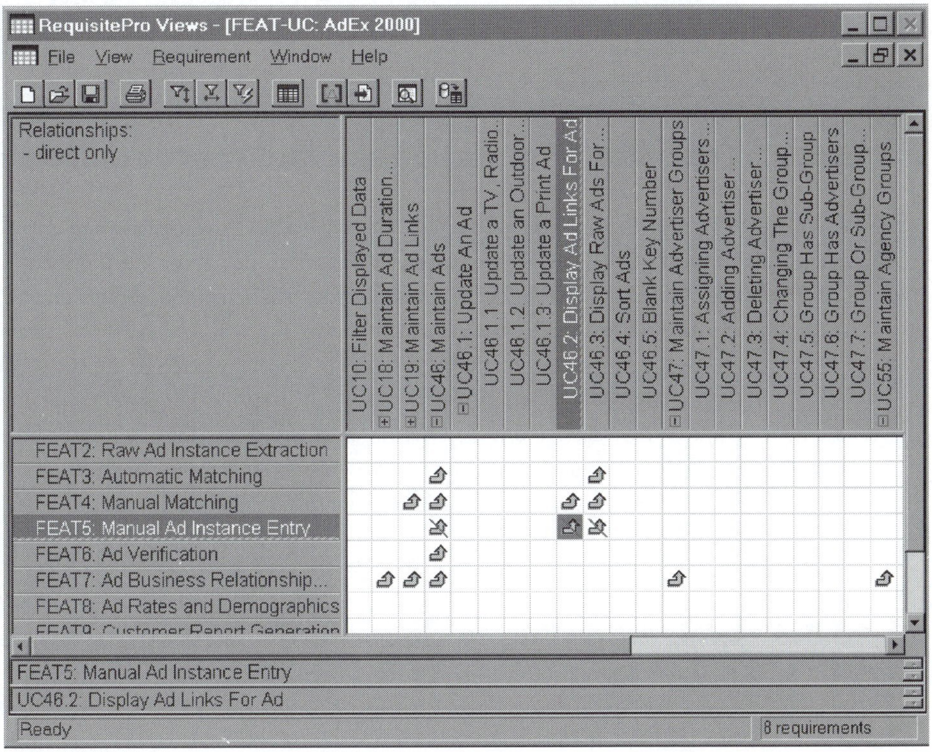

FIGURE 10.6
Traceability
from features
to use cases
and use case
requirements
(courtesy of
ACNielsen AdEx,
Sydney,
Australia.)

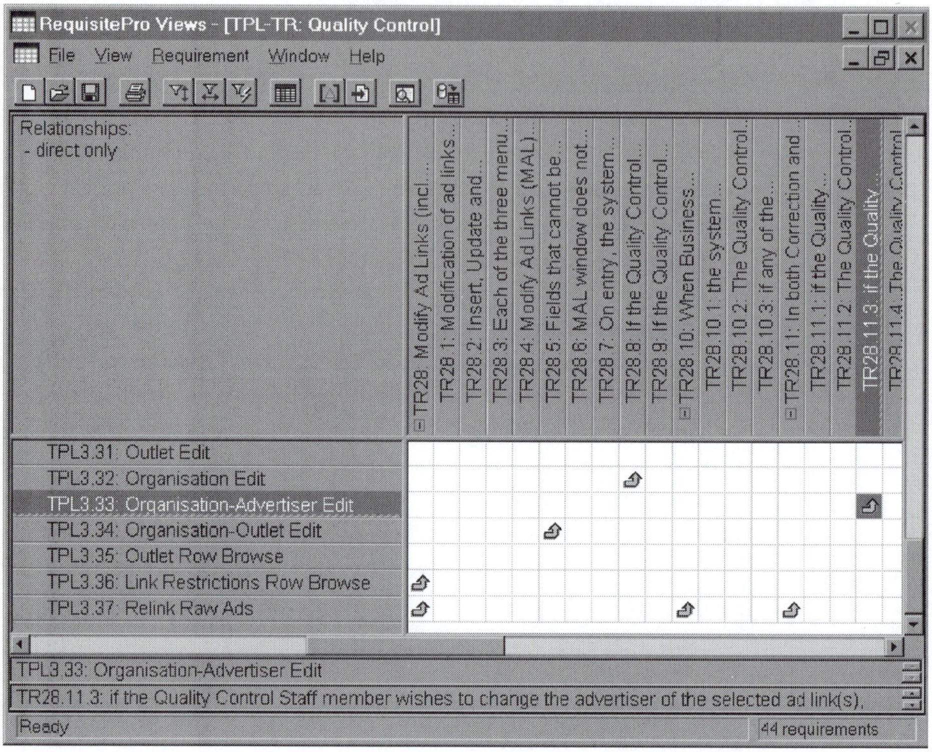

FIGURE 10.7
Traceability from
test plan to test
case and test
requirement
(courtesy of
ACNielsen AdEx,
Sydney,
Australia).

10.5.2 Test plans to test cases and test requirements

A *test plan* document is for the test cases what a business use case document is for the use cases. The test plan identifies the high-level project information and the software components (*test cases*) that should be tested. The test plan describes also the testing strategy for the project, the required test resources, the effort and cost.

Each test case identified in the test plan is to be written as a test case document. Mapping test requirements to test cases and test plans brings similar benefits to the traceability between features, use cases, and use case requirements – the scoping of test capture, scalability, etc.

Figure 10.7 shows the traceability matrix from the test plan to test cases and test requirements within test cases. The hierarchical display of test requirements can be collapsed and expanded.

10.5.3 UML diagrams to documents and requirements

The traceability and change management does not just apply to narrative documents and textual requirements stored in the CASE repository. The repository stores also UML

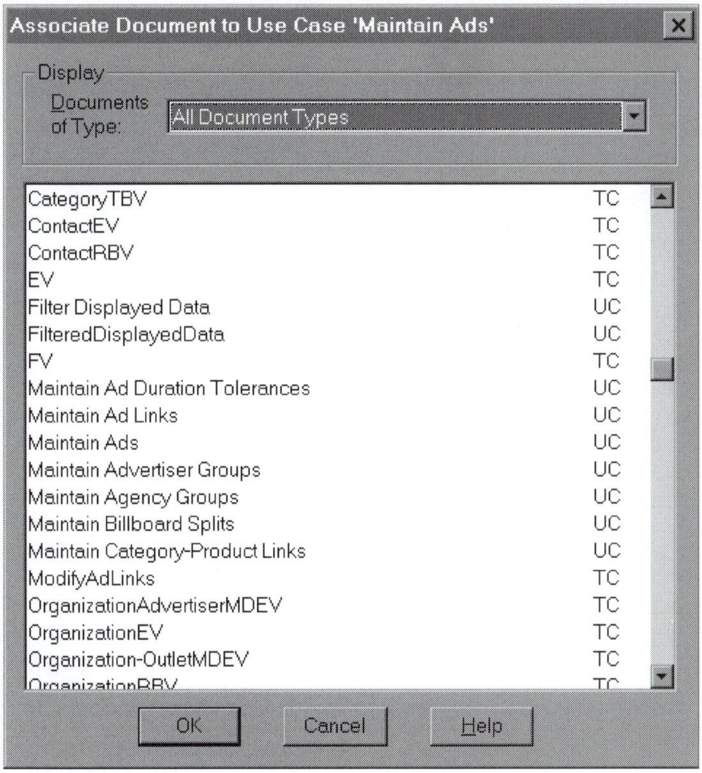

FIGURE 10.8
Hyper-linking
document to use
case graphical
icon (courtesy
of ACNielsen
AdEx, Sydney
Australia).

Associate Document to Use Case 'Maintain Ads'

Display
Documents of Type: All Document Types

CategoryTBV	TC
ContactEV	TC
ContactRBV	TC
EV	TC
Filter Displayed Data	UC
FilteredDisplayedData	UC
FV	TC
Maintain Ad Duration Tolerances	UC
Maintain Ad Links	UC
Maintain Ads	UC
Maintain Advertiser Groups	UC
Maintain Agency Groups	UC
Maintain Billboard Splits	UC
Maintain Category-Product Links	UC
ModifyAdLinks	TC
OrganizationAdvertiserMDEV	TC
OrganizationEV	TC
Organization-OutletMDEV	TC
OrganizationRBV	TC

OK   Cancel   Help

models. The graphical objects in UML diagrams can be hyper-linked to documents and requirements.

The traceability between UML visual artifacts and any other repository records (in particular documents and requirements) can be established for various UML *graphical icons*. Perhaps the most important of these icons are the use cases in use case diagrams.

Figure 10.8 shows the dialog box for hyper-linking a use case graphical icon (`Maintain Ads`) to a document. The hyper-linking is done from within a UML use case diagram. The linked document can be any of the documents in the repository, including those shown in Figure 10.2.

Figure 10.9 shows a dialog box for hyper-linking a use case graphical icon (`Maintain Ads` again) to a use case requirement. In general, it is possible to link the icon to a requirement of any type.

10.5.4 Use case requirements to test requirements

The traceability between the use case requirements and the test requirements is critical in assessing whether the application meets the business requirements established for it. The links

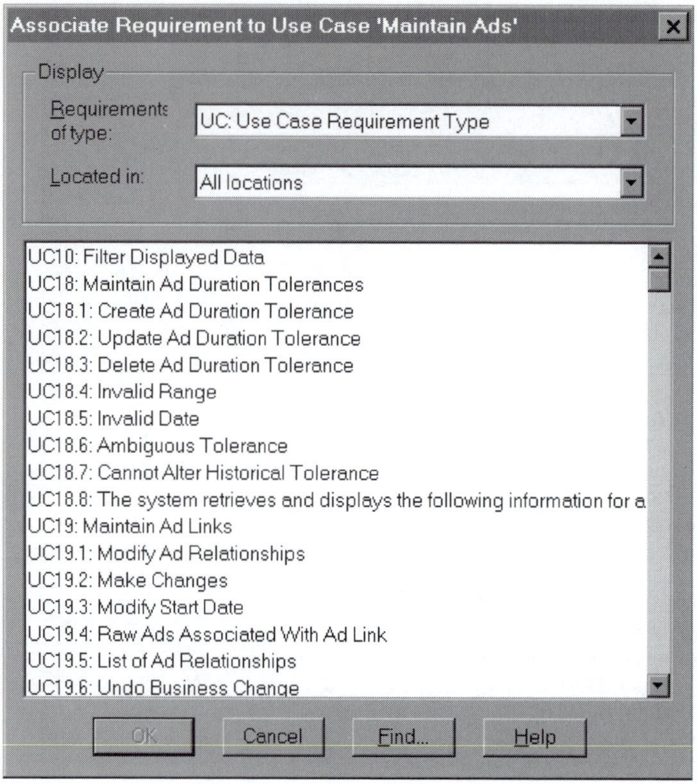

FIGURE 10.9
Hyper-linking
requirement to
use case
graphical icon
(courtesy of
ACNielsen AdEx,
Sydney,
Australia).

between these two requirement types allow the user to track defects via test requirements back to use case requirements and system features (see Figure 10.2).

Figure 10.10 shows the traceability matrix with traces between the use case requirements and test requirements. Note that both the use case requirements and test requirements are hierarchically structured. The hierarchical levels at which the traces are defined can be pre-determined.

10.5.5 Test requirements to defects

Test case documents are written in the form of scripts containing the test requirements to be verified when testing. The scripts are used in *manual* tests but many of these scripts can be *automated* for use in *capture-and-playback* testing tools. Test requirements in test case documents can then be used to establish verification points in these automated tests.

A *verification point* is a requirement in the script that is used (in *regression testing*) to confirm the state of a test object across different versions (builds) of the application under test (AUT). There are various types of verification points (Rational, 2000). A verification point can be set to check that a text has not changed, that numeric values are accurate, that two files are the same, that a file exists, that menu items have not changed, that computation results are as expected, etc.

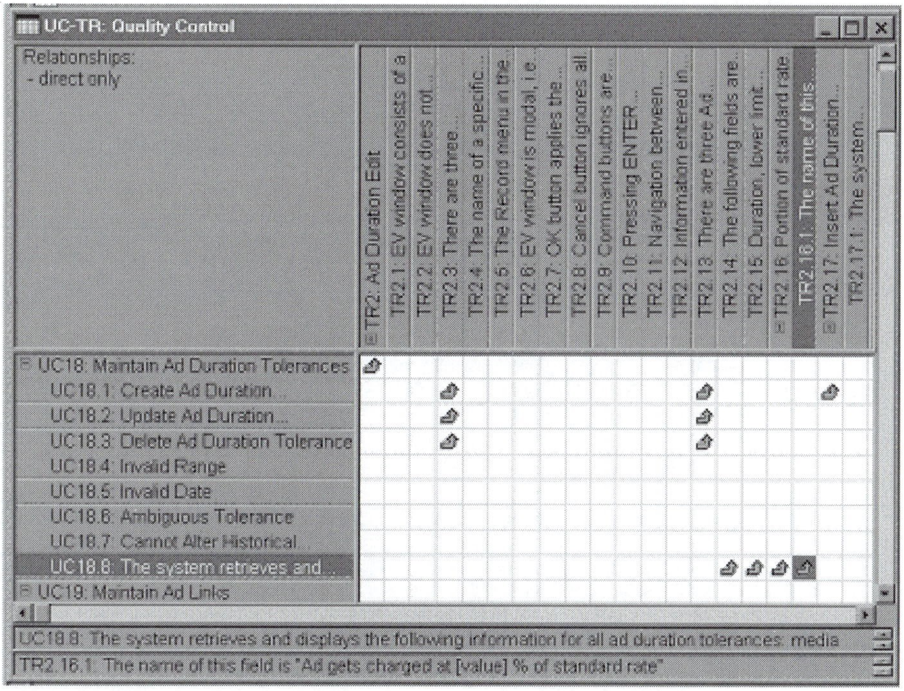

FIGURE 10.10

Traceability
from use case
requirement and
test requirement
(courtesy of
ACNielsen AdEx,
Sydney,
Australia).

The automated testing requires working with two data files – a baseline data file and an actual data file. During *capture*, the verification point records object information in the *baseline data file*. The information is the baseline against which to compare in subsequent tests (*playbacks*). The results of these comparisons are stored in the *actual data file*. Each *failed verification point* needs to be further investigated and, if necessary, entered into the change management tool as a *defect*.

Ultimately all defects – whether discovered in automated or manual tests – must be linked to the test requirements. Figure 10.11 shows a tool that displays all defects in the row browser in the upper part of the window. A currently selected defect can be associated to one or more test requirements. In the example, two test requirements are traced to the highlighted defect.

10.5.6 Use case requirements to enhancements

The defects need to be directly traced to the test requirements. The enhancements (to be implemented in a future release of the product) must have their explanation in the use case requirements. In rare situations when a defect has been converted to an enhancement, the traceability links between use case requirements and test requirements would allow the user to trace the defect to the enhancement.

Figure 10.12 demonstrates that the same tool (see Figure 10.11) can be used to manage enhancements and defects, or indeed any other change requests.

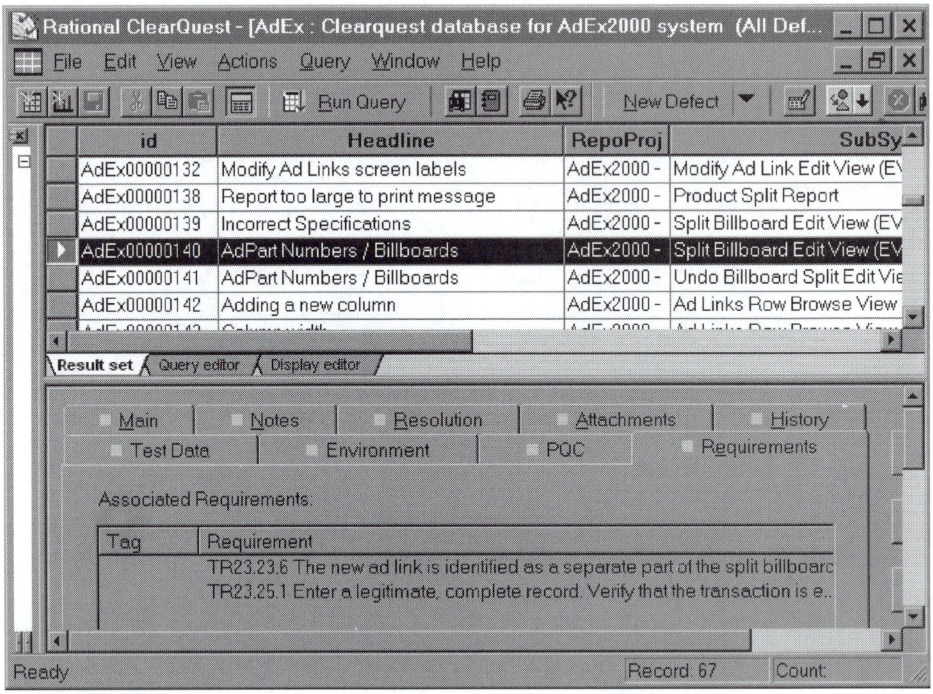

FIGURE 10.11
Traceability from
test requirement
to defect
(courtesy of
ACNielsen AdEx,
Sydney,
Australia).

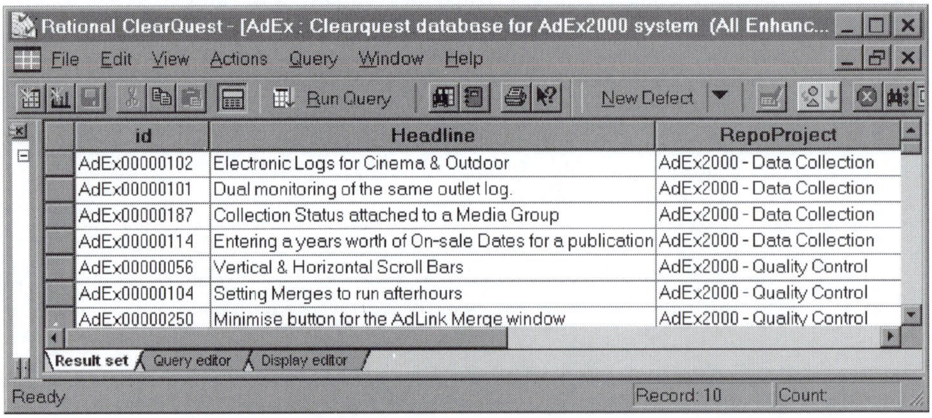

FIGURE 10.12
Enhancements
(courtesy of
ACNielsen AdEx,
Sydney,
Australia).

Summary

In this last chapter of the book, we have addressed the testing and change management issues. The activities of testing and change management span the development lifecycle, but they are of most concern when the project is near its completion. The testing and change management assumes that the traceability links between system artifacts exist and have been properly maintained during the development.

The testing divides into the testing of system services and the testing of system constraints. The *testing of system services* can be non-execution-based or execution-based. The *non-execution-based testing* includes walkthroughs and inspections. The *execution-based testing* can be the *testing to specs* or the *testing to code*.

The *testing of system constraints* includes a large range of relatively disparate tests that relate to such issues as user interface, database, authorization, performance, stress, failover, configuration, and installation. Some of system constraints tests are conducted in parallel with the system services tests; others are done independently.

The testing and change management require specialized *documentation*, such as test plans, test case documents, defect and enhancement documents. *Test requirements* are identified in the *test case documents* and linked to the use case requirements in the use case documents.

A *change request* is normally either a *defect* or an *enhancement*. A change management tool allows submitting a change request and keeping track of it as the developers address it. A vital part of the change management tool relates to the establishing of *traceability* paths between the change requests and other system artifacts, in particular test requirements and use case requirements.

Review questions

R1 How is the walkthrough different from the inspection?

R2 What is the role of the SQA group in the organization?

R3 What is an authorization database? What is its role in system development and testing?

R4 What other system constraints testing is the stress testing closely related to? Explain.

R5 What other system constraints testing is the installation testing closely related to? Explain.

R6 What actions are possible on a submitted change request?

R7 What is a suspect trace? Give an example.

R8 What is a verification point?

R9 Explain the difference between the baseline data file and actual data file.

References

Allen, P. and Frost, S. (1998) *Component-Based Development for Enterprise Systems. Applying the SELECT Perspective*™, Cambridge University Press, 462 pp.

Angell, I.O. and Smithson, S. (1991) *Information Systems Management. Opportunities and Risks*, Macmillan, 248 pp.

Arthur, L.J. (1992) *Rapid Evolutionary Development. Requirements, Prototyping and Software Creation*, John Wiley & Sons, 222 pp.

Bahrami, A. (1999) *Object Oriented Systems Development*, Irwin McGraw-Hill, 412 pp.

Bennett, S. McRobb, S. and Farmer, R. (1999) Object-Oriented Systems Analysis and Design Using UML, McGraw-Hill, 516 pp.

Bochenski, B. (1994) *Implementing Production-Quality Client/Server Systems*, John Wiley & Sons, 442 pp.

Bollinger, T.B. and McGowan, C. (1991) A Critical Look at Software Capability Evaluations, *IEEE Software*, 4, pp. 25–41.

Booch, G. Rumbaugh, J. and Jacobson, I. (1999) *The Unified Modeling Language. User Guide*, Addison-Wesley, 482 pp.

Bourne, K.C. (1997) *Testing Client/Server Systems*, McGraw-Hill, 572 pp.

Brooks, F.P. (1987) No Silver Bullet: Essence and Accidents of Software Engineering, *IEEE Software*, 4, pp. 10–19; reprinted in: *Software Project Management. Readings and Cases* (1997), ed. C.F. Kemerer, Irwin, pp. 2–14.

Buschmann, F. Meunier, R. Rohnert, H. Sommerlad, P. and Stal, M. (1996) *Pattern-Oriented Software Architecture. A System of Patterns*, John Wiley & Sons, 458 pp.

CMM (1995) *The Capability Maturity Model: Guidelines for Improving the Software Process*, Addison-Wesley, 442 pp.

Coad, P. with North, D. and Mayfield, M. (1995) *Object Models. Strategies, Patterns, and Applications*, Yourdon Press, 506 pp.

Collins, D. (1995) *Designing Object-Oriented User Interfaces*, Benjamin/Cummings Publ., 590 pp.

Conallen, J. (2000) *Building Web Applications with UML*, Addison-Wesley, 300 pp.

Constantine, L.L. and Lockwood, L.A.D. (1999) *Software for Use. A Practical Guide to the Models and Methods of Usage-Centered Design*, Addison-Wesley, 579 pp.

Date, C.J. (2000) *An Introduction to Database Systems*, Addison-Wesley, 7th edn., 938 pp.

Davenport, T.H. (1993) *Process Innovation: Reengineering Work through Information Technology*, Harvard Business School Press, 338 pp.

Davenport, T.H. and Short, J. (1990) The New Industrial Engineering. Information Technology and Business Process Redesign. *Sloan Management Review*, Cambridge, Summer, pp. 11, 17.

Eaglestone, B. and Ridley, M. (1998) *Object Databases*, McGraw-Hill, 380 pp.

Eisenberg, A. and Melton, J. (1999) SQL:1999, Formerly Known as SQL3, *ACM SIGMOD Rec.*, 1, pp. 131–138.

Elmasri, R. and Navathe, S.B. (2000) *Fundamentals of Database Systems*, 3rd edn, Addison-Wesley, 956 pp.

Fowler, M. (1997) *Analysis Patterns: Reusable Object Models*, Addison-Wesley, 358 pp.

Fowler, M. (1999) *UML – Current Status for Version 1.3*, http://ourworld.compuserve.com/homepages/Martin_Fowler/umlst.htm, 2 pp.

Fowler, M. and Scott, K. (2000) *UML Distilled. A Brief Guide to The Standard Object Modeling Language*, 2nd edn, Addison-Wesley, 186 pp.

REFERENCES

Fowler, S. (1998) *GUI Design Handbook*, McGraw-Hill, 318 pp.

Galitz, W.O. (1996) *The Essential Guide to User Interface Design. An Introduction to GUI Design Principles and Techniques*, John Wiley & Sons, 626 pp.

Gamma, E. Helm, R. Johnson, R. and Vlissides, J. (1995) *Design Patterns. Elements of Reusable Object-Oriented Software*, Addison-Wesley, 396 pp.

Gray, N.A.B. (1994) *Programming with Class*, John Wiley & Sons, 624 pp.

Hammer, M. (1990) Reengineering Work: Don't Automate, Obliterate, *Harvard Business Review*, Boston, Jul/Aug, p. 104.

Hammer, M. and Champy, J. (1993) *Reengineering the Corporation: A Manifesto for Business Revolution*, Allen & Unwin, 224 pp.

Hammer, M. and Champy, J. (1993) The Promise of Reengineering, *Fortune*, 9, p. 94.

Hammer, M. and Stanton, S. (1993) How Process Enterprises Really Work, *Harvard Business Review*, Boston, Nov/Dec, pp. 108–118.

Harmon, P. and Watson, M. (1998) *Understanding UML: The Developer's Guide. With a Web-Based Application in Java*, Morgan Kaufmann, 368 pp.

Hawryszkiewycz, I. Karagiannis, D. Maciaszek, L. and Teufel, B. (1994) RESPONSE – Requirements Specific Object Model for Workgroup Computing, *Int. J. of Intelligent & Cooperative Information Systems*, 3, pp. 293–318.

Henderson-Sellers, B. (1996) *Object-Oriented Metrics. Measures of Complexity*, Prentice Hall, 230 pp.

Hoffer, J.A. George, J.F. and Valacich, J.S. (1999) *Modern Systems Analysis and Design*, 2nd edn, Addison-Wesley, 854 pp.

Horton, I. (1997) *Beginning Visual C++ 5*, Wrox Press, 1054 pp.

Jacobson, I. (1992) *Object-Oriented Software Engineering. A Use Case Driven Approach*, Addison-Wesley, 524 pp.

Jordan, E.W. and Machesky, J.J. (1990) *Systems Development. Requirements, Evaluation, Design, and Implementation*, PWS-KENT Publ. Company, 648 pp.

Khoshafian, S. Chan, A. Wong, A. and Wong, H.K.T. (1992) *A Guide to Developing Client/Server SQL Applications*, Morgan Kaufmann Publ., 634 pp.

Kimball, R. (1996) *The Data Warehouse Toolkit. Practical Techniques for Building Dimensional Data Warehouses*, John Wiley & Sons, 388 pp.

Kirkwood, J. (1992) *High Performance Relational Database Design*, Ellis Horwood, 266 pp.

Koestler, A. (1967) *The Ghost in the Machine*, Hutchinson, 384 pp.

Koestler, A. (1978) *Janus. A Summing Up*, Hutchinson, 354 pp.

Kotonya, G. and Sommerville, I. (1998) *Requirements Engineering. Processes and Techniques*, John Wiley & Sons, 282 pp.

Kruchten, P. (1999) *The Rational Unified Process*, Addison-Wesley, 256 pp.

Lakos, J. (1996) *Large-Scale C++ Software Design*, Addison-Wesley, 846 pp.

Lee, R.C. and Tepfenhart, W.M. (1997) *UML and C++. A Practical Guide to Object-Oriented Development*, Prentice-Hall, 446 pp.

Lieberherr, K.J. and Holland, I.M. (1989) Assuring Good Style for Object-Oriented Programs, *IEEE Soft.*, 9, pp. 38–48.

Maciaszek, L.A. (1990) *Database Design and Implementation*, Prentice-Hall, 384 pp.

Maciaszek, L.A. (1998) Object Oriented Development of Business Information Systems – Approaches and Misconceptions, *Proc. 2nd Int. Conf. on Business Information Systems BIS'98*, Poznan, Poland, pp. 95–111.

Maciaszek, L.A. (2000) Process Model for Round-Trip Engineering with Relational Database, in: *Challenges of Information Technology Management in the 21st Century, 2000 Information Resources Management Association International Conference*, Anchorage, Alaska, USA, Idea Group Publishing, pp. 468–472.

Maciaszek, L.A. De Troyer, O.M.F Getta J.R. and Bosdriesz, J. (1996a) Generalization versus Aggregation in Object Application Development – the 'AD-HOC' Approach, *Proc. 7th Australasian Conf. on Information Systems ACIS'96*, Vol. 2, Hobart, Tasmania, Australia, pp. 431–442.

Maciaszek, L.A. Getta, J.R. and Bosdriesz, J. (1996b) Restraining Complexity in Object System Development – the 'AD-HOC' Approach, *Proc. 5th Int. Conf. on Information Systems Development ISD'96*, Gdansk, Poland, pp. 425–435.

Maciaszek, L.A. and Wong, K.S. (2000) UML Dialect for Designing Object-Relational Databases, in: *Challenges of Information Technology Management in the 21st Century, 2000 Information Resources Management Association International Conference*, Anchorage, Alaska, USA, Idea Group Publishing, pp. 473–477.

NEXT (1996) *Next Generation Computing. Distributed Objects for Business*, ed. P. Fingar, D. Read and J. Stikeleather, SIGS Books & Multimedia, 306 pp.

ODMG (2000) *The Object Data Standard: ODMG 3.0*, ed. R.G.G. Cattell, D.K. Barry, M. Berler, J. Eastman, D. Jordan, C. Russell, O. Schadow, T. Stanienda and F. Velez, Morgan Kaufmann, 300 pp.

Olsen, D.R. (1998) *Developing User Interfaces*, Morgan Kaufmann Publ., 414 pp.

Page-Jones, M. (2000) *Fundamentals of Object-Oriented Design in UML*, Addison-Wesley, 458 pp.

Paradigm (1997) *Paradigm Plus. Round-trip Engineering with Microsoft Visual C++*, Platinum Technology, 36 pp.

Pfleeger, S.L. (1998) *Software Engineering. Theory and Practice*, Prentice-Hall, 576 pp.

Porter, M. (1985) *Competitive Advantage: Creating and Sustaining Superior Performance*, Free Press, 558 pp.

Porter, M.E. and Millar, V.E. (1985) *How Information Gives You Competitive Advantage*, Harvard Business Review, Jul/Aug, pp. 149–161.

Pressman, R.S. (1997) *Software Engineering. A Practitioner's Approach*, 4th edn, McGraw-Hill, 852 pp.

Quatrani, T. (2000) *Visual Modeling with Rational Rose 2000 and UML*, Addison-Wesley, 256 pp.

Ramakrishnan, R. and Gehrke, J. (2000) *Database Management Systems*, McGraw-Hill, 906 pp.

Rational (1998) *Rational Rose 98. Roundtrip Engineering with C++*, Rational Software Corp., 454 pp.

Rational (2000) *Rational Solutions for Windows*, OnLine Documentation April 2000 Edition, Rational Software Corp.

Riel, A.J. (1996) *Object-Oriented Design Heuristics*, Addison-Wesley, 380 pp.

Robertson, J. and Robertson, S. (2000) *Volere Requirements Specifications Template*, Edition 6.1, Atlantic Systems Guild, http://www.atlsysguild.com, 52 pp.

Robson, W. (1994) *Strategic Management and Information Systems. An Integrated Approach*, Pitman Publ., 570 pp.

Ruble, D.A. (1997) *Practical Analysis and Design for Client/Server and GUI Systems*, Yourdon Press, 516 pp.

Rumbaugh, J. Blaha, M. Premerlani, W. Eddy, F. and Lorensen, W. (1991) *Object-Oriented Modeling and Design*, Prentice-Hall, 500 pp.

Rumbaugh, J. (1994) Getting Started. Using Use Cases to Capture Requirements, *J. Object-Oriented Prog.*, Sept., pp. 8–10, 12, 23.

Rumbaugh, J. Jacobson, I. and Booch, G. (1999) *The Unified Modeling Language Reference Manual*, Addison-Wesley, 550 pp.

Schach, S. (1996) *Classical and Object-Oriented Software Engineering*, 3rd edn, Irwin, 604 pp.

Schmauch, C.H. (1994) *ISO 9000 for Software Deevelopers*, ASQC Quality Press, 156 pp.

Silberschatz, A. Korth, H.F. and Sudershan, S. (1997) *Database System Concepts*, 3rd edn, McGraw-Hill, 864 pp.

Smith, J.M. and Smith, D.C.P. (1977) Database Abstractions: Aggregation and Generalization, *ACM Trans. Database Syst.*, 2, pp. 105–133.

Sommerville, I. and Sawyer, P. (1997) *Requirements Engineering. A Good Practice Guide*, John Wiley & Sons, 392 pp.

Sowa, J.F. and Zachman, J.A. (1992) Extending and Formalizing the Framework for Information Systems Architecture, *IBM Syst. J.*, 3, pp. 590–616.

SQL (2000) *Database Language SQL – Part 2: Foundation (SQL/Foundation)*, ISO-ANSI Working Draft, March 2000, 1170 pp.

Stein, L.A. Lieberman, H. Ungar, D. (1989) A Shared View of Sharing: The Treaty of Orlando, in: *Object-Oriented Concepts, Databases, and Applications*, ed. W. Kim and F.H. Lochovsky, Addison-Wesley, pp. 31–48.

Stevens, P. and Pooley, R. (2000) *Using UML Software Engineering with Objects and Components*, Addison-Wesley, 256 pp.

Stodder, D. (1997) The Database Dozen, *Database Prog. and Design*, Industry in Focus Issue, Dec., pp. 9–24.

Stonebraker, M. and Moore, D. (1996) *Object-Relational DBMSs. The Next Great Wave*, Morgan Kaufmann Publ., 216 pp.

Szyperski, C. (1998) *Component Software. Beyond Object-Oriented Programming*, Addison-Wesley, 412 pp.

Treisman, H. (1994) How to Design a Good Interface Design, *Software Magazine*, Australia, August, pp. 32–36.

Umar, A. (1997) *Object-Oriented Client/Server Internet Environments*, Prentice Hall, 528 pp.

Whitten, J.L. and Bentley, L.D. (1998) *Systems Analysis and Design Methods*, 4th edn, Irwin McGraw-Hill, 724 pp.

Windows (2000) *The Windows Interface Guidelines for Software Design*, MSDN Library, CDROM collection, Microsoft.

Wirfs-Brock, R. and Wilkerson, B. (1989) Object-Oriented Design: A Responsibility-Driven Approach, in: *OOPSLA'89 Proceedings, SIGPLAN Notices*, No. 10, ACM, pp. 71–75.

Wirfs-Brock, R. Wilkerson, B. and Wiener, L. (1990) *Designing Object-Oriented Software*, Prentice-Hall, 342 pp.

Wood, J. and Silver, D. (1995) *Joint Application Development*, 2nd edn, John Wiley & Sons, 402 pp.

Yourdon, E. (1994) *Object-Oriented Systems Design. An Integrated Approach*, Yourdon Press, 400 pp.

Zachman, J.A. (1987) A Framework for Information Systems Architecture, *IBM Syst. J.*, 3, pp. 276–292.

Zachman, J.A. (1999) A Framework for Information Systems Architecture, *IBM Syst. J.*, 2/3, pp. 454–470.

Index